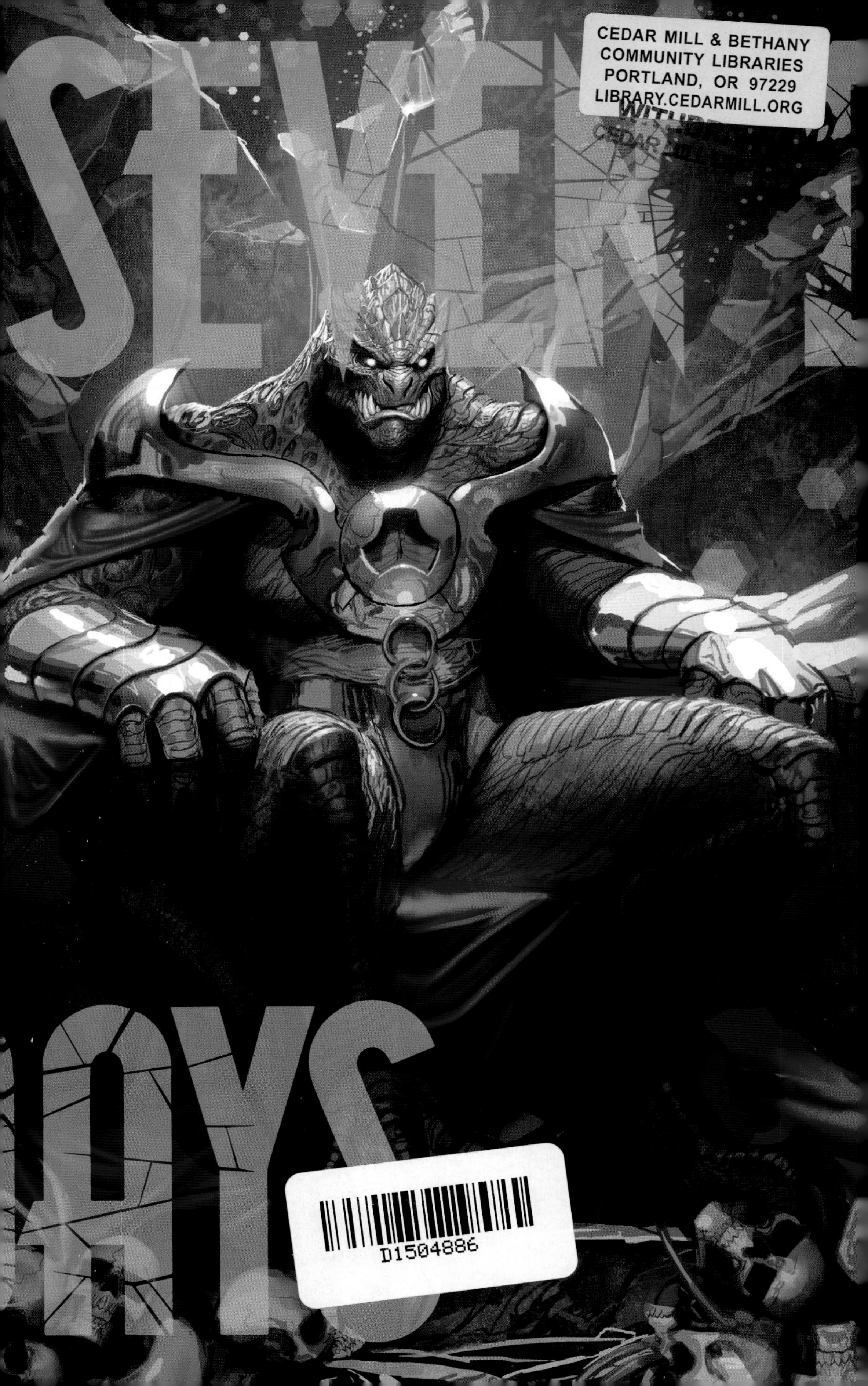
SEVEN
DAYS

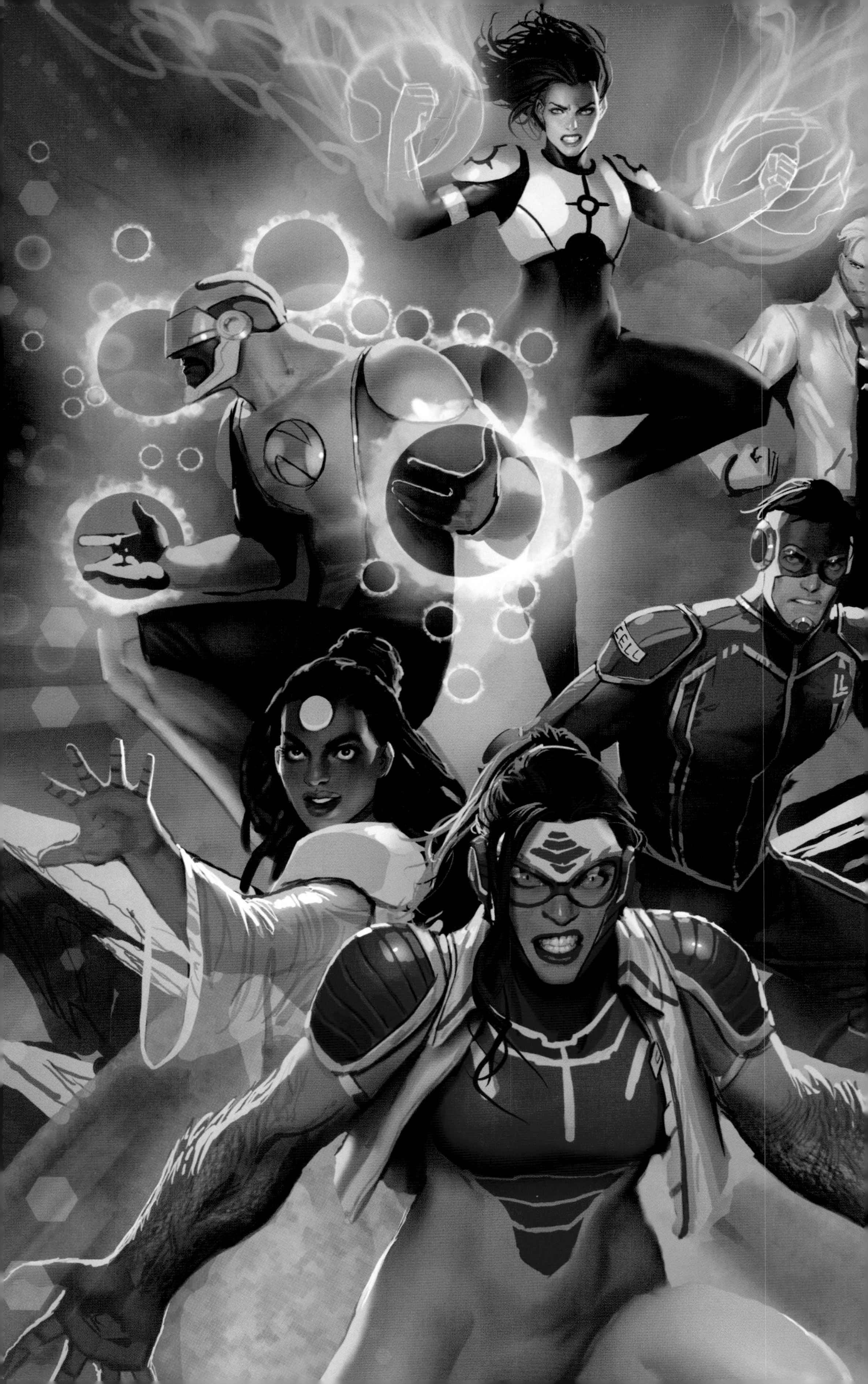

SEVEN DAYS

Written by **GAIL SIMONE**
Pencils by **JOSÉ LUÍS**
Inks by **JONAS TRINDADE**
Lettered by **SAIDA TEMFONTE**
Colored by **MICHELLE MADSEN**

Cover by **CAT STAGGS**
Series Covers by **STJEPAN SEJIC**

DESIREE RODRIGUEZ · Editor
SHAWNA GORE · Senior Editor

ISBN: 9781549303036

Library of Congress Control Number: 2019947384

Seven Days, published 2020, by Oni-Lion Forge Publishing Group, LLC. Copyright 2020 Illustrated Syndicate LLC. Portions of this book were previously published in Seven Days Vol 1, issues 1 - 7. All Rights Reserved. SEVEN DAYS™, ONI PRESS™, ILLUSTRATED SYNDICATE™, CATALYST PRIME™, and their associated distinctive designs, as well as all characters featured in this book and the distinctive names and likenesses thereof, and all related indicia, are trademarks of their respective owners. No similarity between any of the names, characters, persons, or institutions in this issue with those of any living or dead person or institution is intended, and any such similarity which may exist is purely coincidental.

Printed in South Korea through Four Colour Print Group, Louisville, KY.

10 9 8 7 6 5 4 3 2 1

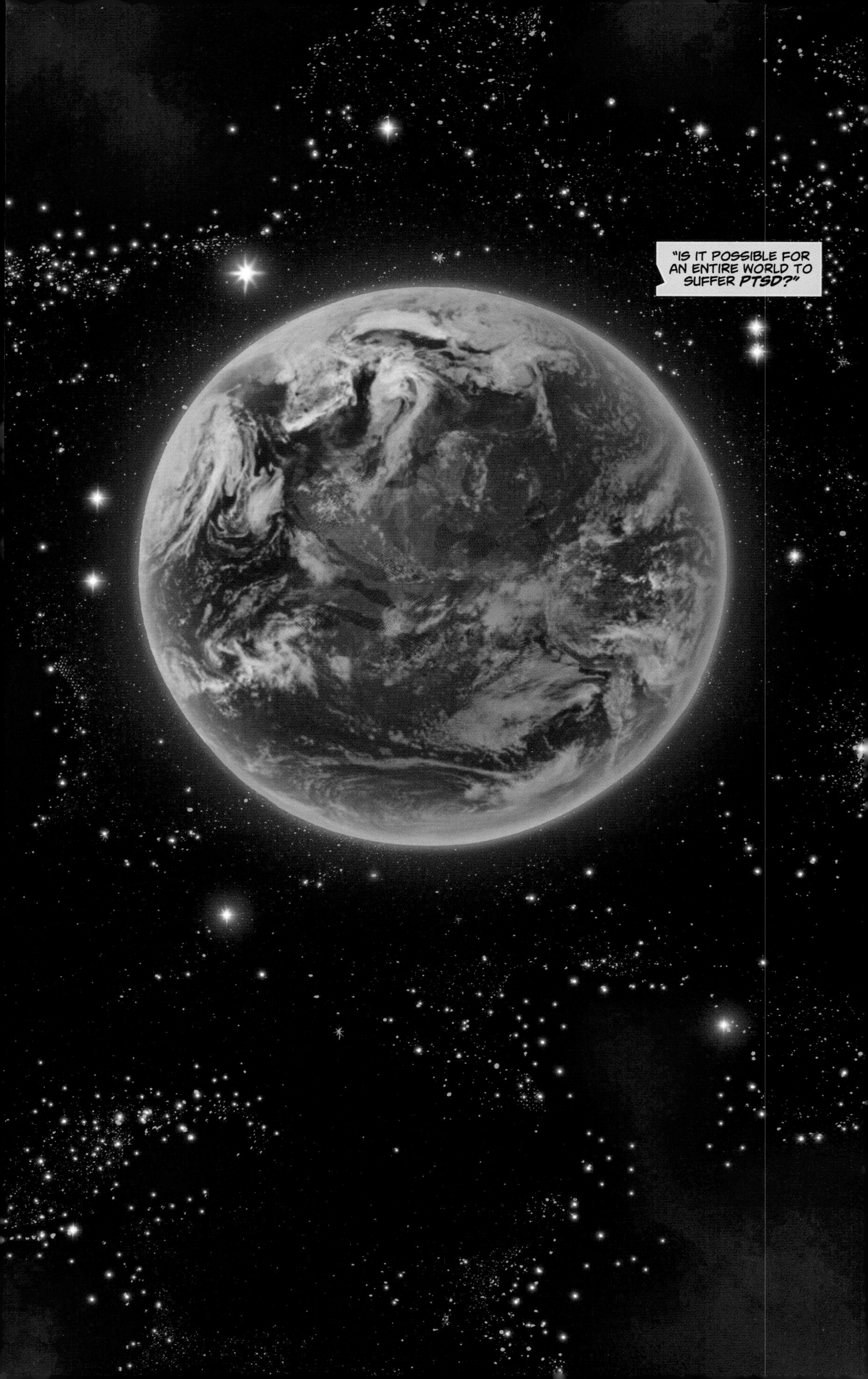
"IS IT POSSIBLE FOR AN ENTIRE WORLD TO SUFFER PTSD?"

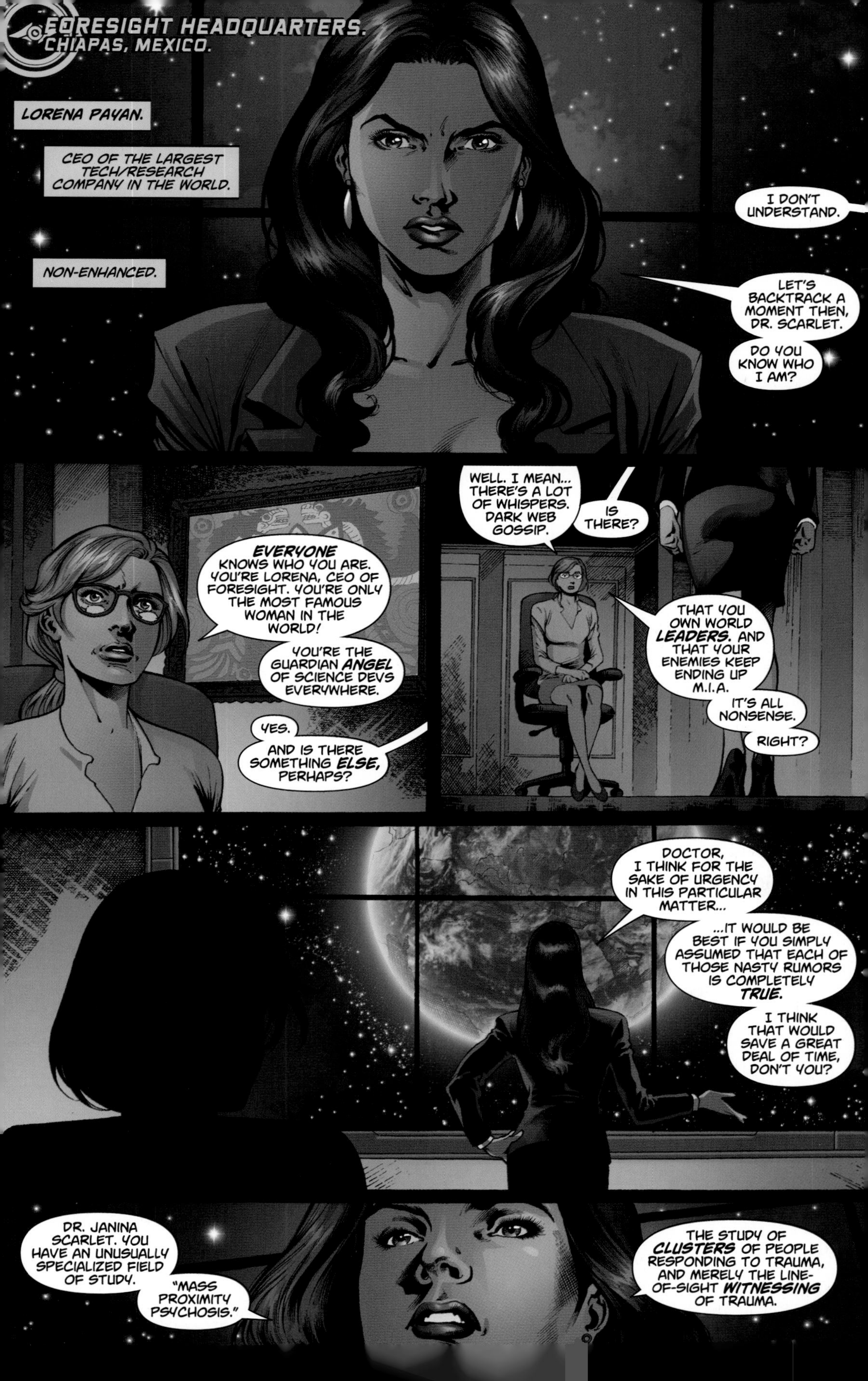
FORESIGHT HEADQUARTERS.
CHIAPAS, MEXICO.
LORENA PAYAN.
CEO OF THE LARGEST TECH/RESEARCH COMPANY IN THE WORLD.
NON-ENHANCED.
I DON'T UNDERSTAND.
LET'S BACKTRACK A MOMENT THEN, DR. SCARLET.
DO YOU KNOW WHO I AM?
EVERYONE KNOWS WHO YOU ARE. YOU'RE LORENA, CEO OF FORESIGHT. YOU'RE ONLY THE MOST FAMOUS WOMAN IN THE WORLD!
YOU'RE THE GUARDIAN ANGEL OF SCIENCE DEVS EVERYWHERE.
YES.
AND IS THERE SOMETHING ELSE, PERHAPS?
WELL. I MEAN... THERE'S A LOT OF WHISPERS. DARK WEB GOSSIP.
IS THERE?
THAT YOU OWN WORLD LEADERS. AND THAT YOUR ENEMIES KEEP ENDING UP M.I.A.
IT'S ALL NONSENSE.
RIGHT?
DOCTOR, I THINK FOR THE SAKE OF URGENCY IN THIS PARTICULAR MATTER...
...IT WOULD BE BEST IF YOU SIMPLY ASSUMED THAT EACH OF THOSE NASTY RUMORS IS COMPLETELY TRUE.
I THINK THAT WOULD SAVE A GREAT DEAL OF TIME, DON'T YOU?
DR. JANINA SCARLET. YOU HAVE AN UNUSUALLY SPECIALIZED FIELD OF STUDY.
"MASS PROXIMITY PSYCHOSIS."
THE STUDY OF CLUSTERS OF PEOPLE RESPONDING TO TRAUMA, AND MERELY THE LINE-OF-SIGHT WITNESSING OF TRAUMA.

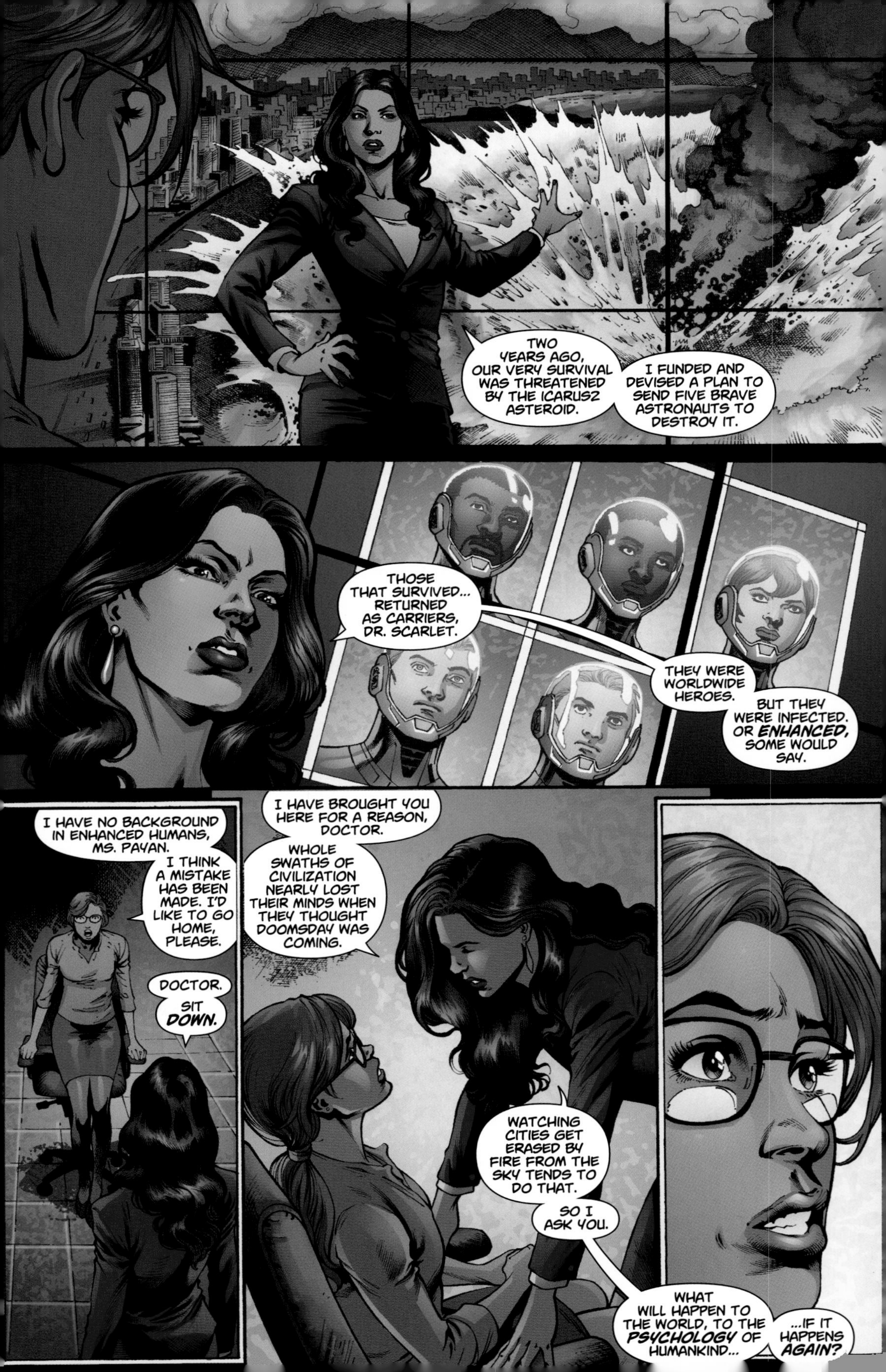
TWO YEARS AGO, OUR VERY SURVIVAL WAS THREATENED BY THE ICARUS2 ASTEROID.
I FUNDED AND DEVISED A PLAN TO SEND FIVE BRAVE ASTRONAUTS TO DESTROY IT.
THOSE THAT SURVIVED... RETURNED AS CARRIERS, DR. SCARLET.
THEY WERE WORLDWIDE HEROES.
BUT THEY WERE INFECTED. OR *ENHANCED,* SOME WOULD SAY.
I HAVE NO BACKGROUND IN ENHANCED HUMANS, MS. PAYAN.
I THINK A MISTAKE HAS BEEN MADE. I'D LIKE TO GO HOME, PLEASE.
DOCTOR.
SIT *DOWN.*
I HAVE BROUGHT YOU HERE FOR A REASON, DOCTOR.
WHOLE SWATHS OF CIVILIZATION NEARLY LOST THEIR MINDS WHEN THEY THOUGHT DOOMSDAY WAS COMING.
WATCHING CITIES GET ERASED BY FIRE FROM THE SKY TENDS TO DO THAT.
SO I ASK YOU.
WHAT WILL HAPPEN TO THE WORLD, TO THE *PSYCHOLOGY* OF HUMANKIND...
...IF IT HAPPENS *AGAIN?*

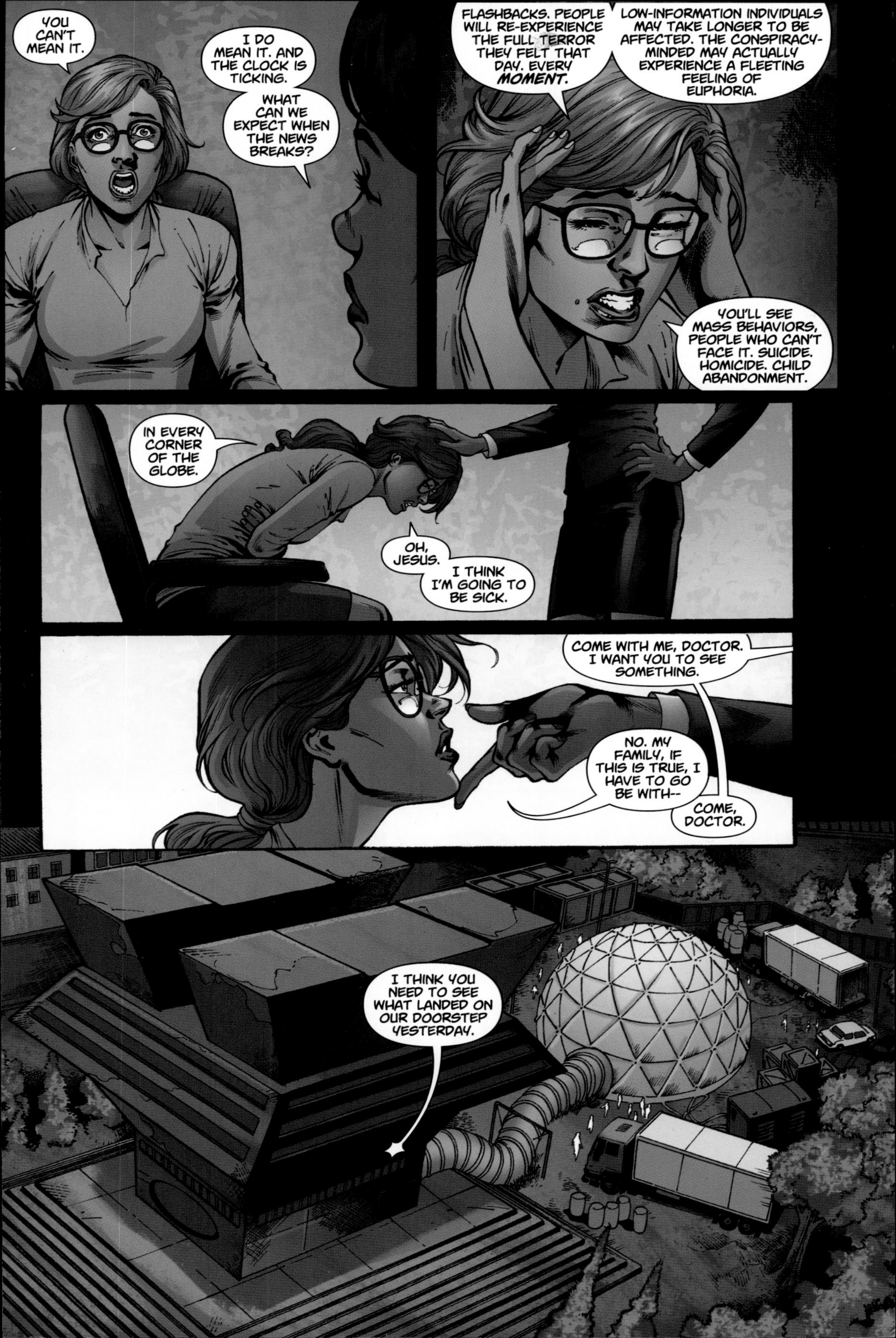
YOU CAN'T MEAN IT.
I DO MEAN IT. AND THE CLOCK IS TICKING.
WHAT CAN WE EXPECT WHEN THE NEWS BREAKS?
FLASHBACKS. PEOPLE WILL RE-EXPERIENCE THE FULL TERROR THEY FELT THAT DAY. EVERY *MOMENT*.
LOW-INFORMATION INDIVIDUALS MAY TAKE LONGER TO BE AFFECTED. THE CONSPIRACY-MINDED MAY ACTUALLY EXPERIENCE A FLEETING FEELING OF EUPHORIA.
YOU'LL SEE MASS BEHAVIORS, PEOPLE WHO CAN'T FACE IT. SUICIDE. HOMICIDE. CHILD ABANDONMENT.
IN EVERY CORNER OF THE GLOBE.
OH, JESUS.
I THINK I'M GOING TO BE SICK.
COME WITH ME, DOCTOR. I WANT YOU TO SEE SOMETHING.
NO. MY FAMILY, IF THIS IS TRUE, I HAVE TO GO BE WITH--
COME, DOCTOR.
I THINK YOU NEED TO SEE WHAT LANDED ON OUR DOORSTEP YESTERDAY.

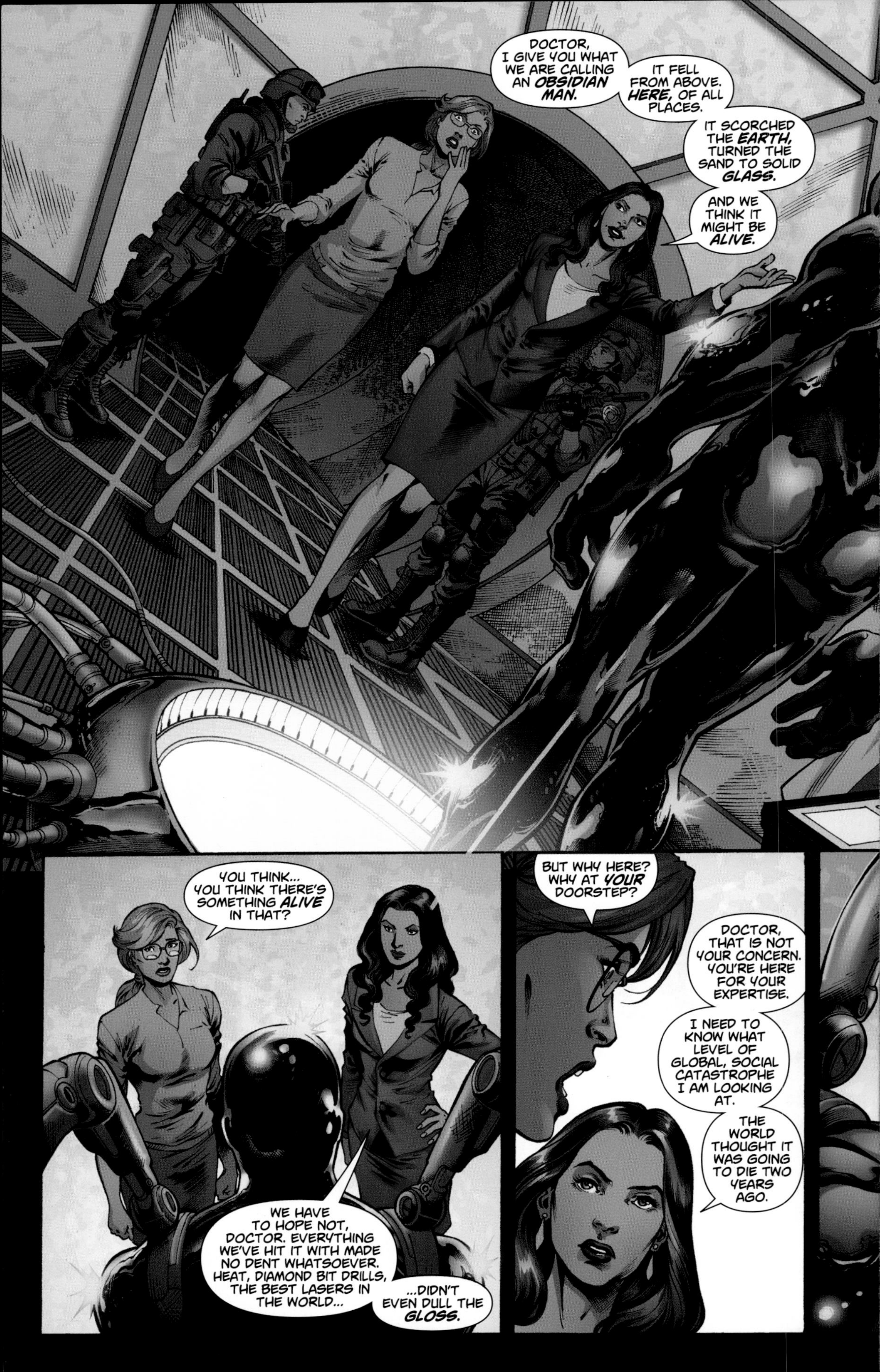
DOCTOR, I GIVE YOU WHAT WE ARE CALLING AN OBSIDIAN MAN.
IT FELL FROM ABOVE. HERE, OF ALL PLACES.
IT SCORCHED THE EARTH, TURNED THE SAND TO SOLID GLASS.
AND WE THINK IT MIGHT BE ALIVE.
YOU THINK... YOU THINK THERE'S SOMETHING ALIVE IN THAT?
WE HAVE TO HOPE NOT, DOCTOR. EVERYTHING WE'VE HIT IT WITH MADE NO DENT WHATSOEVER. HEAT, DIAMOND BIT DRILLS, THE BEST LASERS IN THE WORLD...
...DIDN'T EVEN DULL THE GLOSS.
BUT WHY HERE? WHY AT YOUR DOORSTEP?
DOCTOR, THAT IS NOT YOUR CONCERN. YOU'RE HERE FOR YOUR EXPERTISE.
I NEED TO KNOW WHAT LEVEL OF GLOBAL, SOCIAL CATASTROPHE I AM LOOKING AT.
THE WORLD THOUGHT IT WAS GOING TO DIE TWO YEARS AGO.

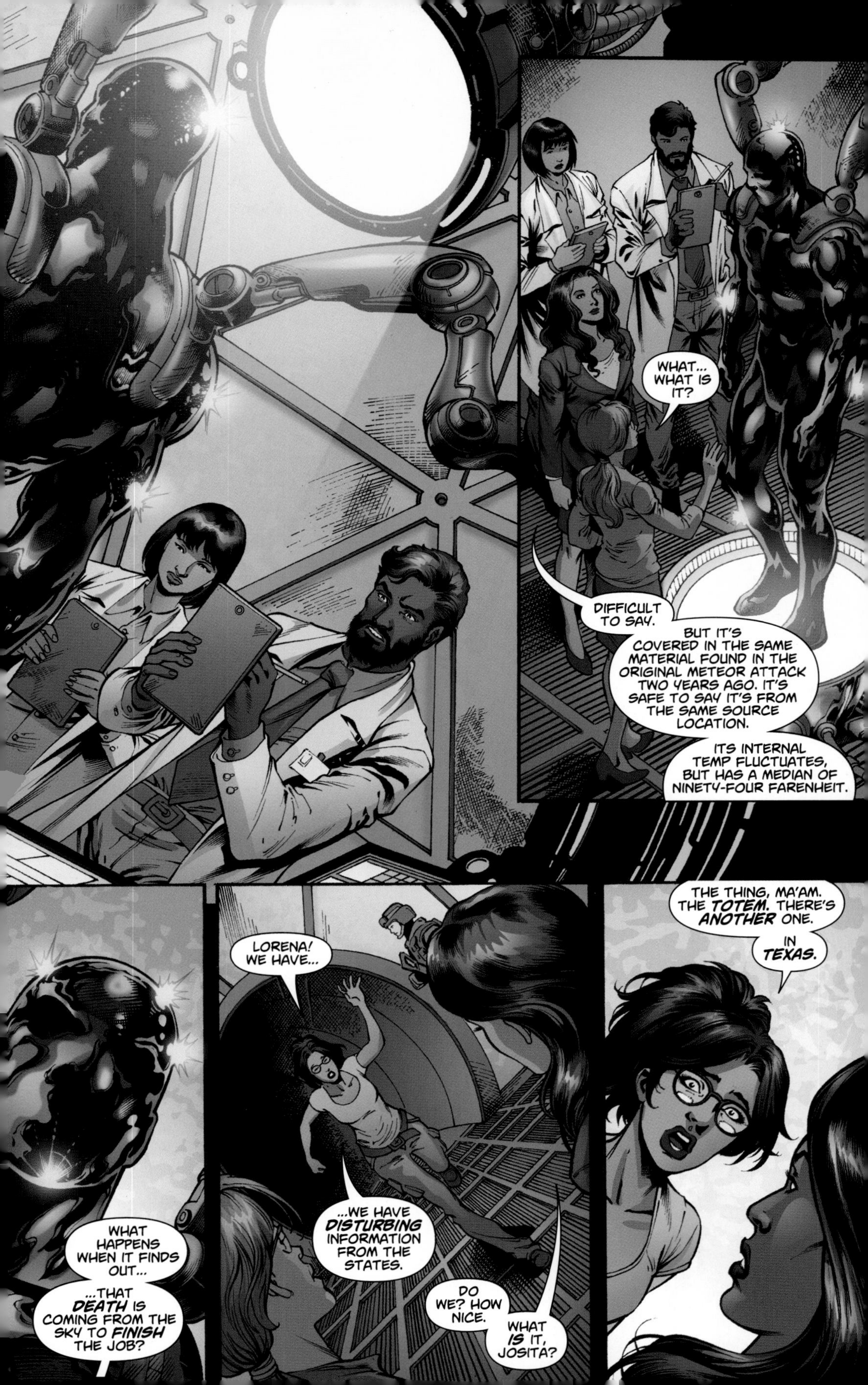
WHAT... WHAT IS IT?
DIFFICULT TO SAY.
BUT IT'S COVERED IN THE SAME MATERIAL FOUND IN THE ORIGINAL METEOR ATTACK TWO YEARS AGO. IT'S SAFE TO SAY IT'S FROM THE SAME SOURCE LOCATION.
ITS INTERNAL TEMP FLUCTUATES, BUT HAS A MEDIAN OF NINETY-FOUR FARENHEIT.
WHAT HAPPENS WHEN IT FINDS OUT...
...THAT DEATH IS COMING FROM THE SKY TO FINISH THE JOB?
LORENA! WE HAVE...
...WE HAVE DISTURBING INFORMATION FROM THE STATES.
DO WE? HOW NICE.
WHAT IS IT, JOSITA?
THE THING, MA'AM. THE TOTEM. THERE'S ANOTHER ONE.
IN TEXAS.

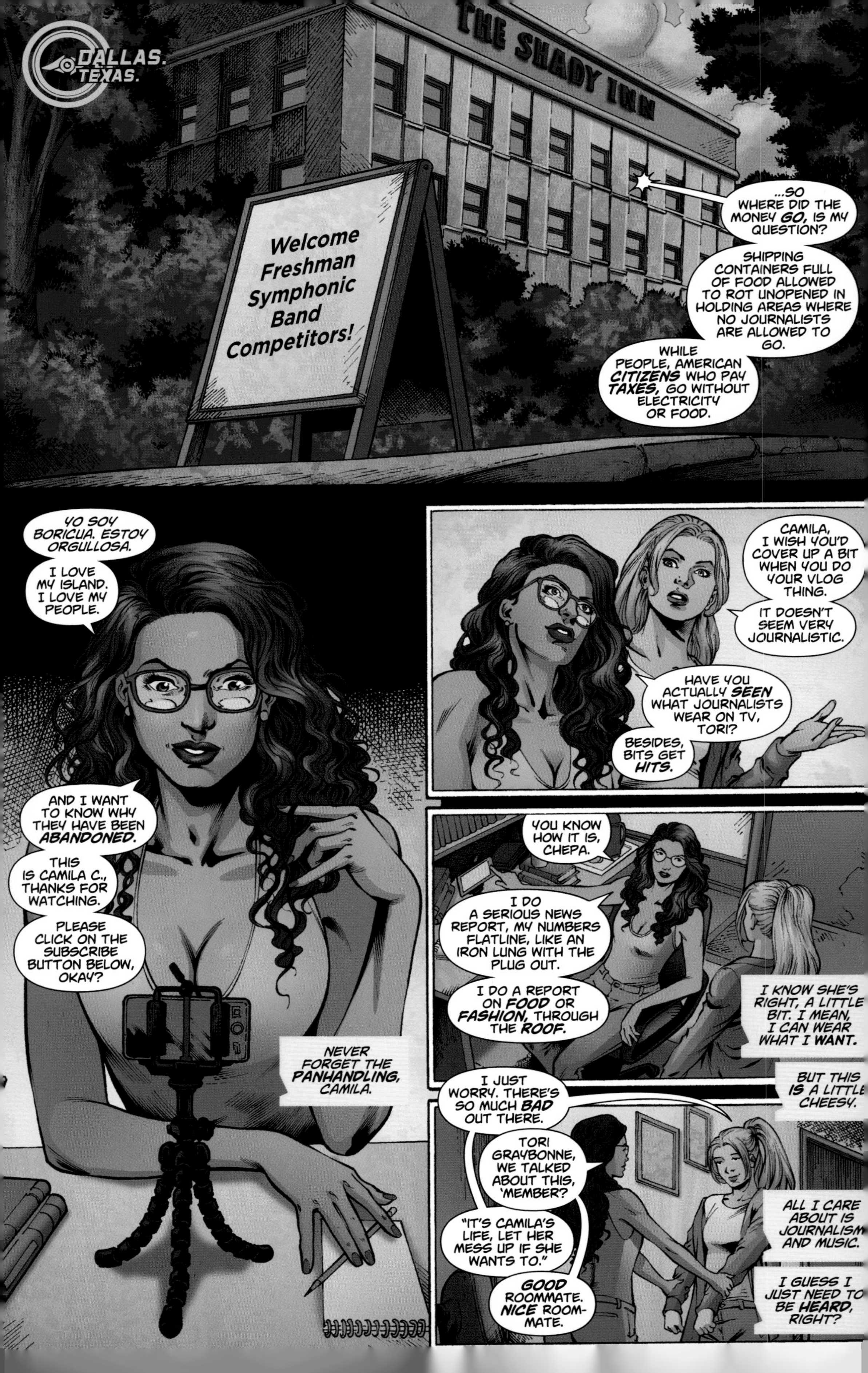
DALLAS. TEXAS.
THE SHADY INN
Welcome Freshman Symphonic Band Competitors!
...SO WHERE DID THE MONEY GO, IS MY QUESTION?
SHIPPING CONTAINERS FULL OF FOOD ALLOWED TO ROT UNOPENED IN HOLDING AREAS WHERE NO JOURNALISTS ARE ALLOWED TO GO.
WHILE PEOPLE, AMERICAN CITIZENS WHO PAY TAXES, GO WITHOUT ELECTRICITY OR FOOD.
YO SOY BORICUA. ESTOY ORGULLOSA.
I LOVE MY ISLAND. I LOVE MY PEOPLE.
AND I WANT TO KNOW WHY THEY HAVE BEEN ABANDONED.
THIS IS CAMILA C., THANKS FOR WATCHING.
PLEASE CLICK ON THE SUBSCRIBE BUTTON BELOW, OKAY?
NEVER FORGET THE PANHANDLING, CAMILA.
CAMILA, I WISH YOU'D COVER UP A BIT WHEN YOU DO YOUR VLOG THING.
IT DOESN'T SEEM VERY JOURNALISTIC.
HAVE YOU ACTUALLY SEEN WHAT JOURNALISTS WEAR ON TV, TORI?
BESIDES, BITS GET HITS.
YOU KNOW HOW IT IS, CHEPA.
I DO A SERIOUS NEWS REPORT, MY NUMBERS FLATLINE, LIKE AN IRON LUNG WITH THE PLUG OUT.
I DO A REPORT ON FOOD OR FASHION, THROUGH THE ROOF.
I KNOW SHE'S RIGHT, A LITTLE BIT. I MEAN, I CAN WEAR WHAT I WANT.
BUT THIS IS A LITTLE CHEESY.
I JUST WORRY. THERE'S SO MUCH BAD OUT THERE.
TORI GRAYBONNE, WE TALKED ABOUT THIS, 'MEMBER?
"IT'S CAMILA'S LIFE, LET HER MESS UP IF SHE WANTS TO."
GOOD ROOMMATE. NICE ROOMMATE.
ALL I CARE ABOUT IS JOURNALISM AND MUSIC.
I GUESS I JUST NEED TO BE HEARD, RIGHT?

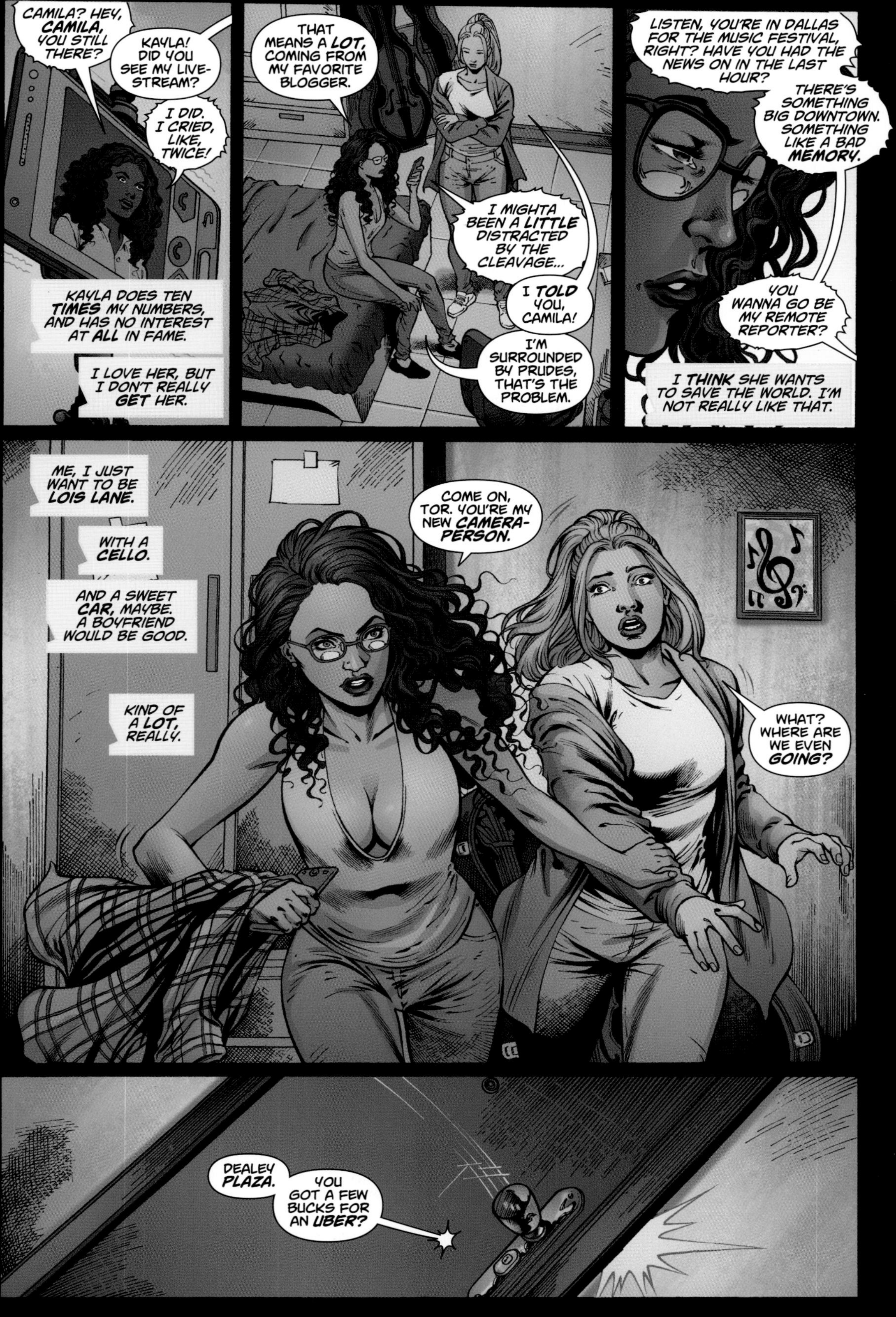

CAMILA? HEY, CAMILA, YOU STILL THERE?
KAYLA! DID YOU SEE MY LIVE-STREAM?
I DID. I CRIED, LIKE, TWICE!
KAYLA DOES TEN TIMES MY NUMBERS, AND HAS NO INTEREST AT ALL IN FAME.
I LOVE HER, BUT I DON'T REALLY GET HER.
THAT MEANS A LOT, COMING FROM MY FAVORITE BLOGGER.
I MIGHTA BEEN A LITTLE DISTRACTED BY THE CLEAVAGE...
I TOLD YOU, CAMILA!
I'M SURROUNDED BY PRUDES, THAT'S THE PROBLEM.
LISTEN, YOU'RE IN DALLAS FOR THE MUSIC FESTIVAL, RIGHT? HAVE YOU HAD THE NEWS ON IN THE LAST HOUR?
THERE'S SOMETHING BIG DOWNTOWN. SOMETHING LIKE A BAD MEMORY.
YOU WANNA GO BE MY REMOTE REPORTER?
I THINK SHE WANTS TO SAVE THE WORLD. I'M NOT REALLY LIKE THAT.
ME, I JUST WANT TO BE LOIS LANE.
WITH A CELLO.
AND A SWEET CAR, MAYBE. A BOYFRIEND WOULD BE GOOD.
KIND OF A LOT, REALLY.
COME ON, TOR. YOU'RE MY NEW CAMERA-PERSON.
WHAT? WHERE ARE WE EVEN GOING?
DEALEY PLAZA.
YOU GOT A FEW BUCKS FOR AN UBER?

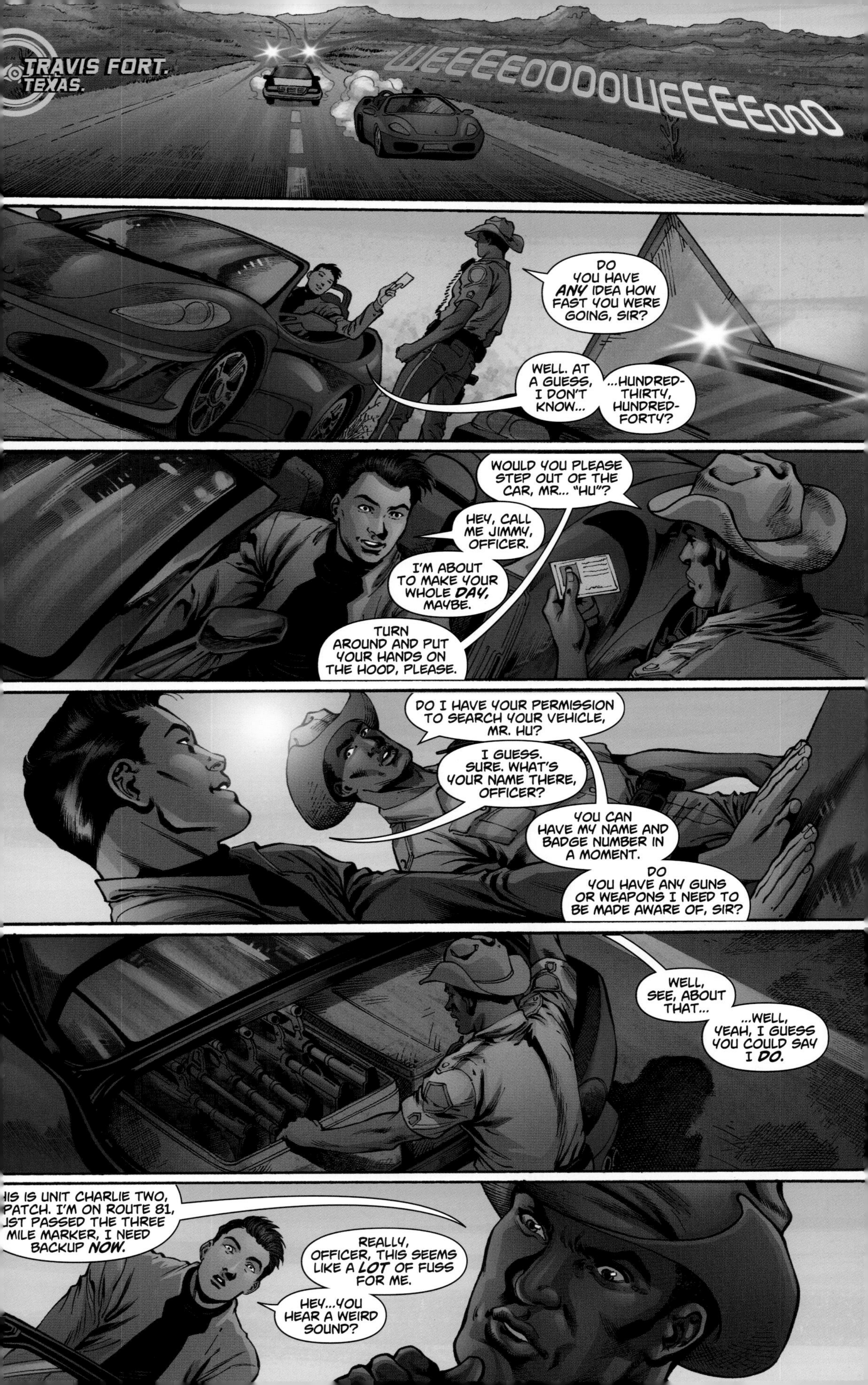
TRAVIS FORT, TEXAS.
WEEEEOOOOWEEEEOOO
DO YOU HAVE ANY IDEA HOW FAST YOU WERE GOING, SIR?
WELL. AT A GUESS, I DON'T KNOW...
...HUNDRED-THIRTY, HUNDRED-FORTY?
WOULD YOU PLEASE STEP OUT OF THE CAR, MR... "HU"?
HEY, CALL ME JIMMY, OFFICER.
I'M ABOUT TO MAKE YOUR WHOLE DAY, MAYBE.
TURN AROUND AND PUT YOUR HANDS ON THE HOOD, PLEASE.
DO I HAVE YOUR PERMISSION TO SEARCH YOUR VEHICLE, MR. HU?
I GUESS. SURE. WHAT'S YOUR NAME THERE, OFFICER?
YOU CAN HAVE MY NAME AND BADGE NUMBER IN A MOMENT.
DO YOU HAVE ANY GUNS OR WEAPONS I NEED TO BE MADE AWARE OF, SIR?
WELL, SEE, ABOUT THAT...
...WELL, YEAH, I GUESS YOU COULD SAY I DO.
HIS IS UNIT CHARLIE TWO, PATCH. I'M ON ROUTE 81, UST PASSED THE THREE MILE MARKER, I NEED BACKUP NOW.
REALLY, OFFICER, THIS SEEMS LIKE A LOT OF FUSS FOR ME.
HEY...YOU HEAR A WEIRD SOUND?

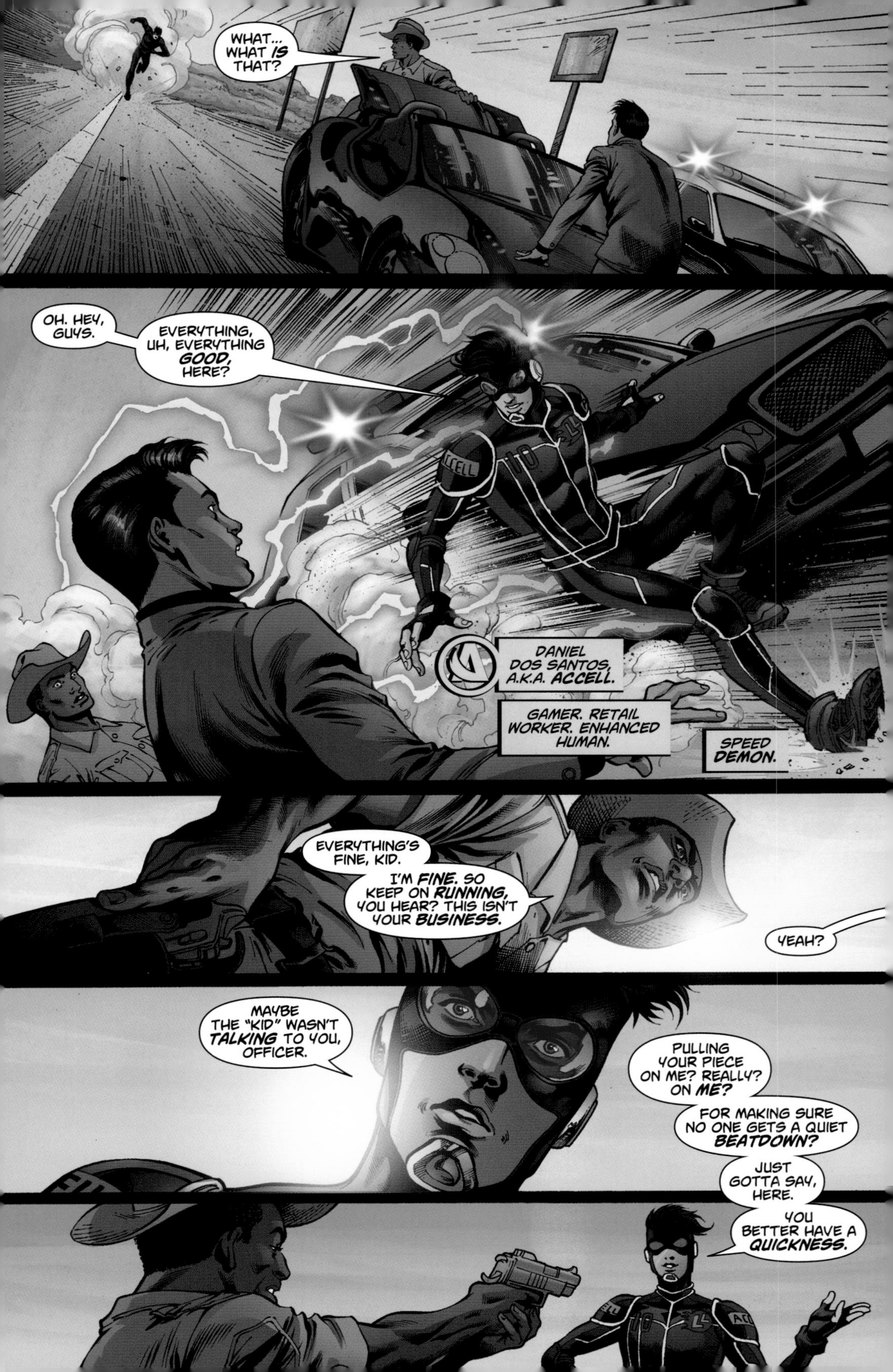
WHAT... WHAT IS THAT?
OH. HEY, GUYS.
EVERYTHING, UH, EVERYTHING GOOD, HERE?
DANIEL DOS SANTOS, A.K.A. ACCELL.
GAMER. RETAIL WORKER. ENHANCED HUMAN.
SPEED DEMON.
EVERYTHING'S FINE, KID.
I'M FINE. SO KEEP ON RUNNING, YOU HEAR? THIS ISN'T YOUR BUSINESS.
YEAH?
MAYBE THE "KID" WASN'T TALKING TO YOU, OFFICER.
PULLING YOUR PIECE ON ME? REALLY? ON ME?
FOR MAKING SURE NO ONE GETS A QUIET BEATDOWN?
JUST GOTTA SAY, HERE.
YOU BETTER HAVE A QUICKNESS.

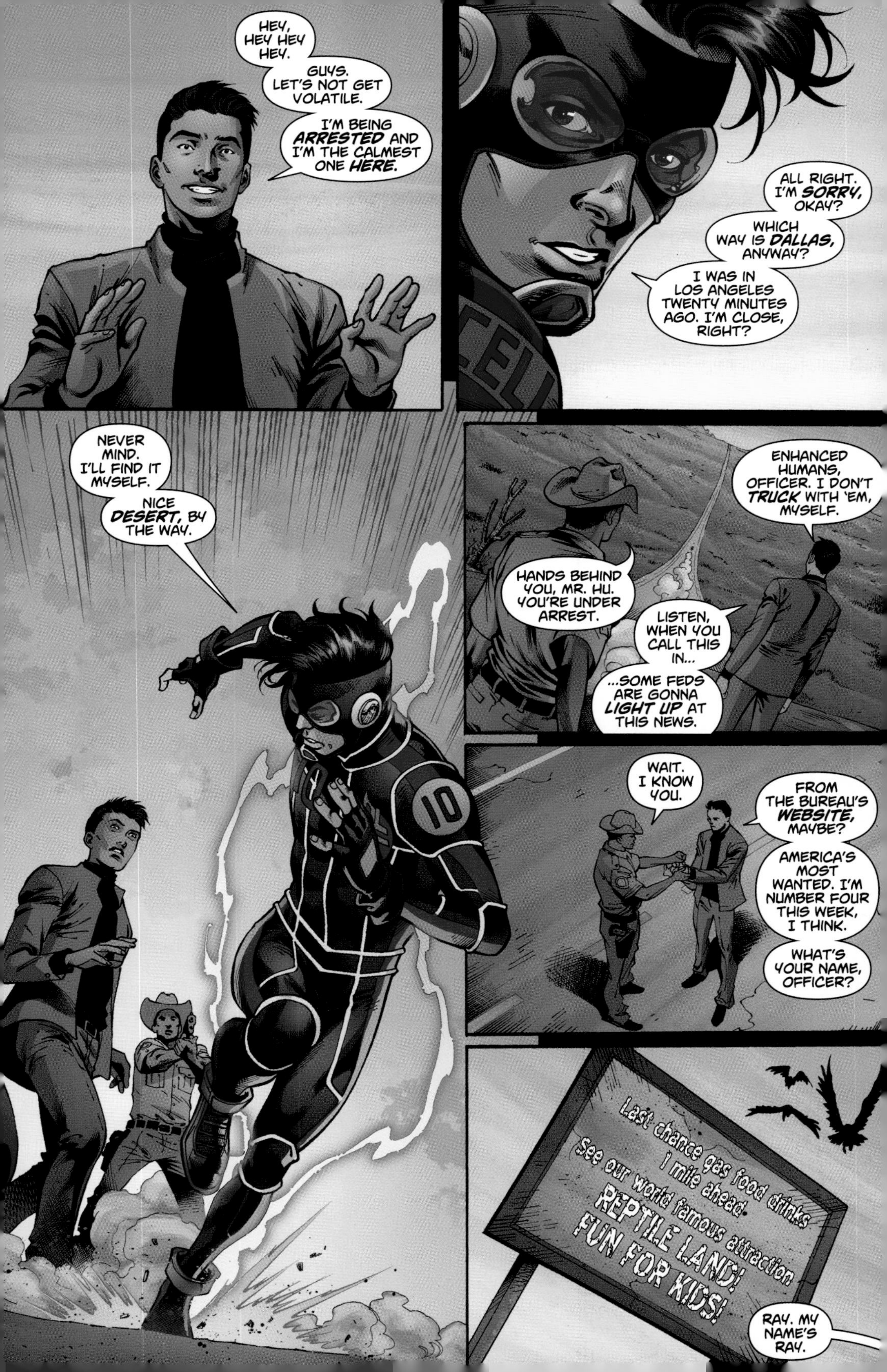
HEY, HEY HEY HEY.
GUYS. LET'S NOT GET VOLATILE.
I'M BEING ARRESTED AND I'M THE CALMEST ONE HERE.
ALL RIGHT. I'M SORRY, OKAY?
WHICH WAY IS DALLAS, ANYWAY?
I WAS IN LOS ANGELES TWENTY MINUTES AGO. I'M CLOSE, RIGHT?
NEVER MIND. I'LL FIND IT MYSELF.
NICE DESERT, BY THE WAY.
10
ENHANCED HUMANS, OFFICER. I DON'T TRUCK WITH 'EM, MYSELF.
HANDS BEHIND YOU, MR. HU. YOU'RE UNDER ARREST.
LISTEN, WHEN YOU CALL THIS IN...
...SOME FEDS ARE GONNA LIGHT UP AT THIS NEWS.
WAIT. I KNOW YOU.
FROM THE BUREAU'S WEBSITE, MAYBE?
AMERICA'S MOST WANTED. I'M NUMBER FOUR THIS WEEK, I THINK.
WHAT'S YOUR NAME, OFFICER?
Last chance gas food drinks
1 mile ahead
See our world famous attraction
REPTILE LAND!
FUN FOR KIDS!
RAY. MY NAME'S RAY.

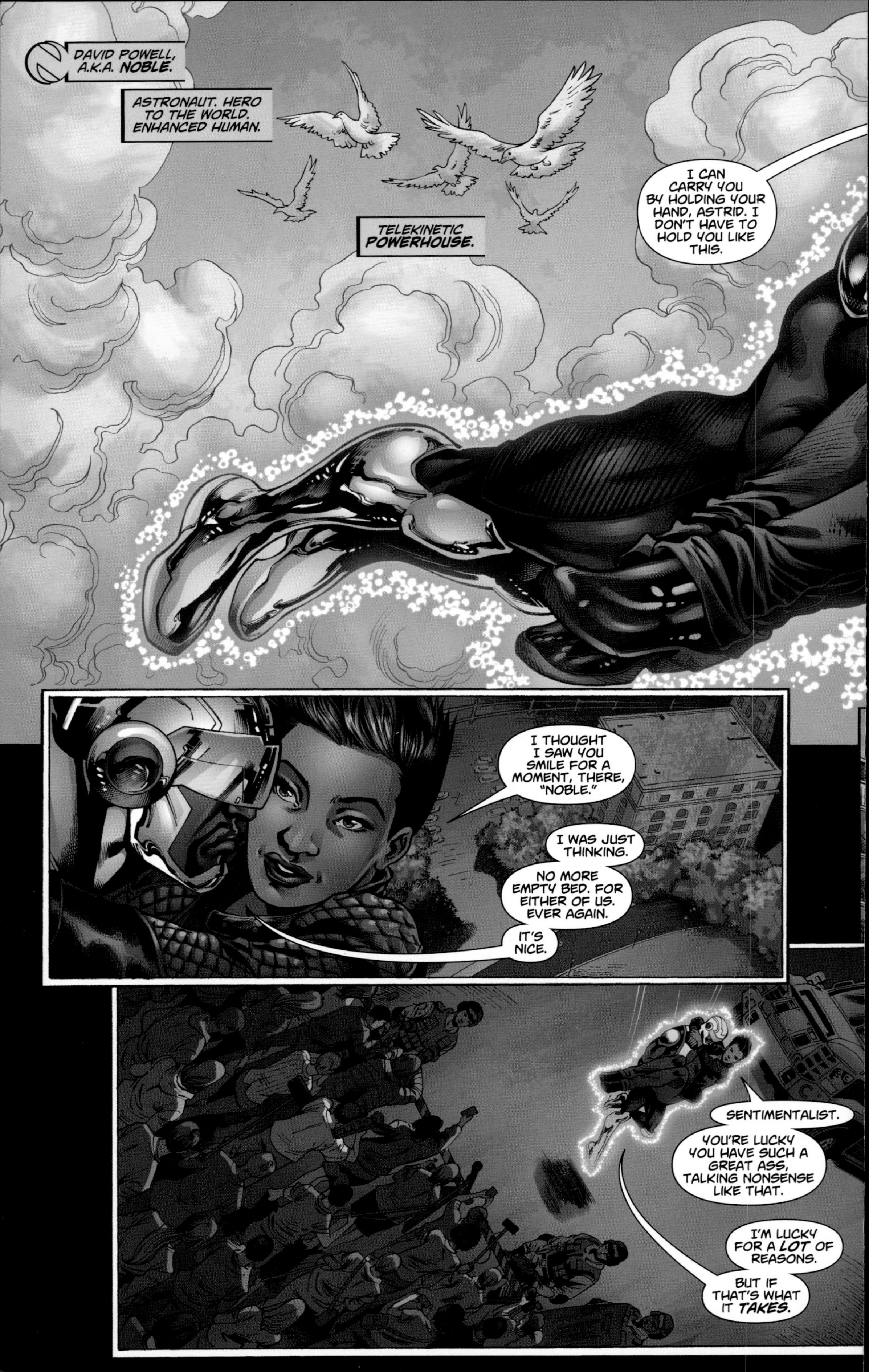
DAVID POWELL, A.K.A. NOBLE.
ASTRONAUT. HERO TO THE WORLD. ENHANCED HUMAN.
TELEKINETIC POWERHOUSE.
I CAN CARRY YOU BY HOLDING YOUR HAND, ASTRID. I DON'T HAVE TO HOLD YOU LIKE THIS.
I THOUGHT I SAW YOU SMILE FOR A MOMENT, THERE, "NOBLE."
I WAS JUST THINKING.
NO MORE EMPTY BED. FOR EITHER OF US. EVER AGAIN.
IT'S NICE.
SENTIMENTALIST.
YOU'RE LUCKY YOU HAVE SUCH A GREAT ASS, TALKING NONSENSE LIKE THAT.
I'M LUCKY FOR A LOT OF REASONS.
BUT IF THAT'S WHAT IT TAKES.

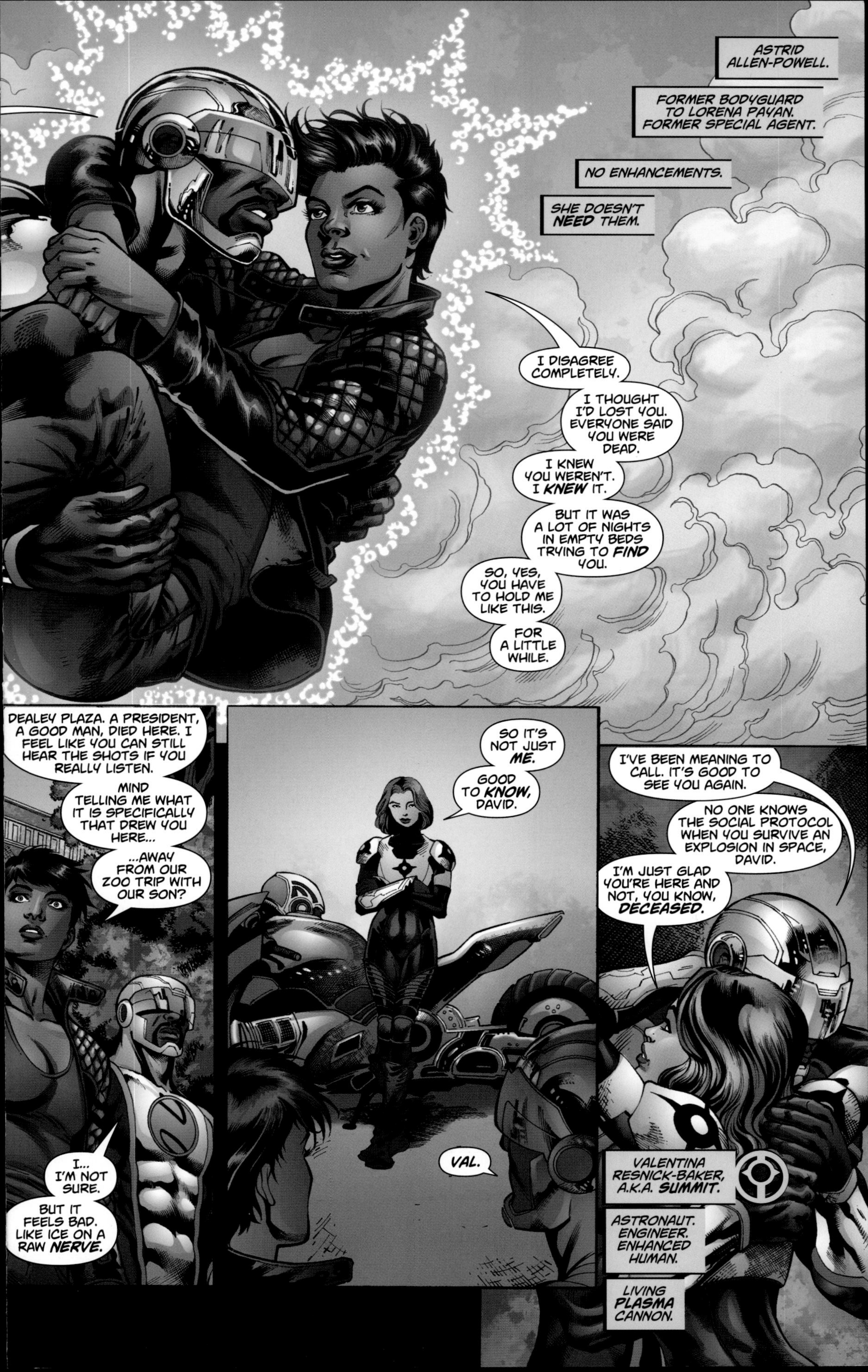
ASTRID ALLEN-POWELL.
FORMER BODYGUARD TO LORENA PAYAN. FORMER SPECIAL AGENT.
NO ENHANCEMENTS.
SHE DOESN'T NEED THEM.
I DISAGREE COMPLETELY.
I THOUGHT I'D LOST YOU. EVERYONE SAID YOU WERE DEAD.
I KNEW YOU WEREN'T. I KNEW IT.
BUT IT WAS A LOT OF NIGHTS IN EMPTY BEDS TRYING TO FIND YOU.
SO, YES, YOU HAVE TO HOLD ME LIKE THIS.
FOR A LITTLE WHILE.
DEALEY PLAZA. A PRESIDENT, A GOOD MAN, DIED HERE. I FEEL LIKE YOU CAN STILL HEAR THE SHOTS IF YOU REALLY LISTEN.
MIND TELLING ME WHAT IT IS SPECIFICALLY THAT DREW YOU HERE...
...AWAY FROM OUR ZOO TRIP WITH OUR SON?
I... I'M NOT SURE.
BUT IT FEELS BAD. LIKE ICE ON A RAW NERVE.
SO IT'S NOT JUST ME.
GOOD TO KNOW, DAVID.
VAL.
I'VE BEEN MEANING TO CALL. IT'S GOOD TO SEE YOU AGAIN.
NO ONE KNOWS THE SOCIAL PROTOCOL WHEN YOU SURVIVE AN EXPLOSION IN SPACE, DAVID.
I'M JUST GLAD YOU'RE HERE AND NOT, YOU KNOW, DECEASED.
VALENTINA RESNICK-BAKER, A.K.A. SUMMIT.
ASTRONAUT. ENGINEER. ENHANCED HUMAN.
LIVING PLASMA CANNON.

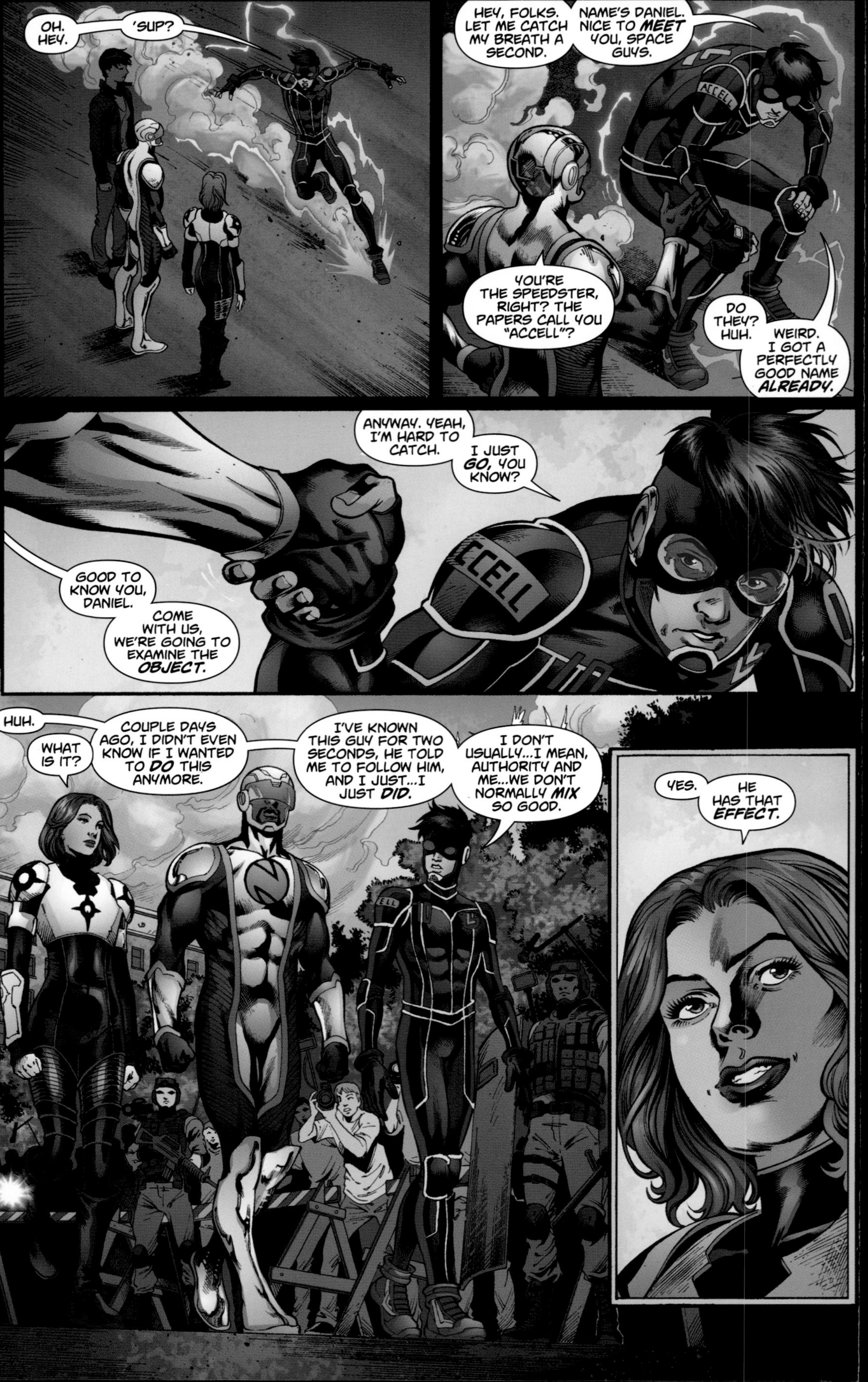
OH. HEY.
'SUP?
HEY, FOLKS. LET ME CATCH MY BREATH A SECOND.
NAME'S DANIEL. NICE TO MEET YOU, SPACE GUYS.
YOU'RE THE SPEEDSTER, RIGHT? THE PAPERS CALL YOU "ACCELL"?
DO THEY? HUH.
WEIRD. I GOT A PERFECTLY GOOD NAME ALREADY.
ANYWAY. YEAH, I'M HARD TO CATCH.
I JUST GO, YOU KNOW?
GOOD TO KNOW YOU, DANIEL.
COME WITH US, WE'RE GOING TO EXAMINE THE OBJECT.
HUH.
WHAT IS IT?
COUPLE DAYS AGO, I DIDN'T EVEN KNOW IF I WANTED TO DO THIS ANYMORE.
I'VE KNOWN THIS GUY FOR TWO SECONDS, HE TOLD ME TO FOLLOW HIM, AND I JUST...I JUST DID.
I DON'T USUALLY...I MEAN, AUTHORITY AND ME...WE DON'T NORMALLY MIX SO GOOD.
YES.
HE HAS THAT EFFECT.

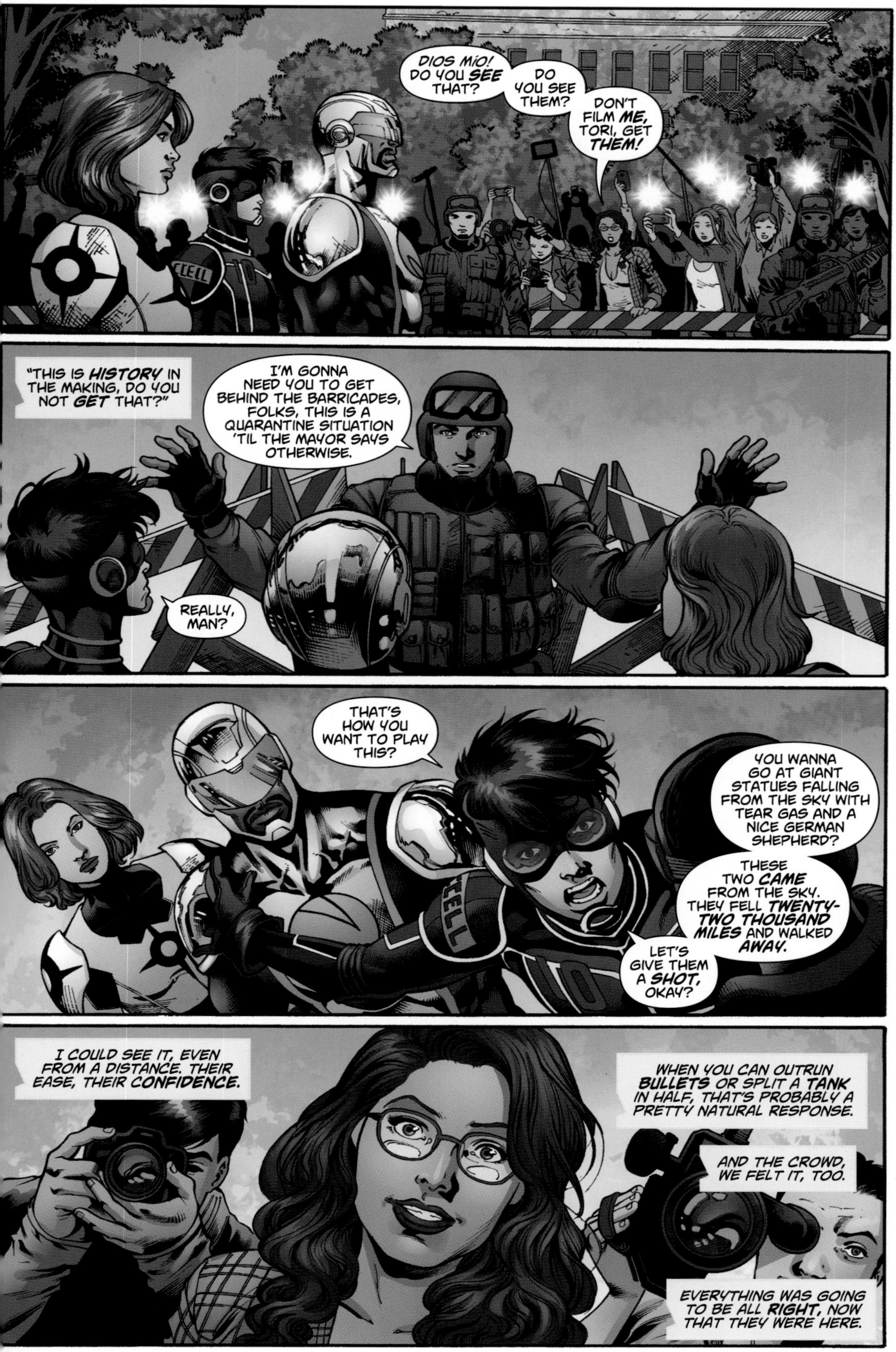
DIOS MÍO! DO YOU SEE THAT?
DO YOU SEE THEM?
DON'T FILM ME, TORI, GET THEM!
"THIS IS HISTORY IN THE MAKING, DO YOU NOT GET THAT?"
I'M GONNA NEED YOU TO GET BEHIND THE BARRICADES, FOLKS, THIS IS A QUARANTINE SITUATION 'TIL THE MAYOR SAYS OTHERWISE.
REALLY, MAN?
THAT'S HOW YOU WANT TO PLAY THIS?
YOU WANNA GO AT GIANT STATUES FALLING FROM THE SKY WITH TEAR GAS AND A NICE GERMAN SHEPHERD?
THESE TWO CAME FROM THE SKY. THEY FELL TWENTY-TWO THOUSAND MILES AND WALKED AWAY.
LET'S GIVE THEM A SHOT, OKAY?
I COULD SEE IT, EVEN FROM A DISTANCE. THEIR EASE, THEIR CONFIDENCE.
WHEN YOU CAN OUTRUN BULLETS OR SPLIT A TANK IN HALF, THAT'S PROBABLY A PRETTY NATURAL RESPONSE.
AND THE CROWD, WE FELT IT, TOO.
EVERYTHING WAS GOING TO BE ALL RIGHT, NOW THAT THEY WERE HERE.

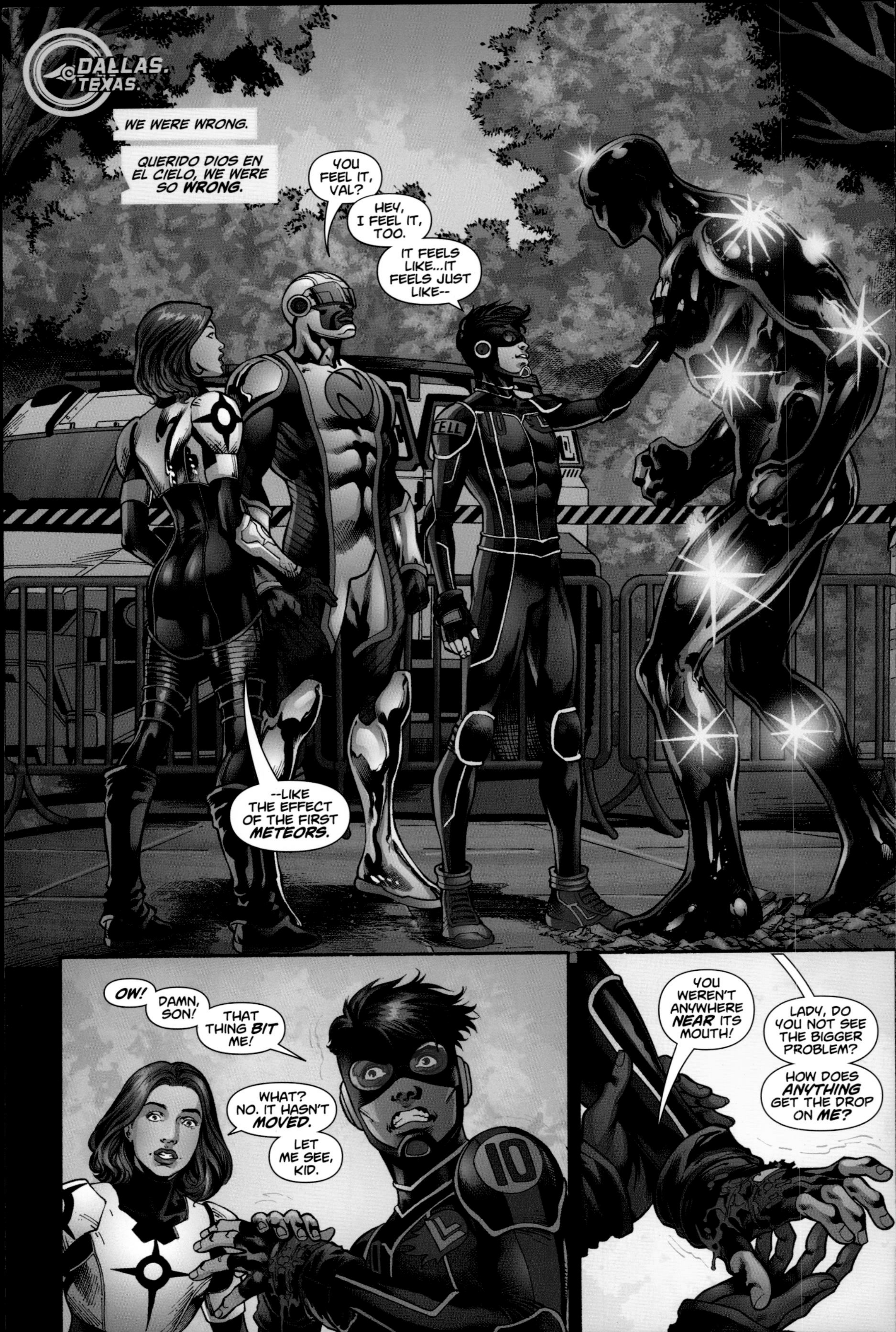

DALLAS, TEXAS.
WE WERE WRONG.
QUERIDO DIOS EN EL CIELO, WE WERE SO WRONG.
YOU FEEL IT, VAL?
HEY, I FEEL IT, TOO.
IT FEELS LIKE...IT FEELS JUST LIKE--
--LIKE THE EFFECT OF THE FIRST METEORS.
OW!
DAMN, SON!
THAT THING BIT ME!
WHAT? NO. IT HASN'T MOVED.
LET ME SEE, KID.
YOU WEREN'T ANYWHERE NEAR ITS MOUTH!
LADY, DO YOU NOT SEE THE BIGGER PROBLEM?
HOW DOES ANYTHING GET THE DROP ON ME?

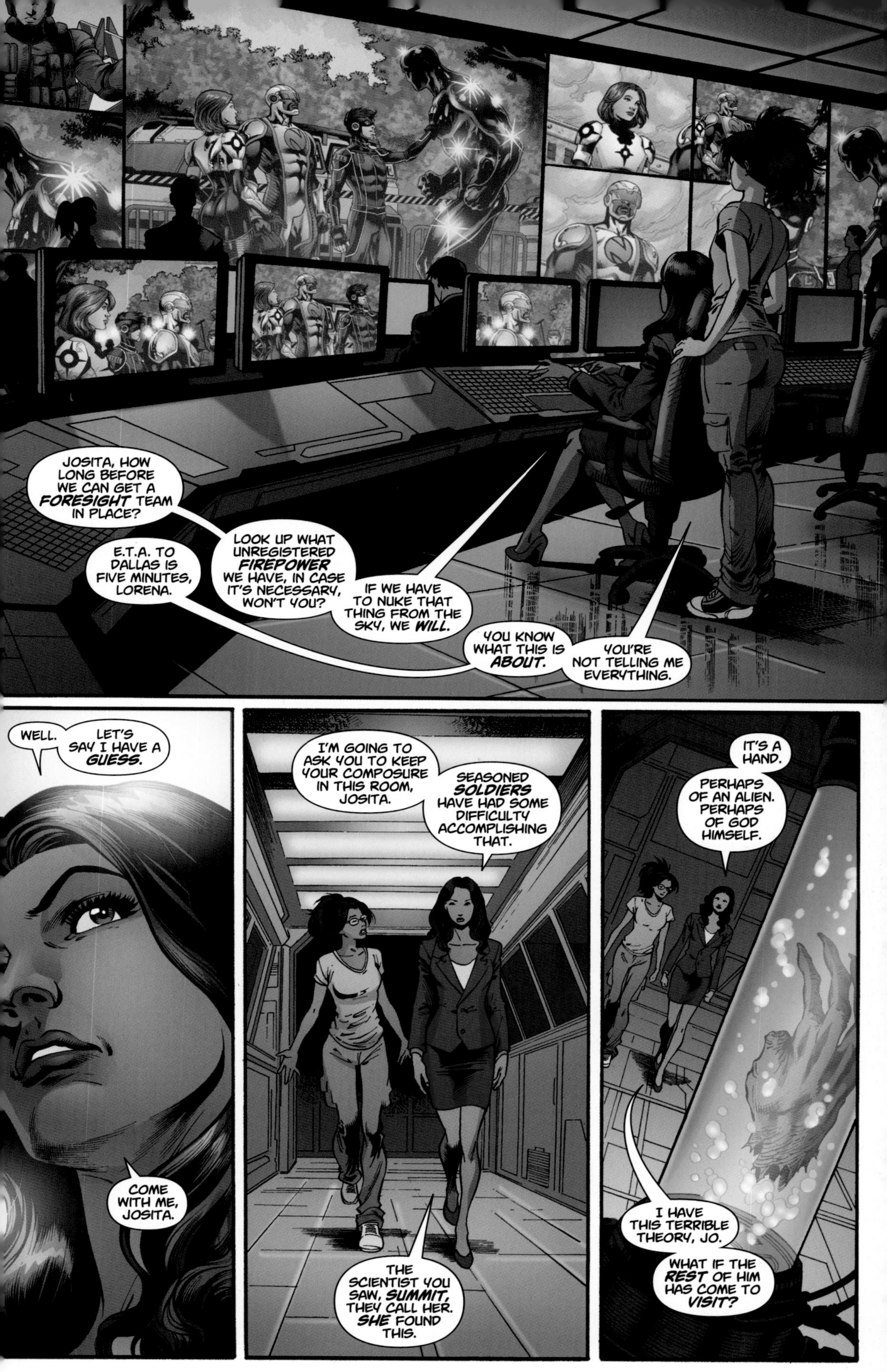
JOSITA, HOW LONG BEFORE WE CAN GET A FORESIGHT TEAM IN PLACE?
E.T.A. TO DALLAS IS FIVE MINUTES, LORENA.
LOOK UP WHAT UNREGISTERED FIREPOWER WE HAVE, IN CASE IT'S NECESSARY, WON'T YOU?
IF WE HAVE TO NUKE THAT THING FROM THE SKY, WE WILL.
YOU KNOW WHAT THIS IS ABOUT.
YOU'RE NOT TELLING ME EVERYTHING.
WELL.
LET'S SAY I HAVE A GUESS.
COME WITH ME, JOSITA.
I'M GOING TO ASK YOU TO KEEP YOUR COMPOSURE IN THIS ROOM, JOSITA.
SEASONED SOLDIERS HAVE HAD SOME DIFFICULTY ACCOMPLISHING THAT.
THE SCIENTIST YOU SAW, SUMMIT, THEY CALL HER. SHE FOUND THIS.
IT'S A HAND.
PERHAPS OF AN ALIEN. PERHAPS OF GOD HIMSELF.
I HAVE THIS TERRIBLE THEORY, JO.
WHAT IF THE REST OF HIM HAS COME TO VISIT?

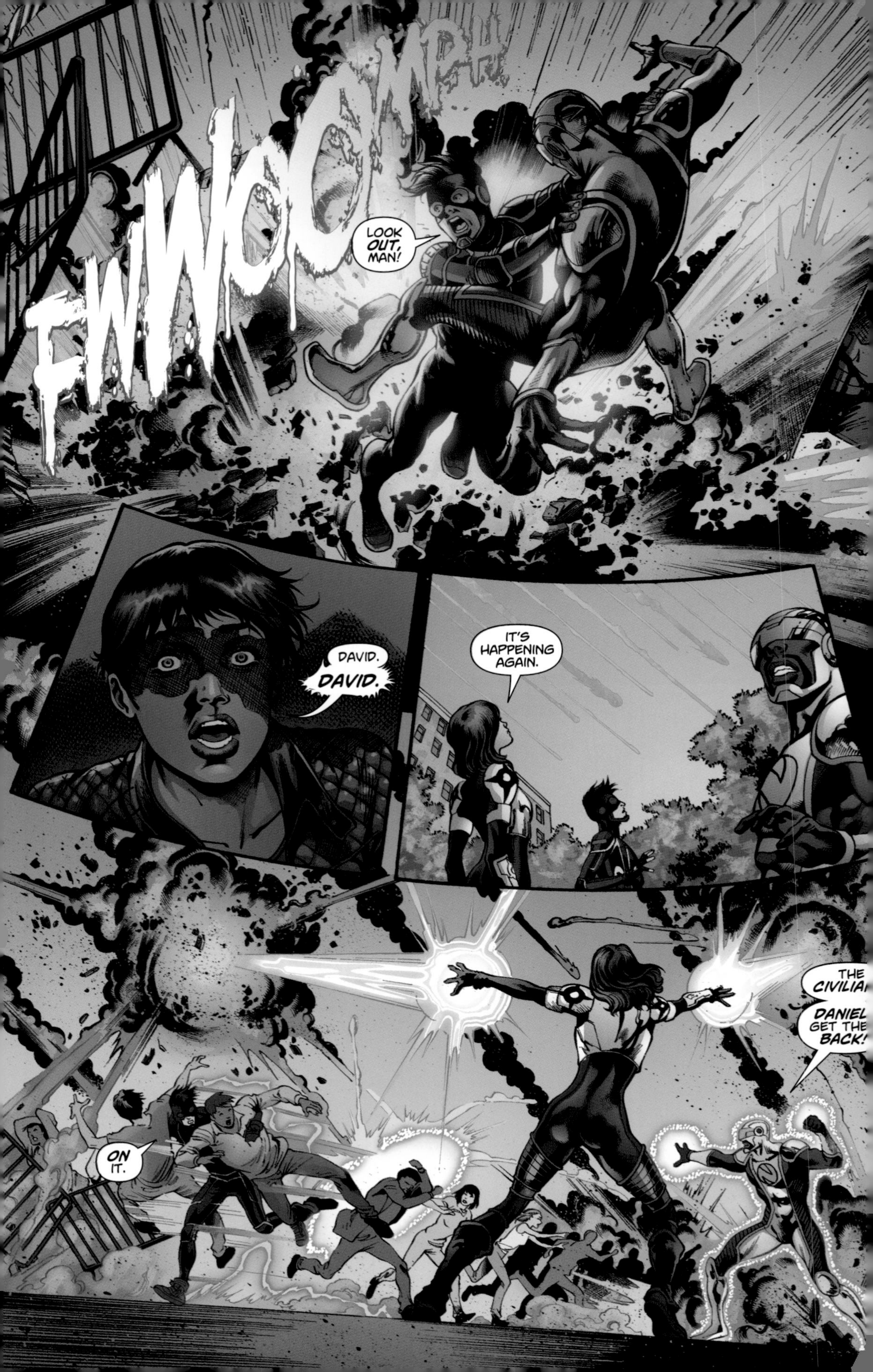
FWOOMPH
LOOK OUT, MAN!
DAVID. DAVID.
IT'S HAPPENING AGAIN.
THE CIVILIA
DANIEL GET THE BACK!
ON IT.

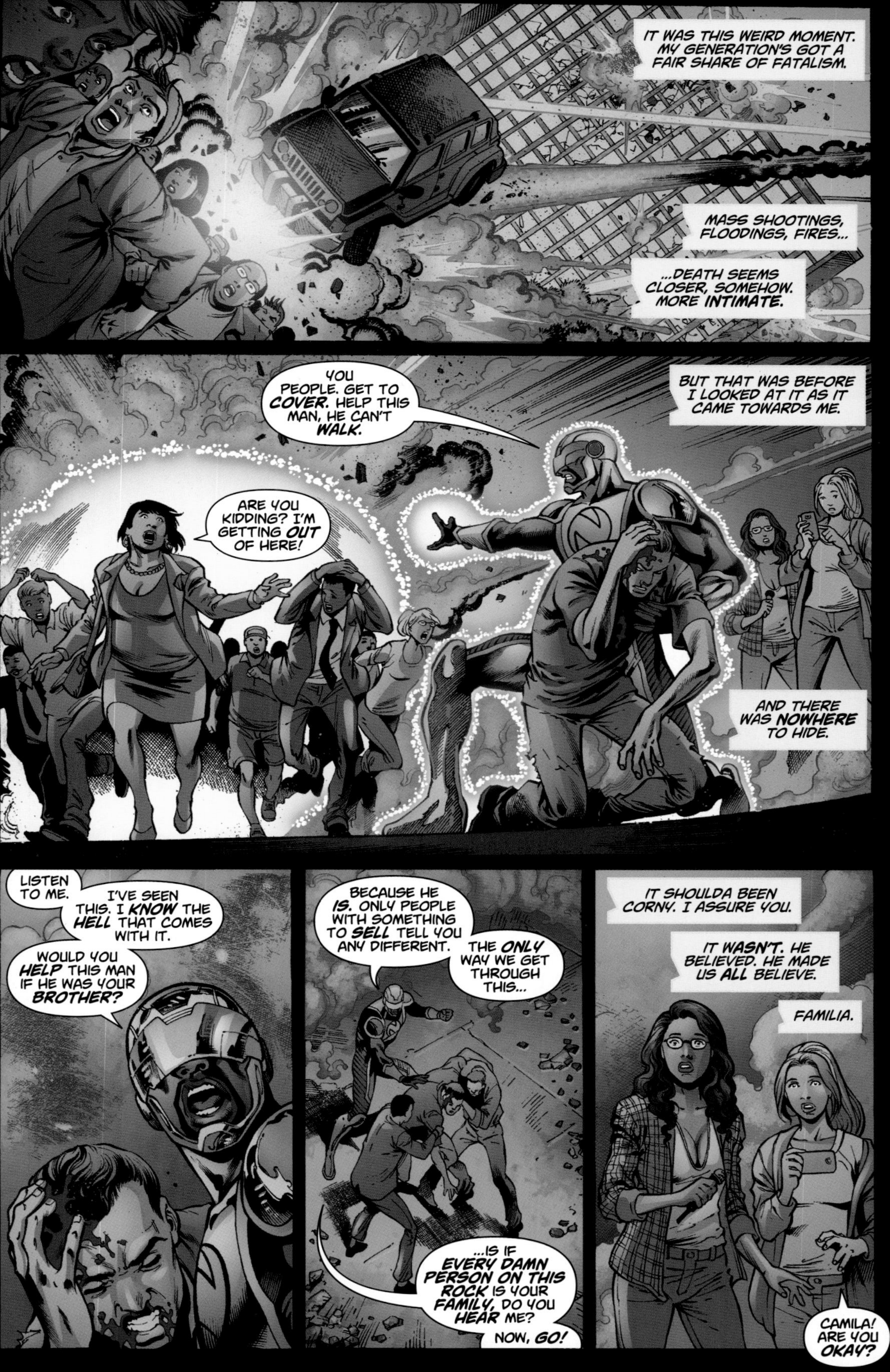
IT WAS THIS WEIRD MOMENT. MY GENERATION'S GOT A FAIR SHARE OF FATALISM.
MASS SHOOTINGS, FLOODINGS, FIRES...
...DEATH SEEMS CLOSER, SOMEHOW. MORE INTIMATE.
YOU PEOPLE. GET TO COVER. HELP THIS MAN, HE CAN'T WALK.
BUT THAT WAS BEFORE I LOOKED AT IT AS IT CAME TOWARDS ME.
ARE YOU KIDDING? I'M GETTING OUT OF HERE!
AND THERE WAS NOWHERE TO HIDE.
LISTEN TO ME.
I'VE SEEN THIS. I KNOW THE HELL THAT COMES WITH IT.
WOULD YOU HELP THIS MAN IF HE WAS YOUR BROTHER?
BECAUSE HE IS. ONLY PEOPLE WITH SOMETHING TO SELL TELL YOU ANY DIFFERENT.
THE ONLY WAY WE GET THROUGH THIS...
...IS IF EVERY DAMN PERSON ON THIS ROCK IS YOUR FAMILY, DO YOU HEAR ME?
NOW, GO!
IT SHOULDA BEEN CORNY. I ASSURE YOU.
IT WASN'T. HE BELIEVED. HE MADE US ALL BELIEVE.
FAMILIA.
CAMILA! ARE YOU OKAY?

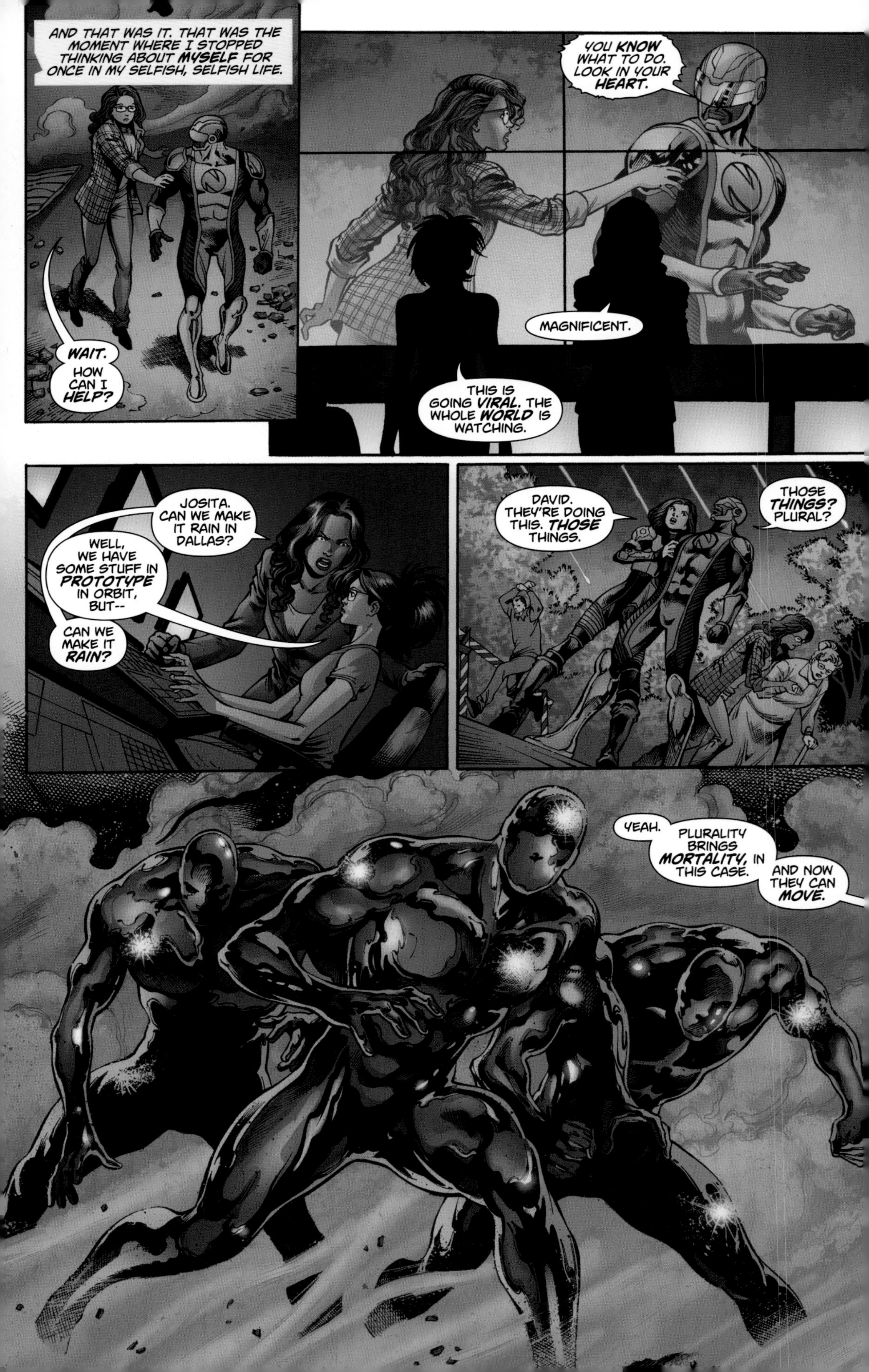
AND THAT WAS IT. THAT WAS THE MOMENT WHERE I STOPPED THINKING ABOUT MYSELF FOR ONCE IN MY SELFISH, SELFISH LIFE.
WAIT. HOW CAN I HELP?
YOU KNOW WHAT TO DO. LOOK IN YOUR HEART.
MAGNIFICENT.
THIS IS GOING VIRAL. THE WHOLE WORLD IS WATCHING.
JOSITA. CAN WE MAKE IT RAIN IN DALLAS?
WELL, WE HAVE SOME STUFF IN PROTOTYPE IN ORBIT, BUT--
CAN WE MAKE IT RAIN?
DAVID. THEY'RE DOING THIS. THOSE THINGS.
THOSE THINGS? PLURAL?
YEAH.
PLURALITY BRINGS MORTALITY, IN THIS CASE.
AND NOW THEY CAN MOVE.

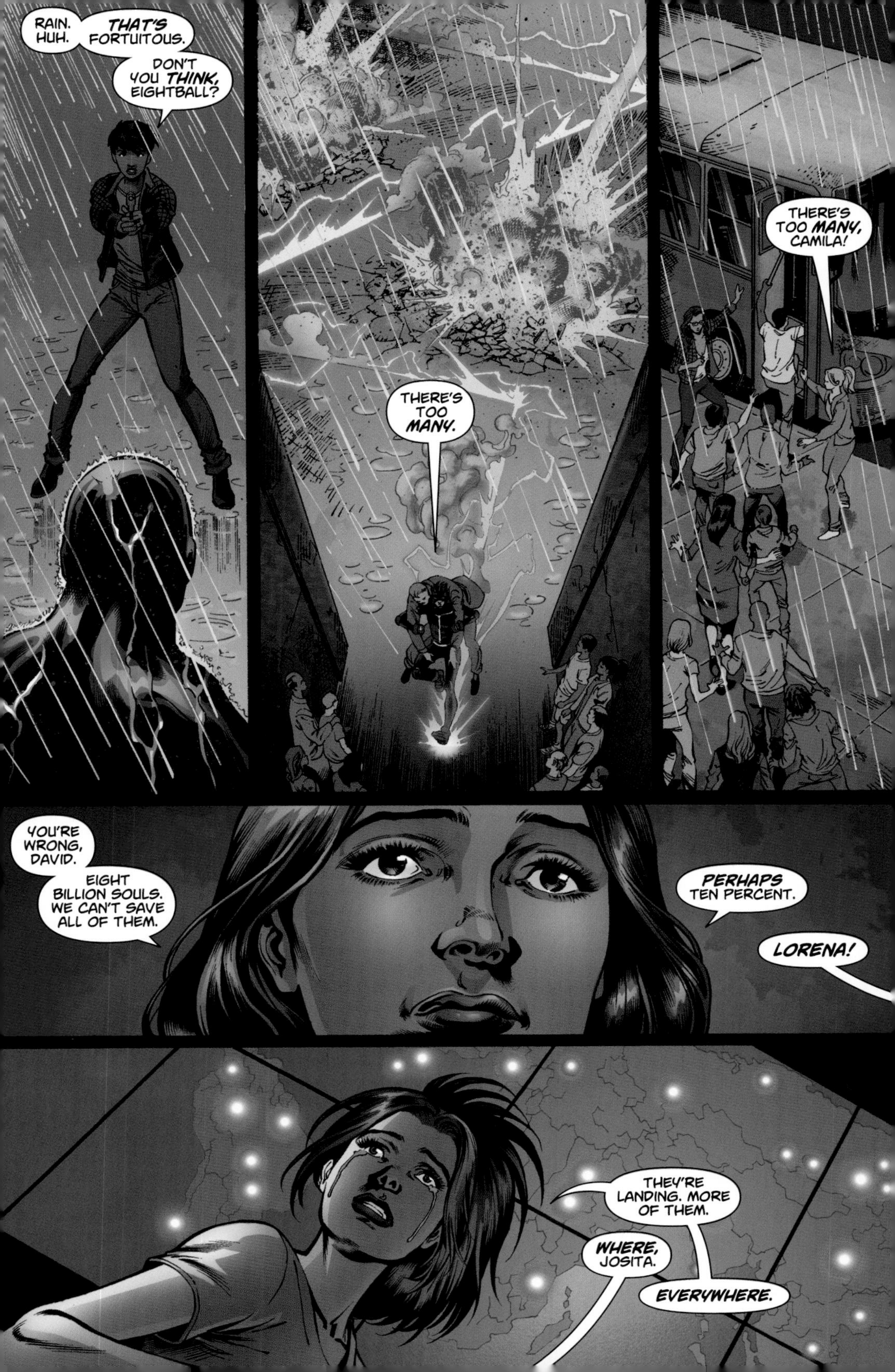
RAIN. HUH.
THAT'S FORTUITOUS.
DON'T YOU THINK, EIGHTBALL?
THERE'S TOO MANY.
THERE'S TOO MANY, CAMILA!
YOU'RE WRONG, DAVID.
EIGHT BILLION SOULS. WE CAN'T SAVE ALL OF THEM.
PERHAPS TEN PERCENT.
LORENA!
THEY'RE LANDING. MORE OF THEM.
WHERE, JOSITA.
EVERYWHERE.

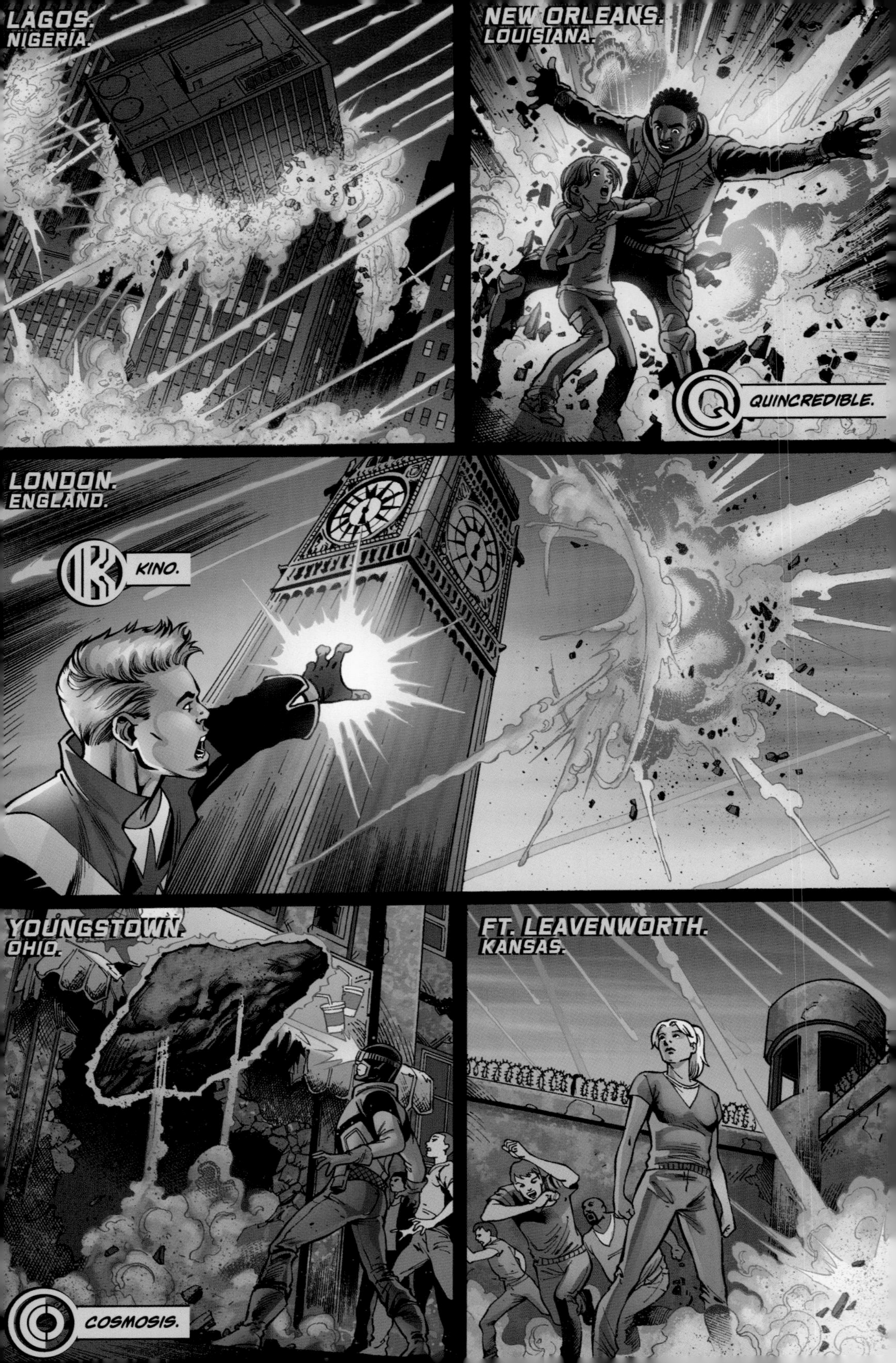
LAGOS.
NIGERIA.
NEW ORLEANS.
LOUISIANA.
QUINCREDIBLE.
LONDON.
ENGLAND.
KINO.
YOUNGSTOWN.
OHIO.
COSMOSIS.
FT. LEAVENWORTH.
KANSAS.

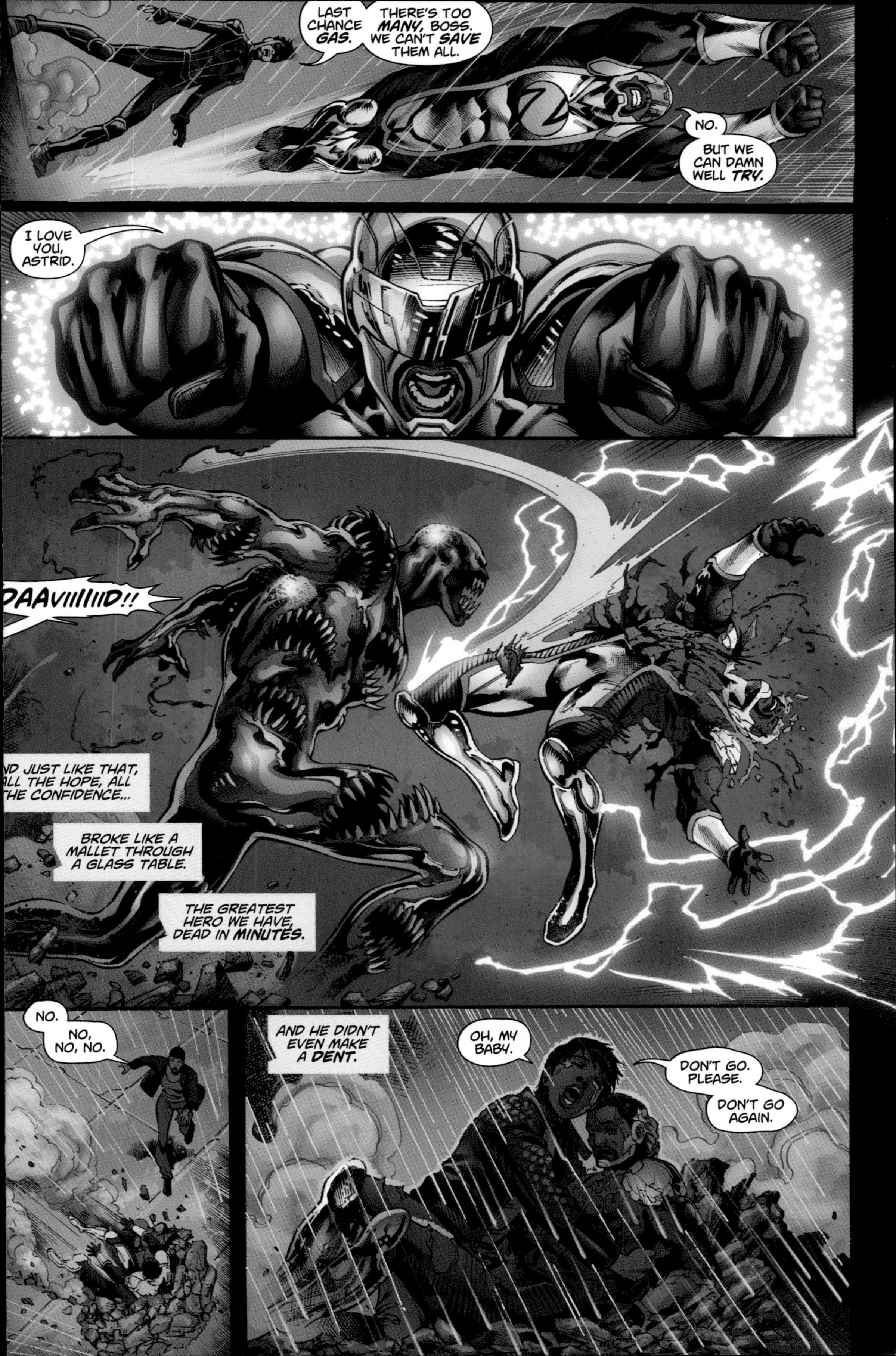
LAST CHANCE GAS.
THERE'S TOO MANY, BOSS. WE CAN'T SAVE THEM ALL.
NO.
BUT WE CAN DAMN WELL TRY.
I LOVE YOU, ASTRID.
DAAVIIIIIID!!
ND JUST LIKE THAT, ALL THE HOPE, ALL THE CONFIDENCE...
BROKE LIKE A MALLET THROUGH A GLASS TABLE.
THE GREATEST HERO WE HAVE, DEAD IN MINUTES.
NO.
NO, NO, NO.
AND HE DIDN'T EVEN MAKE A DENT.
OH, MY BABY.
DON'T GO. PLEASE.
DON'T GO AGAIN.

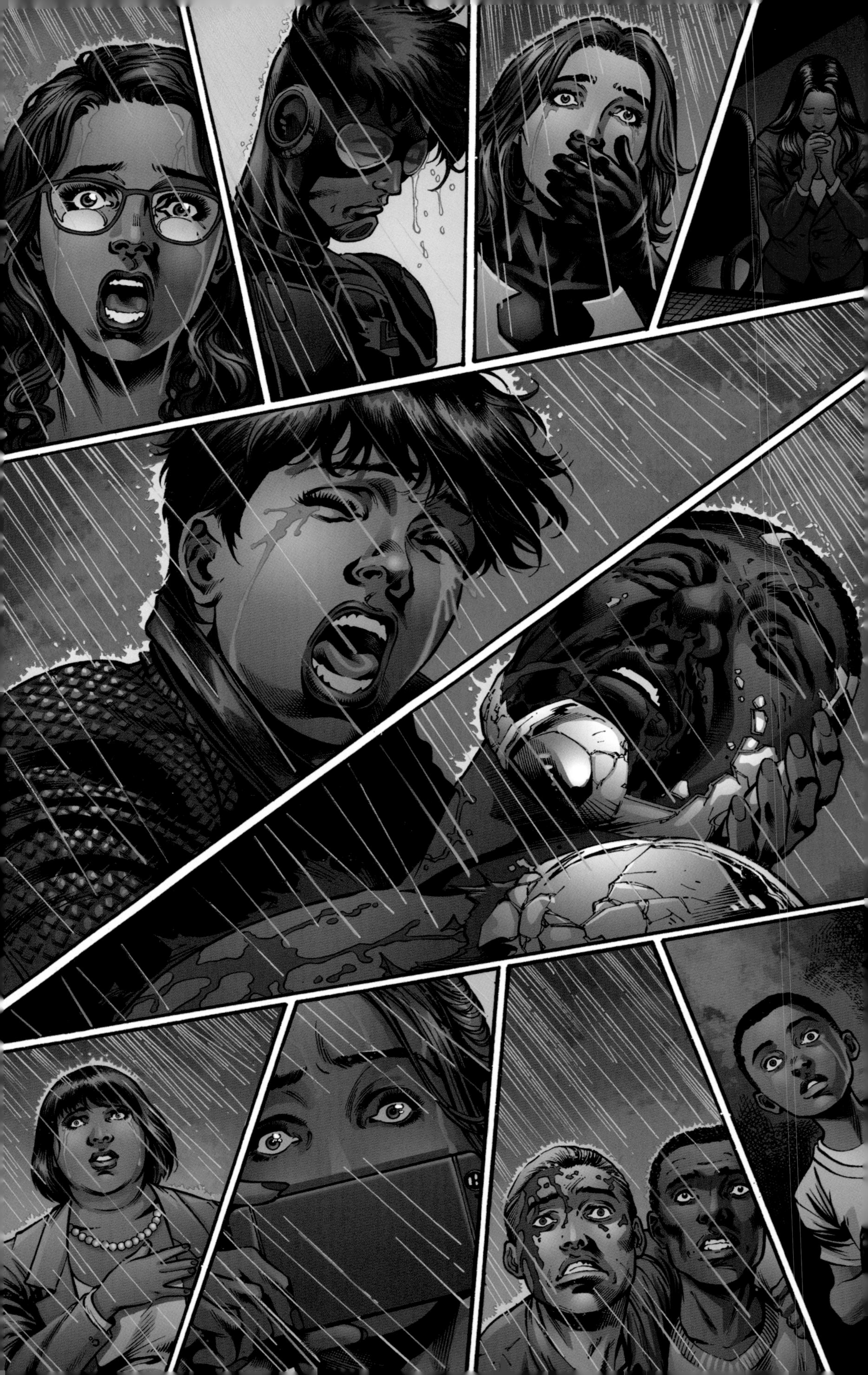

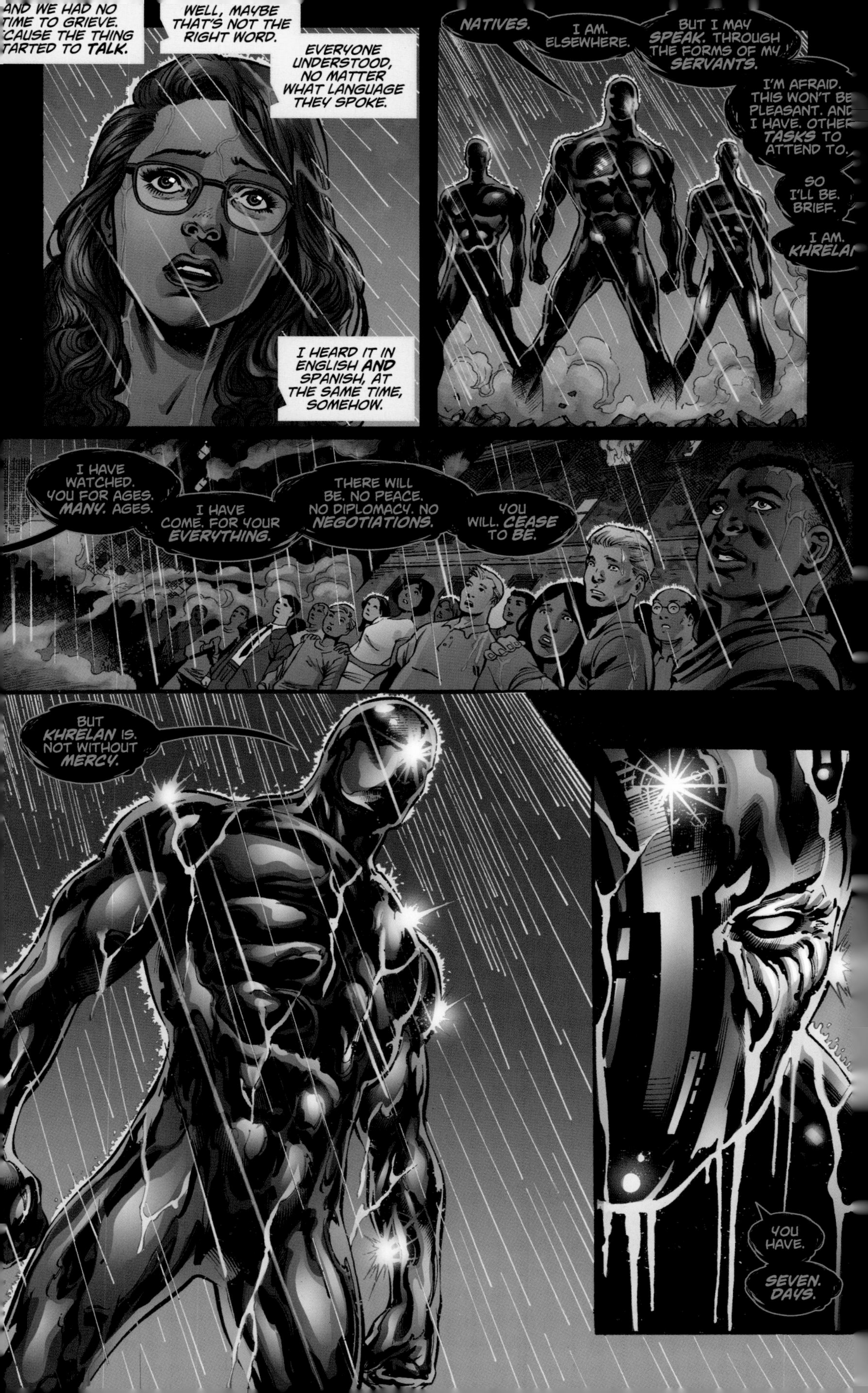
AND WE HAD NO TIME TO GRIEVE. 'CAUSE THE THING STARTED TO TALK.
WELL, MAYBE THAT'S NOT THE RIGHT WORD.
EVERYONE UNDERSTOOD, NO MATTER WHAT LANGUAGE THEY SPOKE.
I HEARD IT IN ENGLISH AND SPANISH, AT THE SAME TIME, SOMEHOW.
NATIVES.
I AM. ELSEWHERE.
BUT I MAY SPEAK. THROUGH THE FORMS OF MY SERVANTS.
I'M AFRAID. THIS WON'T BE PLEASANT. AND I HAVE. OTHER TASKS TO ATTEND TO.
SO I'LL BE. BRIEF.
I AM. KHRELAN
I HAVE WATCHED. YOU FOR AGES. MANY. AGES.
I HAVE COME. FOR YOUR EVERYTHING.
THERE WILL BE. NO PEACE. NO DIPLOMACY. NO NEGOTIATIONS.
YOU WILL. CEASE TO BE.
BUT KHRELAN IS. NOT WITHOUT MERCY.
YOU HAVE.
SEVEN. DAYS.

DAY ONE.

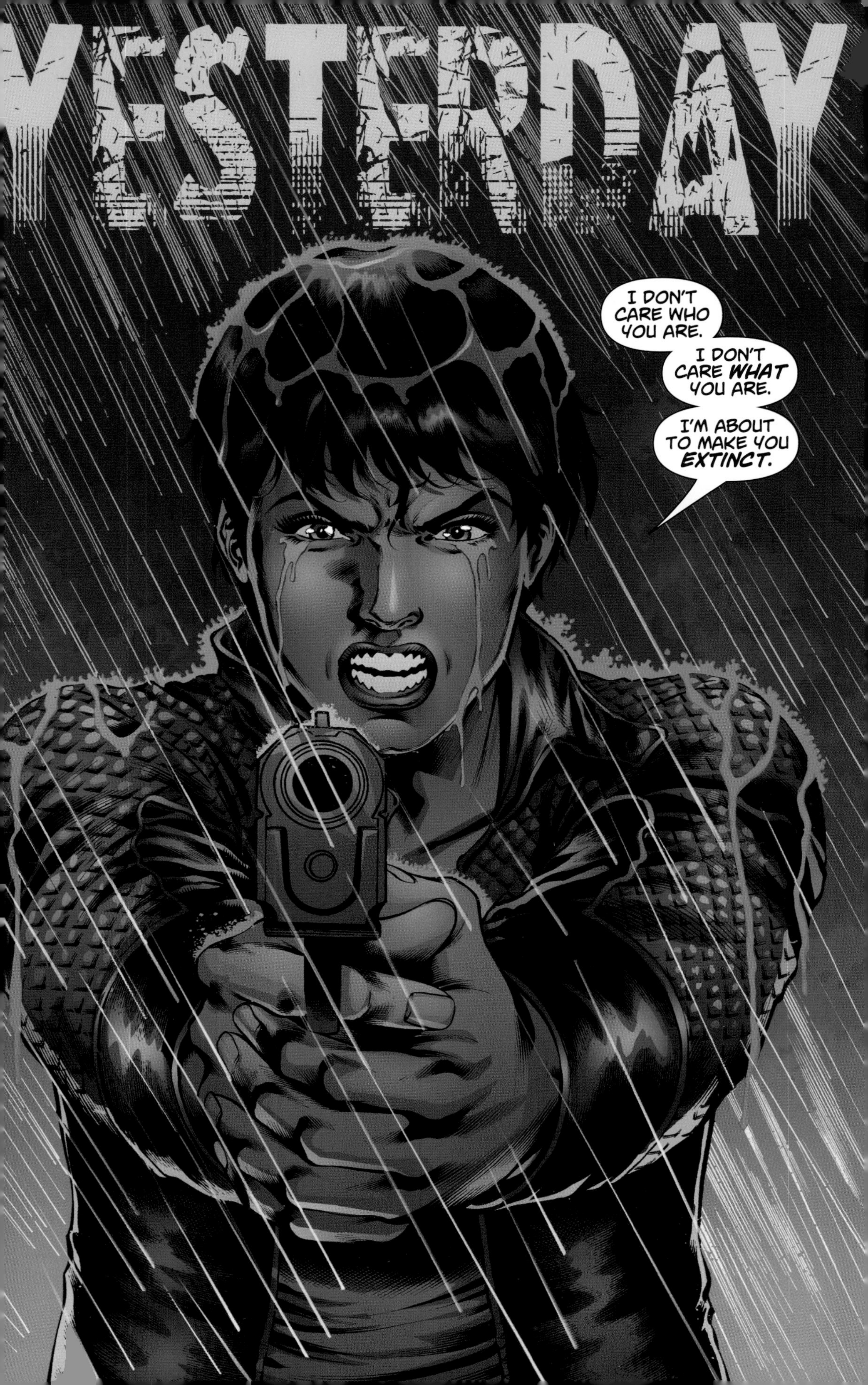
YESTERDAY
I DON'T CARE WHO YOU ARE.
I DON'T CARE WHAT YOU ARE.
I'M ABOUT TO MAKE YOU EXTINCT.

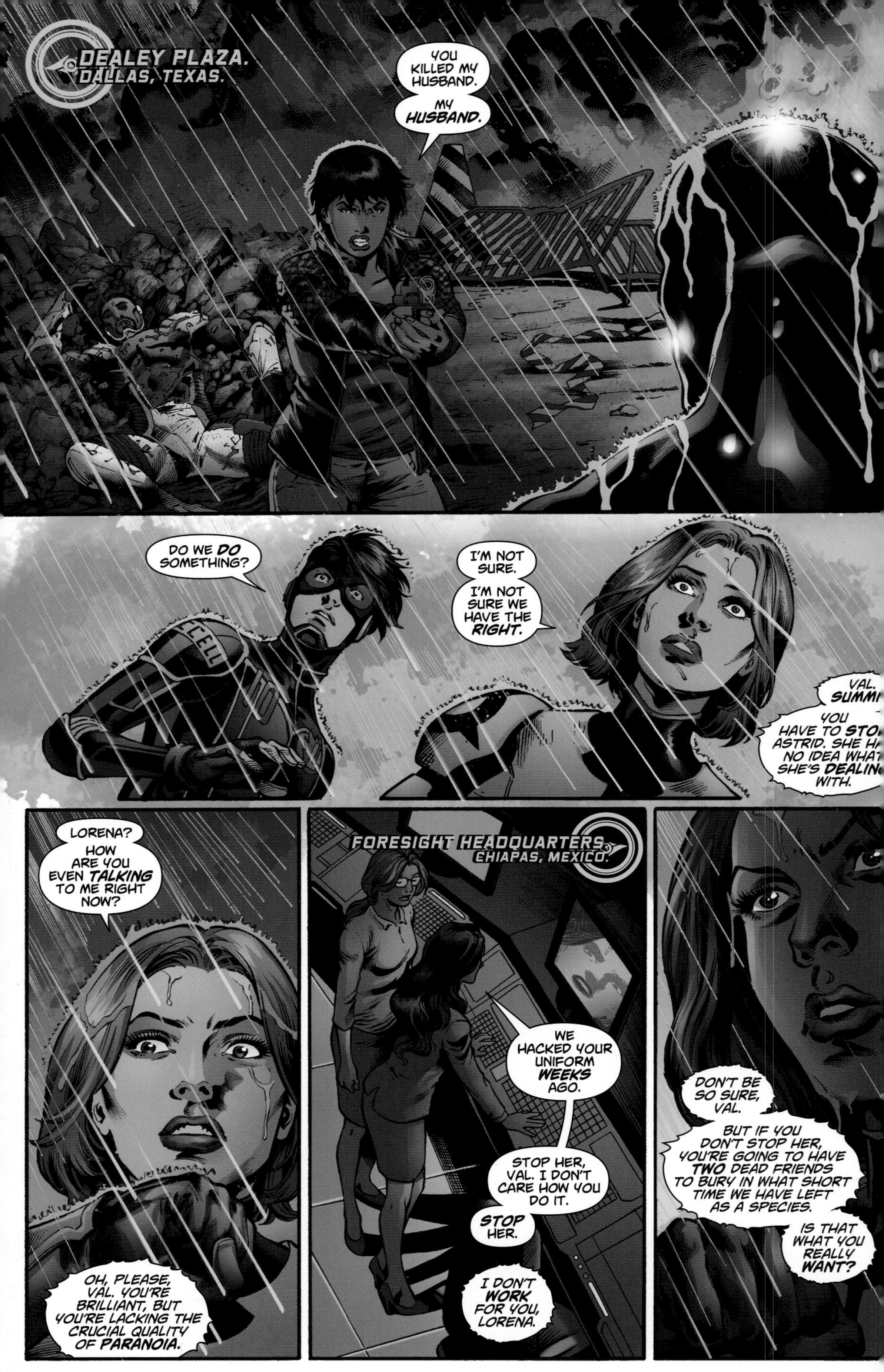
DEALEY PLAZA.
DALLAS, TEXAS.
YOU KILLED MY HUSBAND.
MY HUSBAND.
DO WE DO SOMETHING?
I'M NOT SURE.
I'M NOT SURE WE HAVE THE RIGHT.
VAL. SUMM
YOU HAVE TO STO ASTRID. SHE HA NO IDEA WHAT SHE'S DEALIN WITH.
LORENA?
HOW ARE YOU EVEN TALKING TO ME RIGHT NOW?
OH, PLEASE, VAL. YOU'RE BRILLIANT, BUT YOU'RE LACKING THE CRUCIAL QUALITY OF PARANOIA.
FORESIGHT HEADQUARTERS.
CHIAPAS, MEXICO.
WE HACKED YOUR UNIFORM WEEKS AGO.
STOP HER, VAL. I DON'T CARE HOW YOU DO IT.
STOP HER.
I DON'T WORK FOR YOU, LORENA.
DON'T BE SO SURE, VAL.
BUT IF YOU DON'T STOP HER, YOU'RE GOING TO HAVE TWO DEAD FRIENDS TO BURY IN WHAT SHORT TIME WE HAVE LEFT AS A SPECIES.
IS THAT WHAT YOU REALLY WANT?

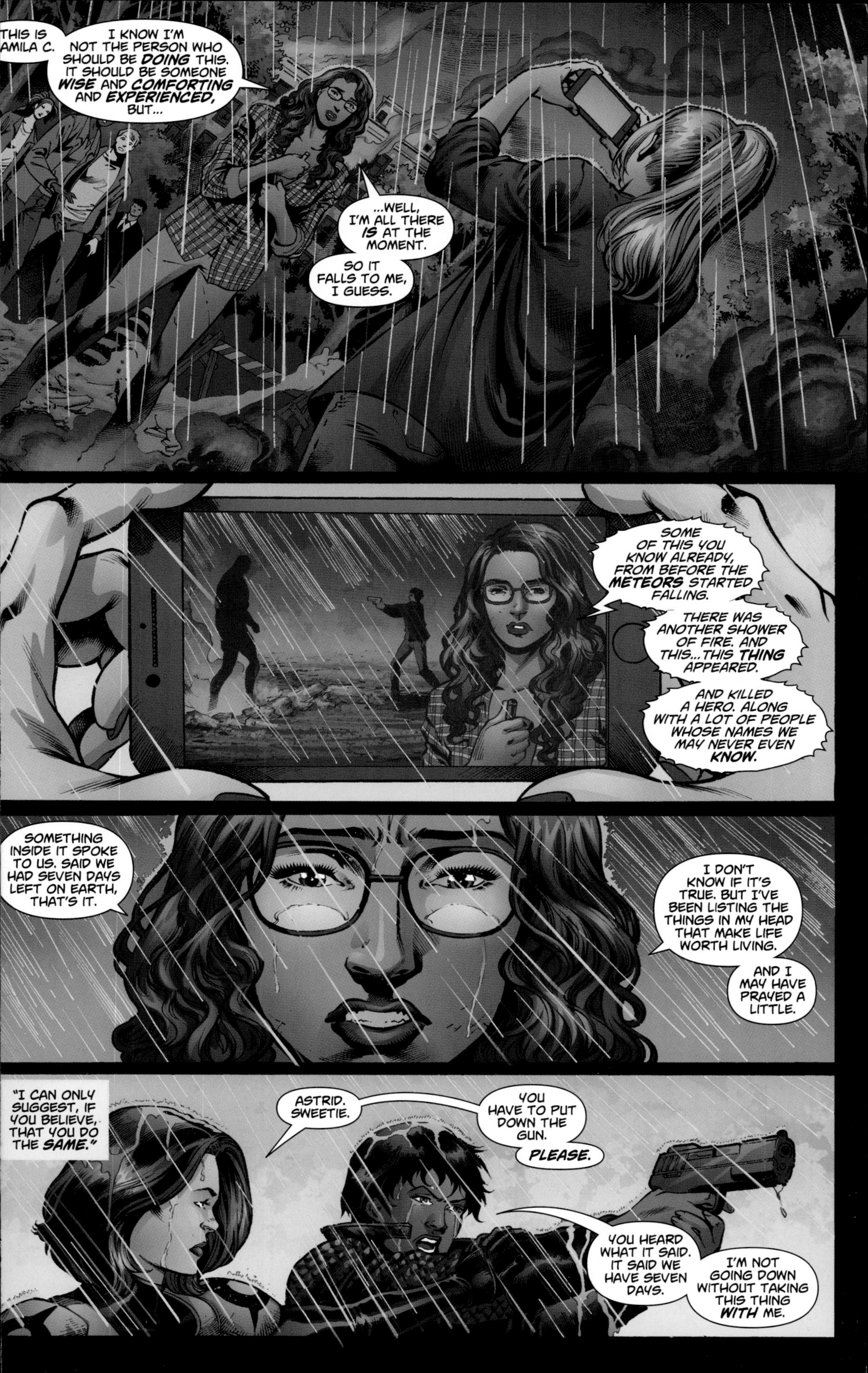
THIS IS AMILA C.
I KNOW I'M NOT THE PERSON WHO SHOULD BE DOING THIS. IT SHOULD BE SOMEONE WISE AND COMFORTING AND EXPERIENCED, BUT...
...WELL, I'M ALL THERE IS AT THE MOMENT.
SO IT FALLS TO ME, I GUESS.
SOME OF THIS YOU KNOW ALREADY, FROM BEFORE THE METEORS STARTED FALLING.
THERE WAS ANOTHER SHOWER OF FIRE. AND THIS...THIS THING APPEARED.
AND KILLED A HERO. ALONG WITH A LOT OF PEOPLE WHOSE NAMES WE MAY NEVER EVEN KNOW.
SOMETHING INSIDE IT SPOKE TO US. SAID WE HAD SEVEN DAYS LEFT ON EARTH, THAT'S IT.
I DON'T KNOW IF IT'S TRUE. BUT I'VE BEEN LISTING THE THINGS IN MY HEAD THAT MAKE LIFE WORTH LIVING.
AND I MAY HAVE PRAYED A LITTLE.
"I CAN ONLY SUGGEST, IF YOU BELIEVE, THAT YOU DO THE SAME."
ASTRID. SWEETIE.
YOU HAVE TO PUT DOWN THE GUN.
PLEASE.
YOU HEARD WHAT IT SAID. IT SAID WE HAVE SEVEN DAYS.
I'M NOT GOING DOWN WITHOUT TAKING THIS THING WITH ME.

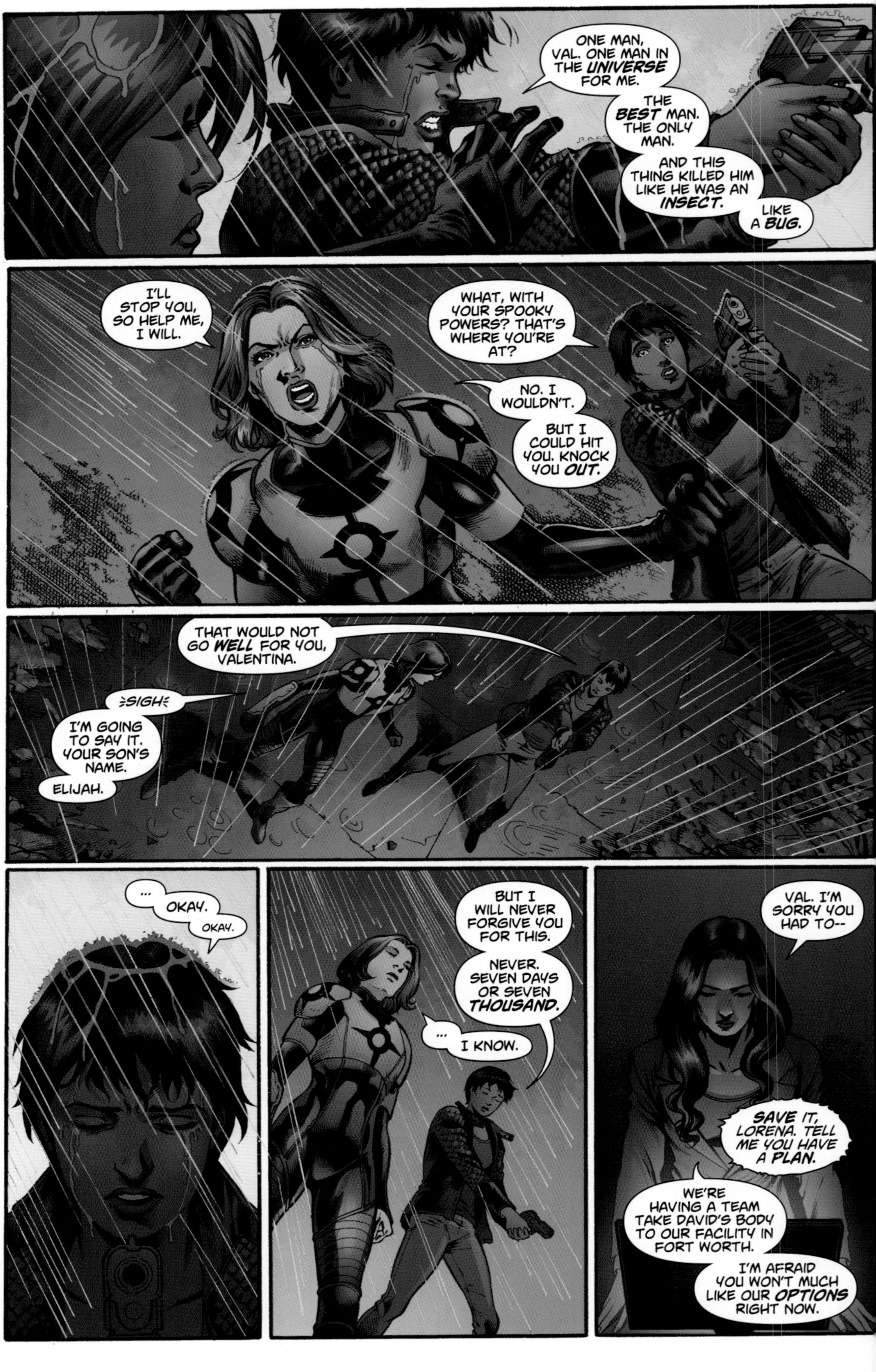
ONE MAN, VAL. ONE MAN IN THE UNIVERSE FOR ME.
THE BEST MAN. THE ONLY MAN.
AND THIS THING KILLED HIM LIKE HE WAS AN INSECT.
LIKE A BUG.
I'LL STOP YOU, SO HELP ME, I WILL.
WHAT, WITH YOUR SPOOKY POWERS? THAT'S WHERE YOU'RE AT?
NO. I WOULDN'T.
BUT I COULD HIT YOU. KNOCK YOU OUT.
THAT WOULD NOT GO WELL FOR YOU, VALENTINA.
SIGH
I'M GOING TO SAY IT. YOUR SON'S NAME.
ELIJAH.
... OKAY.
OKAY.
BUT I WILL NEVER FORGIVE YOU FOR THIS.
NEVER. SEVEN DAYS OR SEVEN THOUSAND.
... I KNOW.
VAL. I'M SORRY YOU HAD TO--
SAVE IT, LORENA. TELL ME YOU HAVE A PLAN.
WE'RE HAVING A TEAM TAKE DAVID'S BODY TO OUR FACILITY IN FORT WORTH.
I'M AFRAID YOU WON'T MUCH LIKE OUR OPTIONS RIGHT NOW.

DAY TWO.

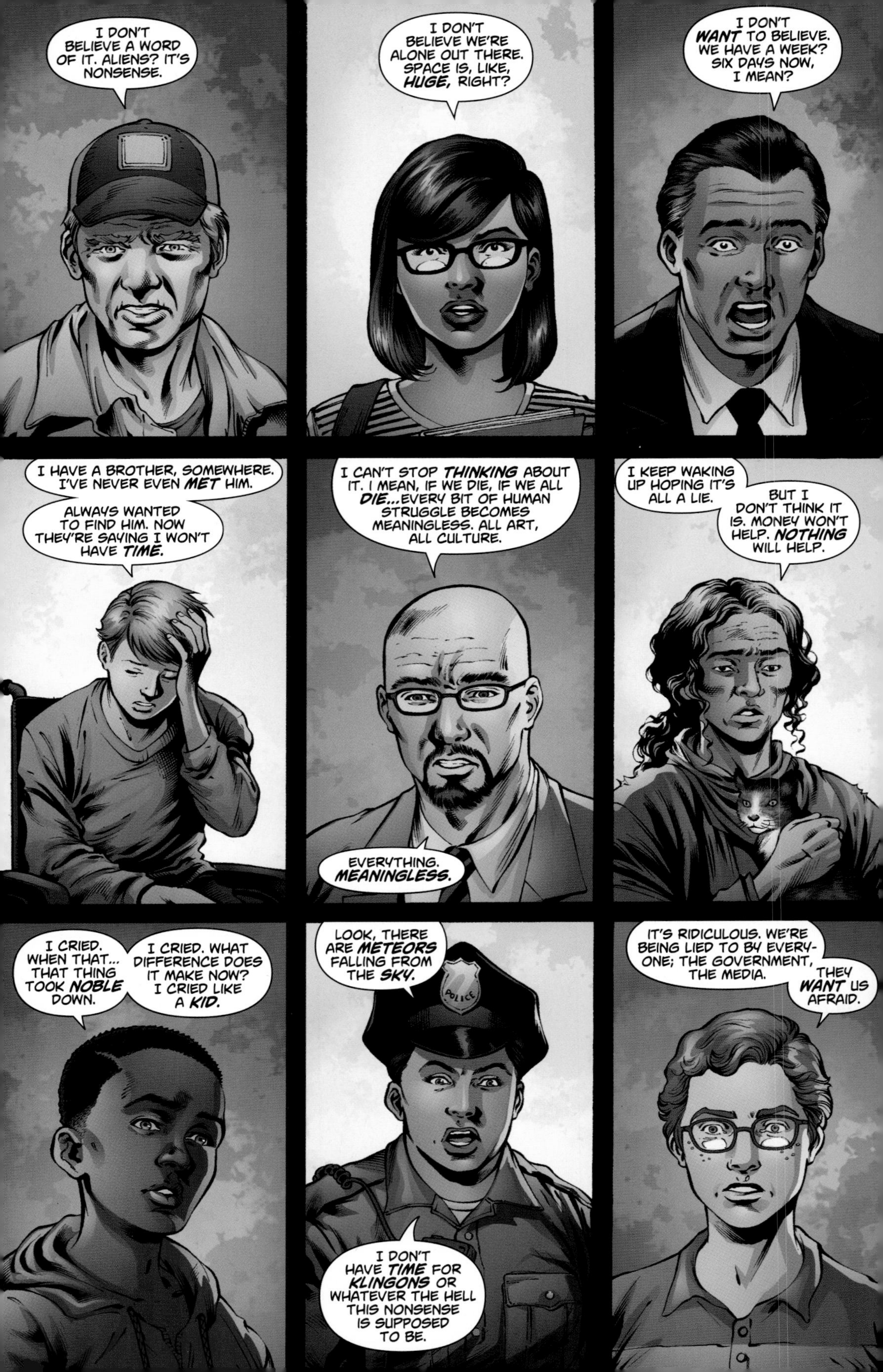
I DON'T BELIEVE A WORD OF IT. ALIENS? IT'S NONSENSE.
I DON'T BELIEVE WE'RE ALONE OUT THERE. SPACE IS, LIKE, HUGE, RIGHT?
I DON'T WANT TO BELIEVE. WE HAVE A WEEK? SIX DAYS NOW, I MEAN?
I HAVE A BROTHER, SOMEWHERE. I'VE NEVER EVEN MET HIM.
ALWAYS WANTED TO FIND HIM. NOW THEY'RE SAYING I WON'T HAVE TIME.
I CAN'T STOP THINKING ABOUT IT. I MEAN, IF WE DIE, IF WE ALL DIE... EVERY BIT OF HUMAN STRUGGLE BECOMES MEANINGLESS. ALL ART, ALL CULTURE.
EVERYTHING. MEANINGLESS.
I KEEP WAKING UP HOPING IT'S ALL A LIE.
BUT I DON'T THINK IT IS. MONEY WON'T HELP. NOTHING WILL HELP.
I CRIED. WHEN THAT... THAT THING TOOK NOBLE DOWN.
I CRIED. WHAT DIFFERENCE DOES IT MAKE NOW? I CRIED LIKE A KID.
LOOK, THERE ARE METEORS FALLING FROM THE SKY.
POLICE
I DON'T HAVE TIME FOR KLINGONS OR WHATEVER THE HELL THIS NONSENSE IS SUPPOSED TO BE.
IT'S RIDICULOUS. WE'RE BEING LIED TO BY EVERY-ONE; THE GOVERNMENT, THE MEDIA.
THEY WANT US AFRAID.

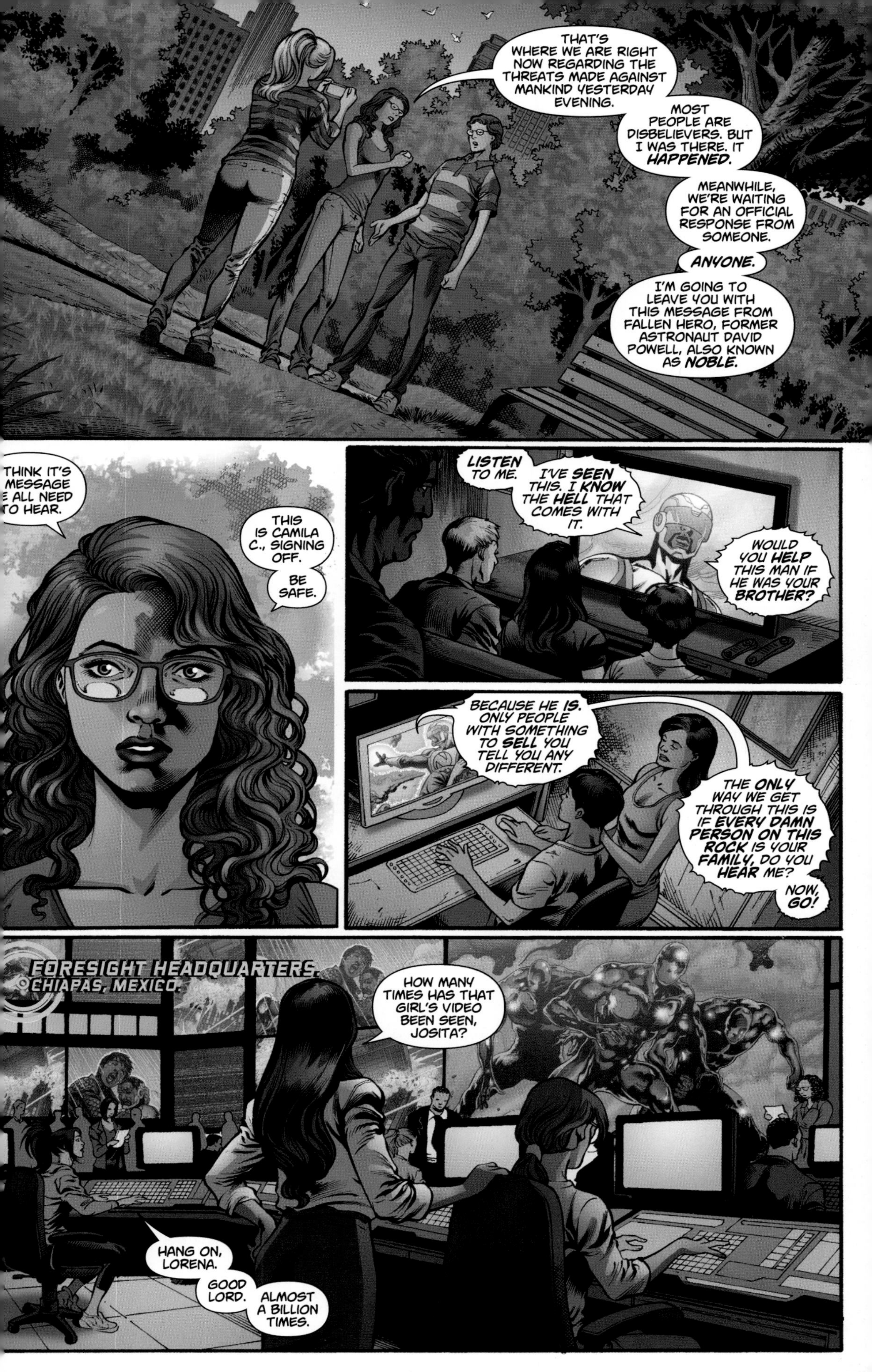
THAT'S WHERE WE ARE RIGHT NOW REGARDING THE THREATS MADE AGAINST MANKIND YESTERDAY EVENING.
MOST PEOPLE ARE DISBELIEVERS. BUT I WAS THERE. IT HAPPENED.
MEANWHILE, WE'RE WAITING FOR AN OFFICIAL RESPONSE FROM SOMEONE.
ANYONE.
I'M GOING TO LEAVE YOU WITH THIS MESSAGE FROM FALLEN HERO, FORMER ASTRONAUT DAVID POWELL, ALSO KNOWN AS NOBLE.
THINK IT'S MESSAGE E ALL NEED TO HEAR.
THIS IS CAMILA C., SIGNING OFF.
BE SAFE.
LISTEN TO ME.
I'VE SEEN THIS. I KNOW THE HELL THAT COMES WITH IT.
WOULD YOU HELP THIS MAN IF HE WAS YOUR BROTHER?
BECAUSE HE IS. ONLY PEOPLE WITH SOMETHING TO SELL YOU TELL YOU ANY DIFFERENT.
THE ONLY WAY WE GET THROUGH THIS IS IF EVERY DAMN PERSON ON THIS ROCK IS YOUR FAMILY, DO YOU HEAR ME?
NOW, GO!
FORESIGHT HEADQUARTERS. CHIAPAS, MEXICO.
HOW MANY TIMES HAS THAT GIRL'S VIDEO BEEN SEEN, JOSITA?
HANG ON, LORENA.
GOOD LORD.
ALMOST A BILLION TIMES.

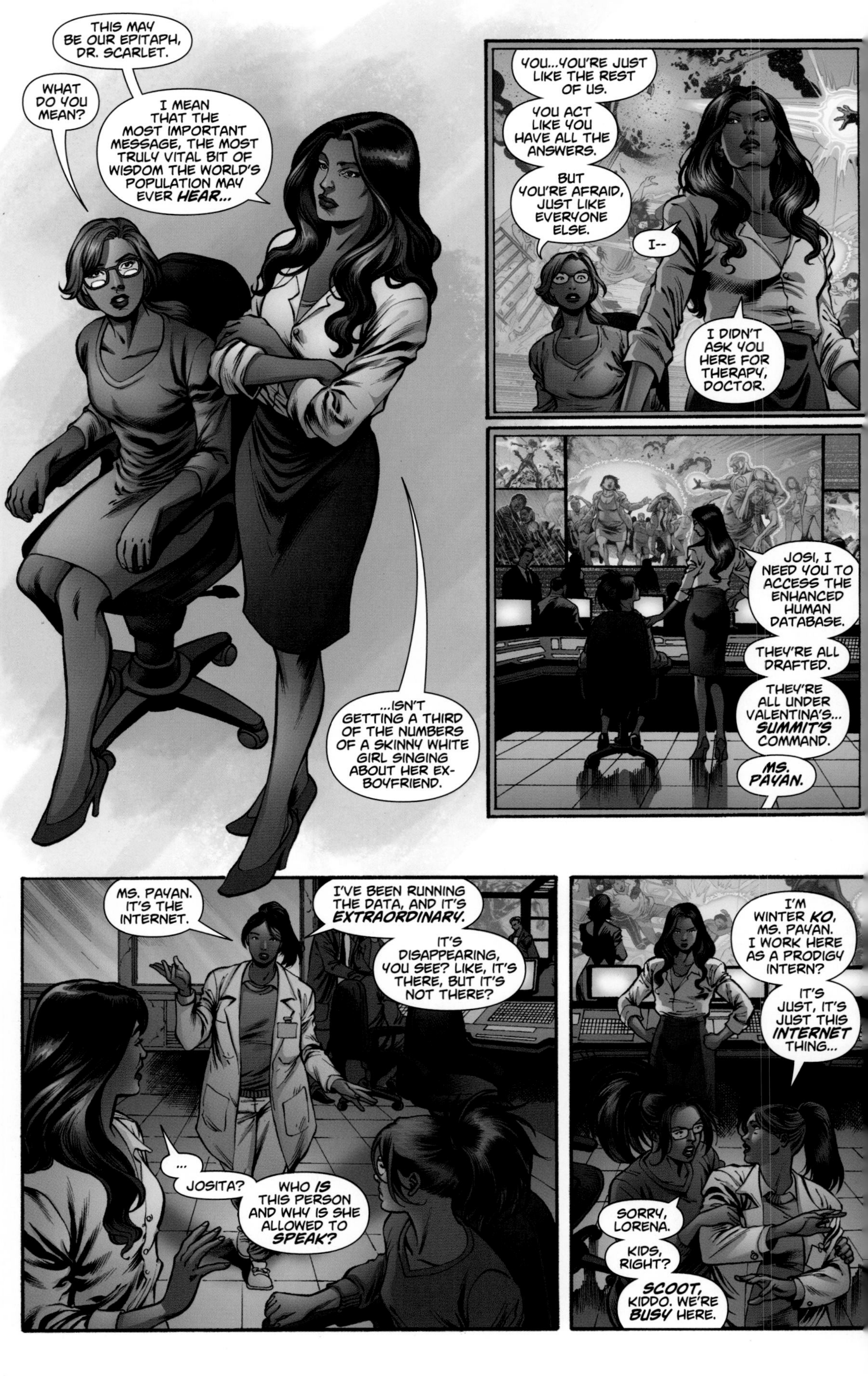
THIS MAY BE OUR EPITAPH, DR. SCARLET.
WHAT DO YOU MEAN?
I MEAN THAT THE MOST IMPORTANT MESSAGE, THE MOST TRULY VITAL BIT OF WISDOM THE WORLD'S POPULATION MAY EVER HEAR...
...ISN'T GETTING A THIRD OF THE NUMBERS OF A SKINNY WHITE GIRL SINGING ABOUT HER EX-BOYFRIEND.
YOU...YOU'RE JUST LIKE THE REST OF US.
YOU ACT LIKE YOU HAVE ALL THE ANSWERS.
BUT YOU'RE AFRAID, JUST LIKE EVERYONE ELSE.
I--
I DIDN'T ASK YOU HERE FOR THERAPY, DOCTOR.
JOSI, I NEED YOU TO ACCESS THE ENHANCED HUMAN DATABASE.
THEY'RE ALL DRAFTED.
THEY'RE ALL UNDER VALENTINA'S... SUMMIT'S COMMAND.
MS. PAYAN.
MS. PAYAN. IT'S THE INTERNET.
I'VE BEEN RUNNING THE DATA, AND IT'S EXTRAORDINARY.
IT'S DISAPPEARING, YOU SEE? LIKE, IT'S THERE, BUT IT'S NOT THERE?
...
JOSITA?
WHO IS THIS PERSON AND WHY IS SHE ALLOWED TO SPEAK?
I'M WINTER KO, MS. PAYAN. I WORK HERE AS A PRODIGY INTERN.
IT'S JUST, IT'S JUST THIS INTERNET THING...
SORRY, LORENA.
KIDS, RIGHT?
SCOOT, KIDDO. WE'RE BUSY HERE.

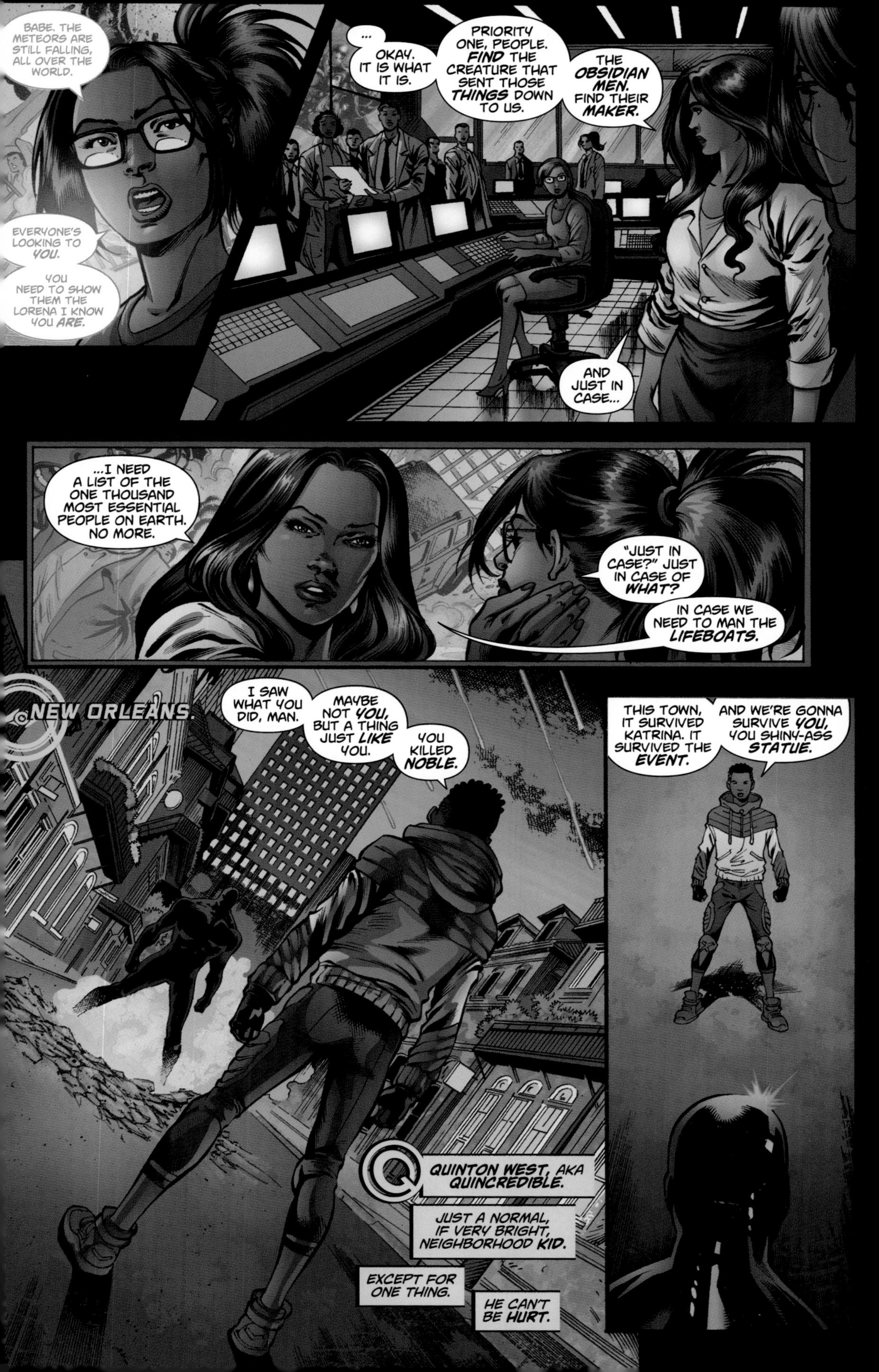
BABE. THE METEORS ARE STILL FALLING, ALL OVER THE WORLD.
EVERYONE'S LOOKING TO YOU.
YOU NEED TO SHOW THEM THE LORENA I KNOW YOU ARE.
...
OKAY. IT IS WHAT IT IS.
PRIORITY ONE, PEOPLE. FIND THE CREATURE THAT SENT THOSE THINGS DOWN TO US.
THE OBSIDIAN MEN. FIND THEIR MAKER.
AND JUST IN CASE...
...I NEED A LIST OF THE ONE THOUSAND MOST ESSENTIAL PEOPLE ON EARTH. NO MORE.
"JUST IN CASE?" JUST IN CASE OF WHAT?
IN CASE WE NEED TO MAN THE LIFEBOATS.
NEW ORLEANS.
I SAW WHAT YOU DID, MAN.
MAYBE NOT YOU, BUT A THING JUST LIKE YOU.
YOU KILLED NOBLE.
QUINTON WEST, AKA QUINCREDIBLE.
JUST A NORMAL, IF VERY BRIGHT, NEIGHBORHOOD KID.
EXCEPT FOR ONE THING.
HE CAN'T BE HURT.
THIS TOWN, IT SURVIVED KATRINA. IT SURVIVED THE EVENT.
AND WE'RE GONNA SURVIVE YOU, YOU SHINY-ASS STATUE.

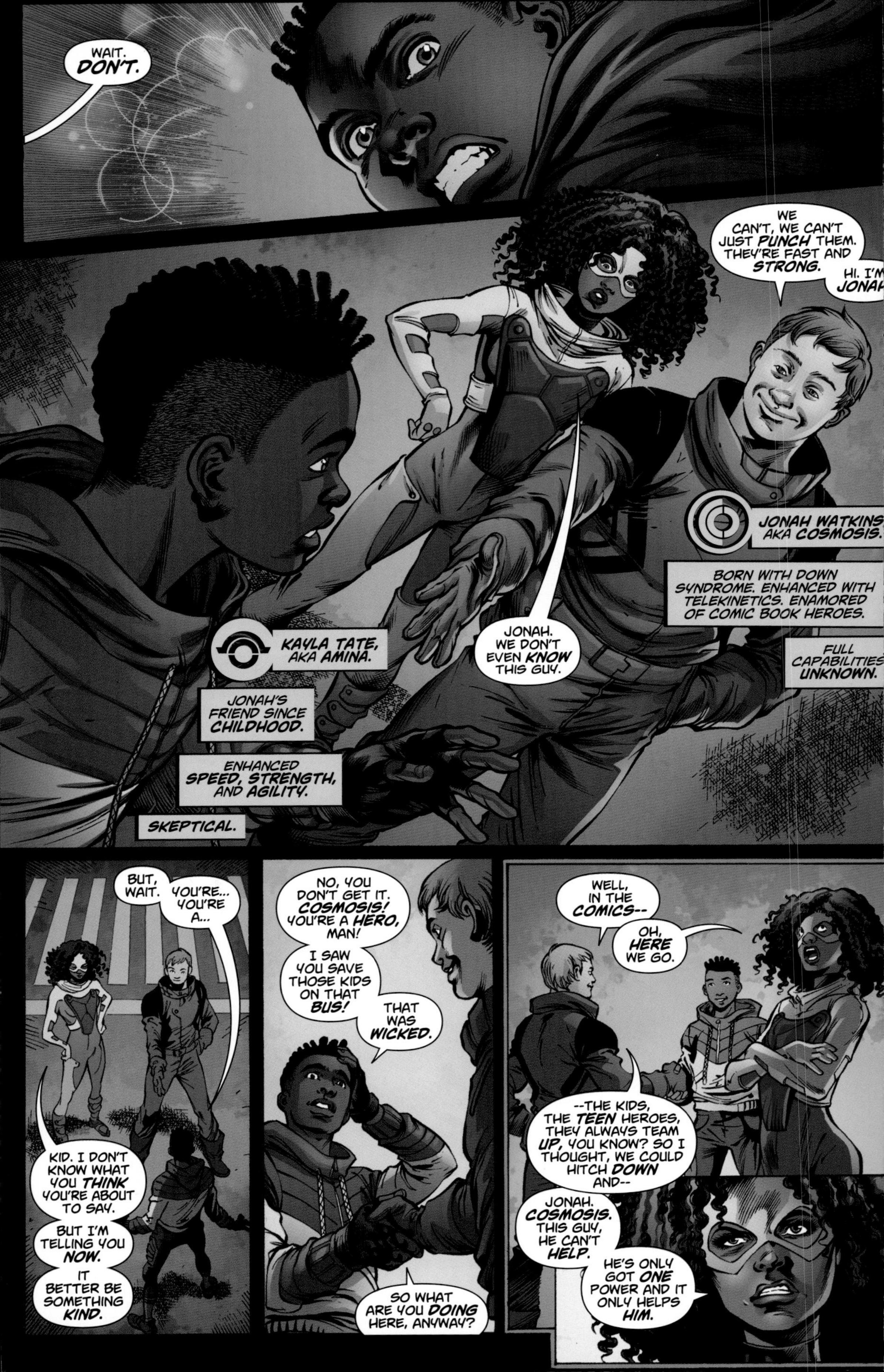
WAIT. DON'T.
WE CAN'T, WE CAN'T JUST PUNCH THEM. THEY'RE FAST AND STRONG.
HI. I'M JONAH
JONAH WATKINS AKA COSMOSIS.
BORN WITH DOWN SYNDROME. ENHANCED WITH TELEKINETICS. ENAMORED OF COMIC BOOK HEROES.
FULL CAPABILITIES UNKNOWN.
JONAH. WE DON'T EVEN KNOW THIS GUY.
KAYLA TATE, AKA AMINA.
JONAH'S FRIEND SINCE CHILDHOOD.
ENHANCED SPEED, STRENGTH, AND AGILITY.
SKEPTICAL.
BUT, WAIT.
YOU'RE... YOU'RE A...
KID. I DON'T KNOW WHAT YOU THINK YOU'RE ABOUT TO SAY.
BUT I'M TELLING YOU NOW.
IT BETTER BE SOMETHING KIND.
NO, YOU DON'T GET IT. COSMOSIS! YOU'RE A HERO, MAN!
I SAW YOU SAVE THOSE KIDS ON THAT BUS!
THAT WAS WICKED.
SO WHAT ARE YOU DOING HERE, ANYWAY?
WELL, IN THE COMICS--
OH, HERE WE GO.
--THE KIDS, THE TEEN HEROES, THEY ALWAYS TEAM UP, YOU KNOW? SO I THOUGHT, WE COULD HITCH DOWN AND--
JONAH. COSMOSIS. THIS GUY, HE CAN'T HELP.
HE'S ONLY GOT ONE POWER AND IT ONLY HELPS HIM.

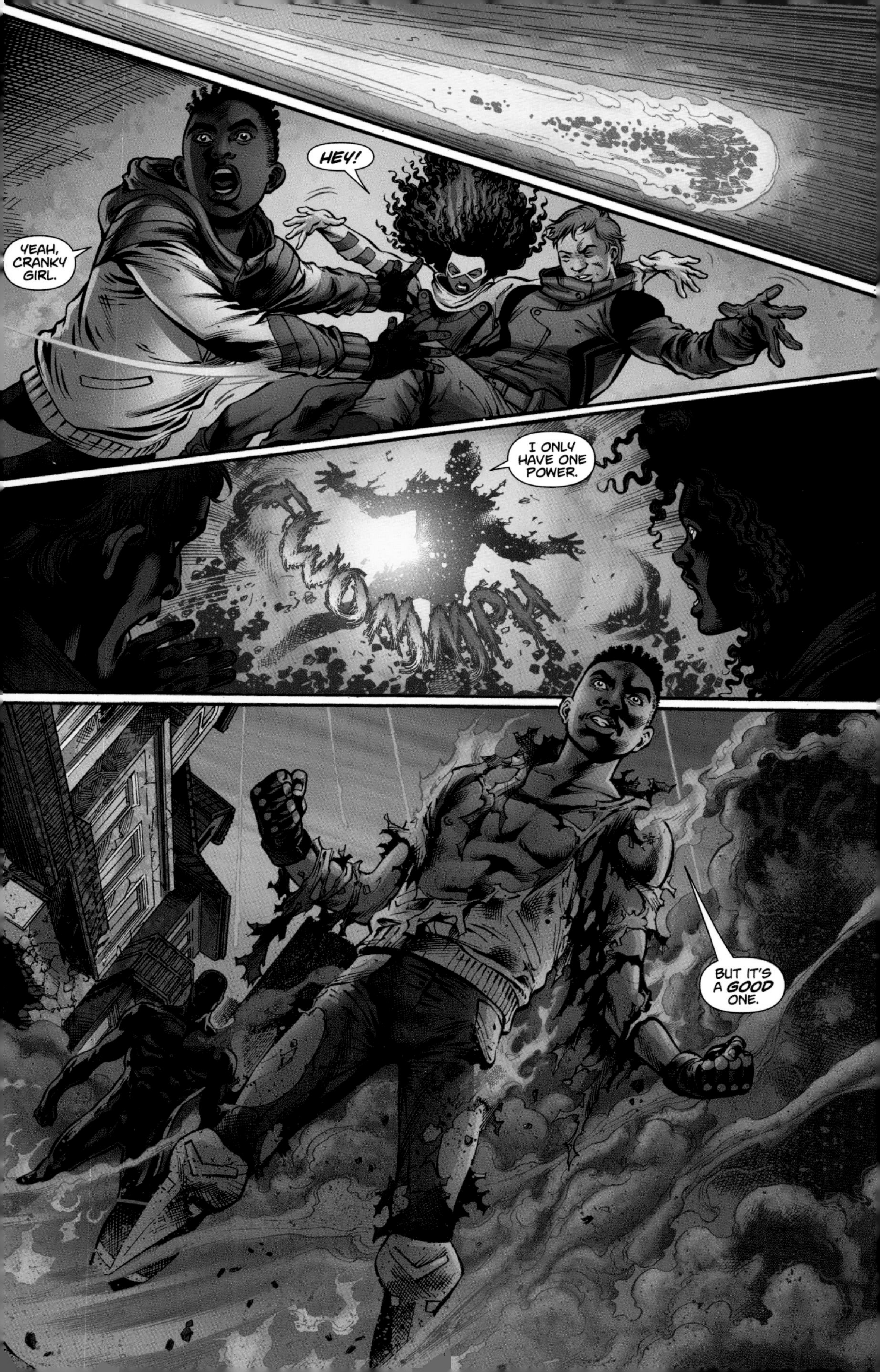

HEY!
YEAH, CRANKY GIRL.
I ONLY HAVE ONE POWER.
WOOMMPH
BUT IT'S A GOOD ONE.

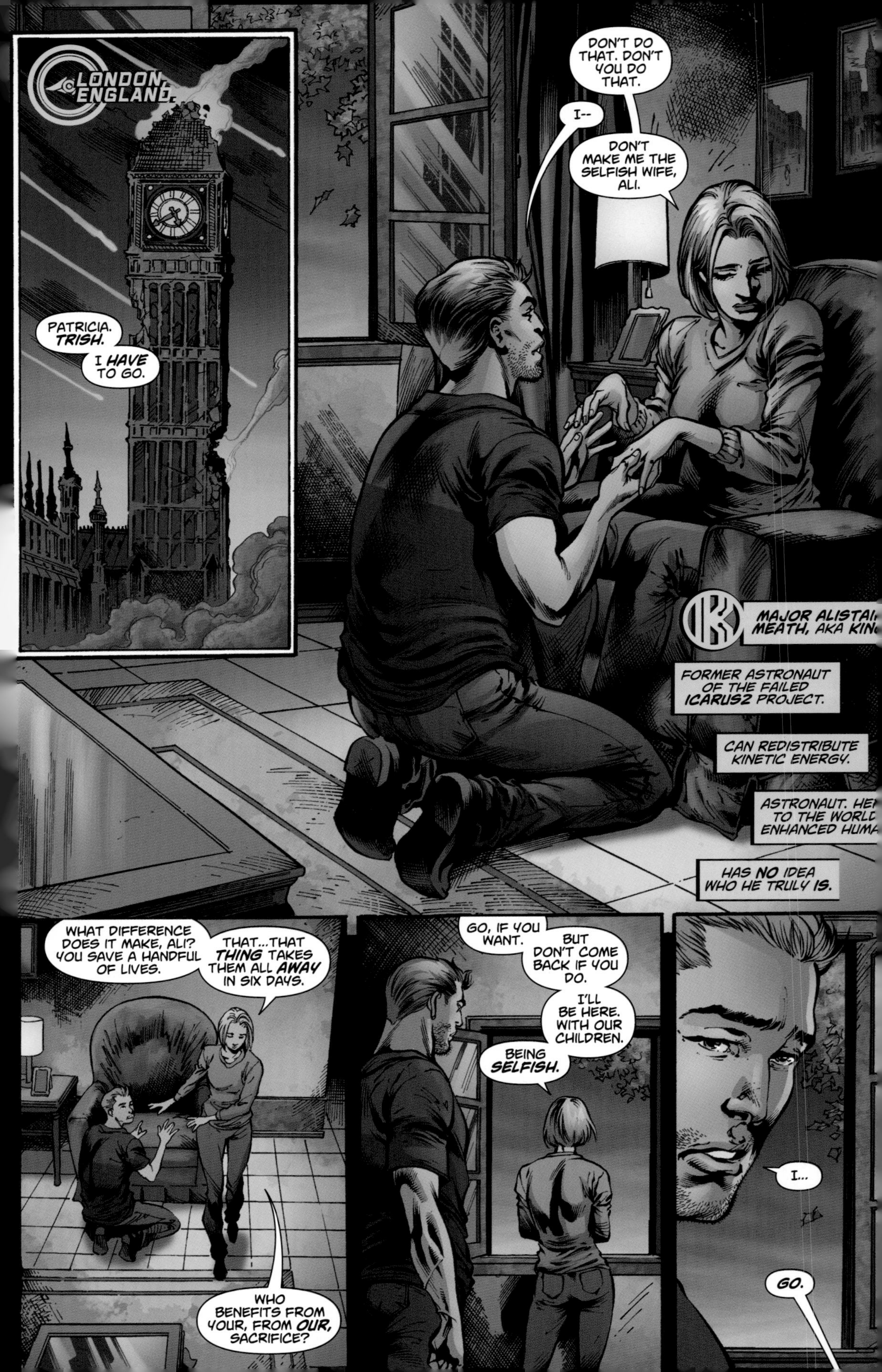
LONDON, ENGLAND.
PATRICIA. *TRISH.*
I *HAVE* TO GO.
DON'T DO THAT. DON'T YOU DO THAT.
I--
DON'T MAKE ME THE SELFISH WIFE, ALI.
MAJOR ALISTAI MEATH, AKA KIN
FORMER ASTRONAUT OF THE FAILED *ICARUS2* PROJECT.
CAN REDISTRIBUTE KINETIC ENERGY.
ASTRONAUT. HE TO THE WORLD ENHANCED HUMA
HAS *NO* IDEA WHO HE TRULY *IS.*
WHAT DIFFERENCE DOES IT MAKE, ALI? YOU SAVE A HANDFUL OF LIVES.
THAT...THAT *THING* TAKES THEM ALL *AWAY* IN SIX DAYS.
WHO BENEFITS FROM YOUR, FROM *OUR,* SACRIFICE?
GO, IF YOU WANT.
BUT DON'T COME BACK IF YOU DO.
I'LL BE HERE. WITH OUR CHILDREN.
BEING *SELFISH.*
I...
GO.

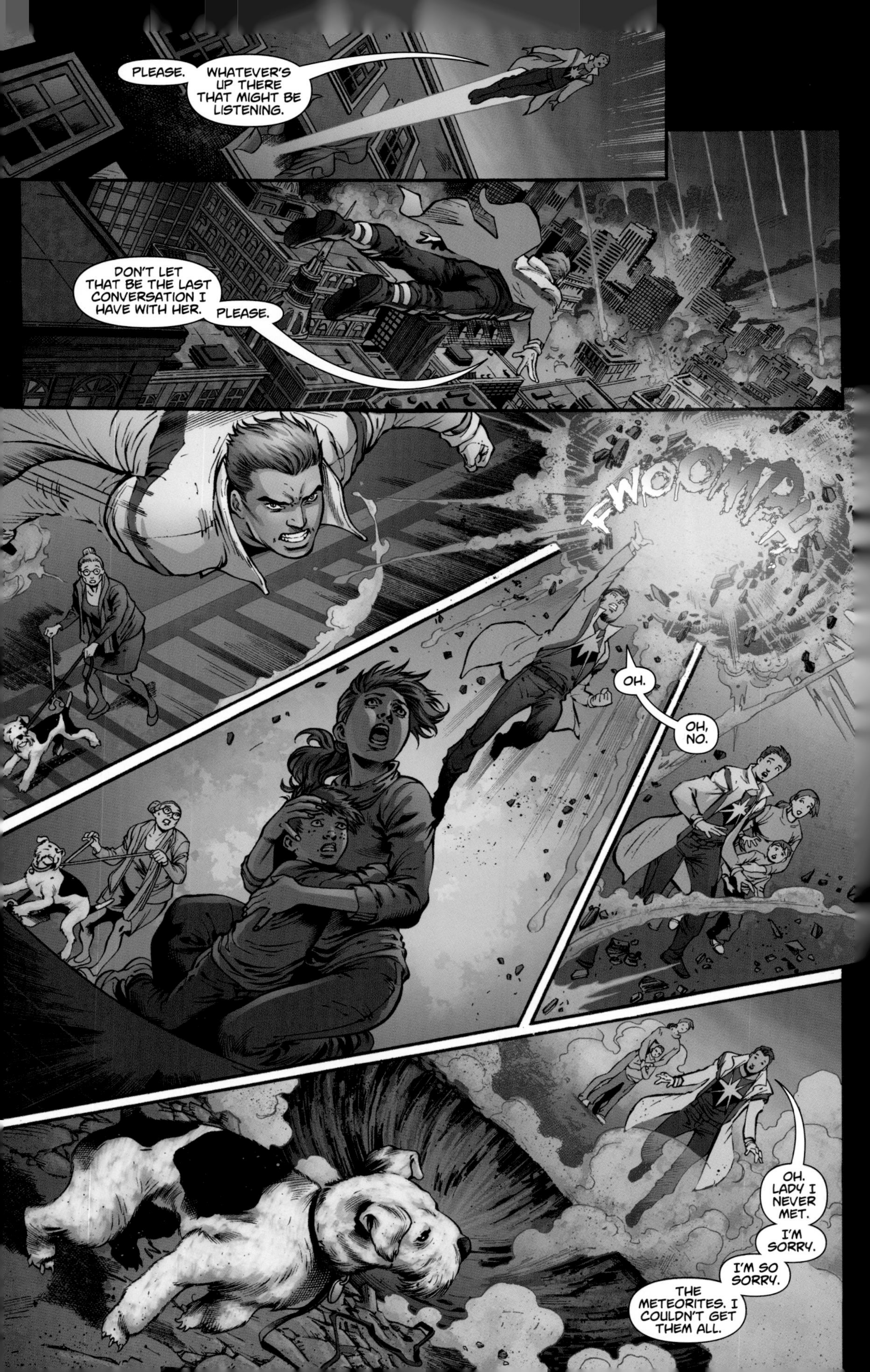
PLEASE.
WHATEVER'S UP THERE THAT MIGHT BE LISTENING.
DON'T LET THAT BE THE LAST CONVERSATION I HAVE WITH HER.
PLEASE.
FWOOMPH
OH.
OH, NO.
OH. LADY I NEVER MET.
I'M SORRY.
I'M SO SORRY.
THE METEORITES. I COULDN'T GET THEM ALL.

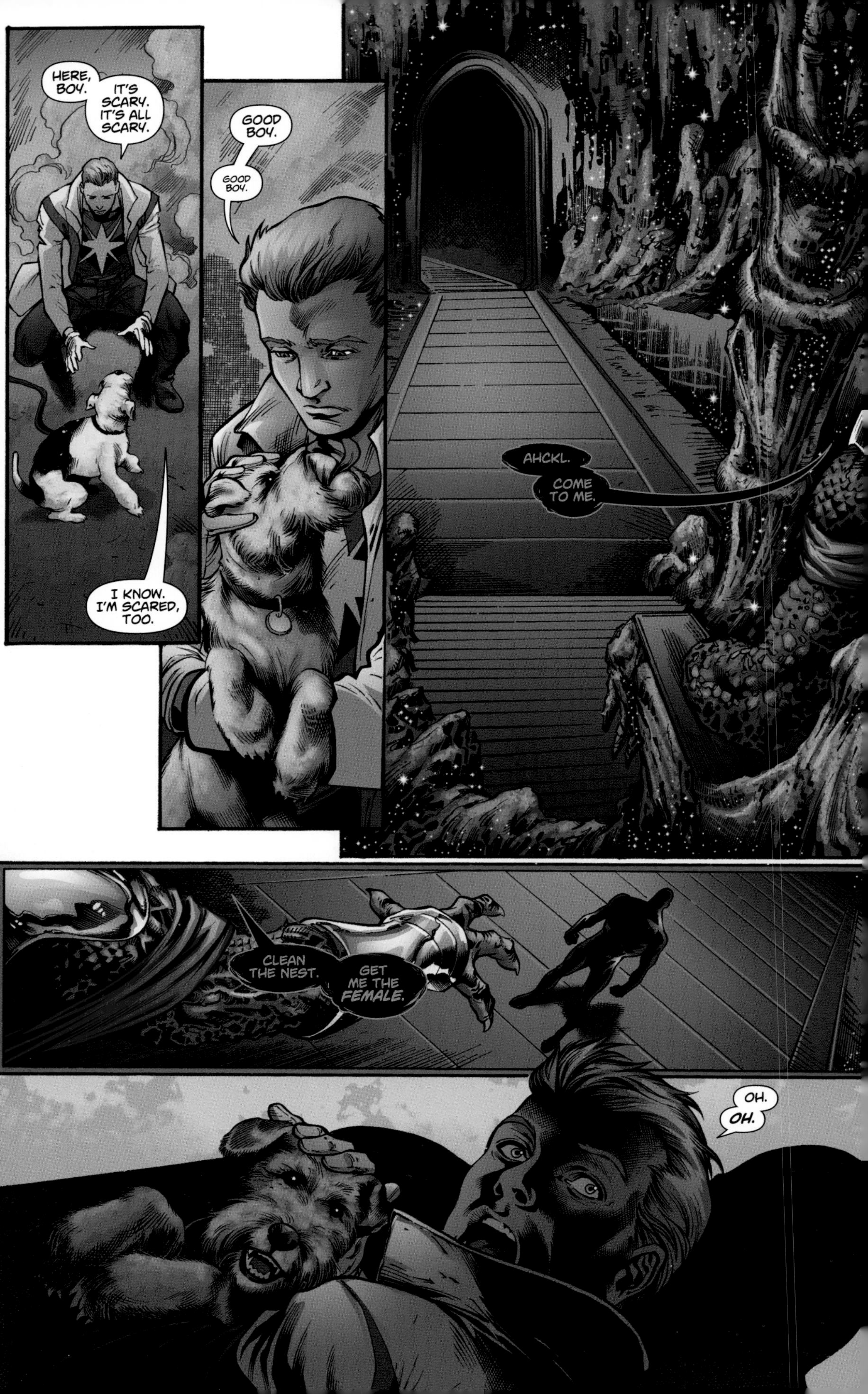
HERE, BOY.
IT'S SCARY. IT'S ALL SCARY.
I KNOW. I'M SCARED, TOO.
GOOD BOY.
GOOD BOY.
AHCKL.
COME TO ME.
CLEAN THE NEST.
GET ME THE FEMALE.
OH.
OH.

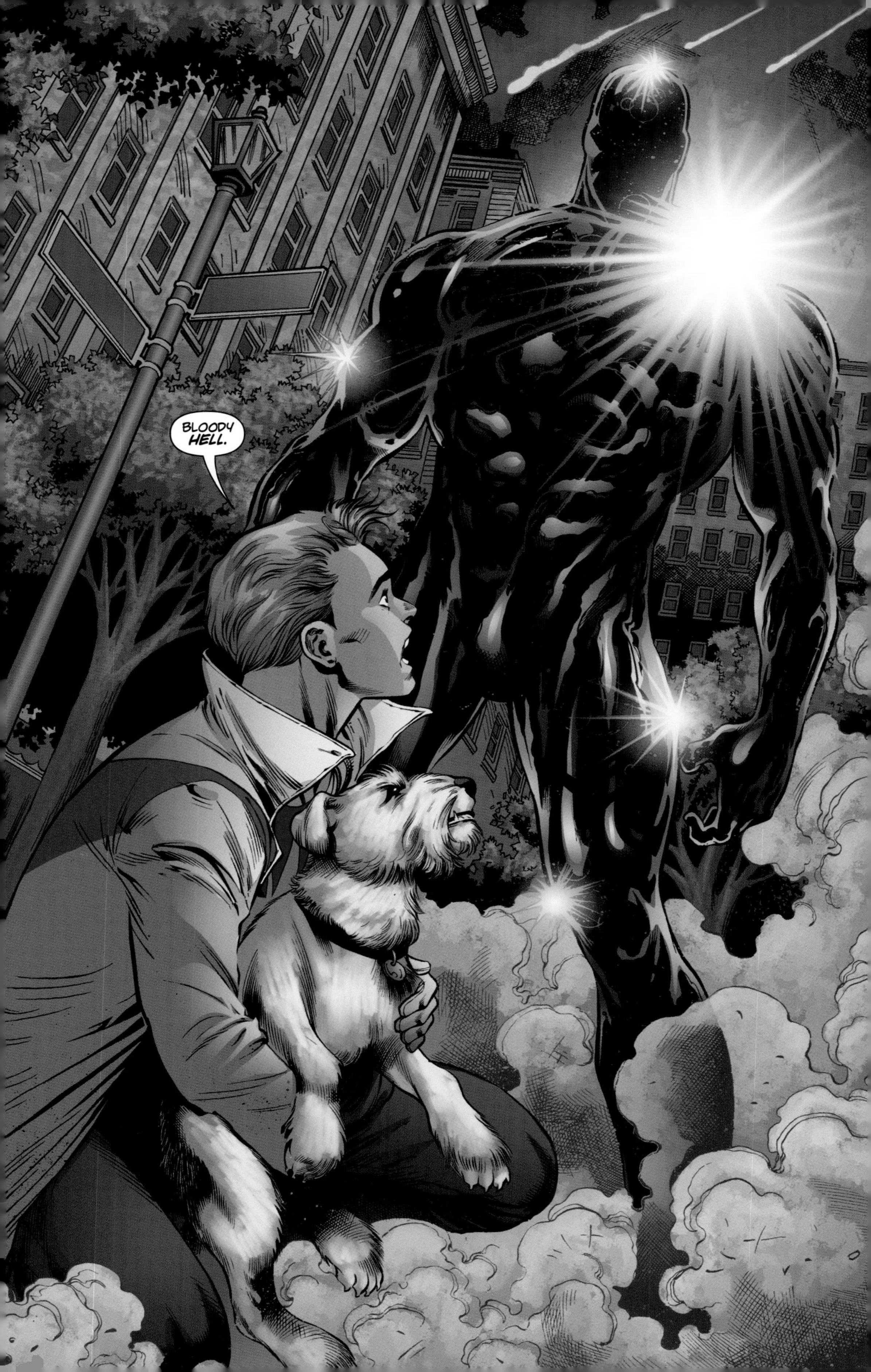
BLOODY HELL.

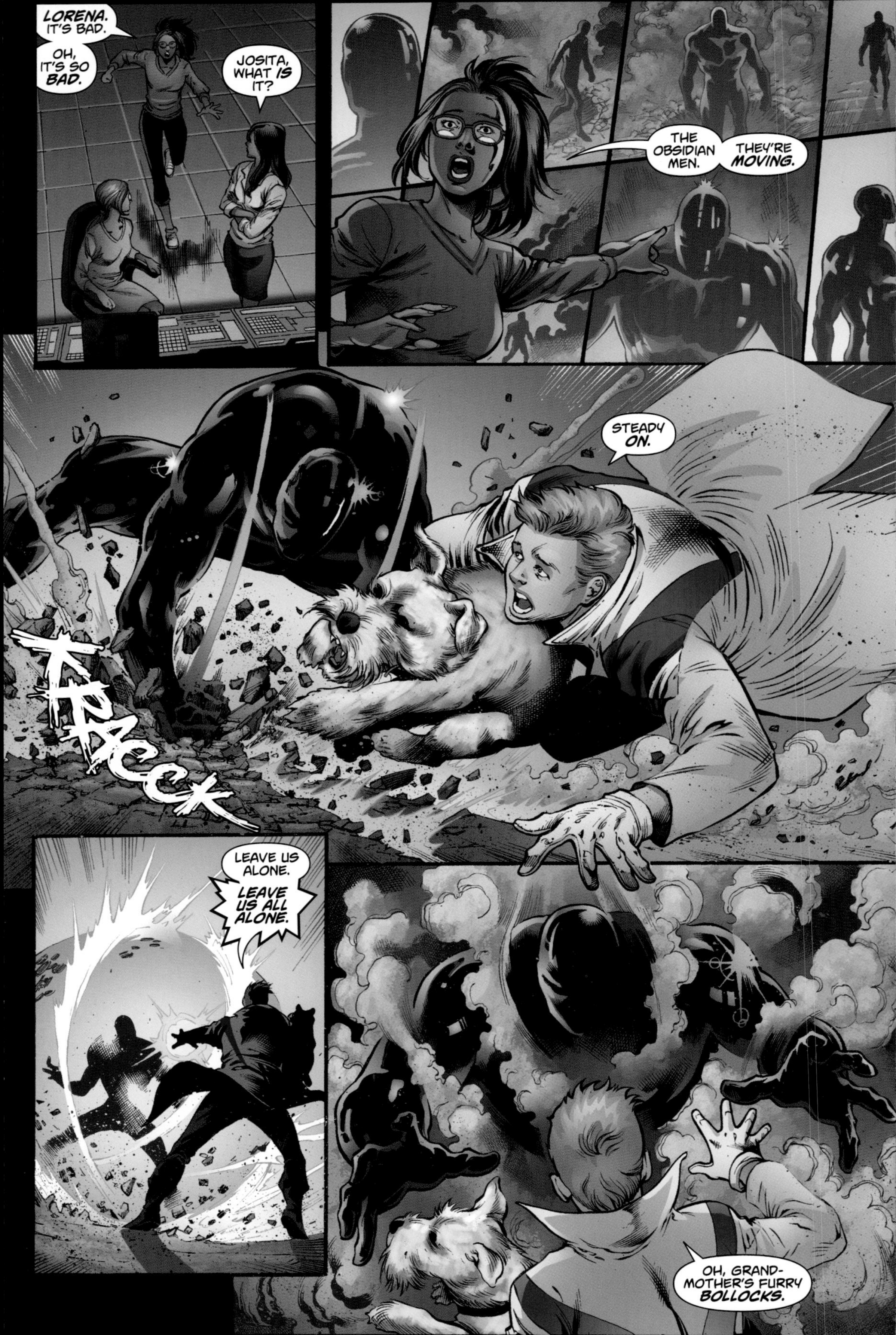
LORENA. IT'S BAD.
OH, IT'S SO BAD.
JOSITA, WHAT IS IT?
THE OBSIDIAN MEN.
THEY'RE MOVING.
STEADY ON.
KRACCK
LEAVE US ALONE.
LEAVE US ALL ALONE.
OH, GRAND-MOTHER'S FURRY BOLLOCKS.

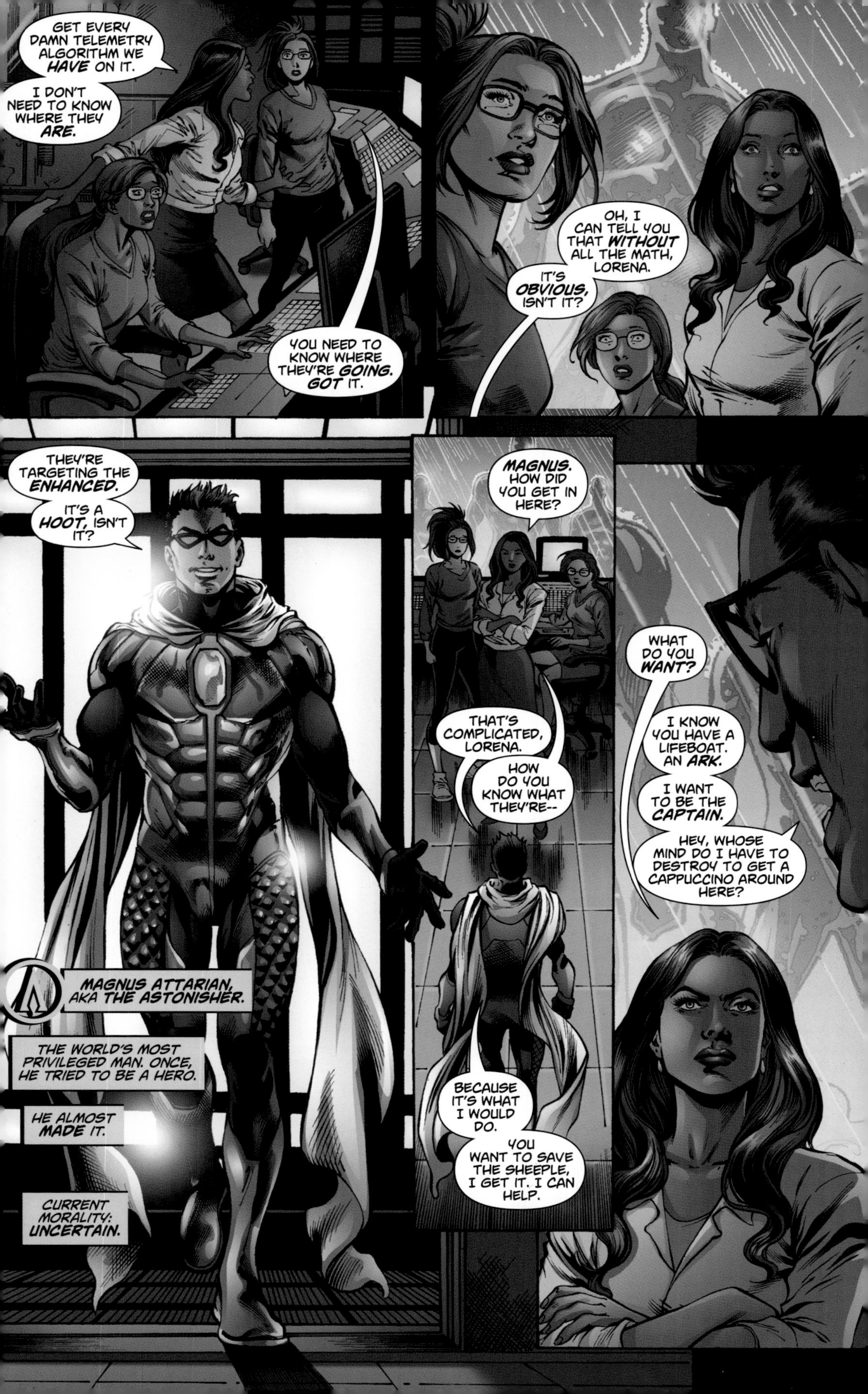
GET EVERY DAMN TELEMETRY ALGORITHM WE HAVE ON IT.
I DON'T NEED TO KNOW WHERE THEY ARE.
YOU NEED TO KNOW WHERE THEY'RE GOING. GOT IT.
OH, I CAN TELL YOU THAT WITHOUT ALL THE MATH, LORENA.
IT'S OBVIOUS, ISN'T IT?
THEY'RE TARGETING THE ENHANCED.
IT'S A HOOT, ISN'T IT?
MAGNUS ATTARIAN, AKA THE ASTONISHER.
THE WORLD'S MOST PRIVILEGED MAN. ONCE, HE TRIED TO BE A HERO.
HE ALMOST MADE IT.
CURRENT MORALITY: UNCERTAIN.
MAGNUS. HOW DID YOU GET IN HERE?
THAT'S COMPLICATED, LORENA.
HOW DO YOU KNOW WHAT THEY'RE--
BECAUSE IT'S WHAT I WOULD DO.
YOU WANT TO SAVE THE SHEEPLE, I GET IT. I CAN HELP.
WHAT DO YOU WANT?
I KNOW YOU HAVE A LIFEBOAT. AN ARK.
I WANT TO BE THE CAPTAIN.
HEY, WHOSE MIND DO I HAVE TO DESTROY TO GET A CAPPUCCINO AROUND HERE?

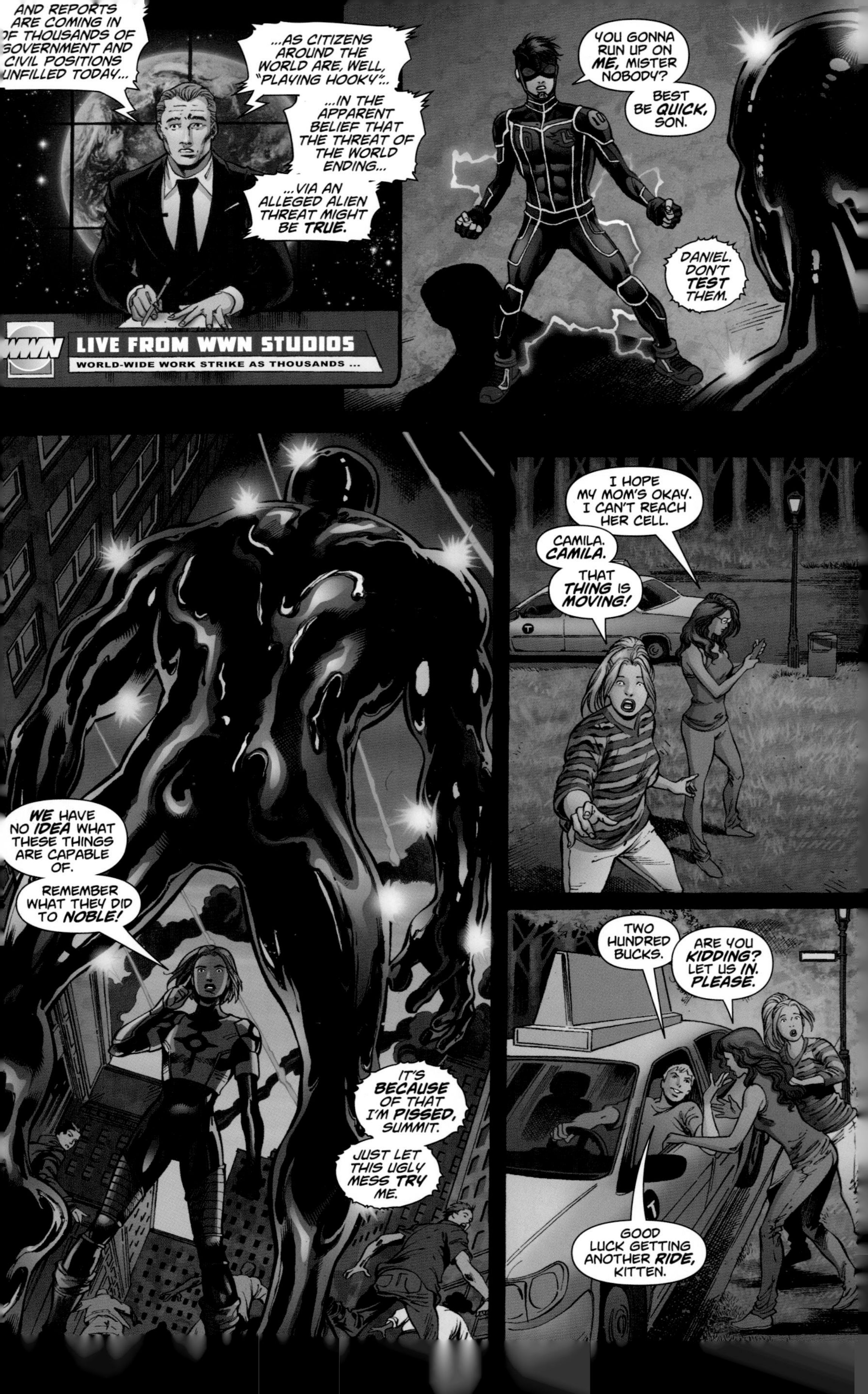

AND REPORTS ARE COMING IN OF THOUSANDS OF GOVERNMENT AND CIVIL POSITIONS UNFILLED TODAY...
...AS CITIZENS AROUND THE WORLD ARE, WELL, "PLAYING HOOKY"...
...IN THE APPARENT BELIEF THAT THE THREAT OF THE WORLD ENDING...
...VIA AN ALLEGED ALIEN THREAT MIGHT BE TRUE.
WWN
LIVE FROM WWN STUDIOS
WORLD-WIDE WORK STRIKE AS THOUSANDS ...
YOU GONNA RUN UP ON ME, MISTER NOBODY?
BEST BE QUICK, SON.
DANIEL. DON'T TEST THEM.
WE HAVE NO IDEA WHAT THESE THINGS ARE CAPABLE OF.
REMEMBER WHAT THEY DID TO NOBLE!
IT'S BECAUSE OF THAT I'M PISSED, SUMMIT.
JUST LET THIS UGLY MESS TRY ME.
I HOPE MY MOM'S OKAY. I CAN'T REACH HER CELL.
CAMILA. CAMILA.
THAT THING IS MOVING!
TWO HUNDRED BUCKS.
ARE YOU KIDDING? LET US IN. PLEASE.
GOOD LUCK GETTING ANOTHER RIDE, KITTEN.

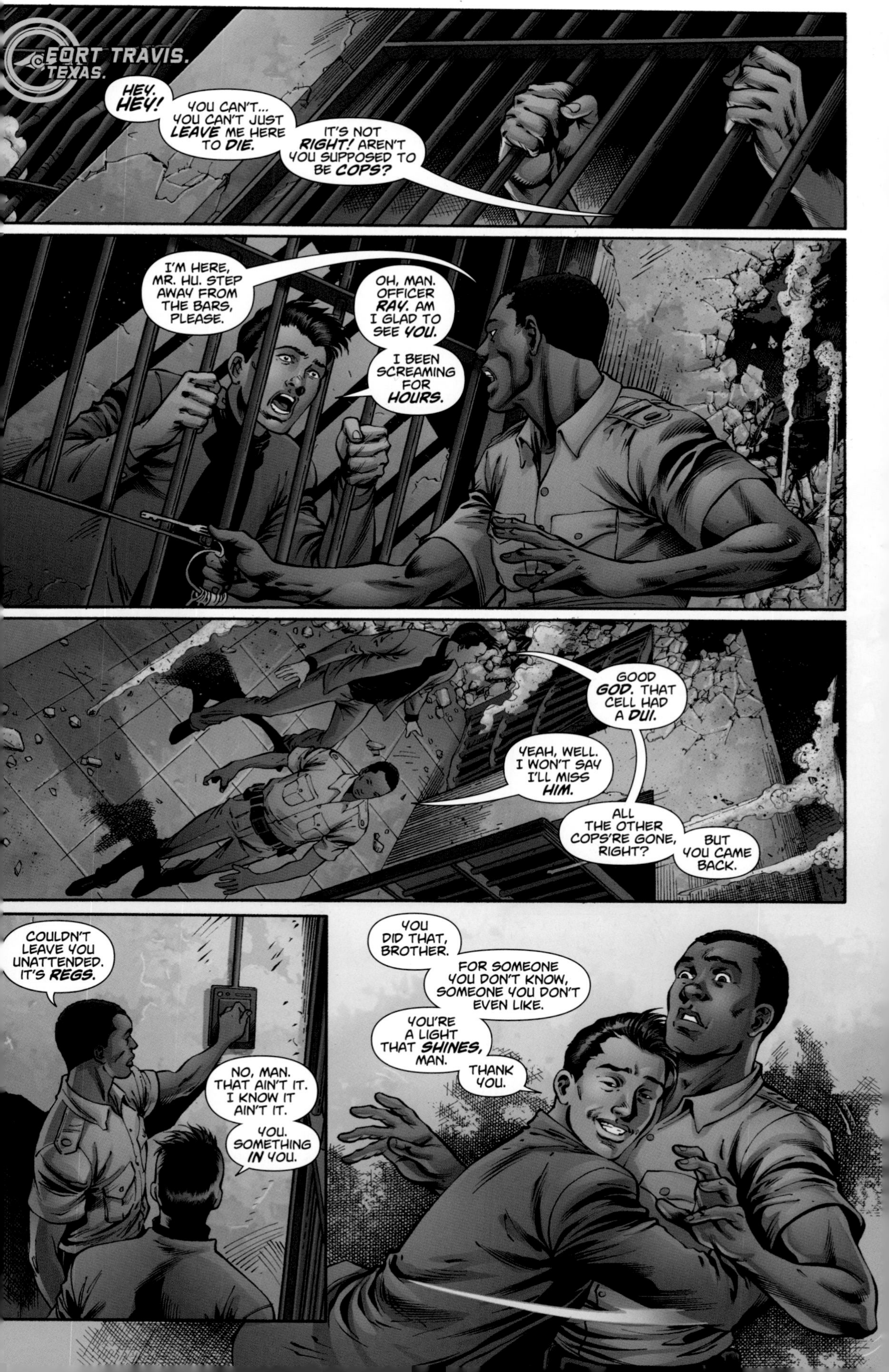
FORT TRAVIS, TEXAS.
HEY, HEY!
YOU CAN'T... YOU CAN'T JUST LEAVE ME HERE TO DIE.
IT'S NOT RIGHT! AREN'T YOU SUPPOSED TO BE COPS?
I'M HERE, MR. HU. STEP AWAY FROM THE BARS, PLEASE.
OH, MAN. OFFICER RAY. AM I GLAD TO SEE YOU.
I BEEN SCREAMING FOR HOURS.
GOOD GOD. THAT CELL HAD A DUI.
YEAH, WELL. I WON'T SAY I'LL MISS HIM.
ALL THE OTHER COPS'RE GONE, RIGHT?
BUT YOU CAME BACK.
COULDN'T LEAVE YOU UNATTENDED. IT'S REGS.
NO, MAN. THAT AIN'T IT. I KNOW IT AIN'T IT.
YOU. SOMETHING IN YOU.
YOU DID THAT, BROTHER.
FOR SOMEONE YOU DON'T KNOW, SOMEONE YOU DON'T EVEN LIKE.
YOU'RE A LIGHT THAT SHINES, MAN.
THANK YOU.

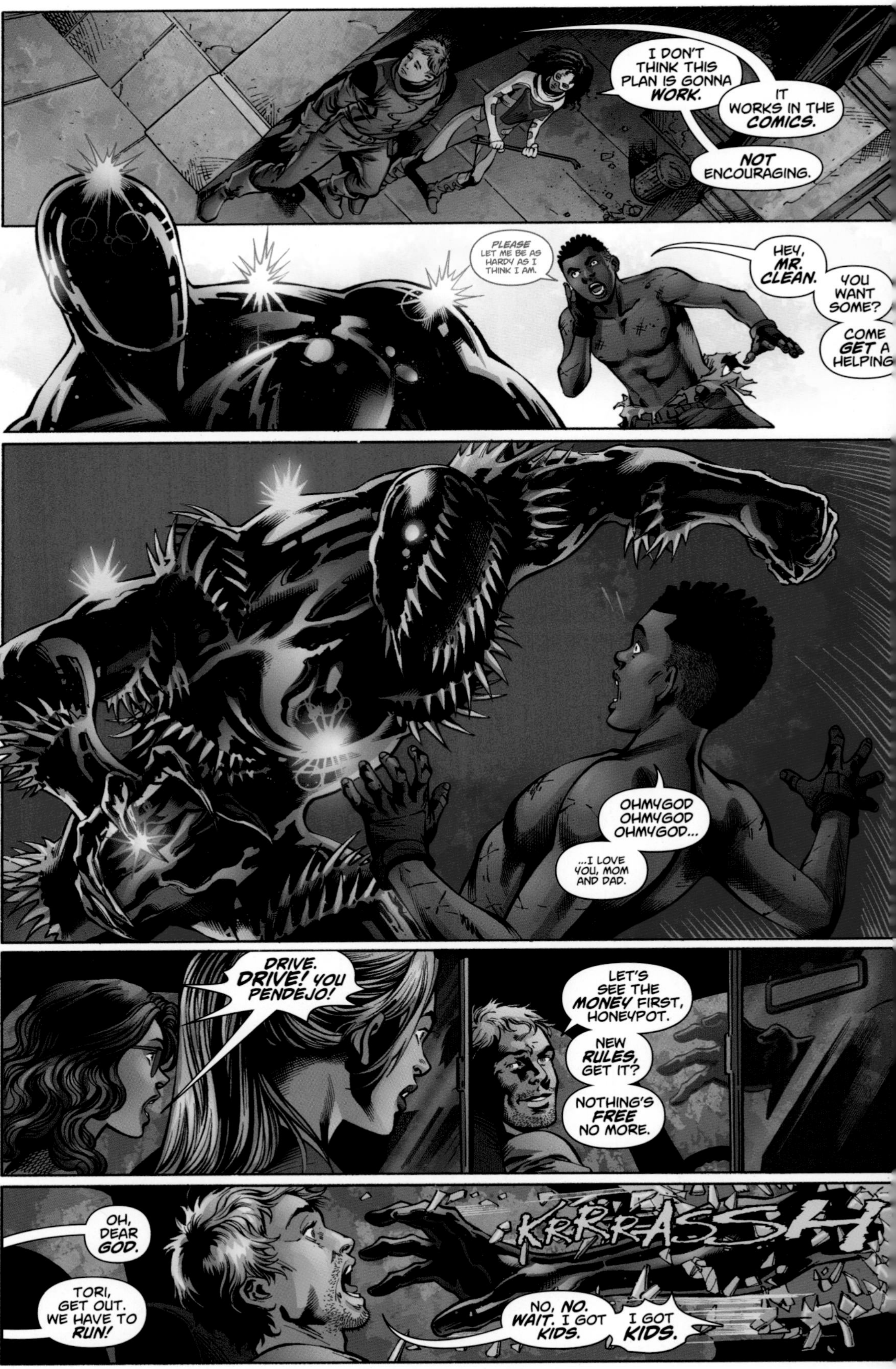
I DON'T THINK THIS PLAN IS GONNA WORK.
IT WORKS IN THE COMICS.
NOT ENCOURAGING.
PLEASE LET ME BE AS HARDY AS I THINK I AM.
HEY, MR. CLEAN.
YOU WANT SOME?
COME GET A HELPING
OHMYGOD OHMYGOD OHMYGOD...
...I LOVE YOU, MOM AND DAD.
DRIVE. DRIVE! YOU PENDEJO!
LET'S SEE THE MONEY FIRST, HONEYPOT.
NEW RULES, GET IT?
NOTHING'S FREE NO MORE.
OH, DEAR GOD.
TORI, GET OUT. WE HAVE TO RUN!
KRRRASSH
NO, NO. WAIT. I GOT KIDS.
I GOT KIDS.

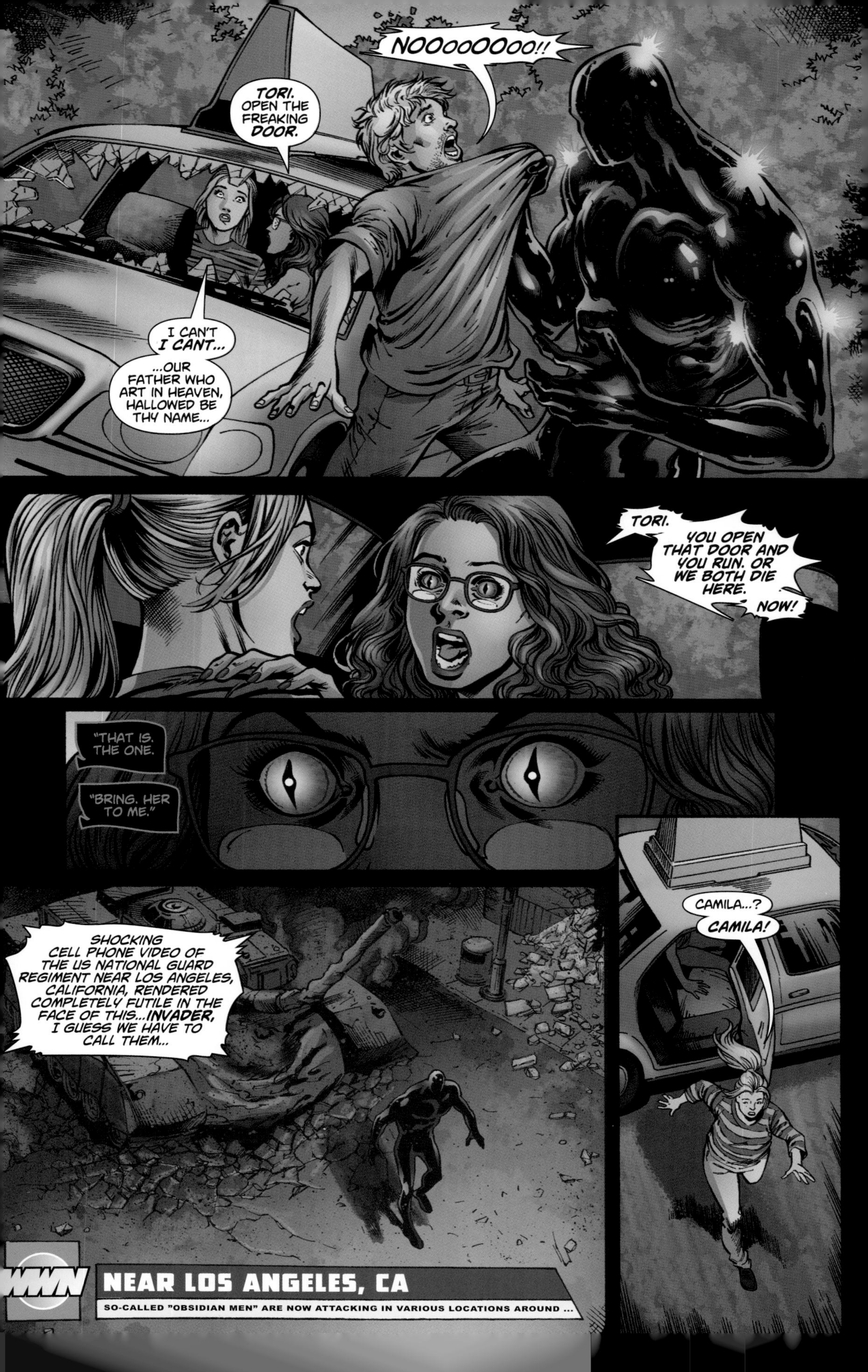
NOOooOOoo!!
TORI. OPEN THE FREAKING DOOR.
I CAN'T I CANT...
...OUR FATHER WHO ART IN HEAVEN, HALLOWED BE THY NAME...
TORI.
YOU OPEN THAT DOOR AND YOU RUN. OR WE BOTH DIE HERE.
NOW!
"THAT IS. THE ONE.
"BRING. HER TO ME."
CAMILA...?
CAMILA!
SHOCKING CELL PHONE VIDEO OF THE US NATIONAL GUARD REGIMENT NEAR LOS ANGELES, CALIFORNIA, RENDERED COMPLETELY FUTILE IN THE FACE OF THIS...INVADER, I GUESS WE HAVE TO CALL THEM...
WWN
NEAR LOS ANGELES, CA
SO-CALLED "OBSIDIAN MEN" ARE NOW ATTACKING IN VARIOUS LOCATIONS AROUND ...

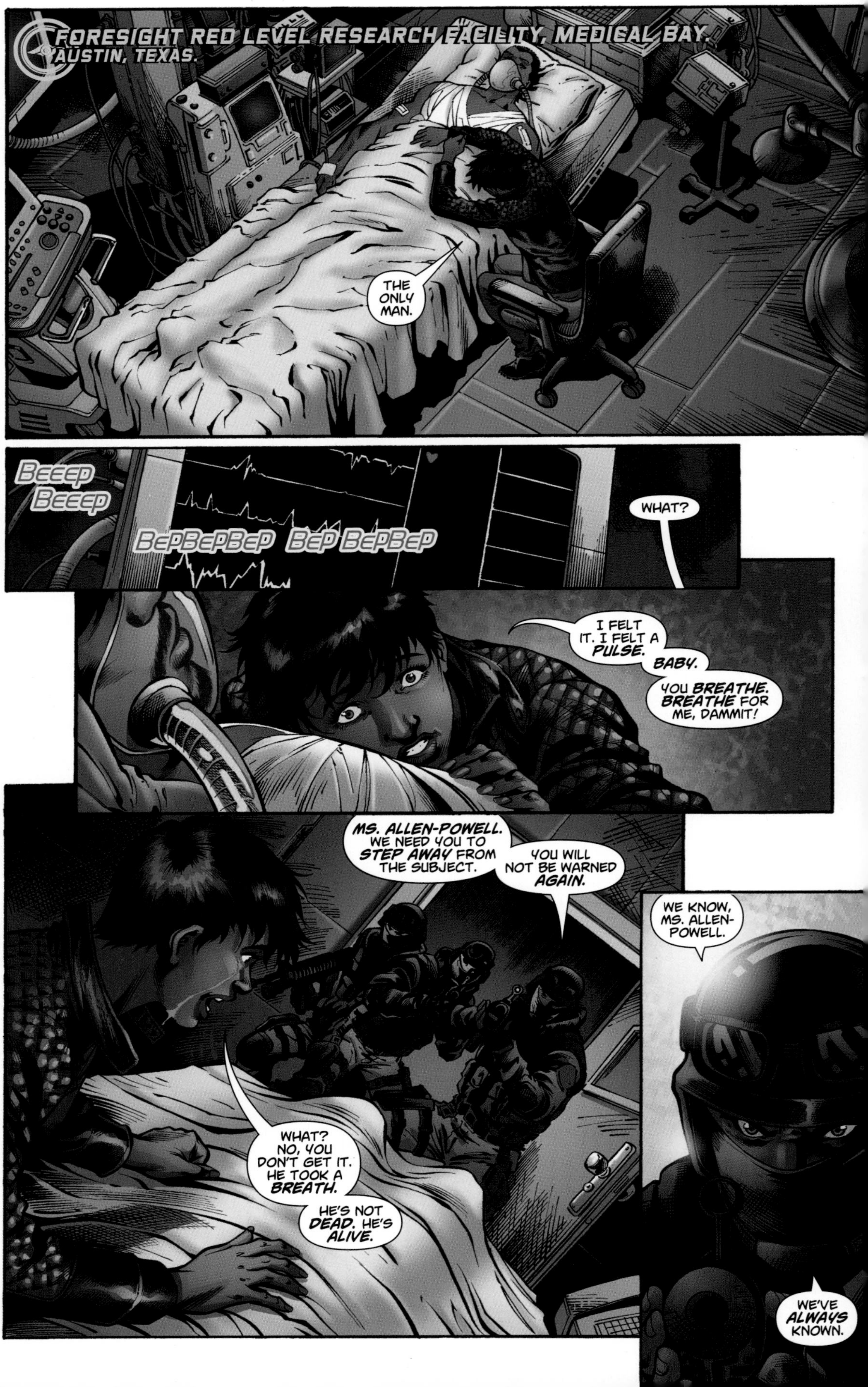
FORESIGHT RED LEVEL RESEARCH FACILITY, MEDICAL BAY.
AUSTIN, TEXAS.
THE ONLY MAN.
Beeep
Beeep
BepBepBep
Bep BepBep
WHAT?
I FELT IT. I FELT A PULSE.
BABY.
YOU BREATHE. BREATHE FOR ME, DAMMIT!
MS. ALLEN-POWELL. WE NEED YOU TO STEP AWAY FROM THE SUBJECT.
YOU WILL NOT BE WARNED AGAIN.
WHAT? NO, YOU DON'T GET IT. HE TOOK A BREATH.
HE'S NOT DEAD. HE'S ALIVE.
WE KNOW, MS. ALLEN-POWELL.
WE'VE ALWAYS KNOWN.

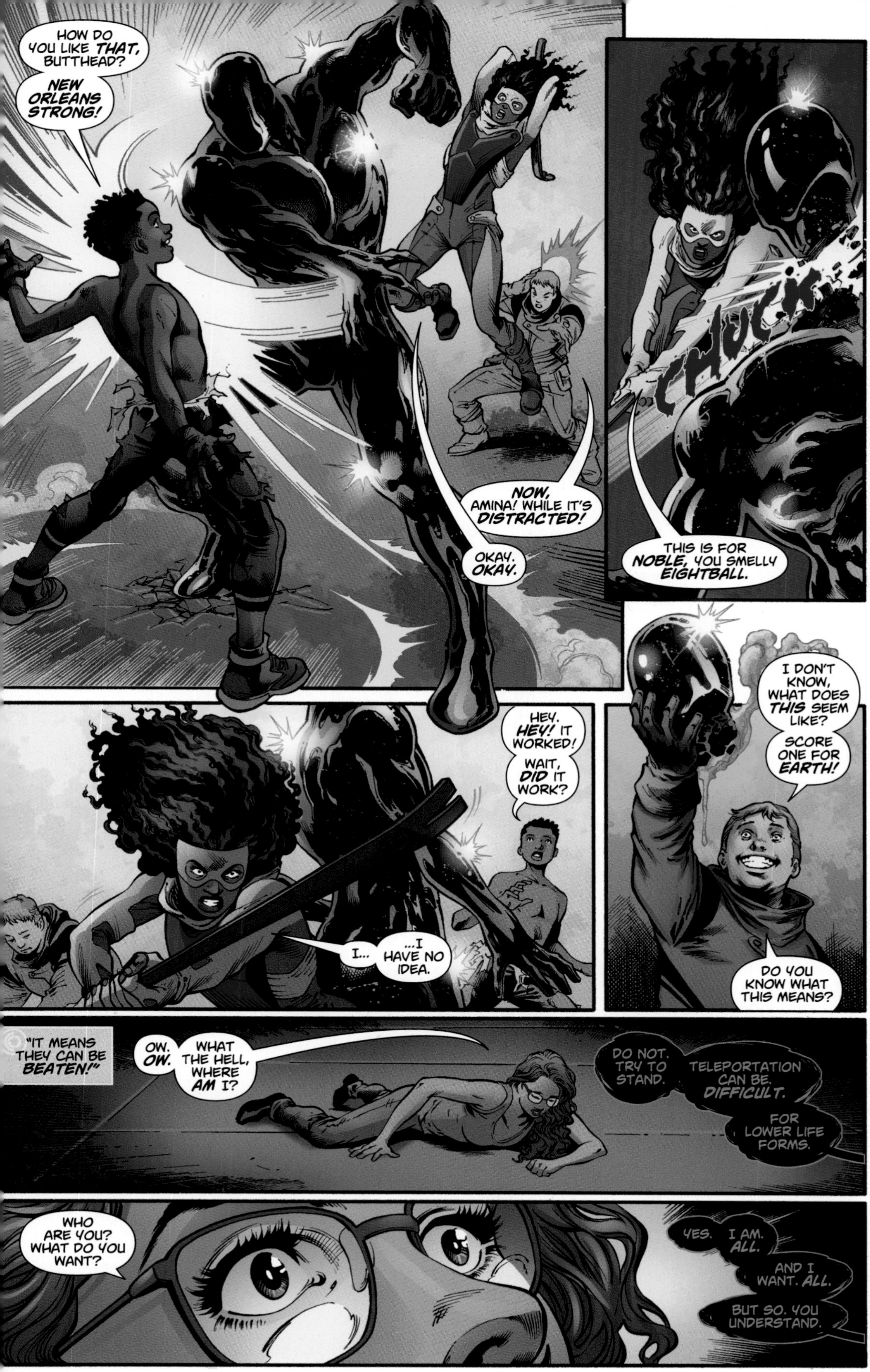
HOW DO YOU LIKE THAT, BUTTHEAD?
NEW ORLEANS STRONG!
NOW, AMINA! WHILE IT'S DISTRACTED!
OKAY. OKAY.
THIS IS FOR NOBLE, YOU SMELLY EIGHTBALL.
CHUCK
HEY. HEY! IT WORKED!
WAIT, DID IT WORK?
I...
...I HAVE NO IDEA.
I DON'T KNOW, WHAT DOES THIS SEEM LIKE?
SCORE ONE FOR EARTH!
DO YOU KNOW WHAT THIS MEANS?
"IT MEANS THEY CAN BE BEATEN!"
OW. OW.
WHAT THE HELL, WHERE AM I?
DO NOT. TRY TO STAND.
TELEPORTATION CAN BE. DIFFICULT.
FOR LOWER LIFE FORMS.
WHO ARE YOU? WHAT DO YOU WANT?
YES. I AM. ALL.
AND I WANT. ALL.
BUT SO. YOU UNDERSTAND.

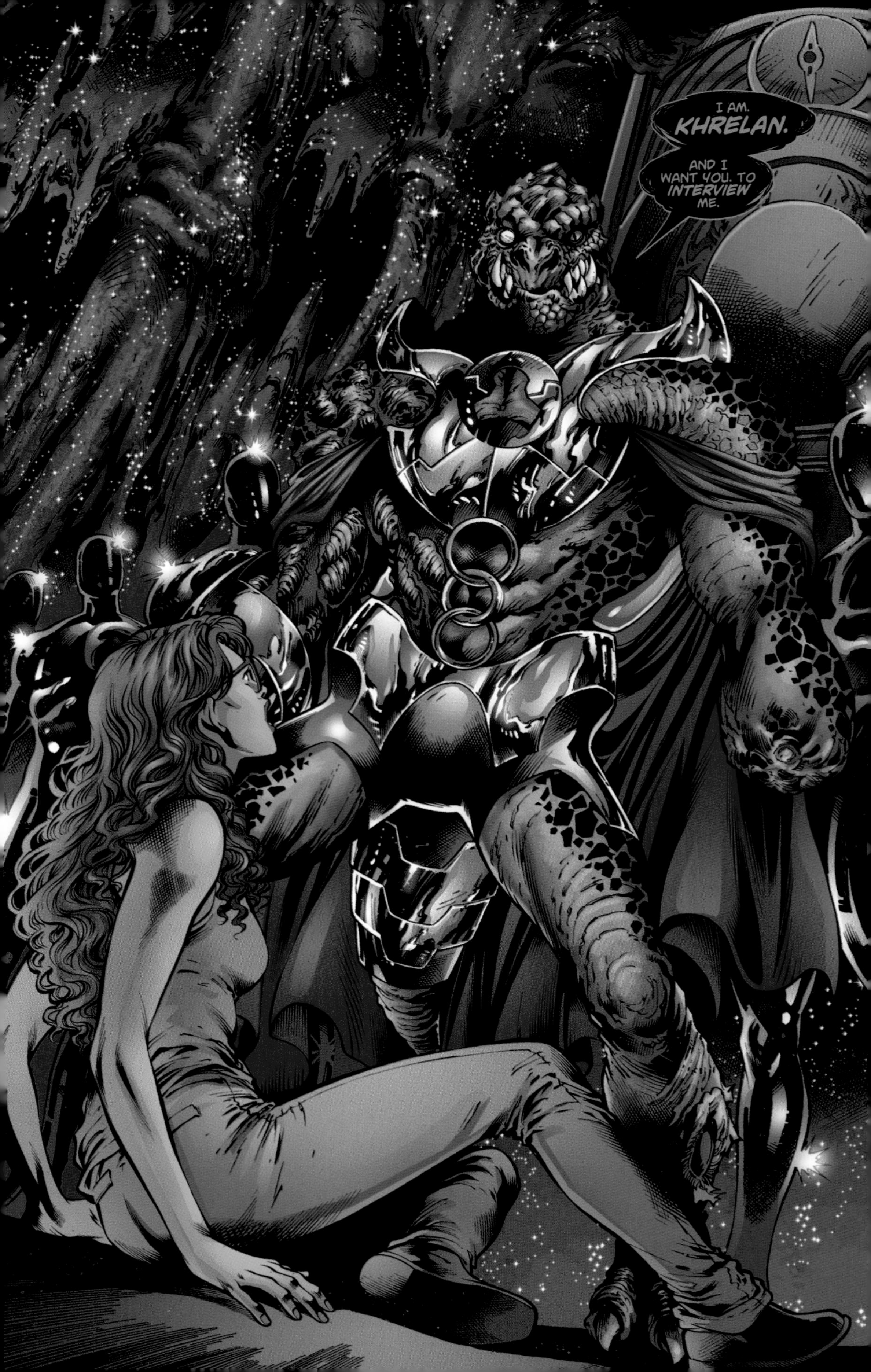
I AM. KHRELAN.
AND I WANT YOU. TO INTERVIEW ME.

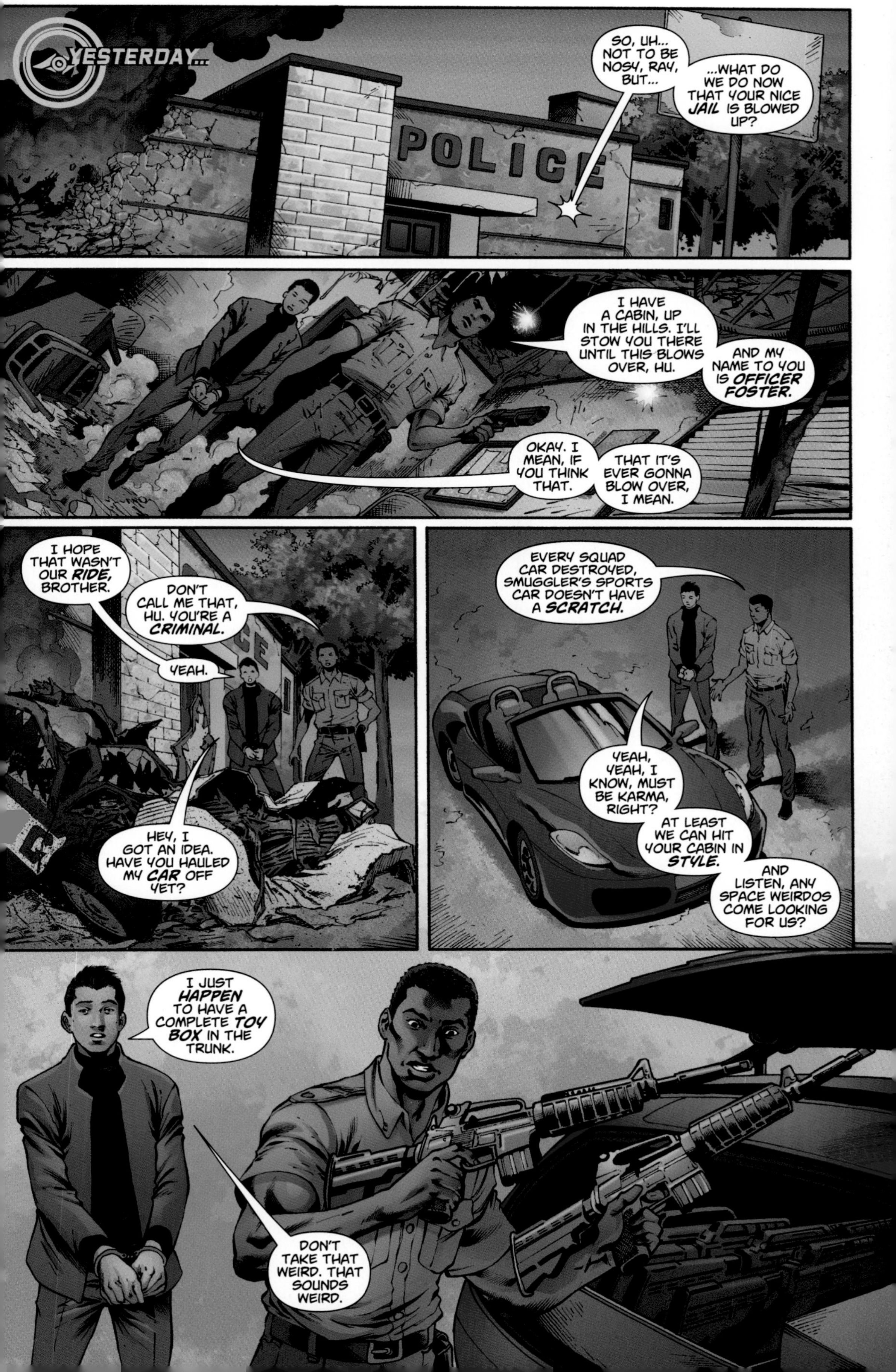
YESTERDAY...
SO, UH... NOT TO BE NOSY, RAY, BUT...
...WHAT DO WE DO NOW THAT YOUR NICE JAIL IS BLOWED UP?
POLICE
I HAVE A CABIN, UP IN THE HILLS. I'LL STOW YOU THERE UNTIL THIS BLOWS OVER, HU.
AND MY NAME TO YOU IS OFFICER FOSTER.
OKAY. I MEAN, IF YOU THINK THAT.
THAT IT'S EVER GONNA BLOW OVER, I MEAN.
I HOPE THAT WASN'T OUR RIDE, BROTHER.
DON'T CALL ME THAT, HU. YOU'RE A CRIMINAL.
YEAH.
HEY, I GOT AN IDEA. HAVE YOU HAULED MY CAR OFF YET?
EVERY SQUAD CAR DESTROYED, SMUGGLER'S SPORTS CAR DOESN'T HAVE A SCRATCH.
YEAH, YEAH, I KNOW, MUST BE KARMA, RIGHT?
AT LEAST WE CAN HIT YOUR CABIN IN STYLE.
AND LISTEN, ANY SPACE WEIRDOS COME LOOKING FOR US?
I JUST HAPPEN TO HAVE A COMPLETE TOY BOX IN THE TRUNK.
DON'T TAKE THAT WEIRD. THAT SOUNDS WEIRD.

DAY THREE.

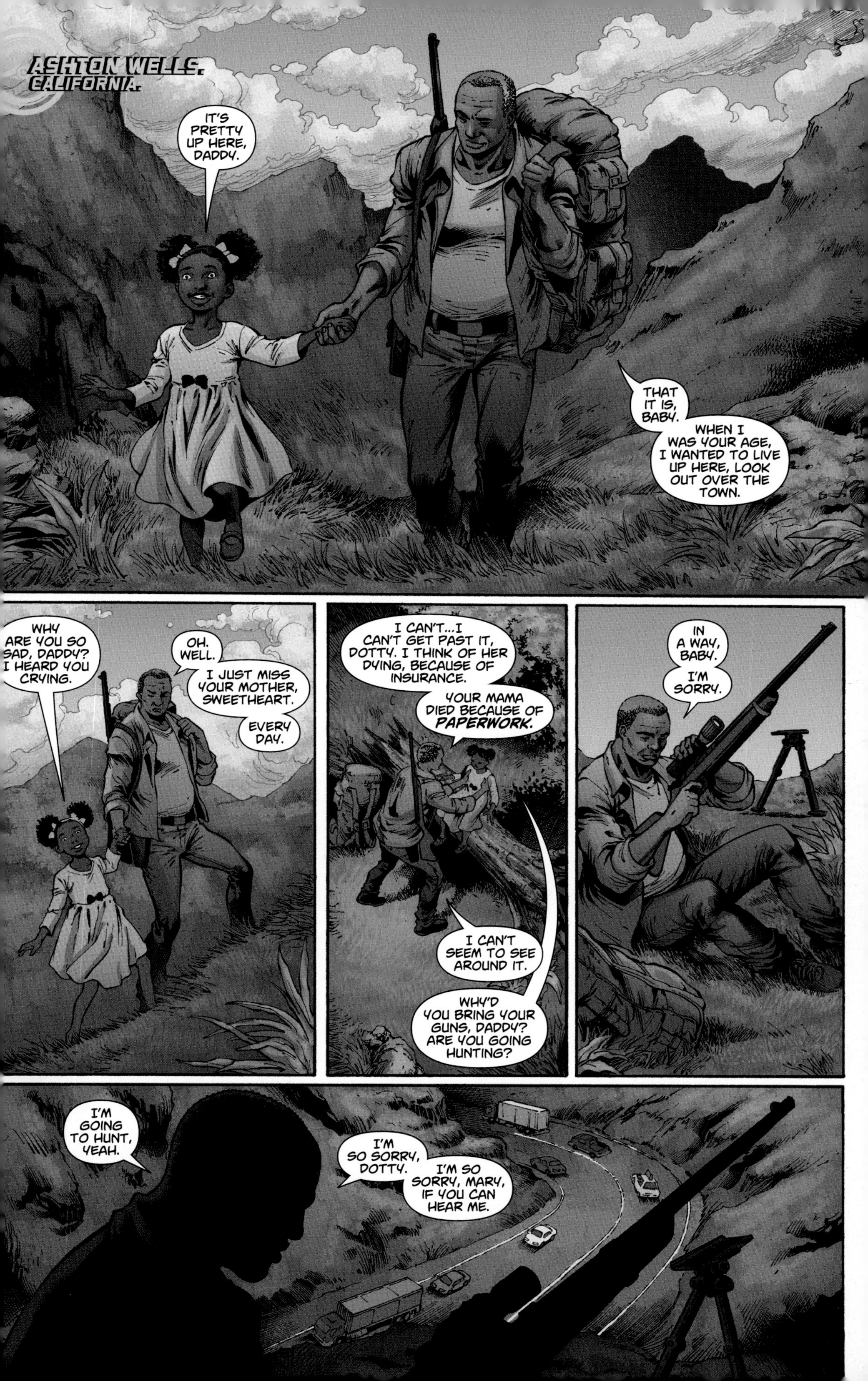
ASHTON WELLS, CALIFORNIA.
IT'S PRETTY UP HERE, DADDY.
THAT IT IS, BABY.
WHEN I WAS YOUR AGE, I WANTED TO LIVE UP HERE, LOOK OUT OVER THE TOWN.
WHY ARE YOU SO SAD, DADDY? I HEARD YOU CRYING.
OH. WELL.
I JUST MISS YOUR MOTHER, SWEETHEART.
EVERY DAY.
I CAN'T...I CAN'T GET PAST IT, DOTTY. I THINK OF HER DYING, BECAUSE OF INSURANCE.
YOUR MAMA DIED BECAUSE OF PAPERWORK.
I CAN'T SEEM TO SEE AROUND IT.
WHY'D YOU BRING YOUR GUNS, DADDY? ARE YOU GOING HUNTING?
IN A WAY, BABY.
I'M SORRY.
I'M GOING TO HUNT, YEAH.
I'M SO SORRY, DOTTY.
I'M SO SORRY, MARY, IF YOU CAN HEAR ME.

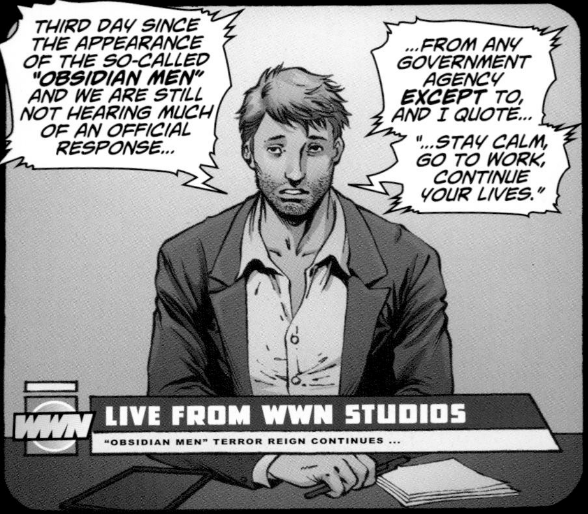
THIRD DAY SINCE THE APPEARANCE OF THE SO-CALLED "OBSIDIAN MEN" AND WE ARE STILL NOT HEARING MUCH OF AN OFFICIAL RESPONSE...
...FROM ANY GOVERNMENT AGENCY EXCEPT TO, AND I QUOTE...
"...STAY CALM, GO TO WORK, CONTINUE YOUR LIVES."
LIVE FROM WWN STUDIOS
"OBSIDIAN MEN" TERROR REIGN CONTINUES ...

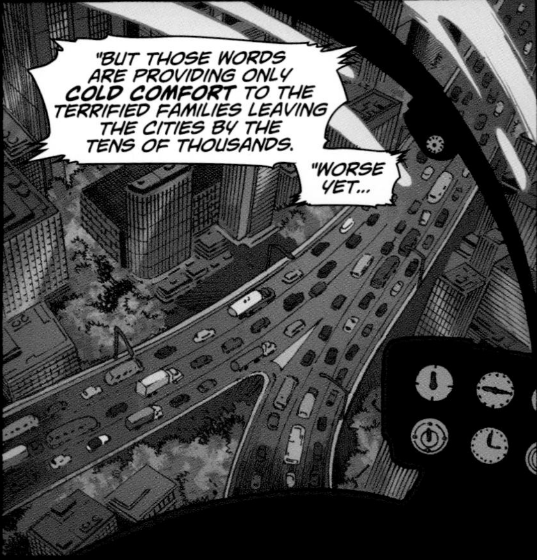
"BUT THOSE WORDS ARE PROVIDING ONLY COLD COMFORT TO THE TERRIFIED FAMILIES LEAVING THE CITIES BY THE TENS OF THOUSANDS.
"WORSE YET...

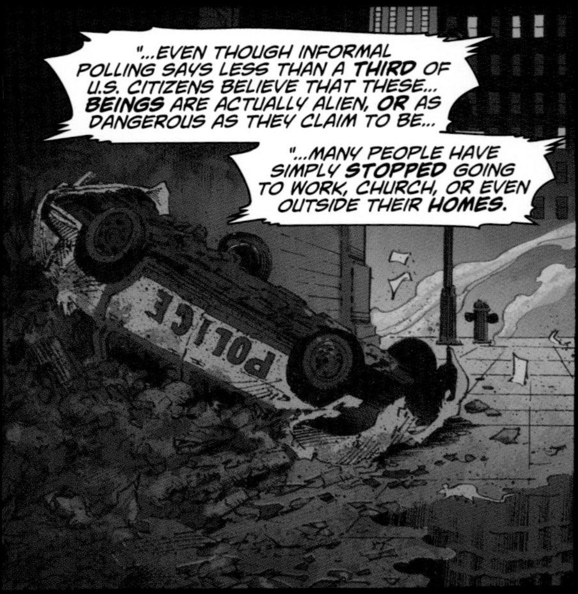
"...EVEN THOUGH INFORMAL POLLING SAYS LESS THAN A THIRD OF U.S. CITIZENS BELIEVE THAT THESE... BEINGS ARE ACTUALLY ALIEN, OR AS DANGEROUS AS THEY CLAIM TO BE...
"...MANY PEOPLE HAVE SIMPLY STOPPED GOING TO WORK, CHURCH, OR EVEN OUTSIDE THEIR HOMES.
POLICE

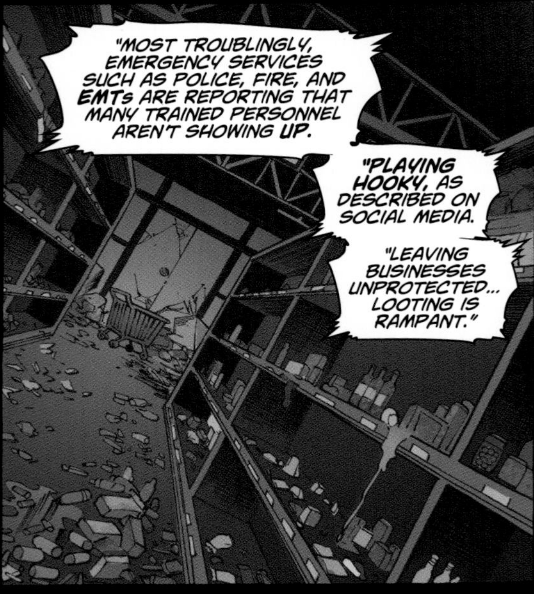
"MOST TROUBLINGLY, EMERGENCY SERVICES SUCH AS POLICE, FIRE, AND EMTs ARE REPORTING THAT MANY TRAINED PERSONNEL AREN'T SHOWING UP.
"PLAYING HOOKY, AS DESCRIBED ON SOCIAL MEDIA.
"LEAVING BUSINESSES UNPROTECTED... LOOTING IS RAMPANT."

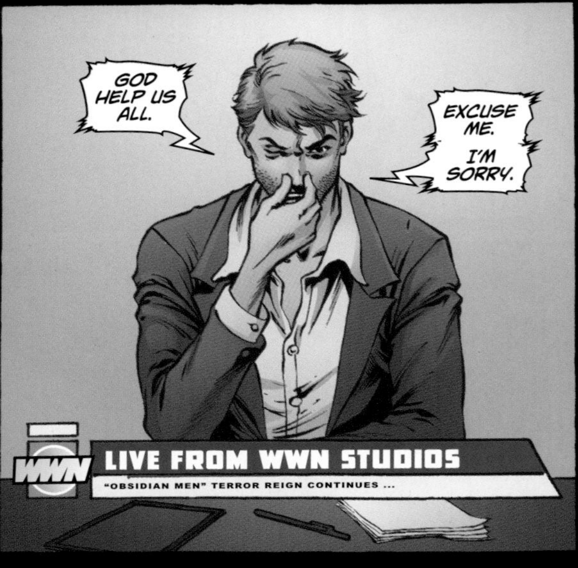
GOD HELP US ALL.
EXCUSE ME.
I'M SORRY.
LIVE FROM WWN STUDIOS
"OBSIDIAN MEN" TERROR REIGN CONTINUES ...

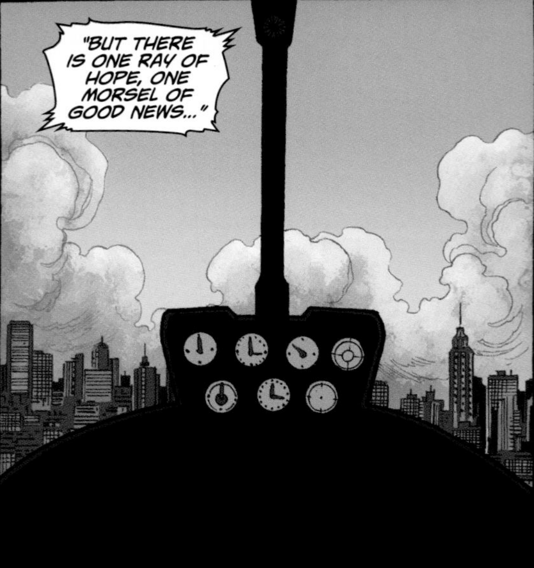
"BUT THERE IS ONE RAY OF HOPE, ONE MORSEL OF GOOD NEWS..."

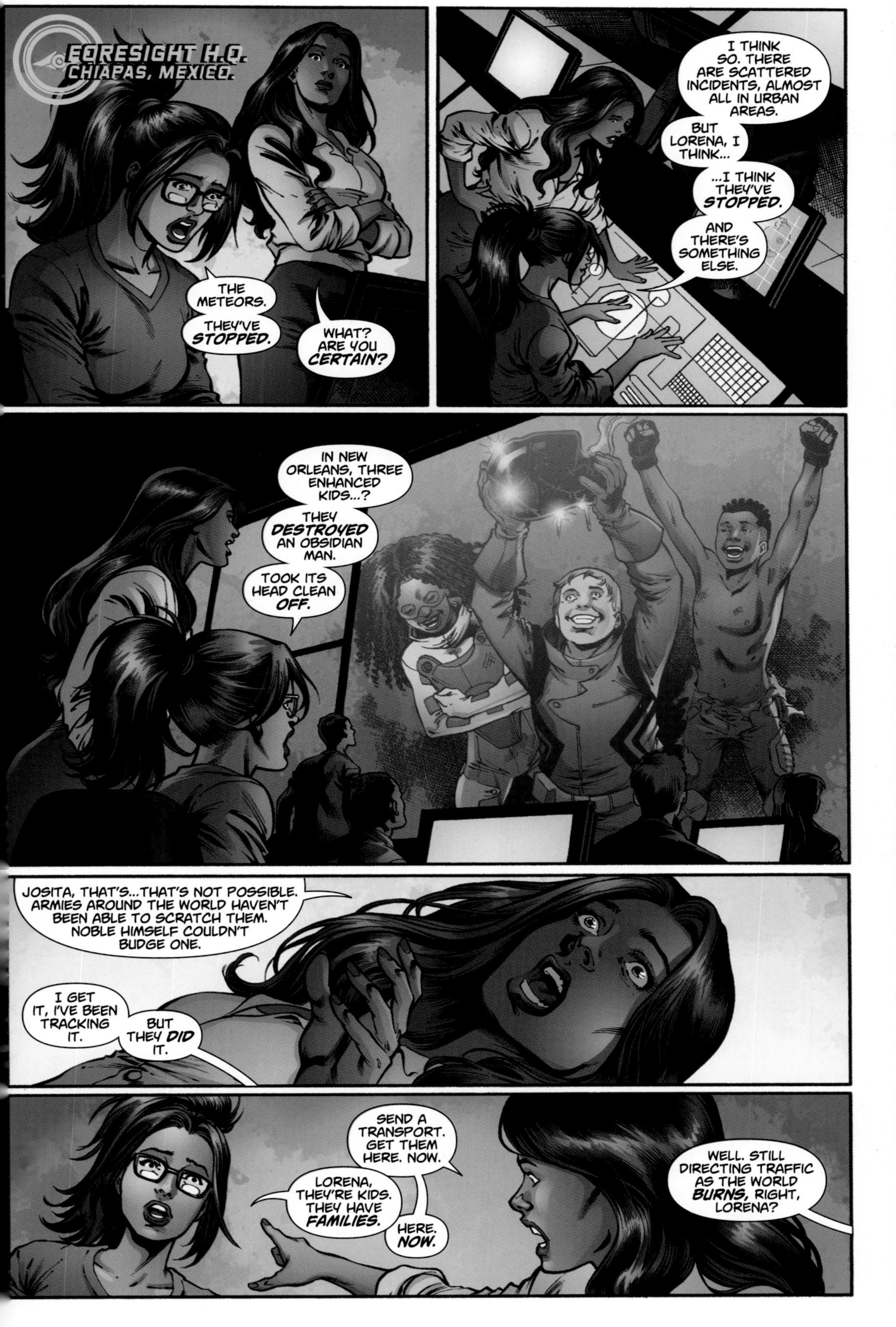
FORESIGHT H.Q. CHIAPAS, MEXICO.
THE METEORS.
THEY'VE STOPPED.
WHAT? ARE YOU CERTAIN?
I THINK SO. THERE ARE SCATTERED INCIDENTS, ALMOST ALL IN URBAN AREAS.
BUT LORENA, I THINK...
...I THINK THEY'VE STOPPED.
AND THERE'S SOMETHING ELSE.
IN NEW ORLEANS, THREE ENHANCED KIDS...?
THEY DESTROYED AN OBSIDIAN MAN.
TOOK ITS HEAD CLEAN OFF.
JOSITA, THAT'S...THAT'S NOT POSSIBLE. ARMIES AROUND THE WORLD HAVEN'T BEEN ABLE TO SCRATCH THEM. NOBLE HIMSELF COULDN'T BUDGE ONE.
I GET IT, I'VE BEEN TRACKING IT.
BUT THEY DID IT.
SEND A TRANSPORT. GET THEM HERE. NOW.
LORENA, THEY'RE KIDS. THEY HAVE FAMILIES.
HERE. NOW.
WELL. STILL DIRECTING TRAFFIC AS THE WORLD BURNS, RIGHT, LORENA?

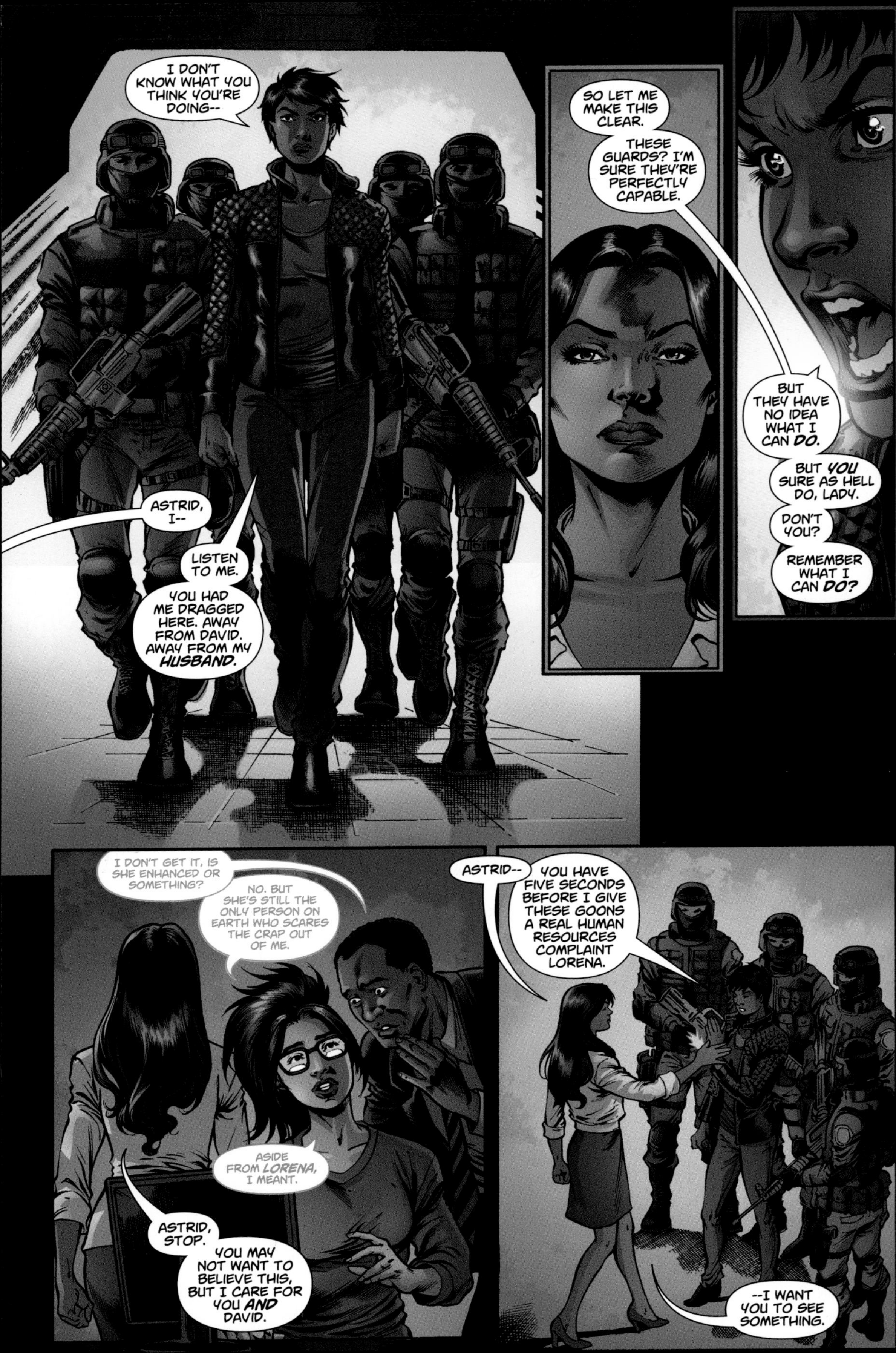
I DON'T KNOW WHAT YOU THINK YOU'RE DOING--
ASTRID, I--
LISTEN TO ME.
YOU HAD ME DRAGGED HERE. AWAY FROM DAVID. AWAY FROM MY HUSBAND.
SO LET ME MAKE THIS CLEAR.
THESE GUARDS? I'M SURE THEY'RE PERFECTLY CAPABLE.
BUT THEY HAVE NO IDEA WHAT I CAN DO.
BUT YOU SURE AS HELL DO, LADY.
DON'T YOU?
REMEMBER WHAT I CAN DO?
I DON'T GET IT, IS SHE ENHANCED OR SOMETHING?
NO. BUT SHE'S STILL THE ONLY PERSON ON EARTH WHO SCARES THE CRAP OUT OF ME.
ASIDE FROM LORENA, I MEANT.
ASTRID, STOP.
YOU MAY NOT WANT TO BELIEVE THIS, BUT I CARE FOR YOU AND DAVID.
ASTRID--
YOU HAVE FIVE SECONDS BEFORE I GIVE THESE GOONS A REAL HUMAN RESOURCES COMPLAINT LORENA.
--I WANT YOU TO SEE SOMETHING.

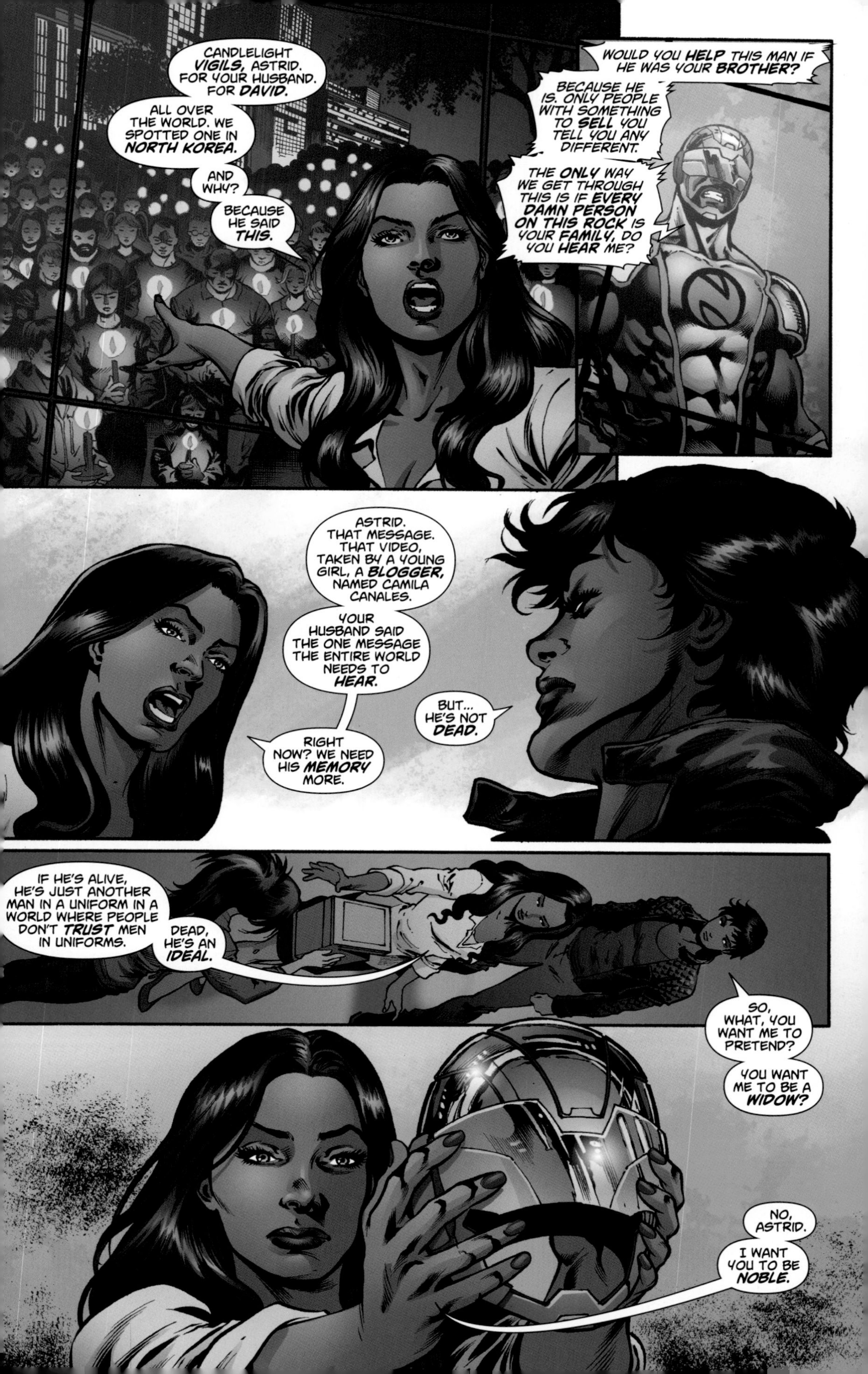
CANDLELIGHT VIGILS, ASTRID. FOR YOUR HUSBAND. FOR DAVID.
ALL OVER THE WORLD. WE SPOTTED ONE IN NORTH KOREA.
AND WHY?
BECAUSE HE SAID THIS.
WOULD YOU HELP THIS MAN IF HE WAS YOUR BROTHER?
BECAUSE HE IS. ONLY PEOPLE WITH SOMETHING TO SELL YOU TELL YOU ANY DIFFERENT.
THE ONLY WAY WE GET THROUGH THIS IS IF EVERY DAMN PERSON ON THIS ROCK IS YOUR FAMILY, DO YOU HEAR ME?
ASTRID. THAT MESSAGE. THAT VIDEO, TAKEN BY A YOUNG GIRL, A BLOGGER, NAMED CAMILA CANALES.
YOUR HUSBAND SAID THE ONE MESSAGE THE ENTIRE WORLD NEEDS TO HEAR.
BUT... HE'S NOT DEAD.
RIGHT NOW? WE NEED HIS MEMORY MORE.
IF HE'S ALIVE, HE'S JUST ANOTHER MAN IN A UNIFORM IN A WORLD WHERE PEOPLE DON'T TRUST MEN IN UNIFORMS.
DEAD, HE'S AN IDEAL.
SO, WHAT, YOU WANT ME TO PRETEND?
YOU WANT ME TO BE A WIDOW?
NO, ASTRID.
I WANT YOU TO BE NOBLE.

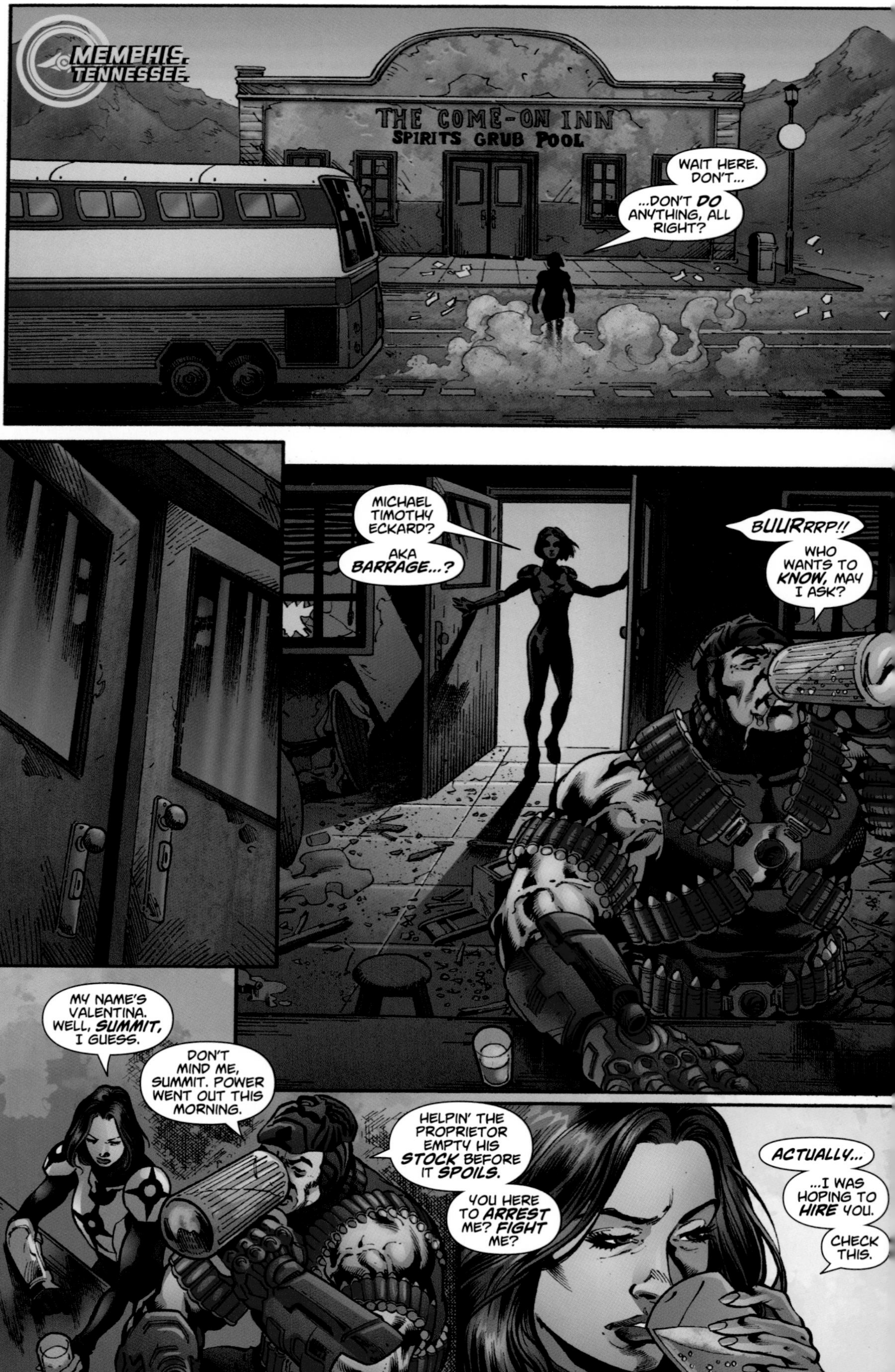
MEMPHIS, TENNESSEE
THE COME-ON INN
SPIRITS GRUB POOL
WAIT HERE. DON'T...
...DON'T DO ANYTHING, ALL RIGHT?
MICHAEL TIMOTHY ECKARD?
AKA BARRAGE...?
BUURRRP!!
WHO WANTS TO KNOW, MAY I ASK?
MY NAME'S VALENTINA. WELL, SUMMIT, I GUESS.
DON'T MIND ME, SUMMIT. POWER WENT OUT THIS MORNING.
HELPIN' THE PROPRIETOR EMPTY HIS STOCK BEFORE IT SPOILS.
YOU HERE TO ARREST ME? FIGHT ME?
ACTUALLY...
...I WAS HOPING TO HIRE YOU.
CHECK THIS.

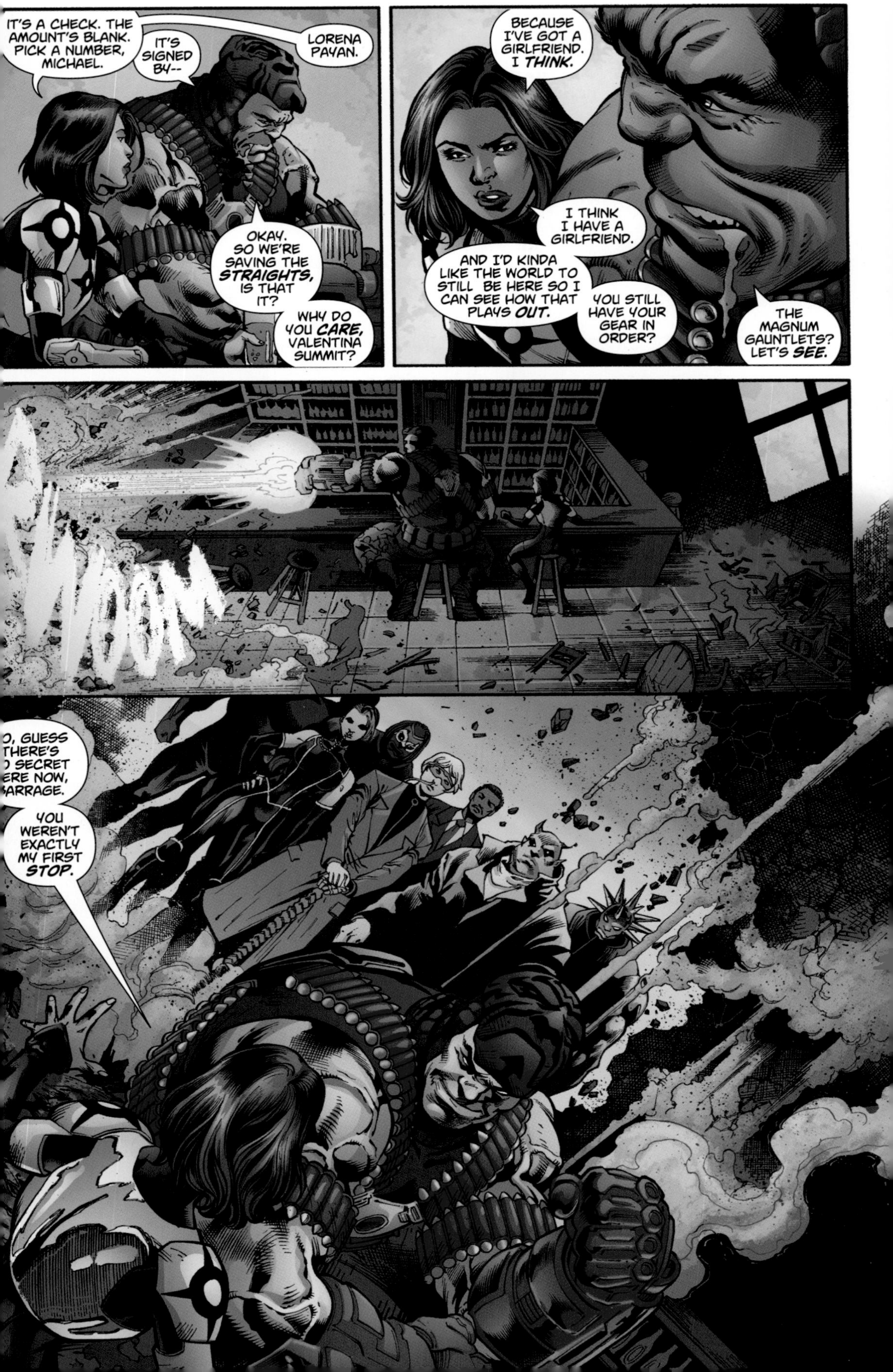
IT'S A CHECK. THE AMOUNT'S BLANK. PICK A NUMBER, MICHAEL.
IT'S SIGNED BY--
LORENA PAYAN.
OKAY. SO WE'RE SAVING THE STRAIGHTS, IS THAT IT?
WHY DO YOU CARE, VALENTINA SUMMIT?
BECAUSE I'VE GOT A GIRLFRIEND. I THINK.
I THINK I HAVE A GIRLFRIEND.
AND I'D KINDA LIKE THE WORLD TO STILL BE HERE SO I CAN SEE HOW THAT PLAYS OUT.
YOU STILL HAVE YOUR GEAR IN ORDER?
THE MAGNUM GAUNTLETS? LET'S SEE.
VOOOM
O, GUESS THERE'S O SECRET ERE NOW, ARRAGE.
YOU WEREN'T EXACTLY MY FIRST STOP.

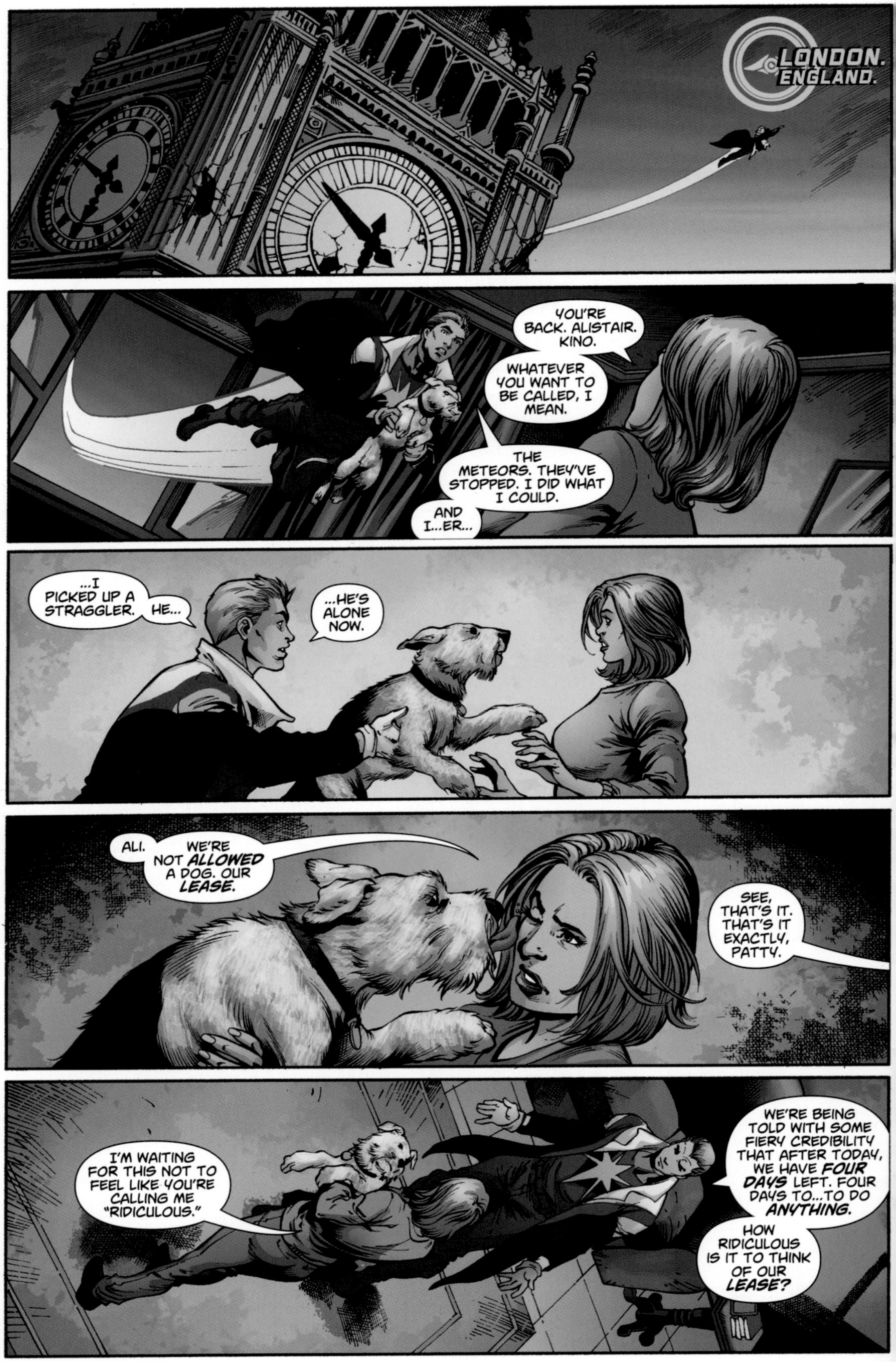
LONDON. ENGLAND.
YOU'RE BACK. ALISTAIR. KINO.
WHATEVER YOU WANT TO BE CALLED, I MEAN.
THE METEORS. THEY'VE STOPPED. I DID WHAT I COULD.
AND I...ER...
...I PICKED UP A STRAGGLER. HE...
...HE'S ALONE NOW.
ALI. WE'RE NOT ALLOWED A DOG. OUR LEASE.
SEE, THAT'S IT. THAT'S IT EXACTLY, PATTY.
WE'RE BEING TOLD WITH SOME FIERY CREDIBILITY THAT AFTER TODAY, WE HAVE FOUR DAYS LEFT. FOUR DAYS TO...TO DO ANYTHING.
HOW RIDICULOUS IS IT TO THINK OF OUR LEASE?
I'M WAITING FOR THIS NOT TO FEEL LIKE YOU'RE CALLING ME "RIDICULOUS."

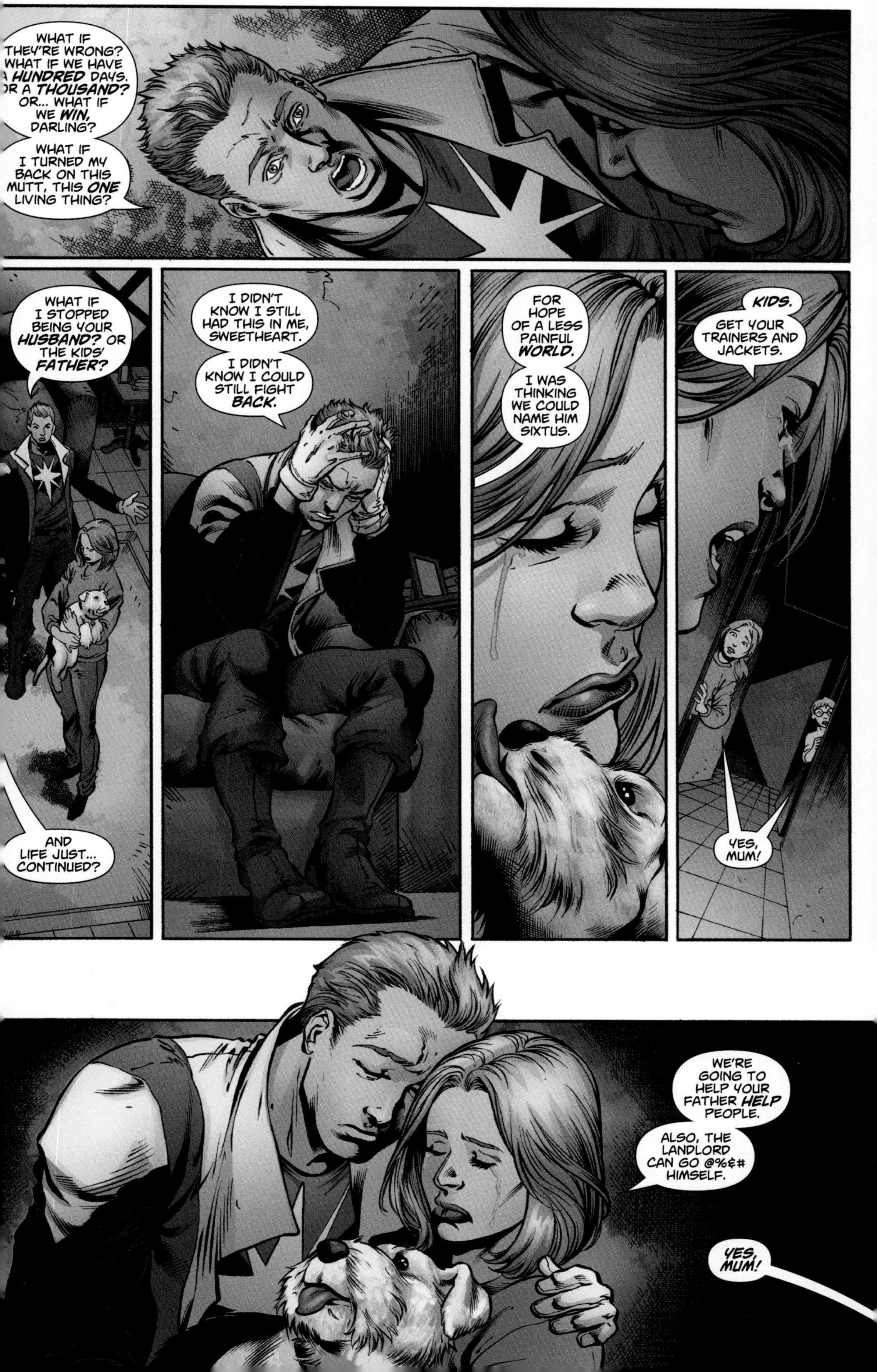

WHAT IF THEY'RE WRONG? WHAT IF WE HAVE A HUNDRED DAYS. OR A THOUSAND? OR... WHAT IF WE WIN, DARLING?
WHAT IF I TURNED MY BACK ON THIS MUTT, THIS ONE LIVING THING?
WHAT IF I STOPPED BEING YOUR HUSBAND? OR THE KIDS' FATHER?
AND LIFE JUST... CONTINUED?
I DIDN'T KNOW I STILL HAD THIS IN ME, SWEETHEART.
I DIDN'T KNOW I COULD STILL FIGHT BACK.
FOR HOPE OF A LESS PAINFUL WORLD.
I WAS THINKING WE COULD NAME HIM SIXTUS.
KIDS.
GET YOUR TRAINERS AND JACKETS.
YES, MUM!
WE'RE GOING TO HELP YOUR FATHER HELP PEOPLE.
ALSO, THE LANDLORD CAN GO @%&# HIMSELF.
YES, MUM!

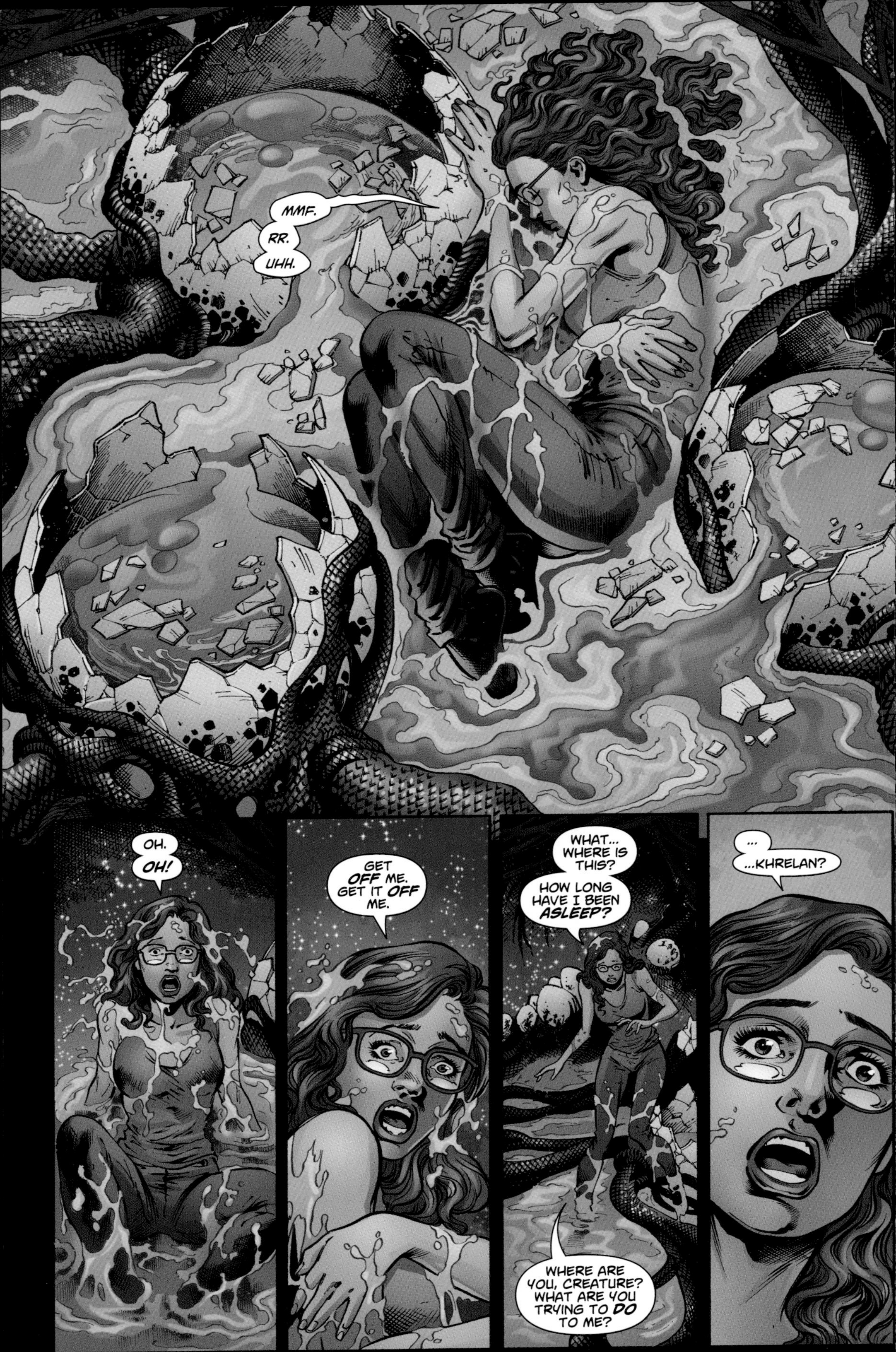
MMF.
RR.
UHH.
OH.
OH!
GET OFF ME. GET IT OFF ME.
WHAT... WHERE IS THIS?
HOW LONG HAVE I BEEN ASLEEP?
WHERE ARE YOU, CREATURE? WHAT ARE YOU TRYING TO DO TO ME?
...
...KHRELAN?

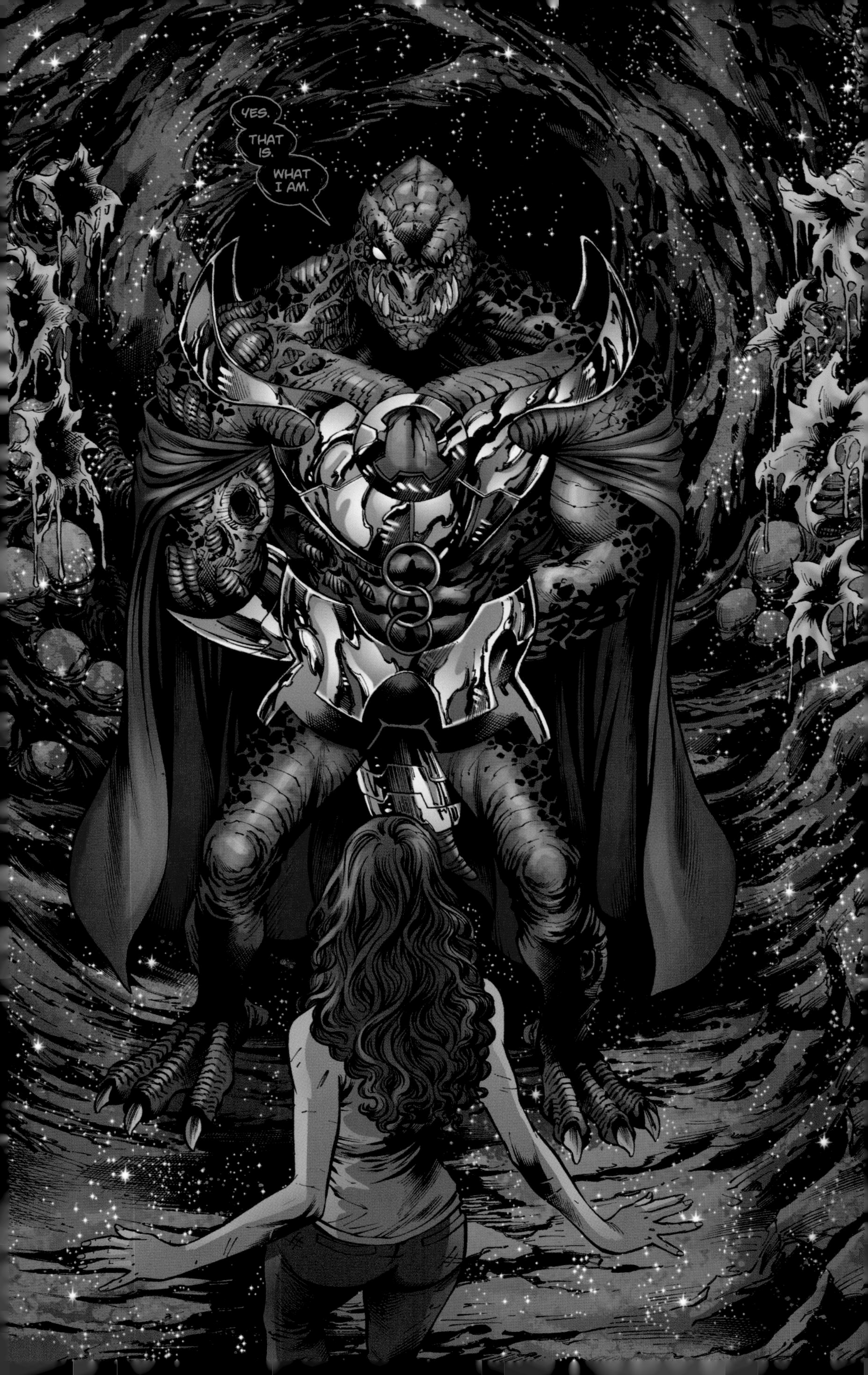
YES.
THAT IS.
WHAT I AM.

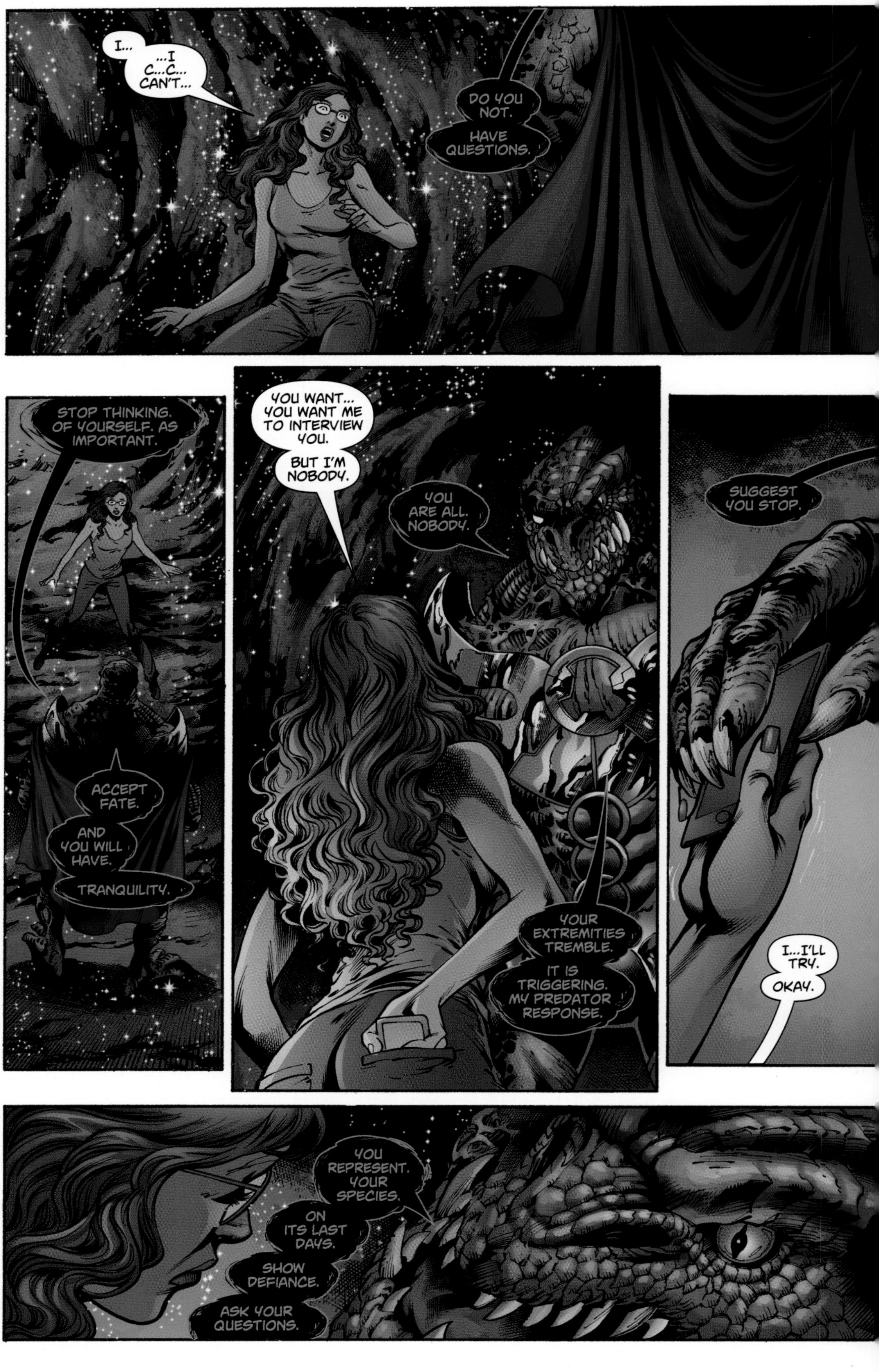
I...
...I C...C... CAN'T...
DO YOU NOT.
HAVE QUESTIONS.
STOP THINKING. OF YOURSELF. AS IMPORTANT.
ACCEPT FATE.
AND YOU WILL HAVE.
TRANQUILITY.
YOU WANT... YOU WANT ME TO INTERVIEW YOU.
BUT I'M NOBODY.
YOU ARE ALL. NOBODY.
YOUR EXTREMITIES TREMBLE.
IT IS TRIGGERING. MY PREDATOR RESPONSE.
SUGGEST YOU STOP.
I...I'LL TRY.
OKAY.
YOU REPRESENT. YOUR SPECIES.
ON ITS LAST DAYS.
SHOW DEFIANCE.
ASK YOUR QUESTIONS.

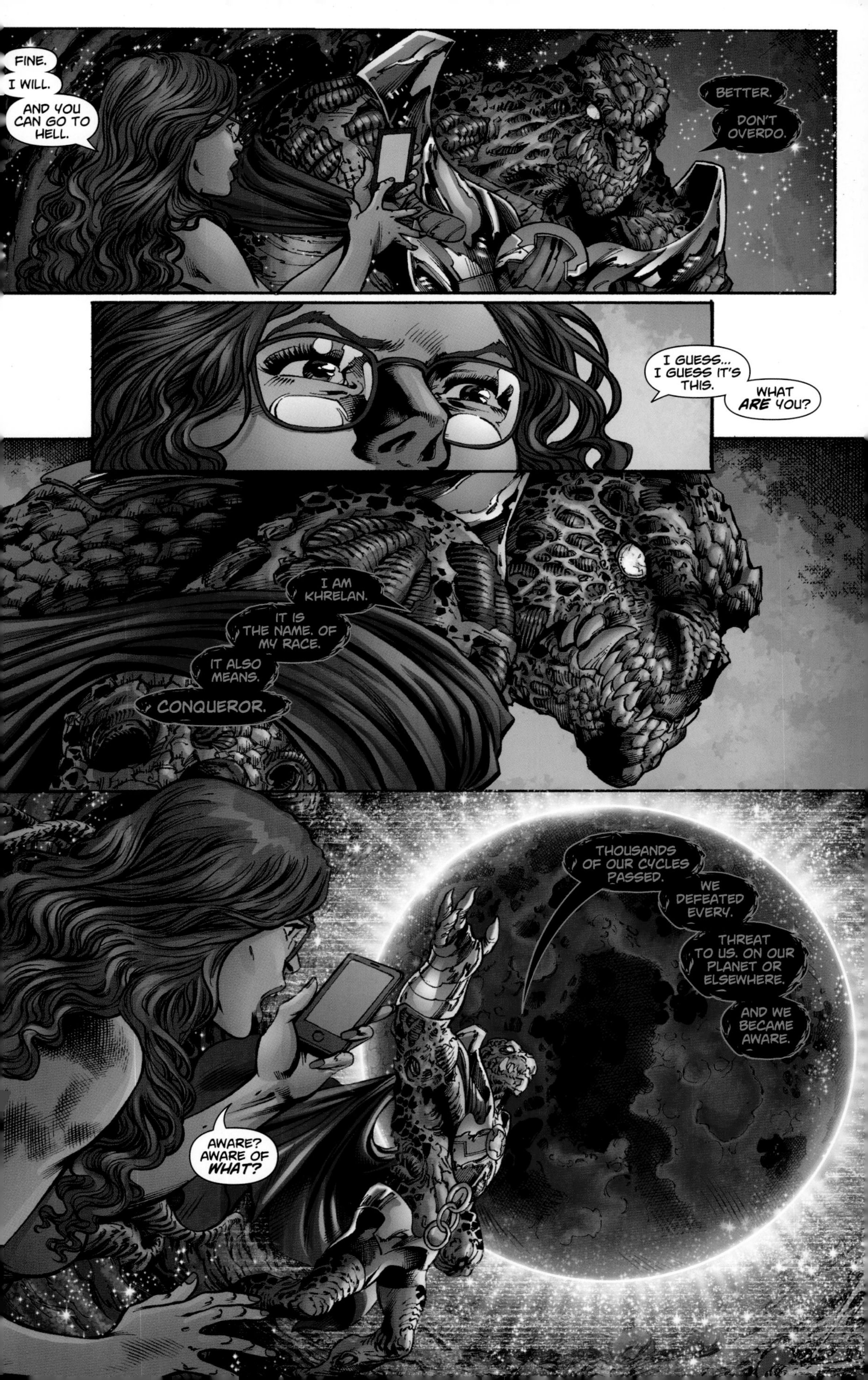
FINE.
I WILL.
AND YOU CAN GO TO HELL.
BETTER.
DON'T OVERDO.
I GUESS... I GUESS IT'S THIS.
WHAT ***ARE*** YOU?
I AM KHRELAN.
IT IS THE NAME. OF MY RACE.
IT ALSO MEANS.
CONQUEROR.
THOUSANDS OF OUR CYCLES PASSED.
WE DEFEATED EVERY.
THREAT TO US. ON OUR PLANET OR ELSEWHERE.
AND WE BECAME AWARE.
AWARE? AWARE OF ***WHAT?***

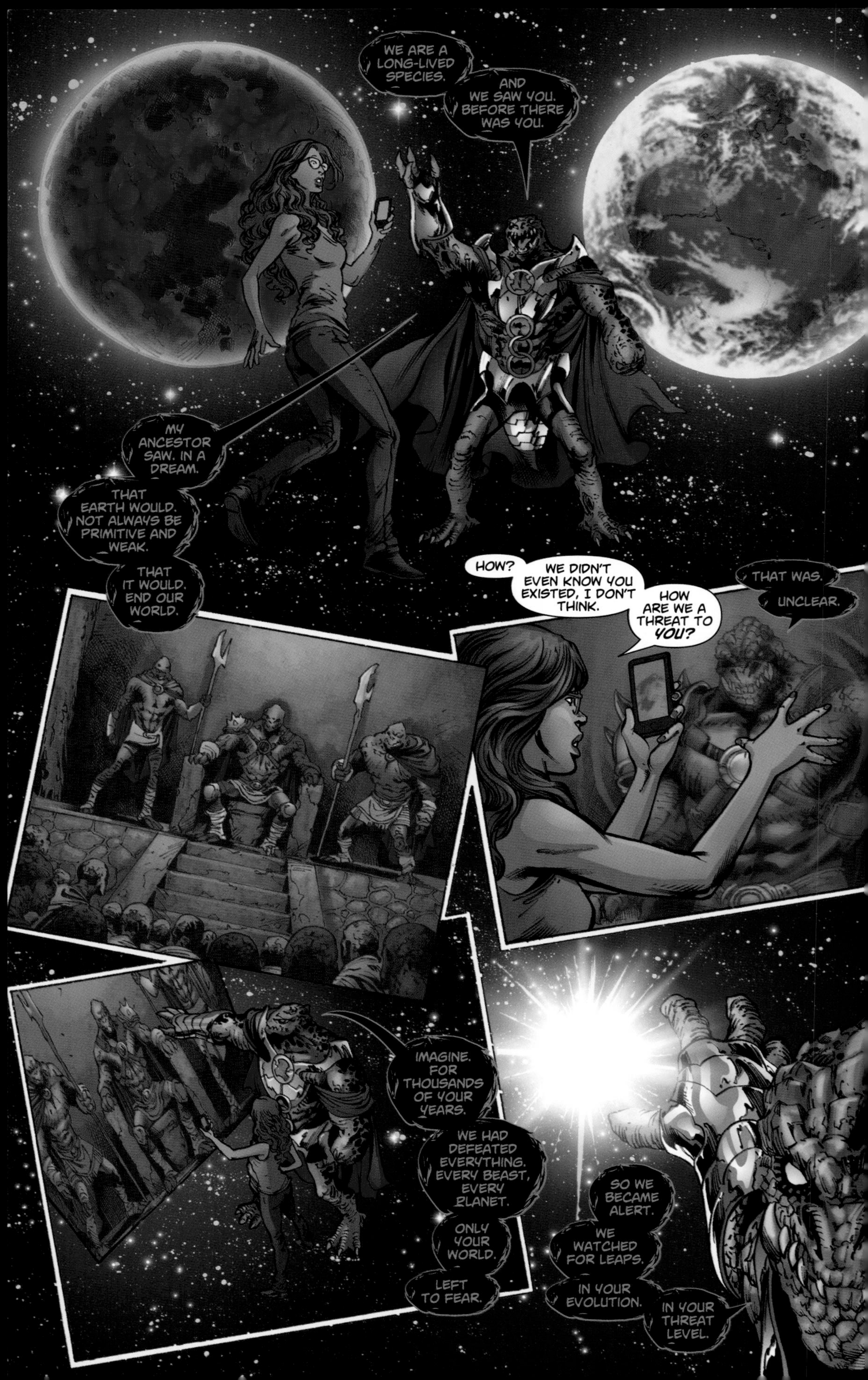
WE ARE A LONG-LIVED SPECIES.
AND WE SAW YOU. BEFORE THERE WAS YOU.
MY ANCESTOR SAW. IN A DREAM.
THAT EARTH WOULD. NOT ALWAYS BE PRIMITIVE AND WEAK.
THAT IT WOULD. END OUR WORLD.
HOW?
WE DIDN'T EVEN KNOW YOU EXISTED, I DON'T THINK.
HOW ARE WE A THREAT TO YOU?
THAT WAS.
UNCLEAR.
IMAGINE. FOR THOUSANDS OF YOUR YEARS.
WE HAD DEFEATED EVERYTHING. EVERY BEAST, EVERY PLANET.
ONLY YOUR WORLD.
LEFT TO FEAR.
SO WE BECAME ALERT.
WE WATCHED FOR LEAPS.
IN YOUR EVOLUTION.
IN YOUR THREAT LEVEL.

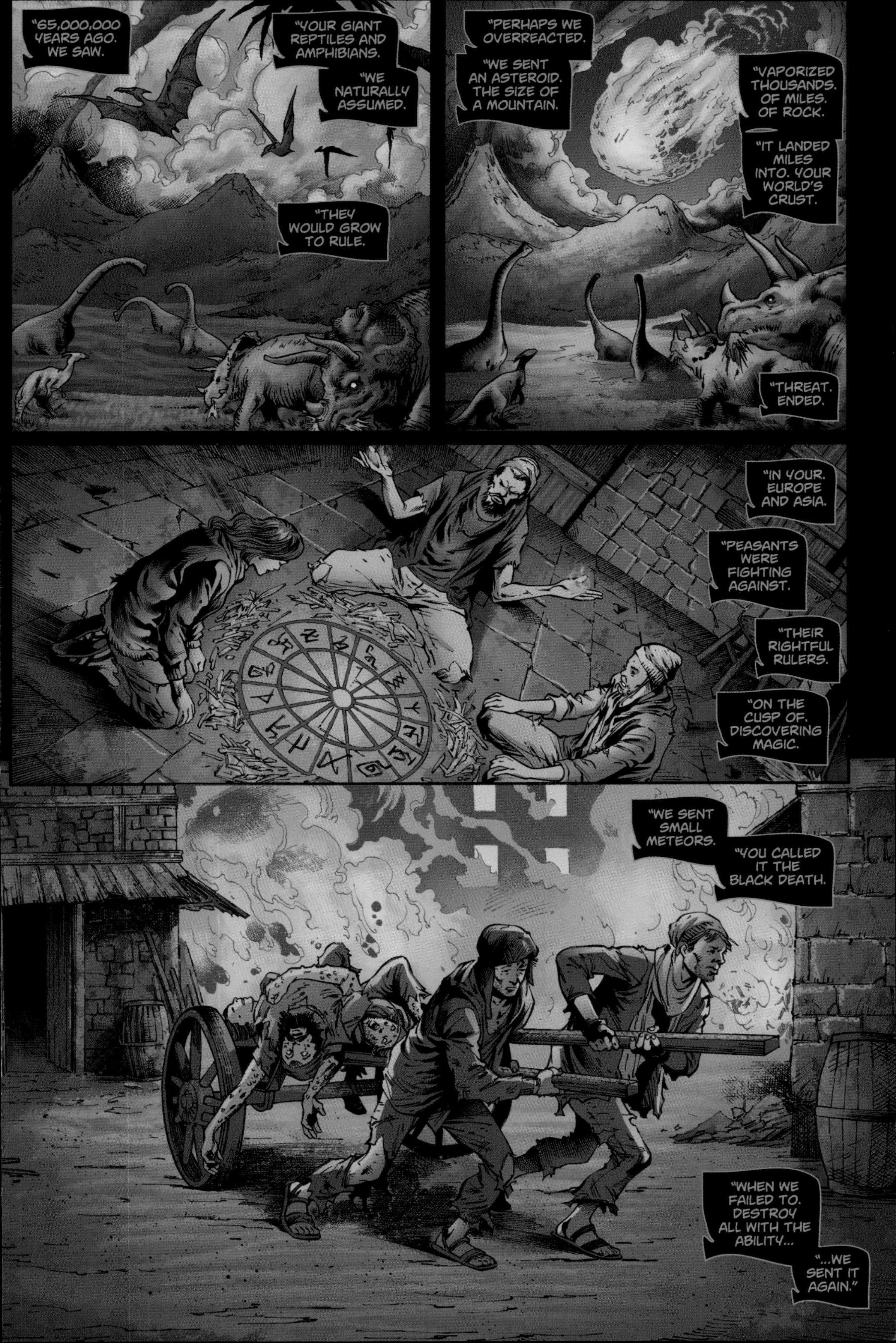
"65,000,000 YEARS AGO. WE SAW.
"YOUR GIANT REPTILES AND AMPHIBIANS.
"WE NATURALLY ASSUMED.
"THEY WOULD GROW TO RULE.
"PERHAPS WE OVERREACTED.
"WE SENT AN ASTEROID. THE SIZE OF A MOUNTAIN.
"VAPORIZED THOUSANDS. OF MILES. OF ROCK.
"IT LANDED MILES INTO. YOUR WORLD'S CRUST.
"THREAT. ENDED.
"IN YOUR. EUROPE AND ASIA.
"PEASANTS WERE FIGHTING AGAINST.
"THEIR RIGHTFUL RULERS.
"ON THE CUSP OF. DISCOVERING MAGIC.
"WE SENT SMALL METEORS.
"YOU CALLED IT THE BLACK DEATH.
"WHEN WE FAILED TO. DESTROY ALL WITH THE ABILITY...
"...WE SENT IT AGAIN."

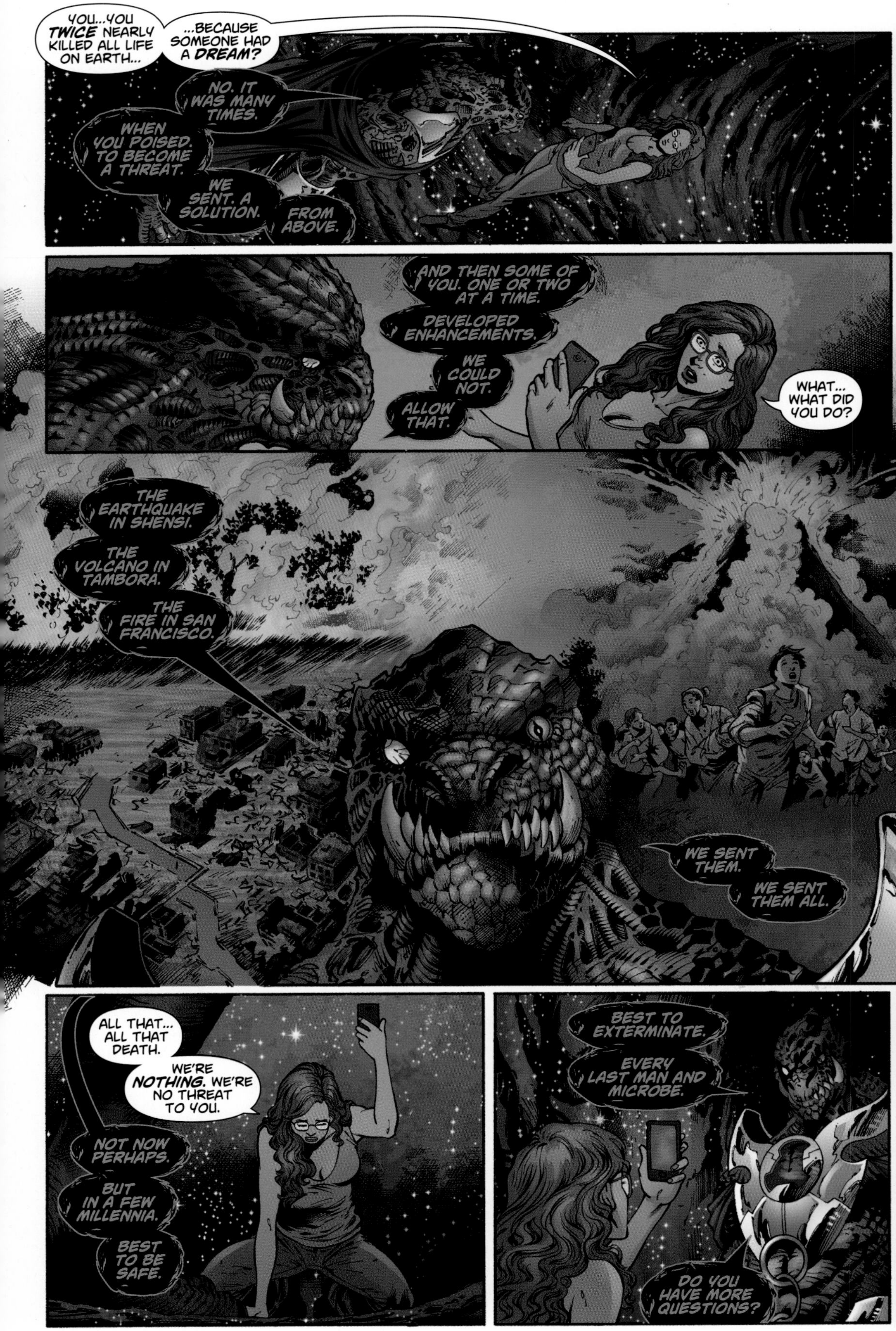
YOU...YOU TWICE NEARLY KILLED ALL LIFE ON EARTH...
...BECAUSE SOMEONE HAD A DREAM?
NO. IT WAS MANY TIMES.
WHEN YOU POISED. TO BECOME A THREAT.
WE SENT. A SOLUTION.
FROM ABOVE.
AND THEN SOME OF YOU. ONE OR TWO AT A TIME.
DEVELOPED ENHANCEMENTS.
WE COULD NOT.
ALLOW THAT.
WHAT... WHAT DID YOU DO?
THE EARTHQUAKE IN SHENSI.
THE VOLCANO IN TAMBORA.
THE FIRE IN SAN FRANCISCO.
WE SENT THEM.
WE SENT THEM ALL.
ALL THAT... ALL THAT DEATH.
WE'RE NOTHING. WE'RE NO THREAT TO YOU.
NOT NOW PERHAPS.
BUT IN A FEW MILLENNIA.
BEST TO BE SAFE.
BEST TO EXTERMINATE.
EVERY LAST MAN AND MICROBE.
DO YOU HAVE MORE QUESTIONS?

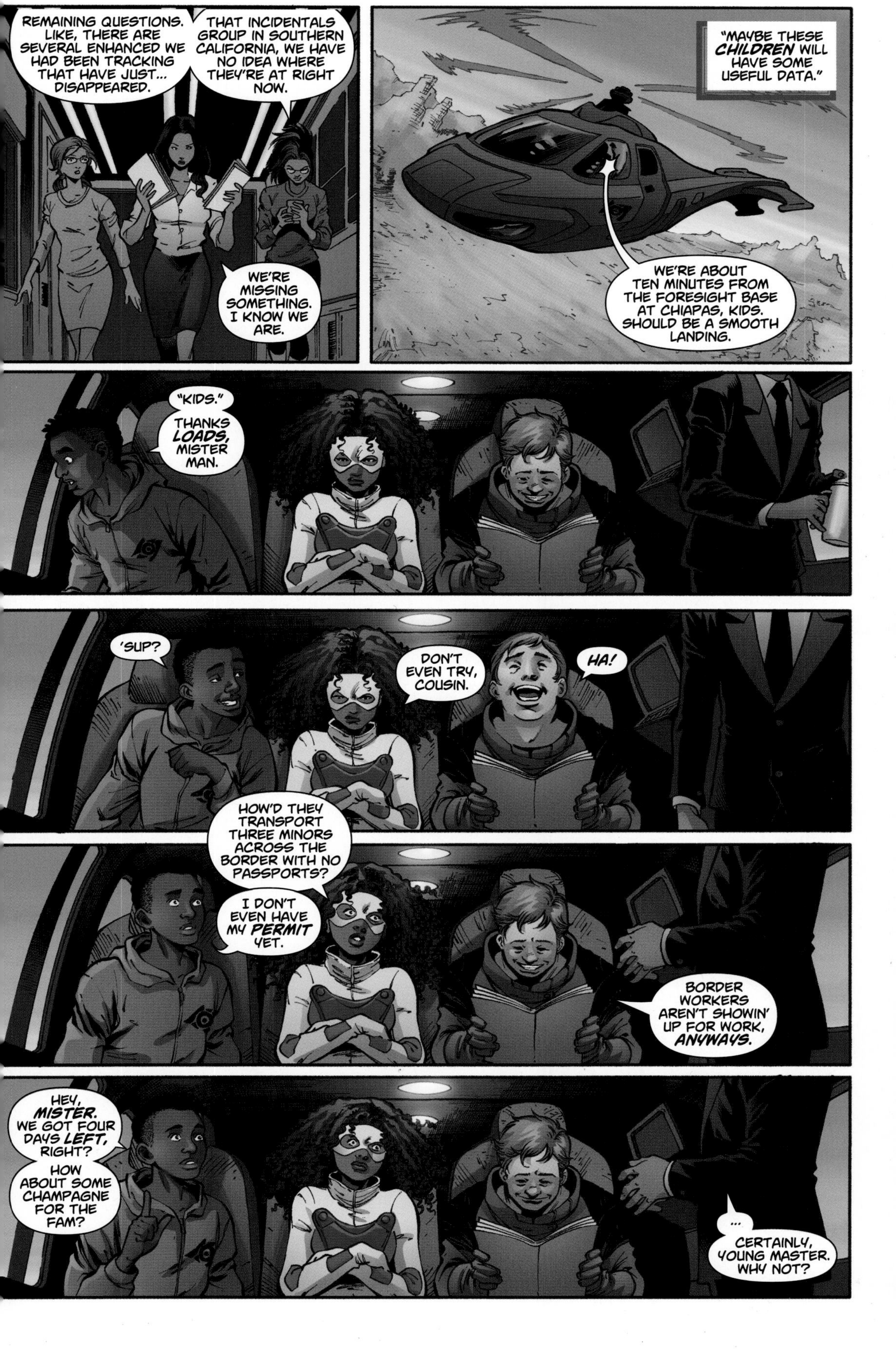
REMAINING QUESTIONS. LIKE, THERE ARE SEVERAL ENHANCED WE HAD BEEN TRACKING THAT HAVE JUST... DISAPPEARED.
THAT INCIDENTALS GROUP IN SOUTHERN CALIFORNIA, WE HAVE NO IDEA WHERE THEY'RE AT RIGHT NOW.
WE'RE MISSING SOMETHING. I KNOW WE ARE.
"MAYBE THESE CHILDREN WILL HAVE SOME USEFUL DATA."
WE'RE ABOUT TEN MINUTES FROM THE FORESIGHT BASE AT CHIAPAS, KIDS. SHOULD BE A SMOOTH LANDING.
"KIDS." THANKS LOADS, MISTER MAN.
'SUP?
DON'T EVEN TRY, COUSIN.
HA!
HOW'D THEY TRANSPORT THREE MINORS ACROSS THE BORDER WITH NO PASSPORTS?
I DON'T EVEN HAVE MY PERMIT YET.
BORDER WORKERS AREN'T SHOWIN' UP FOR WORK, ANYWAYS.
HEY, MISTER. WE GOT FOUR DAYS LEFT, RIGHT?
HOW ABOUT SOME CHAMPAGNE FOR THE FAM?
...
CERTAINLY, YOUNG MASTER. WHY NOT?

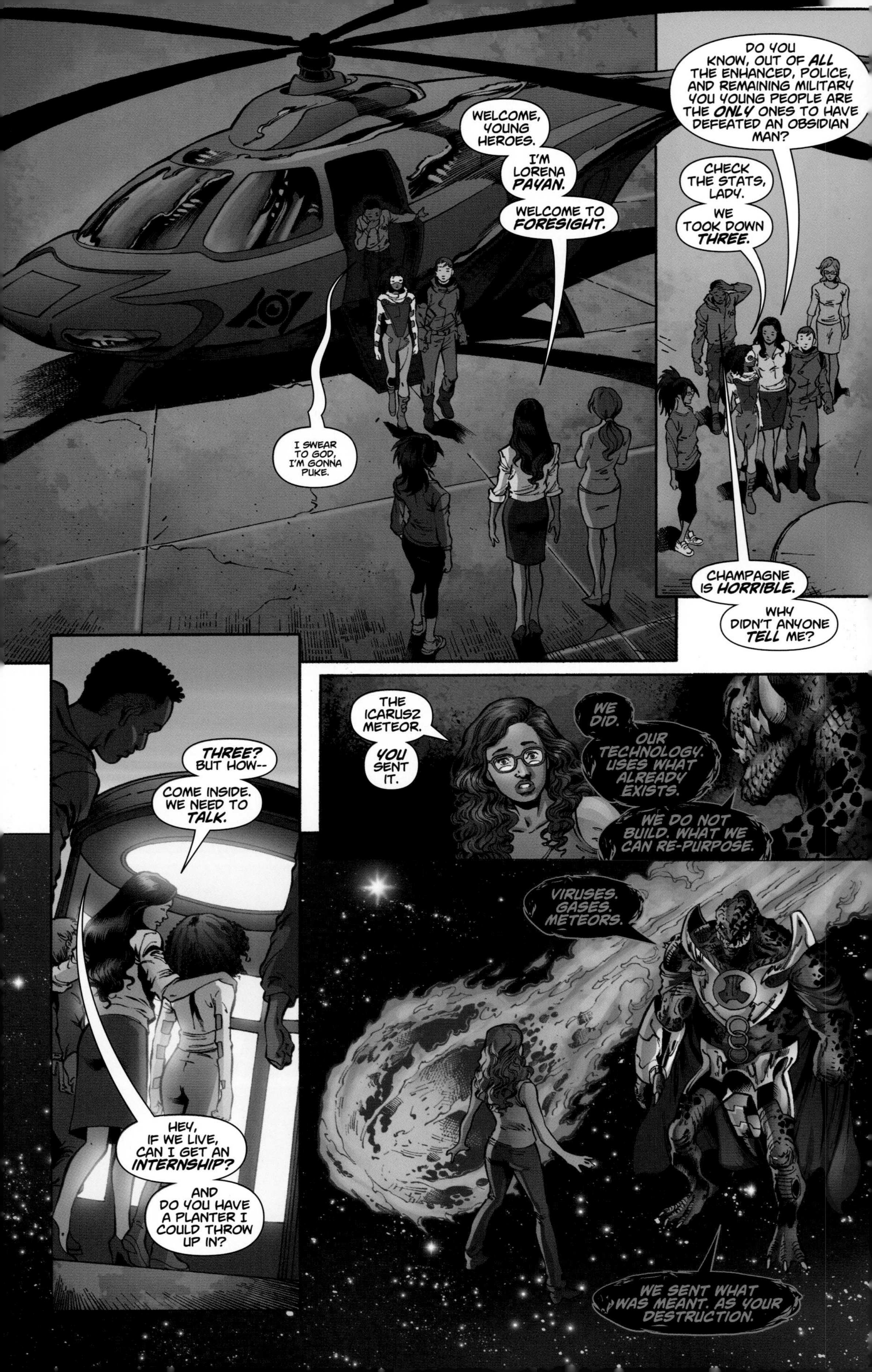
WELCOME, YOUNG HEROES.
I'M LORENA PAYAN.
WELCOME TO FORESIGHT.
I SWEAR TO GOD, I'M GONNA PUKE.
DO YOU KNOW, OUT OF ALL THE ENHANCED, POLICE, AND REMAINING MILITARY YOU YOUNG PEOPLE ARE THE ONLY ONES TO HAVE DEFEATED AN OBSIDIAN MAN?
CHECK THE STATS, LADY.
WE TOOK DOWN THREE.
CHAMPAGNE IS HORRIBLE.
WHY DIDN'T ANYONE TELL ME?
THREE? BUT HOW--
COME INSIDE. WE NEED TO TALK.
HEY, IF WE LIVE, CAN I GET AN INTERNSHIP?
AND DO YOU HAVE A PLANTER I COULD THROW UP IN?
THE ICARUS2 METEOR.
YOU SENT IT.
WE DID.
OUR TECHNOLOGY. USES WHAT ALREADY EXISTS.
WE DO NOT BUILD. WHAT WE CAN RE-PURPOSE.
VIRUSES. GASES. METEORS.
WE SENT WHAT WAS MEANT. AS YOUR DESTRUCTION.

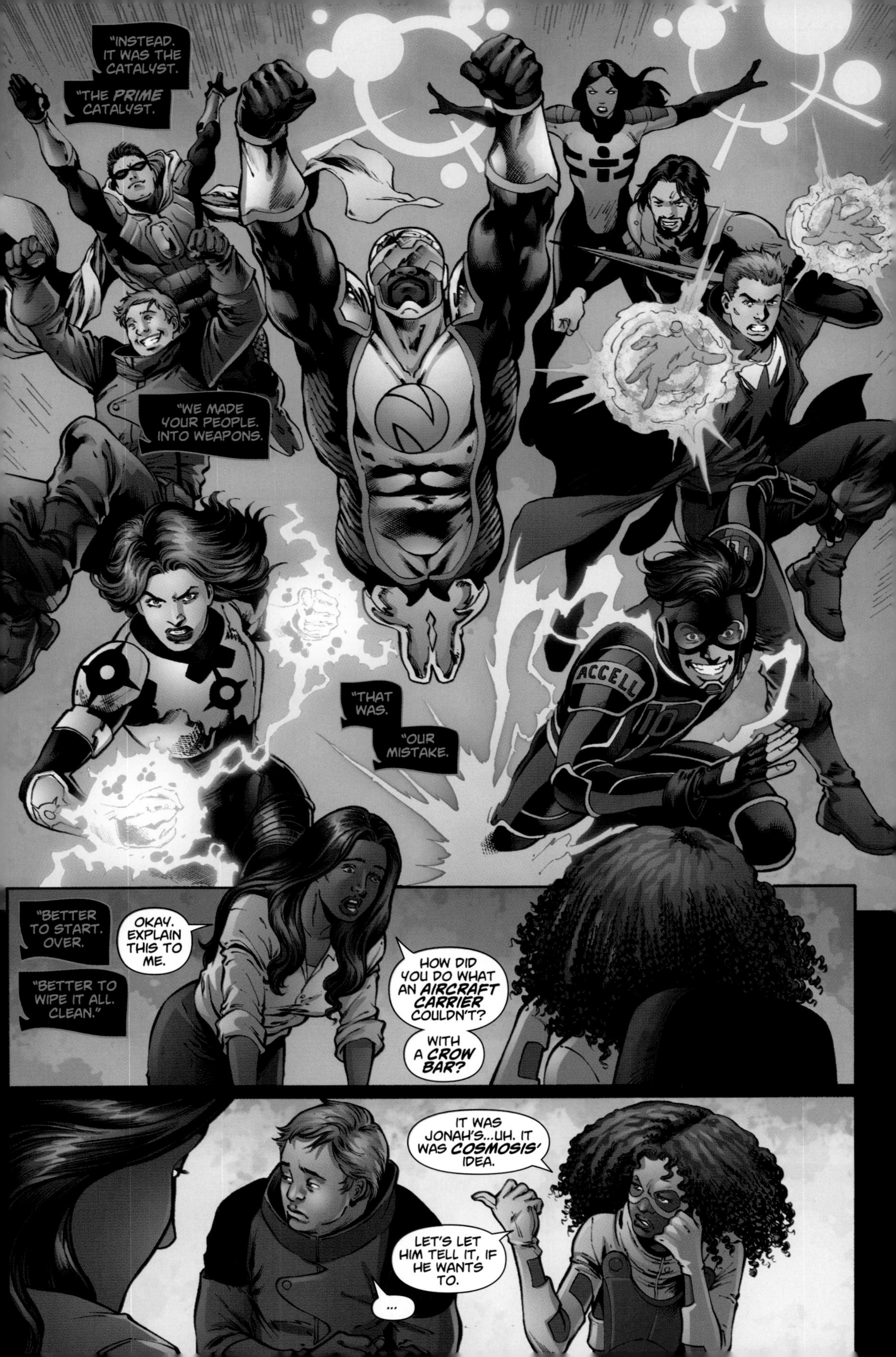
"INSTEAD. IT WAS THE CATALYST.
"THE PRIME CATALYST.
"WE MADE YOUR PEOPLE. INTO WEAPONS.
ACCELL
10
"THAT WAS.
"OUR MISTAKE.
"BETTER TO START. OVER.
"BETTER TO WIPE IT ALL. CLEAN."
OKAY. EXPLAIN THIS TO ME.
HOW DID YOU DO WHAT AN AIRCRAFT CARRIER COULDN'T?
WITH A CROW BAR?
IT WAS JONAH'S...UH. IT WAS COSMOSIS' IDEA.
LET'S LET HIM TELL IT, IF HE WANTS TO.
...

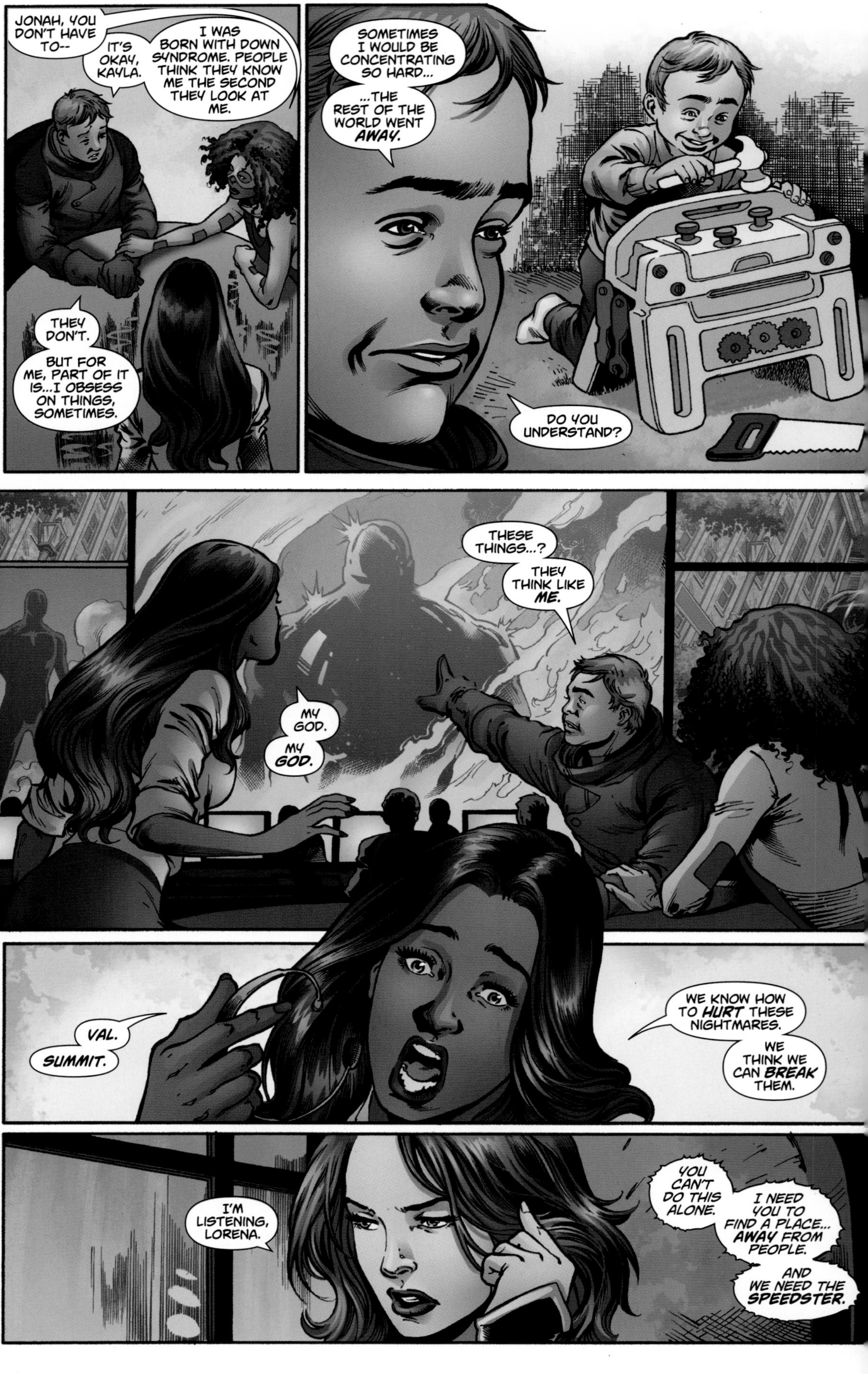
JONAH, YOU DON'T HAVE TO--
IT'S OKAY, KAYLA.
I WAS BORN WITH DOWN SYNDROME. PEOPLE THINK THEY KNOW ME THE SECOND THEY LOOK AT ME.
THEY DON'T.
BUT FOR ME, PART OF IT IS...I OBSESS ON THINGS, SOMETIMES.
SOMETIMES I WOULD BE CONCENTRATING SO HARD...
...THE REST OF THE WORLD WENT AWAY.
DO YOU UNDERSTAND?
THESE THINGS...?
THEY THINK LIKE ME.
MY GOD.
MY GOD.
VAL.
SUMMIT.
WE KNOW HOW TO HURT THESE NIGHTMARES.
WE THINK WE CAN BREAK THEM.
I'M LISTENING, LORENA.
YOU CAN'T DO THIS ALONE.
I NEED YOU TO FIND A PLACE... AWAY FROM PEOPLE.
AND WE NEED THE SPEEDSTER.

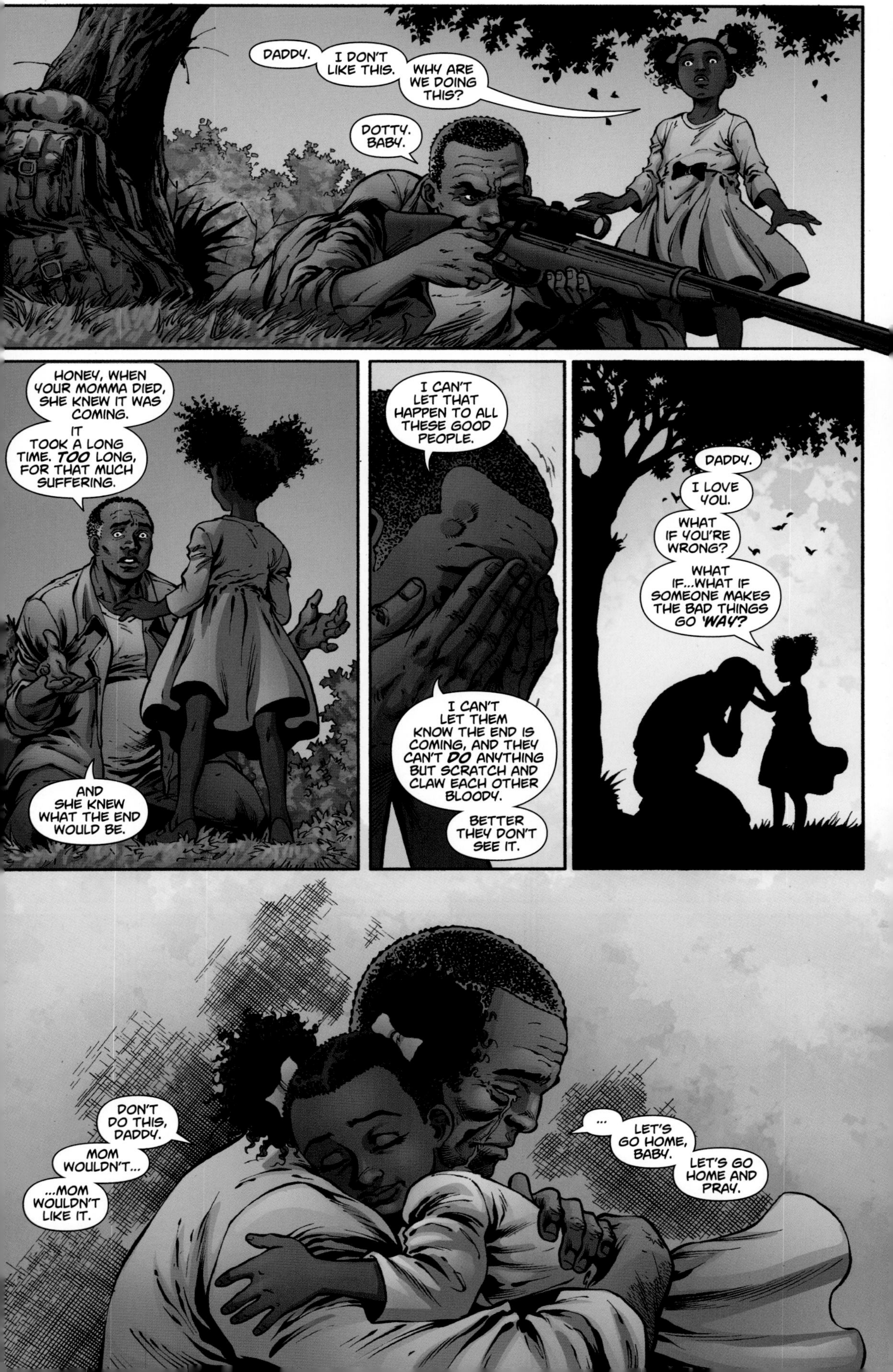
DADDY.
I DON'T LIKE THIS.
WHY ARE WE DOING THIS?
DOTTY. BABY.
HONEY, WHEN YOUR MOMMA DIED, SHE KNEW IT WAS COMING.
IT TOOK A LONG TIME. TOO LONG, FOR THAT MUCH SUFFERING.
AND SHE KNEW WHAT THE END WOULD BE.
I CAN'T LET THAT HAPPEN TO ALL THESE GOOD PEOPLE.
I CAN'T LET THEM KNOW THE END IS COMING, AND THEY CAN'T DO ANYTHING BUT SCRATCH AND CLAW EACH OTHER BLOODY.
BETTER THEY DON'T SEE IT.
DADDY.
I LOVE YOU.
WHAT IF YOU'RE WRONG?
WHAT IF...WHAT IF SOMEONE MAKES THE BAD THINGS GO 'WAY?
DON'T DO THIS, DADDY.
MOM WOULDN'T...
...MOM WOULDN'T LIKE IT.
...
LET'S GO HOME, BABY.
LET'S GO HOME AND PRAY.

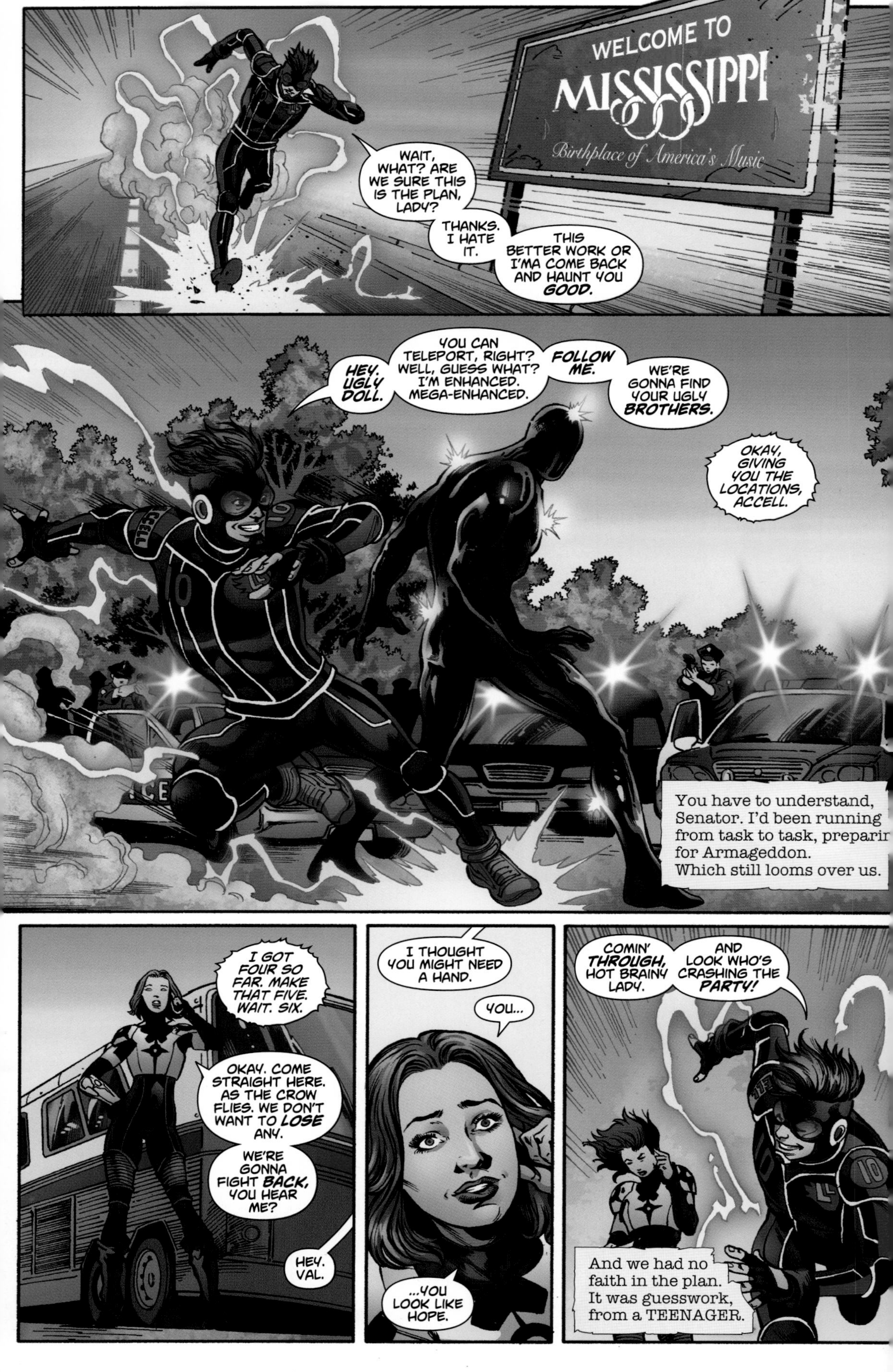
WELCOME TO
MISSISSIPPI
Birthplace of America's Music
WAIT, WHAT? ARE WE SURE THIS IS THE PLAN, LADY?
THANKS. I HATE IT.
THIS BETTER WORK OR I'MA COME BACK AND HAUNT YOU GOOD.
HEY. UGLY DOLL.
YOU CAN TELEPORT, RIGHT? WELL, GUESS WHAT? I'M ENHANCED. MEGA-ENHANCED.
FOLLOW ME.
WE'RE GONNA FIND YOUR UGLY BROTHERS.
OKAY, GIVING YOU THE LOCATIONS, ACCELL.
You have to understand, Senator. I'd been running from task to task, preparir for Armageddon. Which still looms over us.
I GOT FOUR SO FAR. MAKE THAT FIVE. WAIT. SIX.
OKAY. COME STRAIGHT HERE. AS THE CROW FLIES. WE DON'T WANT TO LOSE ANY.
WE'RE GONNA FIGHT BACK, YOU HEAR ME?
HEY. VAL.
I THOUGHT YOU MIGHT NEED A HAND.
YOU...
...YOU LOOK LIKE HOPE.
COMIN' THROUGH, HOT BRAINY LADY.
AND LOOK WHO'S CRASHING THE PARTY!
And we had no faith in the plan. It was guesswork, from a TEENAGER.

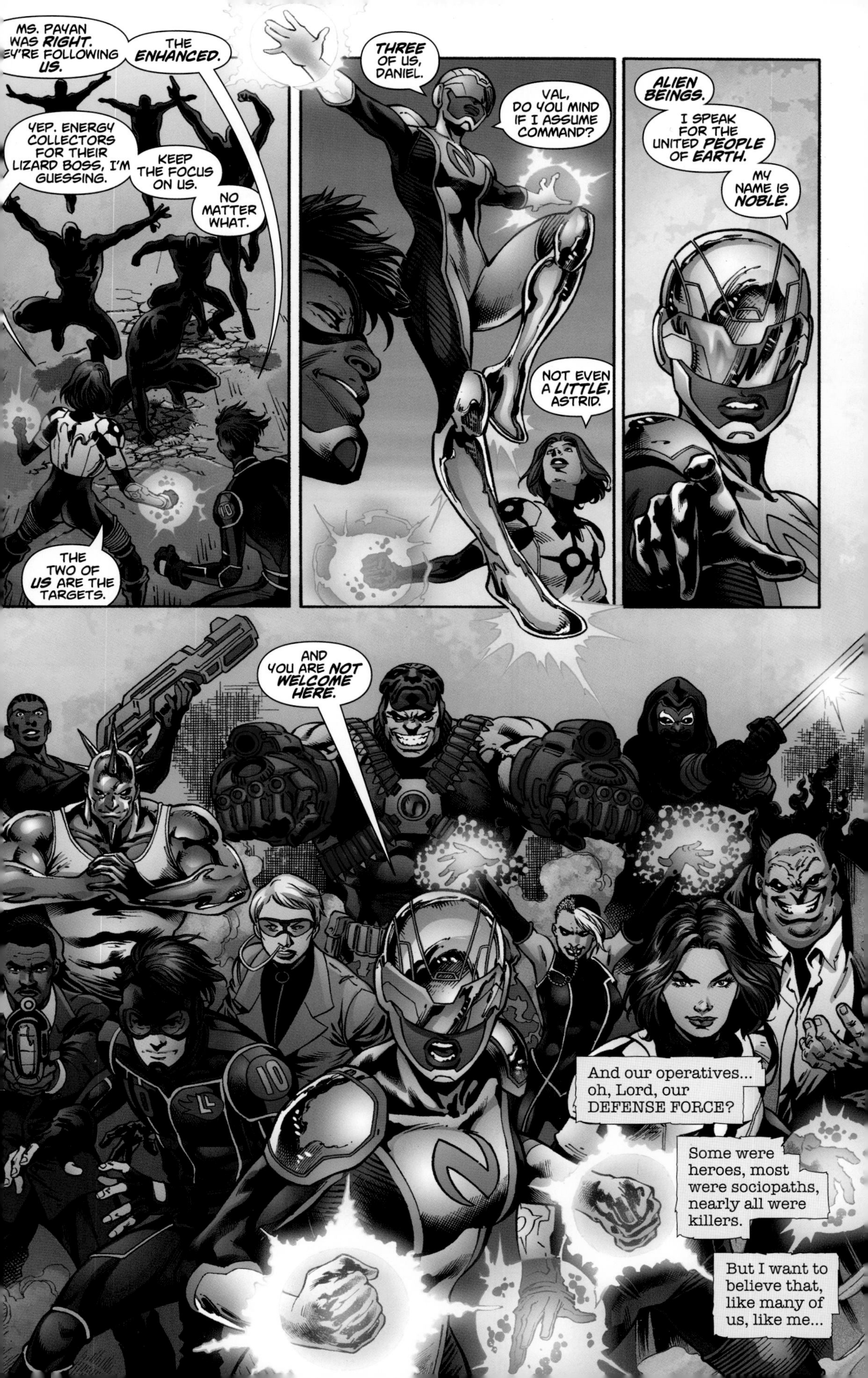

MS. PAYAN WAS **RIGHT**. ...EY'RE FOLLOWING **US**.
THE **ENHANCED**.
YEP. ENERGY COLLECTORS FOR THEIR LIZARD BOSS, I'M GUESSING.
KEEP THE FOCUS ON US.
NO MATTER WHAT.
THE TWO OF **US** ARE THE TARGETS.
THREE OF US, DANIEL.
VAL, DO YOU MIND IF I ASSUME COMMAND?
NOT EVEN A **LITTLE**, ASTRID.
ALIEN BEINGS.
I SPEAK FOR THE UNITED **PEOPLE** OF **EARTH**.
MY NAME IS **NOBLE**.
AND YOU ARE **NOT WELCOME HERE**.
And our operatives... oh, Lord, our DEFENSE FORCE?
Some were heroes, most were sociopaths, nearly all were killers.
But I want to believe that, like many of us, like me...

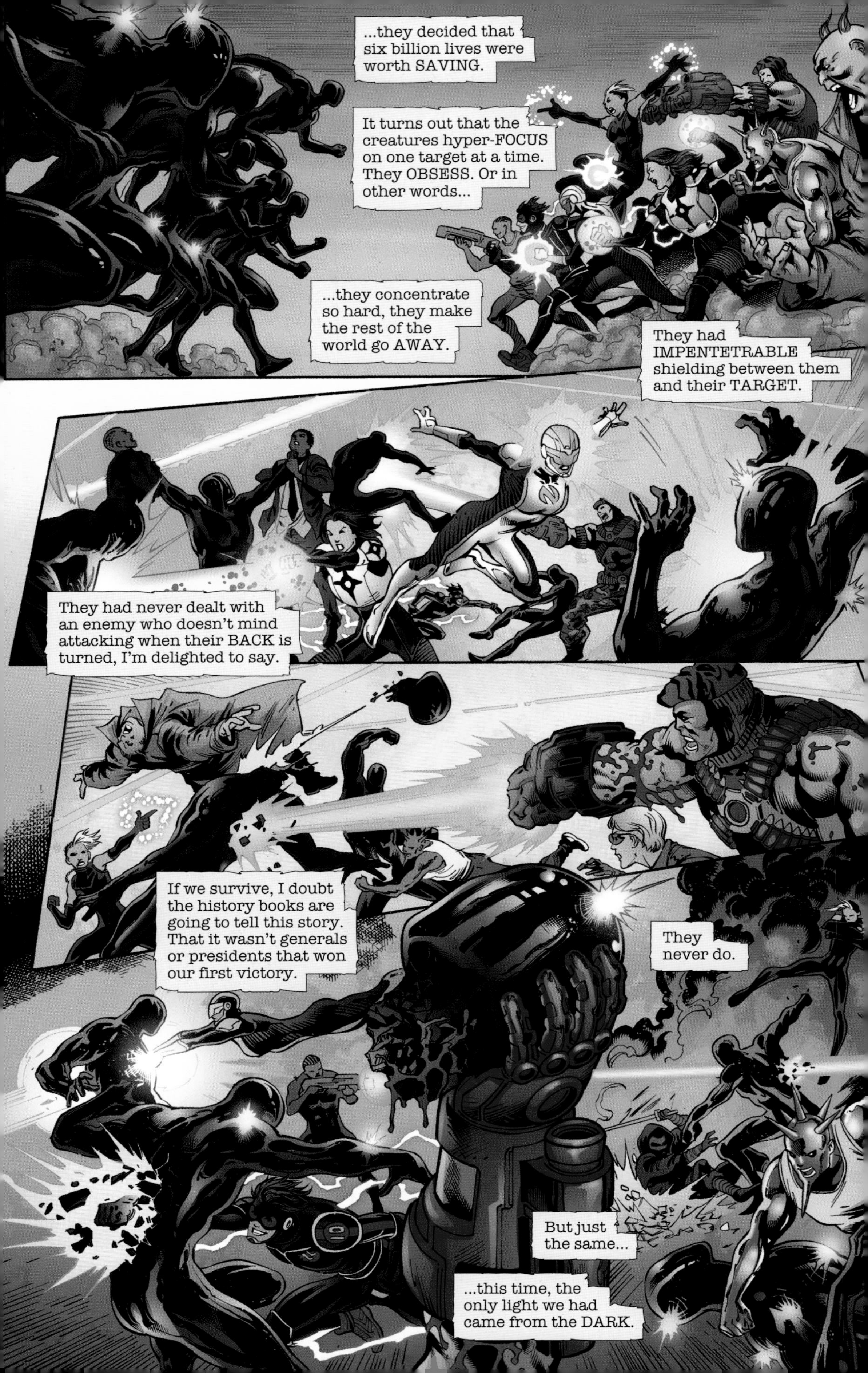
...they decided that six billion lives were worth SAVING.
It turns out that the creatures hyper-FOCUS on one target at a time. They OBSESS. Or in other words...
...they concentrate so hard, they make the rest of the world go AWAY.
They had IMPENTETRABLE shielding between them and their TARGET.
They had never dealt with an enemy who doesn't mind attacking when their BACK is turned, I'm delighted to say.
If we survive, I doubt the history books are going to tell this story. That it wasn't generals or presidents that won our first victory.
They never do.
But just the same...
...this time, the only light we had came from the DARK.

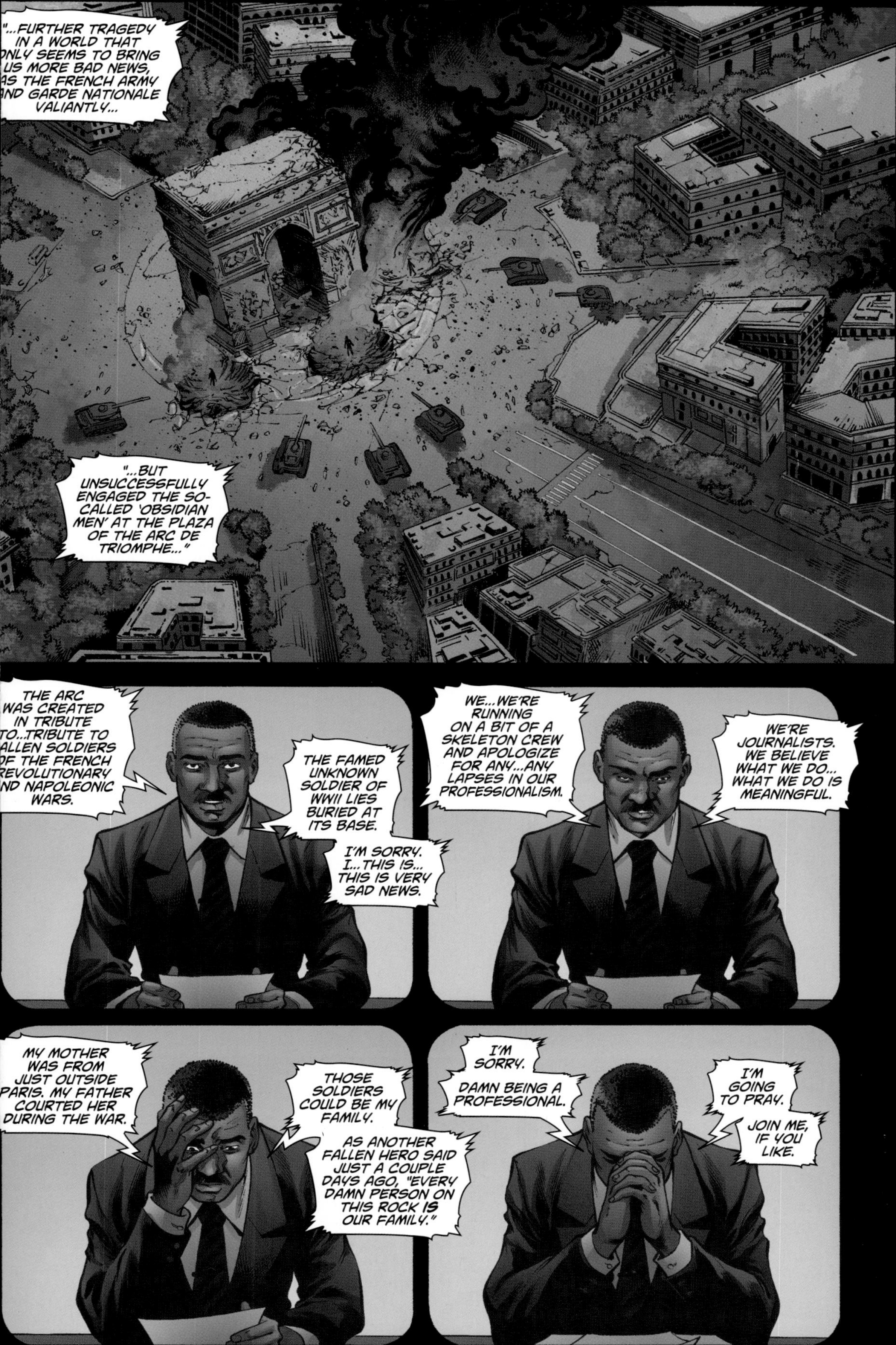
"...FURTHER TRAGEDY IN A WORLD THAT ONLY SEEMS TO BRING US MORE BAD NEWS, AS THE FRENCH ARMY AND GARDE NATIONALE VALIANTLY...
"...BUT UNSUCCESSFULLY ENGAGED THE SO-CALLED 'OBSIDIAN MEN' AT THE PLAZA OF THE ARC DE TRIOMPHE..."
THE ARC WAS CREATED IN TRIBUTE TO...TRIBUTE TO FALLEN SOLDIERS OF THE FRENCH REVOLUTIONARY AND NAPOLEONIC WARS.
THE FAMED UNKNOWN SOLDIER OF WWII LIES BURIED AT ITS BASE.
I'M SORRY. I...THIS IS... THIS IS VERY SAD NEWS.
WE...WE'RE RUNNING ON A BIT OF A SKELETON CREW AND APOLOGIZE FOR ANY...ANY LAPSES IN OUR PROFESSIONALISM.
WE'RE JOURNALISTS. WE BELIEVE WHAT WE DO... WHAT WE DO IS MEANINGFUL.
MY MOTHER WAS FROM JUST OUTSIDE PARIS. MY FATHER COURTED HER DURING THE WAR.
THOSE SOLDIERS COULD BE MY FAMILY.
AS ANOTHER FALLEN HERO SAID JUST A COUPLE DAYS AGO, "EVERY DAMN PERSON ON THIS ROCK IS OUR FAMILY."
I'M SORRY.
DAMN BEING A PROFESSIONAL.
I'M GOING TO PRAY.
JOIN ME, IF YOU LIKE.

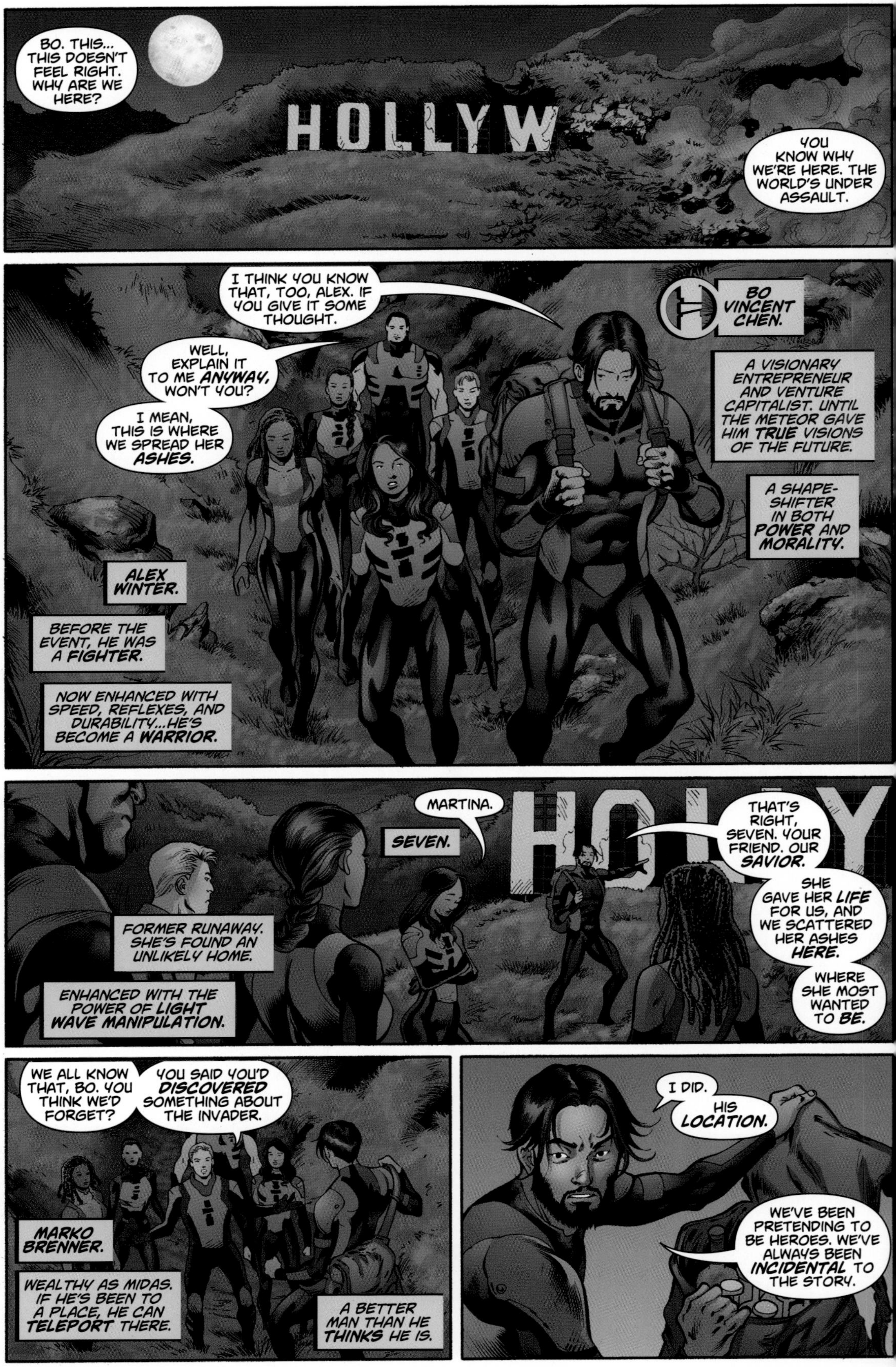
BO. THIS... THIS DOESN'T FEEL RIGHT. WHY ARE WE HERE?
HOLLYW
YOU KNOW WHY WE'RE HERE. THE WORLD'S UNDER ASSAULT.
I THINK YOU KNOW THAT, TOO, ALEX. IF YOU GIVE IT SOME THOUGHT.
BO VINCENT CHEN.
A VISIONARY ENTREPRENEUR AND VENTURE CAPITALIST. UNTIL THE METEOR GAVE HIM TRUE VISIONS OF THE FUTURE.
A SHAPE-SHIFTER IN BOTH POWER AND MORALITY.
WELL, EXPLAIN IT TO ME ANYWAY, WON'T YOU?
I MEAN, THIS IS WHERE WE SPREAD HER ASHES.
ALEX WINTER.
BEFORE THE EVENT, HE WAS A FIGHTER.
NOW ENHANCED WITH SPEED, REFLEXES, AND DURABILITY...HE'S BECOME A WARRIOR.
SEVEN.
MARTINA.
FORMER RUNAWAY. SHE'S FOUND AN UNLIKELY HOME.
ENHANCED WITH THE POWER OF LIGHT WAVE MANIPULATION.
THAT'S RIGHT, SEVEN. YOUR FRIEND. OUR SAVIOR.
SHE GAVE HER LIFE FOR US, AND WE SCATTERED HER ASHES HERE.
WHERE SHE MOST WANTED TO BE.
WE ALL KNOW THAT, BO. YOU THINK WE'D FORGET?
YOU SAID YOU'D DISCOVERED SOMETHING ABOUT THE INVADER.
MARKO BRENNER.
WEALTHY AS MIDAS. IF HE'S BEEN TO A PLACE, HE CAN TELEPORT THERE.
A BETTER MAN THAN HE THINKS HE IS.
I DID.
HIS LOCATION.
WE'VE BEEN PRETENDING TO BE HEROES. WE'VE ALWAYS BEEN INCIDENTAL TO THE STORY.

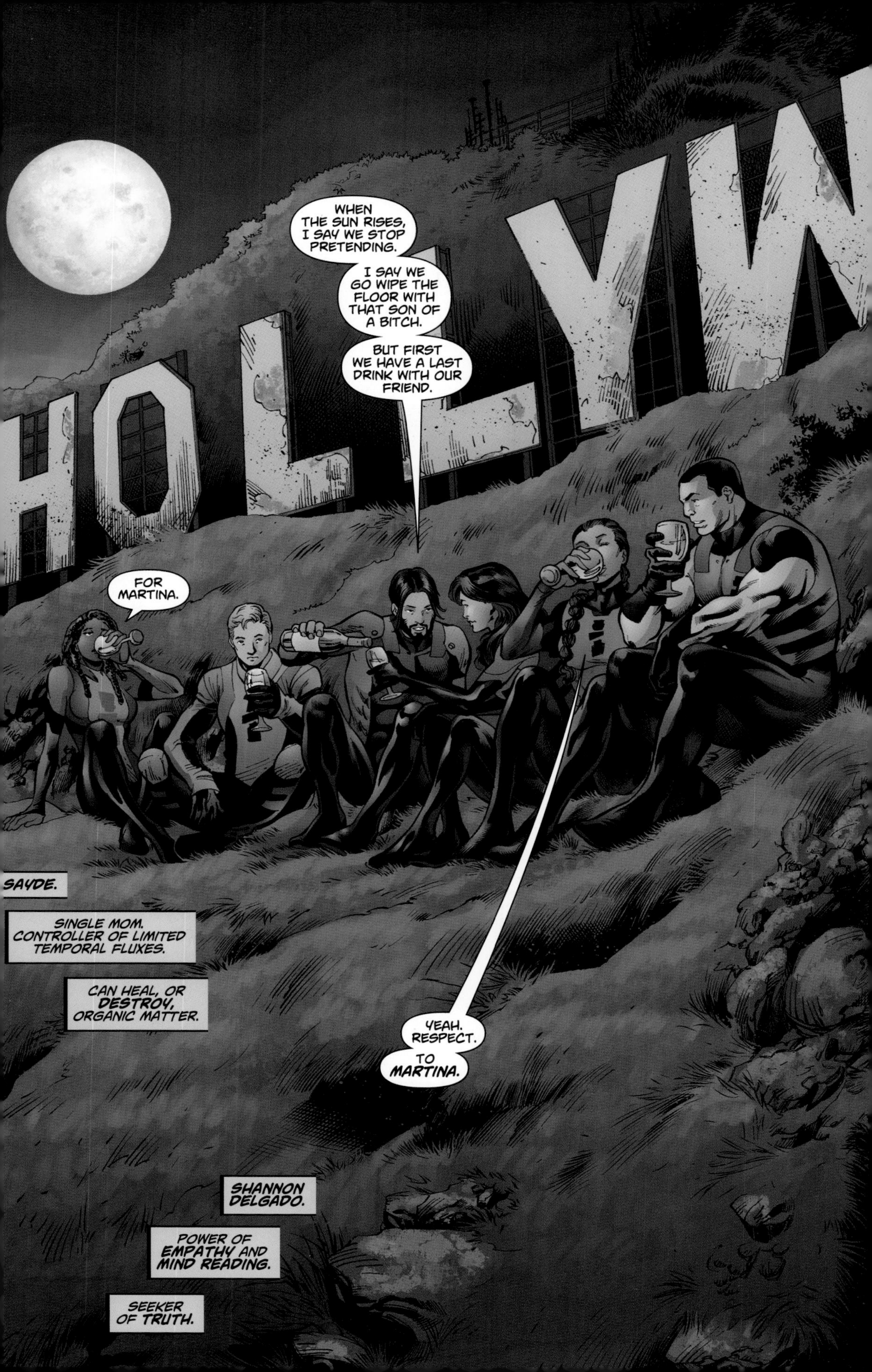
WHEN THE SUN RISES, I SAY WE STOP PRETENDING.
I SAY WE GO WIPE THE FLOOR WITH THAT SON OF A BITCH.
BUT FIRST WE HAVE A LAST DRINK WITH OUR FRIEND.
FOR MARTINA.
SAYDE.
SINGLE MOM. CONTROLLER OF LIMITED TEMPORAL FLUXES.
CAN HEAL, OR DESTROY, ORGANIC MATTER.
YEAH. RESPECT.
TO MARTINA.
SHANNON DELGADO.
POWER OF EMPATHY AND MIND READING.
SEEKER OF TRUTH.

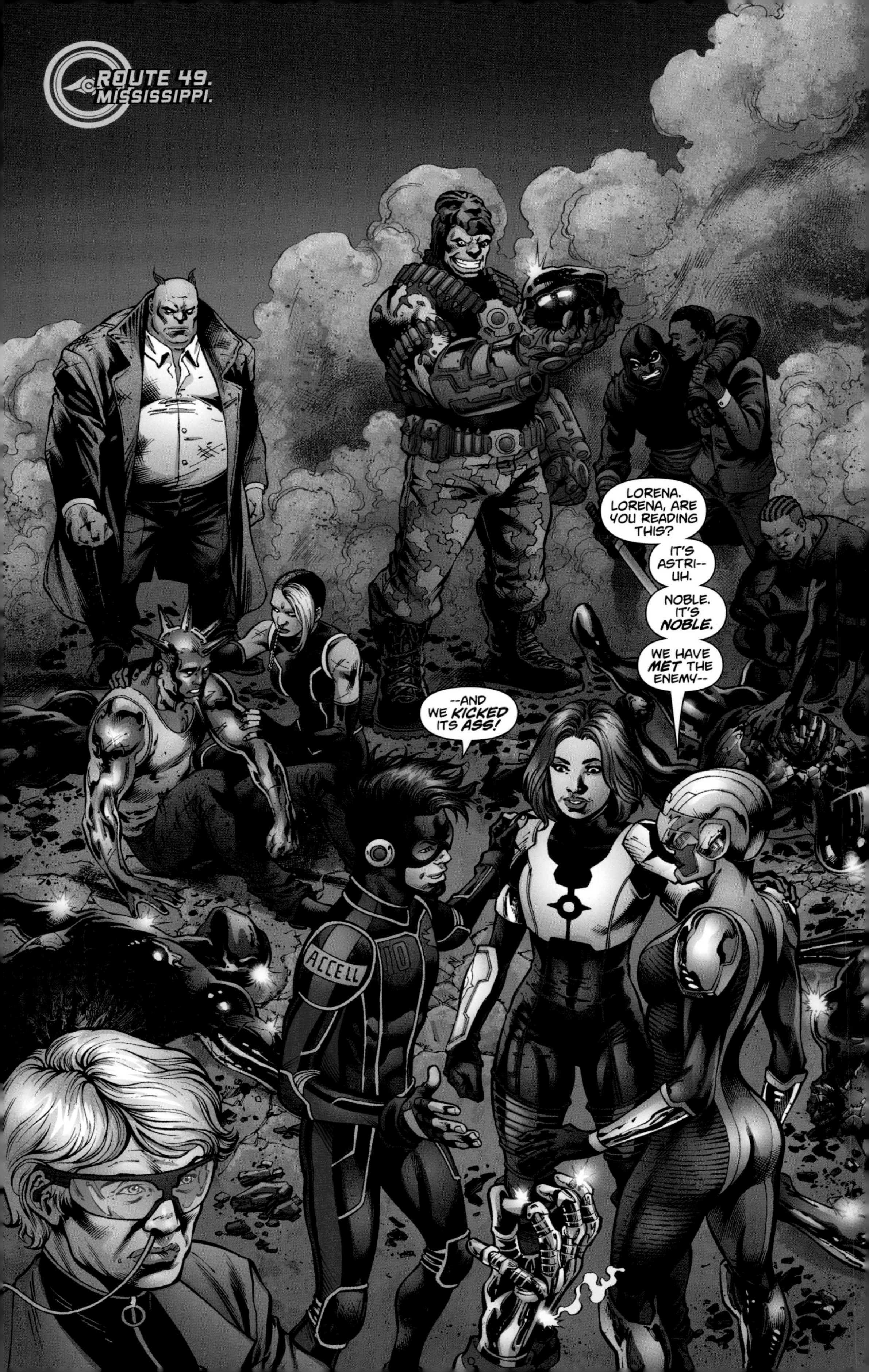
ROUTE 49.
MISSISSIPPI.
LORENA. LORENA, ARE YOU READING THIS?
IT'S ASTRI-- UH.
NOBLE. IT'S NOBLE.
WE HAVE MET THE ENEMY--
--AND WE KICKED ITS ASS!
ACCELL

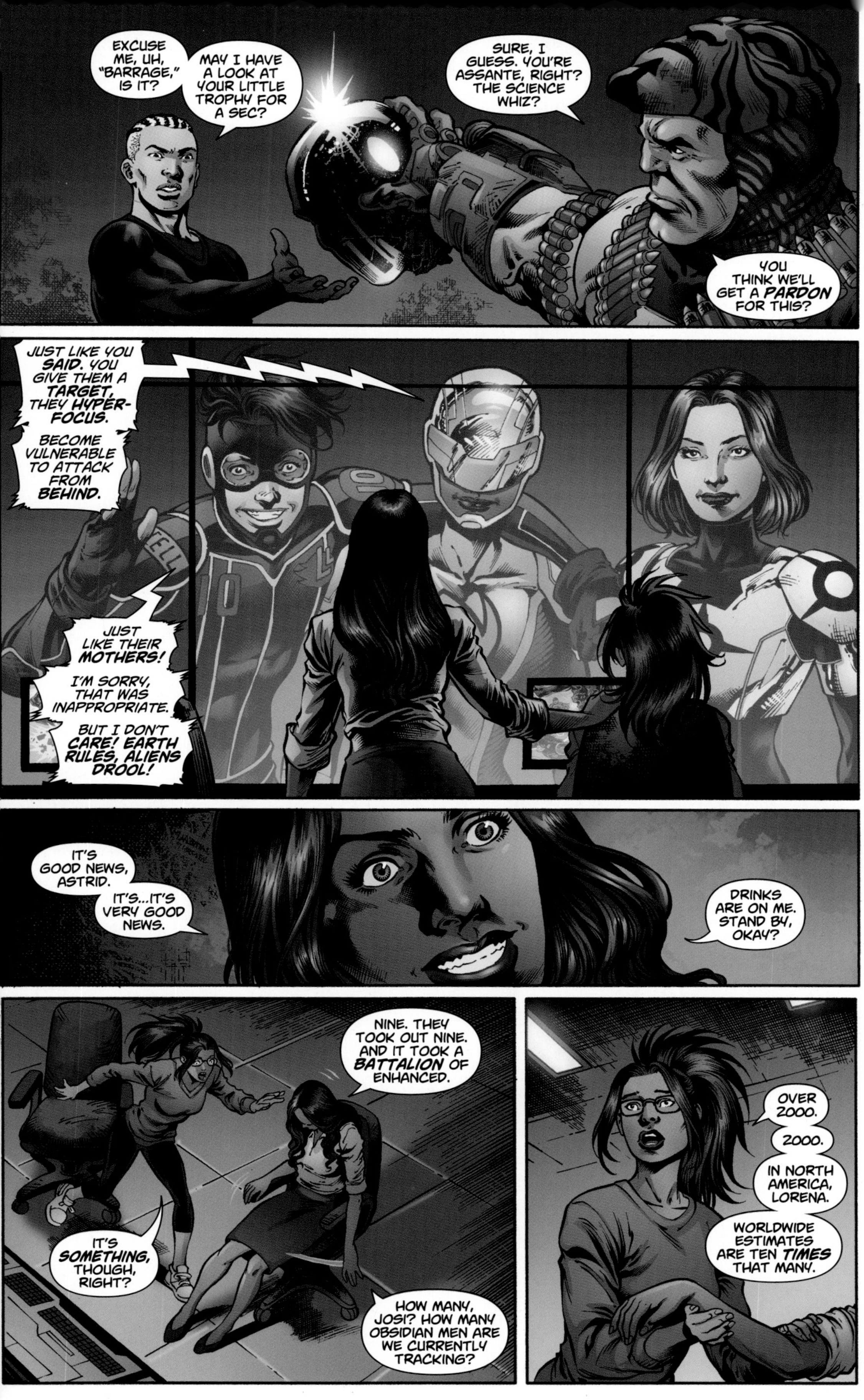
EXCUSE ME, UH, "BARRAGE," IS IT?
MAY I HAVE A LOOK AT YOUR LITTLE TROPHY FOR A SEC?
SURE, I GUESS. YOU'RE ASSANTE, RIGHT? THE SCIENCE WHIZ?
YOU THINK WE'LL GET A PARDON FOR THIS?
JUST LIKE YOU SAID. YOU GIVE THEM A TARGET, THEY HYPER-FOCUS.
BECOME VULNERABLE TO ATTACK FROM BEHIND.
JUST LIKE THEIR MOTHERS!
I'M SORRY, THAT WAS INAPPROPRIATE.
BUT I DON'T CARE! EARTH RULES, ALIENS DROOL!
IT'S GOOD NEWS, ASTRID.
IT'S...IT'S VERY GOOD NEWS.
DRINKS ARE ON ME. STAND BY, OKAY?
NINE. THEY TOOK OUT NINE. AND IT TOOK A BATTALION OF ENHANCED.
IT'S SOMETHING, THOUGH, RIGHT?
HOW MANY, JOSI? HOW MANY OBSIDIAN MEN ARE WE CURRENTLY TRACKING?
OVER 2000.
2000.
IN NORTH AMERICA, LORENA.
WORLDWIDE ESTIMATES ARE TEN TIMES THAT MANY.

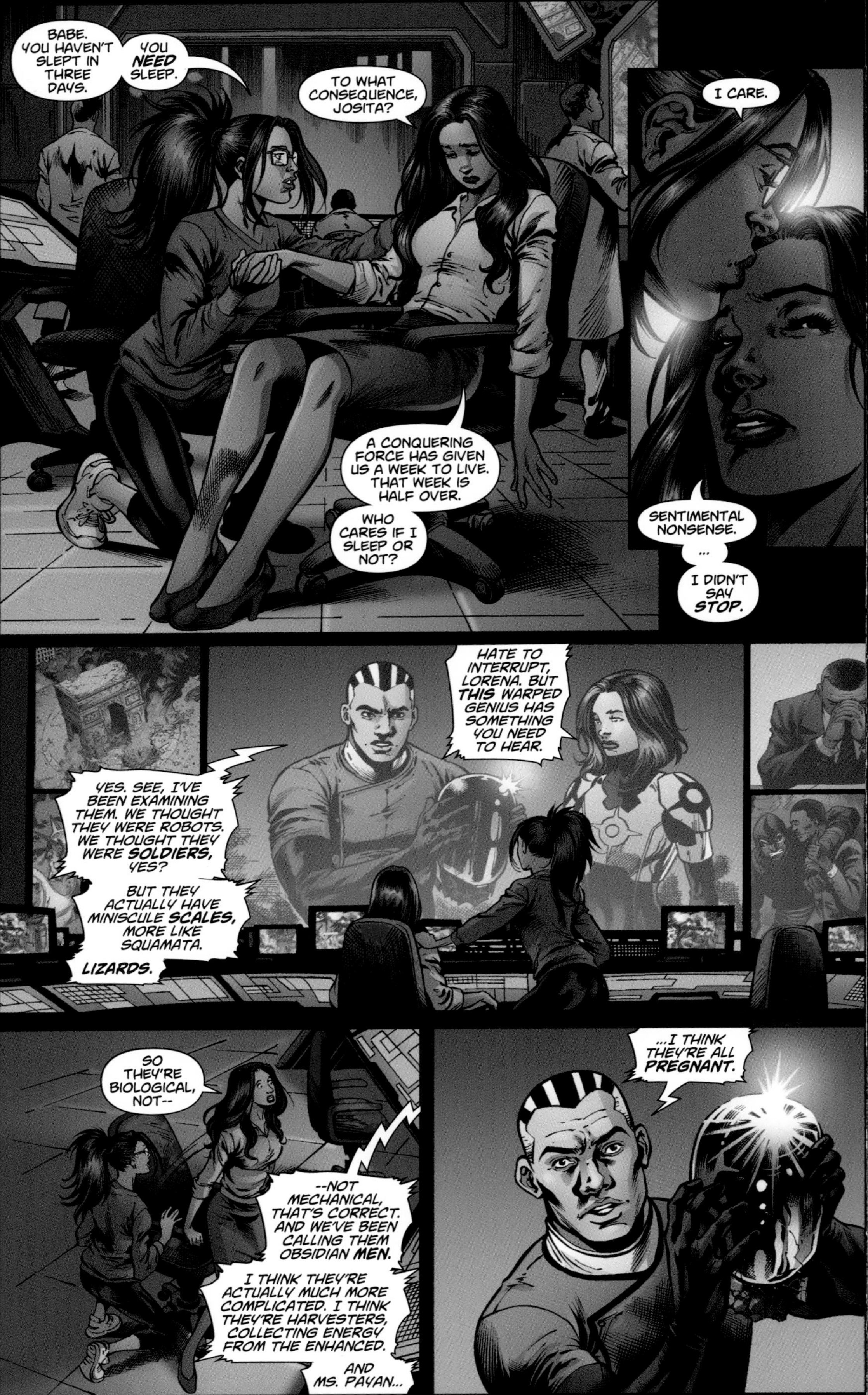
BABE. YOU HAVEN'T SLEPT IN THREE DAYS.
YOU NEED SLEEP.
TO WHAT CONSEQUENCE, JOSITA?
A CONQUERING FORCE HAS GIVEN US A WEEK TO LIVE. THAT WEEK IS HALF OVER.
WHO CARES IF I SLEEP OR NOT?
I CARE.
SENTIMENTAL NONSENSE.
...
I DIDN'T SAY STOP.
HATE TO INTERRUPT, LORENA. BUT THIS WARPED GENIUS HAS SOMETHING YOU NEED TO HEAR.
YES. SEE, I'VE BEEN EXAMINING THEM. WE THOUGHT THEY WERE ROBOTS. WE THOUGHT THEY WERE SOLDIERS, YES?
BUT THEY ACTUALLY HAVE MINISCULE SCALES, MORE LIKE SQUAMATA.
LIZARDS.
SO THEY'RE BIOLOGICAL, NOT--
--NOT MECHANICAL, THAT'S CORRECT. AND WE'VE BEEN CALLING THEM OBSIDIAN MEN.
I THINK THEY'RE ACTUALLY MUCH MORE COMPLICATED. I THINK THEY'RE HARVESTERS, COLLECTING ENERGY FROM THE ENHANCED.
AND MS. PAYAN...
...I THINK THEY'RE ALL PREGNANT.

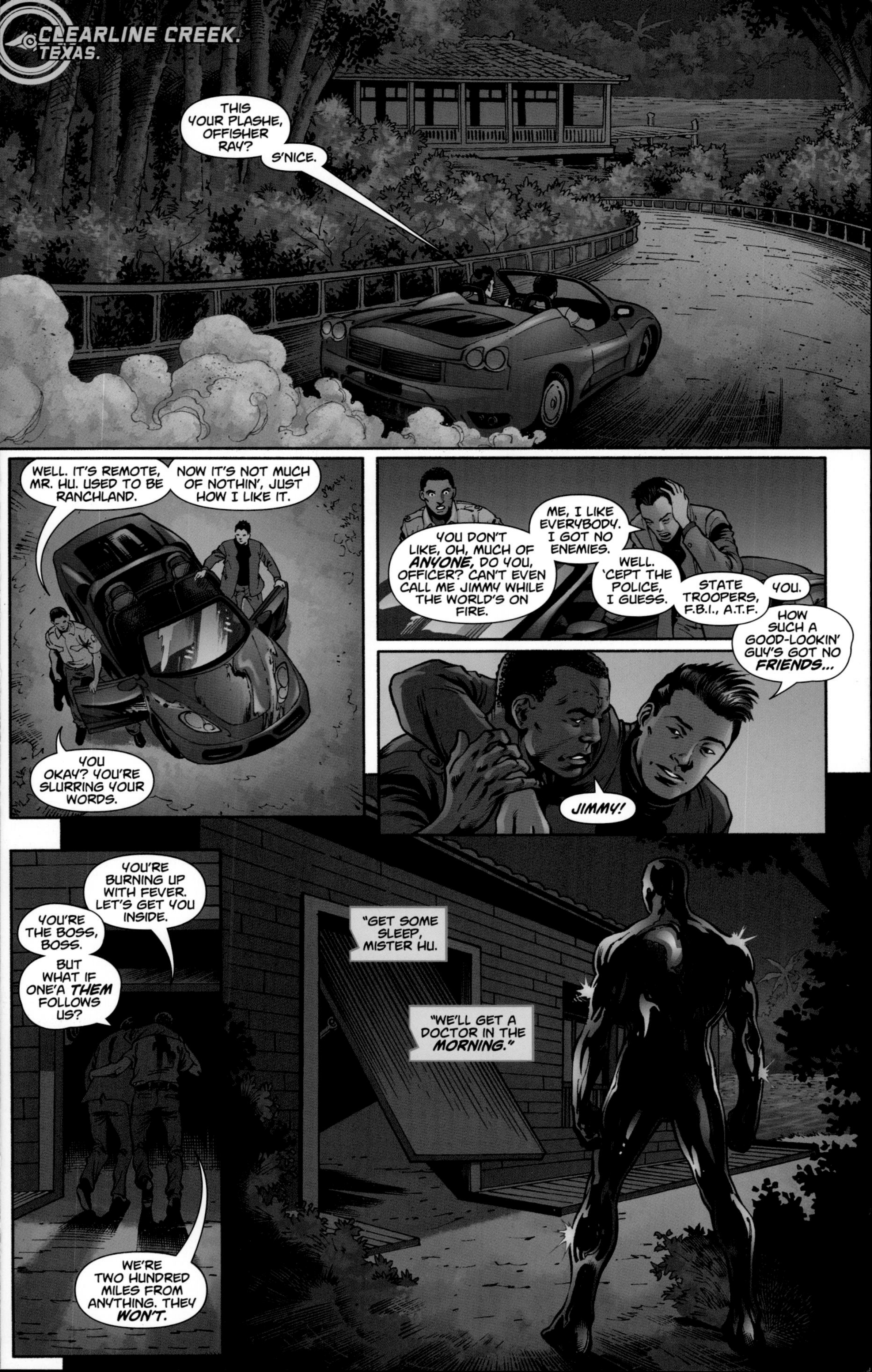
CLEARLINE CREEK. TEXAS.
THIS YOUR PLASHE, OFFISHER RAY?
S'NICE.
WELL. IT'S REMOTE, MR. HU. USED TO BE RANCHLAND.
NOW IT'S NOT MUCH OF NOTHIN', JUST HOW I LIKE IT.
YOU OKAY? YOU'RE SLURRING YOUR WORDS.
YOU DON'T LIKE, OH, MUCH OF ANYONE, DO YOU, OFFICER? CAN'T EVEN CALL ME JIMMY WHILE THE WORLD'S ON FIRE.
ME, I LIKE EVERYBODY. I GOT NO ENEMIES.
WELL. 'CEPT THE POLICE, I GUESS.
STATE TROOPERS, F.B.I., A.T.F.
YOU.
HOW SUCH A GOOD-LOOKIN' GUY'S GOT NO FRIENDS...
JIMMY!
YOU'RE BURNING UP WITH FEVER. LET'S GET YOU INSIDE.
YOU'RE THE BOSS, BOSS.
BUT WHAT IF ONE'A THEM FOLLOWS US?
WE'RE TWO HUNDRED MILES FROM ANYTHING. THEY WON'T.
"GET SOME SLEEP, MISTER HU.
"WE'LL GET A DOCTOR IN THE MORNING."

DAY FOUR.

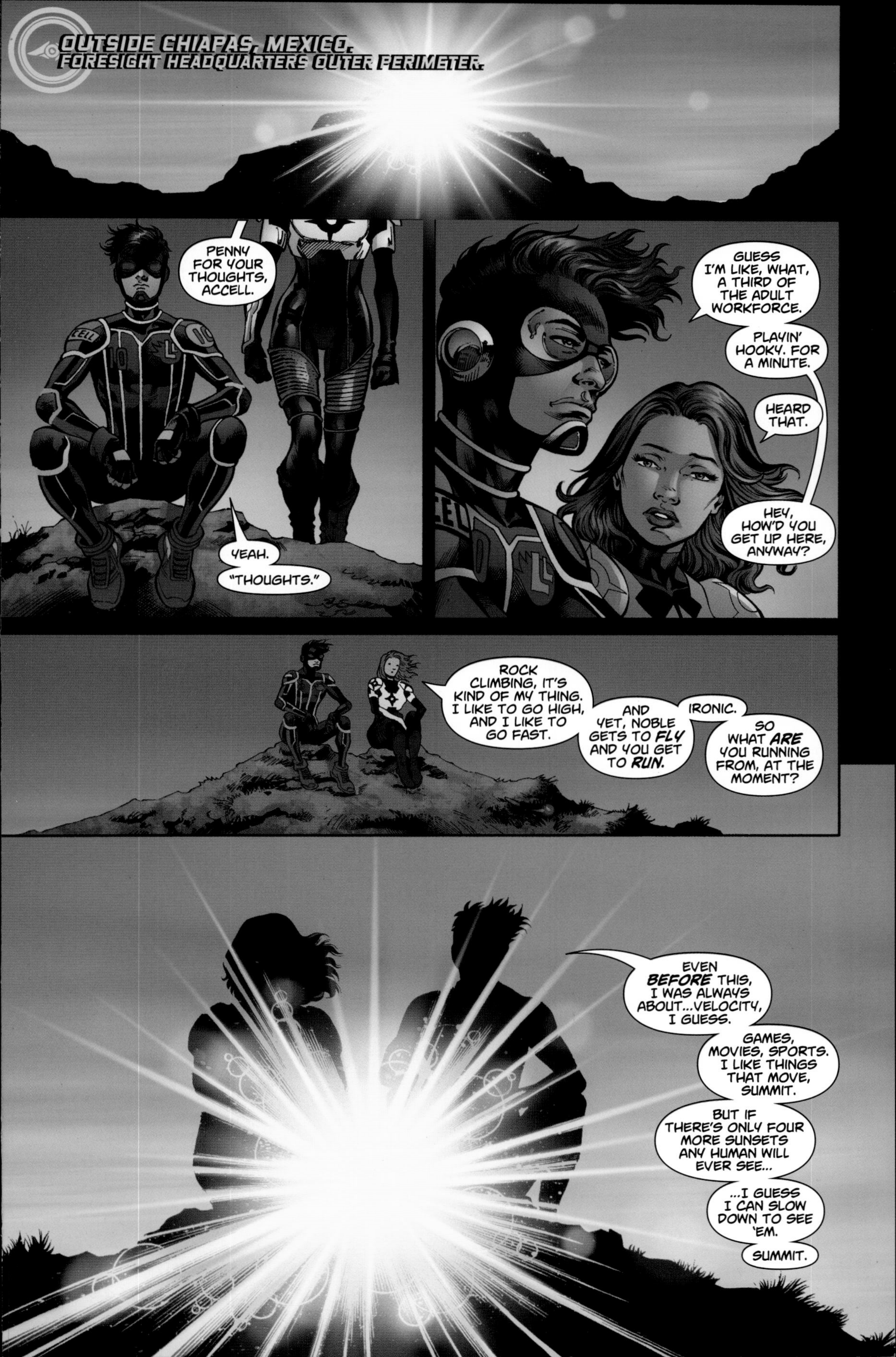
OUTSIDE CHIAPAS, MEXICO.
FORESIGHT HEADQUARTERS OUTER PERIMETER.
PENNY FOR YOUR THOUGHTS, ACCELL.
YEAH.
"THOUGHTS."
GUESS I'M LIKE, WHAT, A THIRD OF THE ADULT WORKFORCE.
PLAYIN' HOOKY. FOR A MINUTE.
HEARD THAT.
HEY, HOW'D YOU GET UP HERE, ANYWAY?
ROCK CLIMBING, IT'S KIND OF MY THING. I LIKE TO GO HIGH, AND I LIKE TO GO FAST.
AND YET, NOBLE GETS TO FLY AND YOU GET TO RUN.
IRONIC.
SO WHAT ARE YOU RUNNING FROM, AT THE MOMENT?
EVEN BEFORE THIS, I WAS ALWAYS ABOUT...VELOCITY, I GUESS.
GAMES, MOVIES, SPORTS. I LIKE THINGS THAT MOVE, SUMMIT.
BUT IF THERE'S ONLY FOUR MORE SUNSETS ANY HUMAN WILL EVER SEE...
...I GUESS I CAN SLOW DOWN TO SEE 'EM.
SUMMIT.

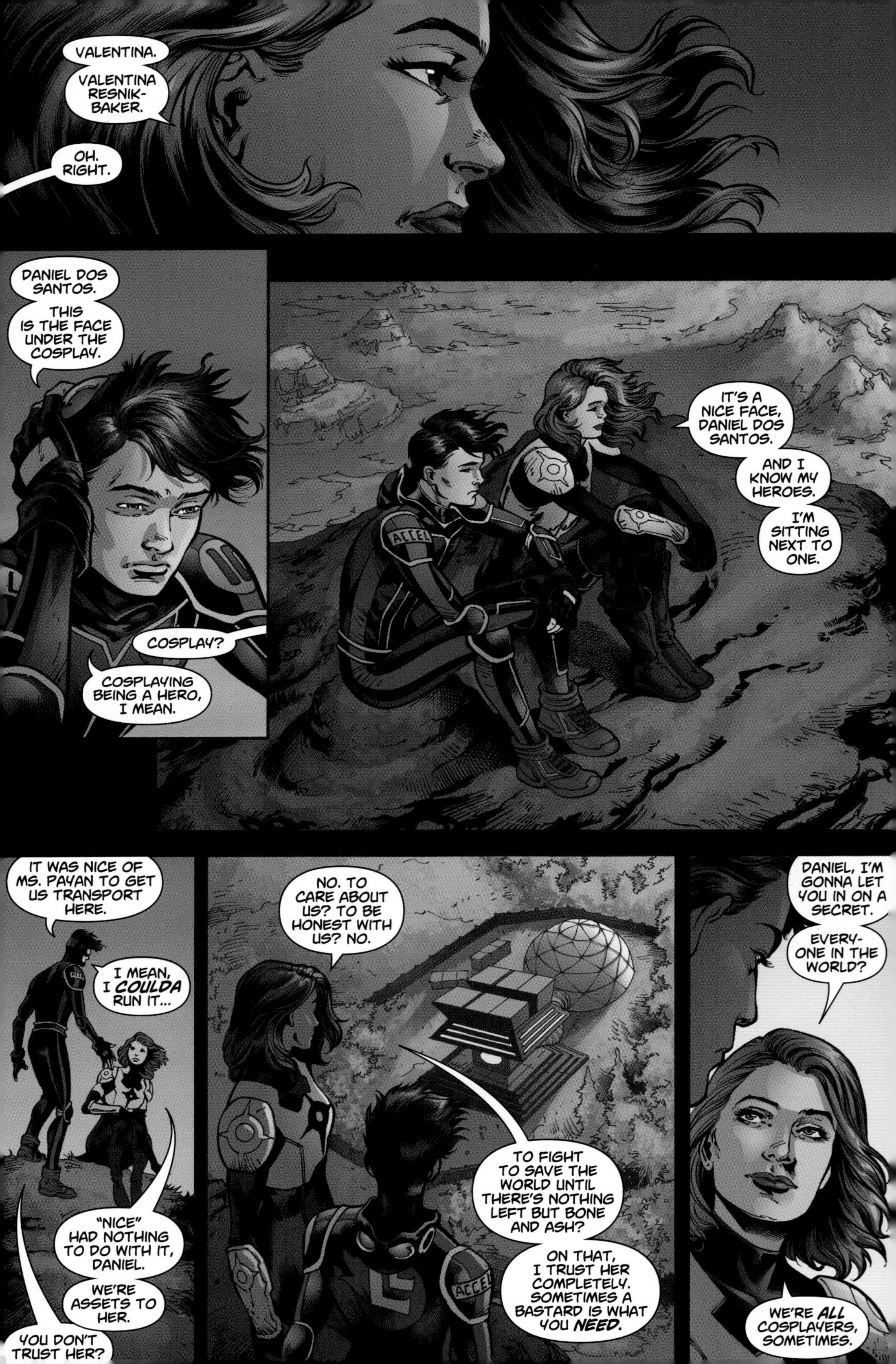
VALENTINA.
VALENTINA RESNIK-BAKER.
OH. RIGHT.
DANIEL DOS SANTOS.
THIS IS THE FACE UNDER THE COSPLAY.
COSPLAY?
COSPLAYING BEING A HERO, I MEAN.
IT'S A NICE FACE, DANIEL DOS SANTOS.
AND I KNOW MY HEROES.
I'M SITTING NEXT TO ONE.
ACCEL
IT WAS NICE OF MS. PAYAN TO GET US TRANSPORT HERE.
I MEAN, I COULDA RUN IT...
"NICE" HAD NOTHING TO DO WITH IT, DANIEL.
WE'RE ASSETS TO HER.
YOU DON'T TRUST HER?
NO. TO CARE ABOUT US? TO BE HONEST WITH US? NO.
TO FIGHT TO SAVE THE WORLD UNTIL THERE'S NOTHING LEFT BUT BONE AND ASH?
ON THAT, I TRUST HER COMPLETELY. SOMETIMES A BASTARD IS WHAT YOU NEED.
DANIEL, I'M GONNA LET YOU IN ON A SECRET.
EVERY-ONE IN THE WORLD?
WE'RE ALL COSPLAYERS, SOMETIMES.

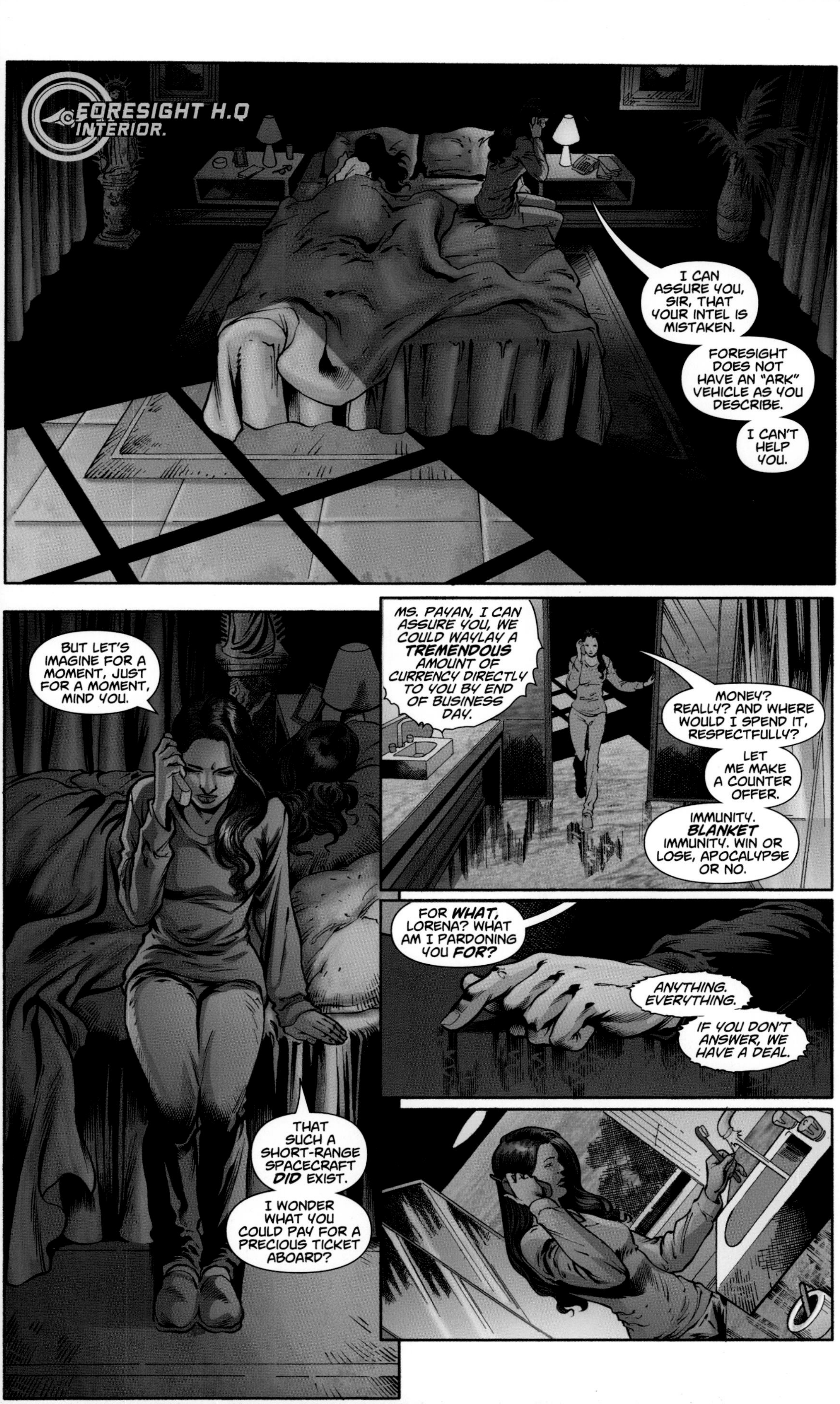
FORESIGHT H.Q INTERIOR.
I CAN ASSURE YOU, SIR, THAT YOUR INTEL IS MISTAKEN.
FORESIGHT DOES NOT HAVE AN "ARK" VEHICLE AS YOU DESCRIBE.
I CAN'T HELP YOU.
BUT LET'S IMAGINE FOR A MOMENT, JUST FOR A MOMENT, MIND YOU.
THAT SUCH A SHORT-RANGE SPACECRAFT DID EXIST.
I WONDER WHAT YOU COULD PAY FOR A PRECIOUS TICKET ABOARD?
MS. PAYAN, I CAN ASSURE YOU, WE COULD WAYLAY A TREMENDOUS AMOUNT OF CURRENCY DIRECTLY TO YOU BY END OF BUSINESS DAY.
MONEY? REALLY? AND WHERE WOULD I SPEND IT, RESPECTFULLY?
LET ME MAKE A COUNTER OFFER.
IMMUNITY. BLANKET IMMUNITY. WIN OR LOSE, APOCALYPSE OR NO.
FOR WHAT, LORENA? WHAT AM I PARDONING YOU FOR?
ANYTHING. EVERYTHING.
IF YOU DON'T ANSWER, WE HAVE A DEAL.

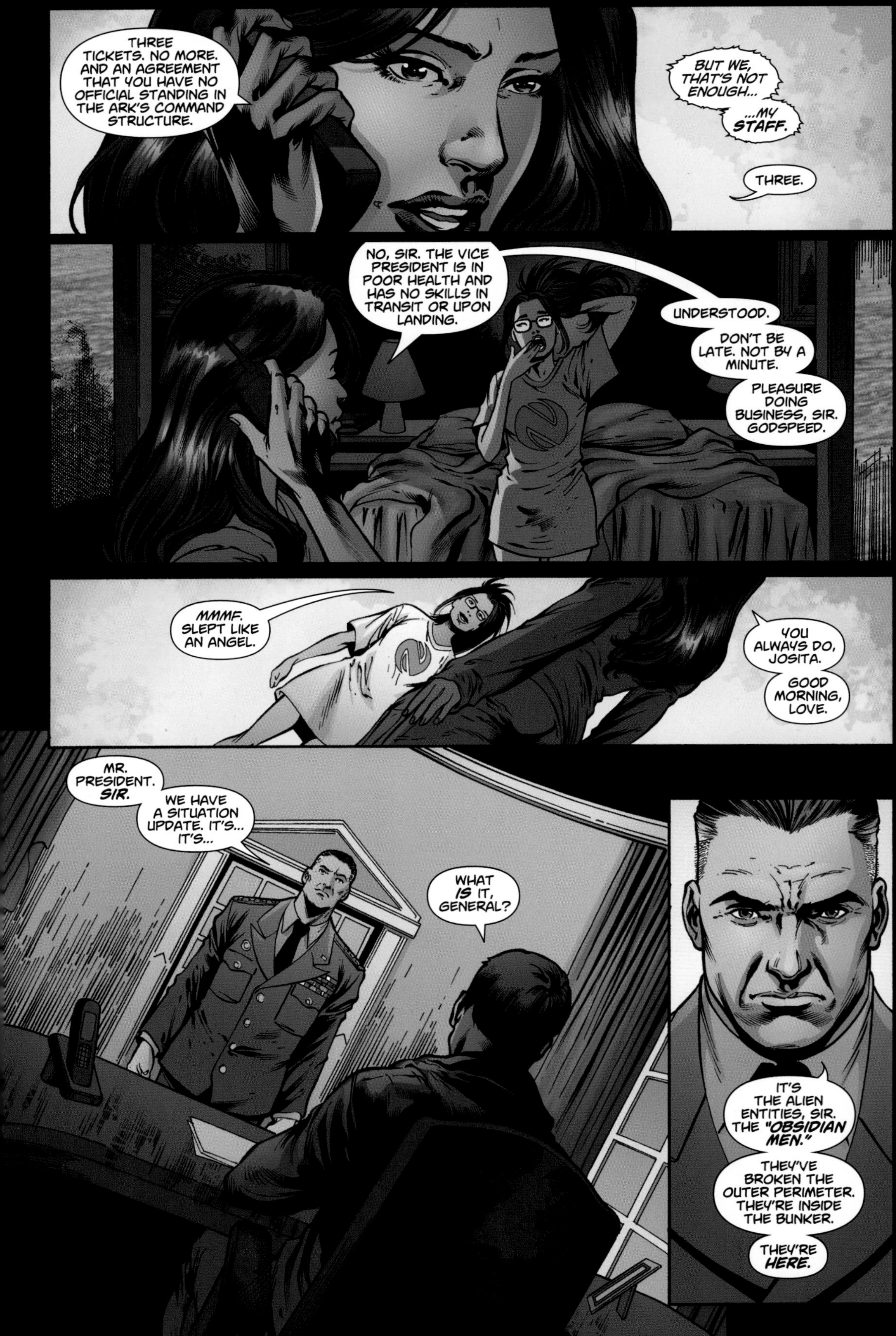
THREE TICKETS. NO MORE. AND AN AGREEMENT THAT YOU HAVE NO OFFICIAL STANDING IN THE ARK'S COMMAND STRUCTURE.
BUT WE, THAT'S NOT ENOUGH...
...MY STAFF.
THREE.
NO, SIR. THE VICE PRESIDENT IS IN POOR HEALTH AND HAS NO SKILLS IN TRANSIT OR UPON LANDING.
UNDERSTOOD.
DON'T BE LATE. NOT BY A MINUTE.
PLEASURE DOING BUSINESS, SIR. GODSPEED.
MMMF. SLEPT LIKE AN ANGEL.
YOU ALWAYS DO, JOSITA.
GOOD MORNING, LOVE.
MR. PRESIDENT. SIR.
WE HAVE A SITUATION UPDATE. IT'S... IT'S...
WHAT IS IT, GENERAL?
IT'S THE ALIEN ENTITIES, SIR. THE "OBSIDIAN MEN."
THEY'VE BROKEN THE OUTER PERIMETER. THEY'RE INSIDE THE BUNKER.
THEY'RE HERE.

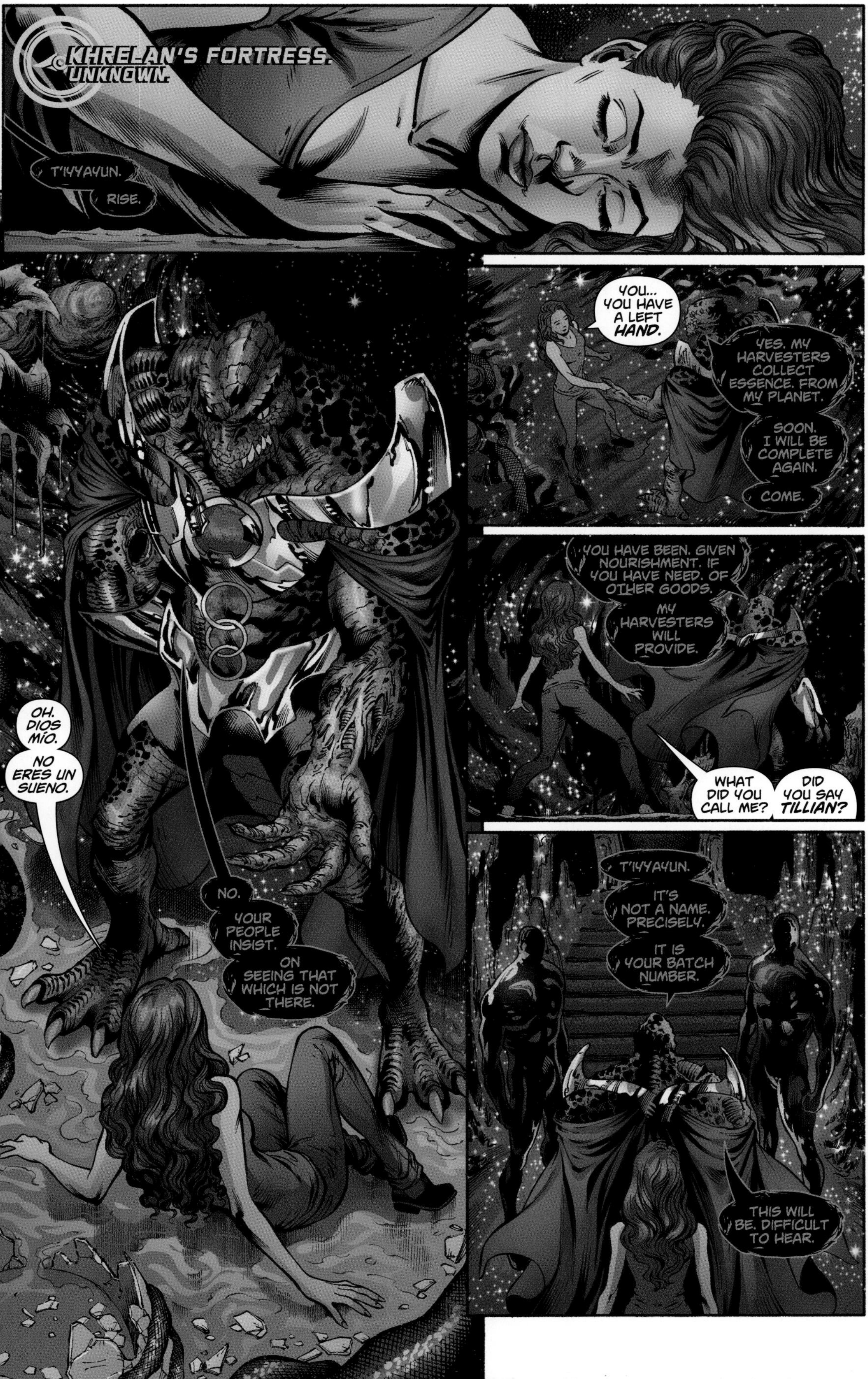
KHRELAN'S FORTRESS. UNKNOWN.
T'IYYAYUN.
RISE.
OH. DIOS MÍO.
NO ERES UN SUENO.
NO.
YOUR PEOPLE INSIST.
ON SEEING THAT WHICH IS NOT THERE.
YOU... YOU HAVE A LEFT HAND.
YES. MY HARVESTERS COLLECT ESSENCE. FROM MY PLANET.
SOON. I WILL BE COMPLETE AGAIN.
COME.
YOU HAVE BEEN. GIVEN NOURISHMENT. IF YOU HAVE NEED. OF OTHER GOODS.
MY HARVESTERS WILL PROVIDE.
WHAT DID YOU CALL ME?
DID YOU SAY TILLIAN?
T'IYYAYUN.
IT'S NOT A NAME. PRECISELY.
IT IS YOUR BATCH NUMBER.
THIS WILL BE. DIFFICULT TO HEAR.

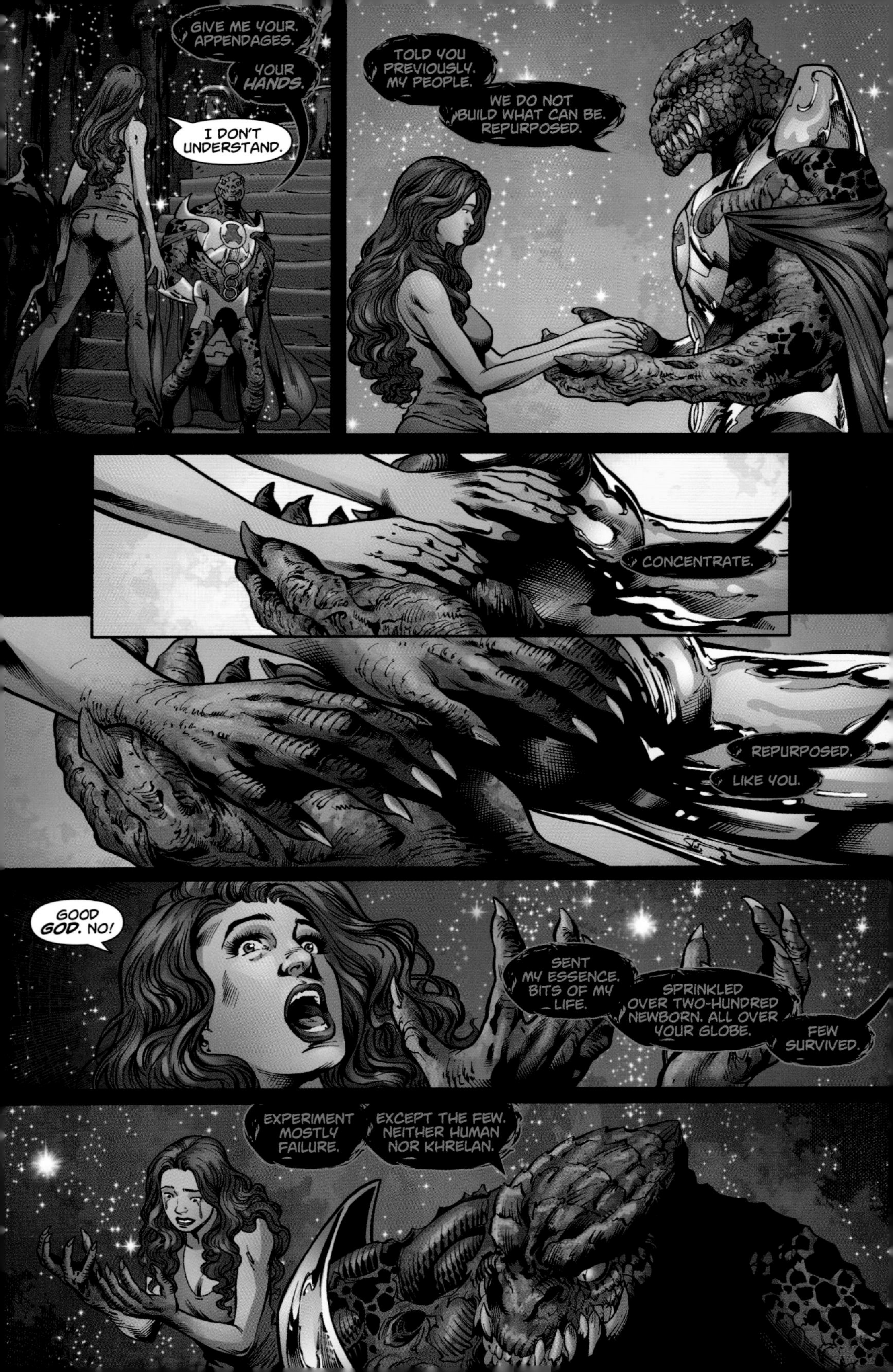

GIVE ME YOUR. APPENDAGES.
YOUR HANDS.
I DON'T UNDERSTAND.
TOLD YOU PREVIOUSLY. MY PEOPLE.
WE DO NOT BUILD WHAT CAN BE. REPURPOSED.
CONCENTRATE.
REPURPOSED.
LIKE YOU.
GOOD GOD. NO!
SENT MY ESSENCE. BITS OF MY LIFE.
SPRINKLED OVER TWO-HUNDRED NEWBORN. ALL OVER YOUR GLOBE.
FEW SURVIVED.
EXPERIMENT MOSTLY FAILURE.
EXCEPT THE FEW. NEITHER HUMAN NOR KHRELAN.

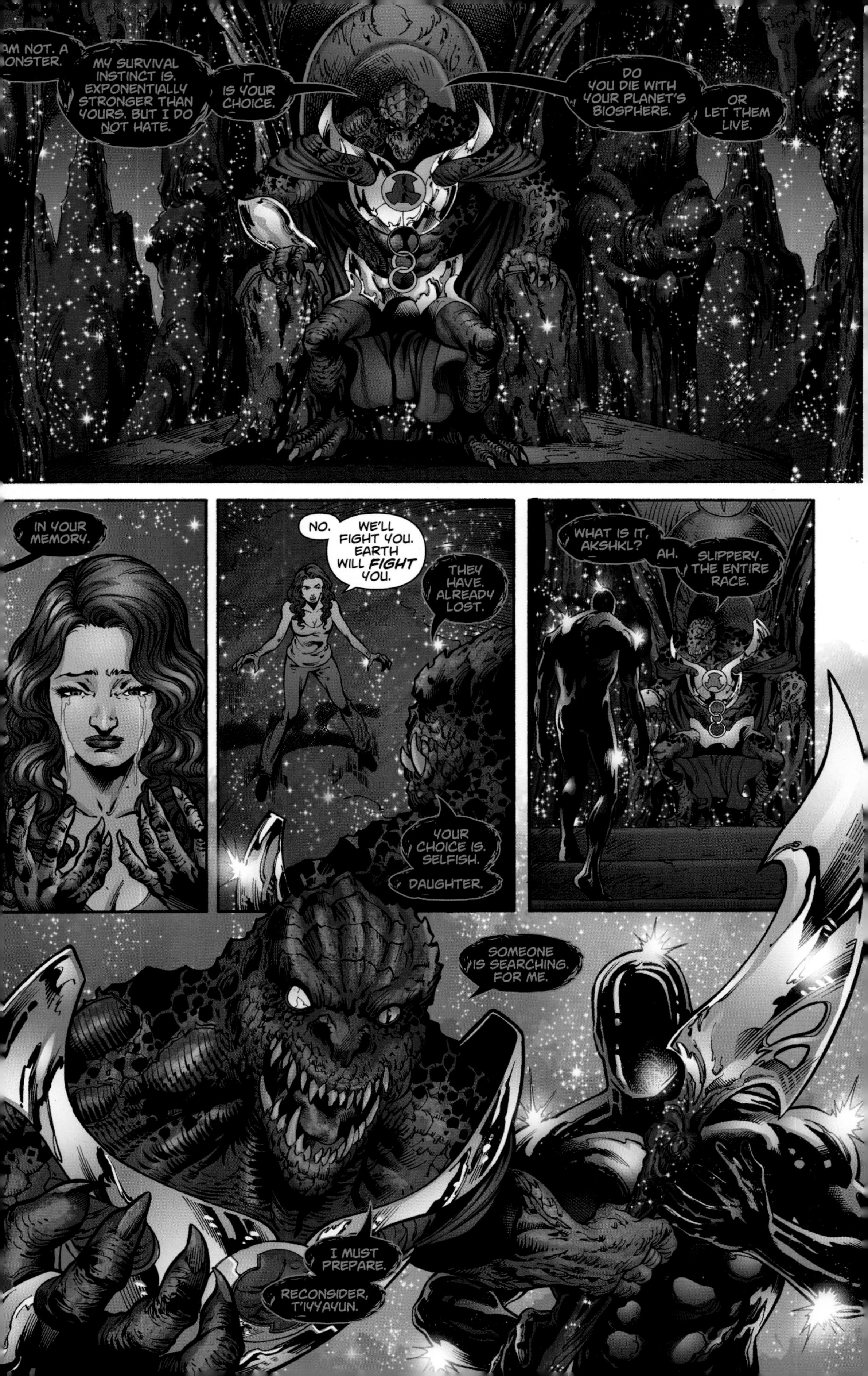

AM NOT. A
ONSTER.
MY SURVIVAL INSTINCT IS. EXPONENTIALLY STRONGER THAN YOURS. BUT I DO NOT HATE.
IT IS YOUR CHOICE.
DO YOU DIE WITH YOUR PLANET'S BIOSPHERE.
OR LET THEM LIVE.
IN YOUR MEMORY.
NO.
WE'LL FIGHT YOU. EARTH WILL FIGHT YOU.
THEY HAVE. ALREADY LOST.
YOUR CHOICE IS. SELFISH.
DAUGHTER.
WHAT IS IT, AKSHKL?
AH.
SLIPPERY. THE ENTIRE RACE.
SOMEONE IS SEARCHING. FOR ME.
I MUST PREPARE.
RECONSIDER, T'IYYAYUN.

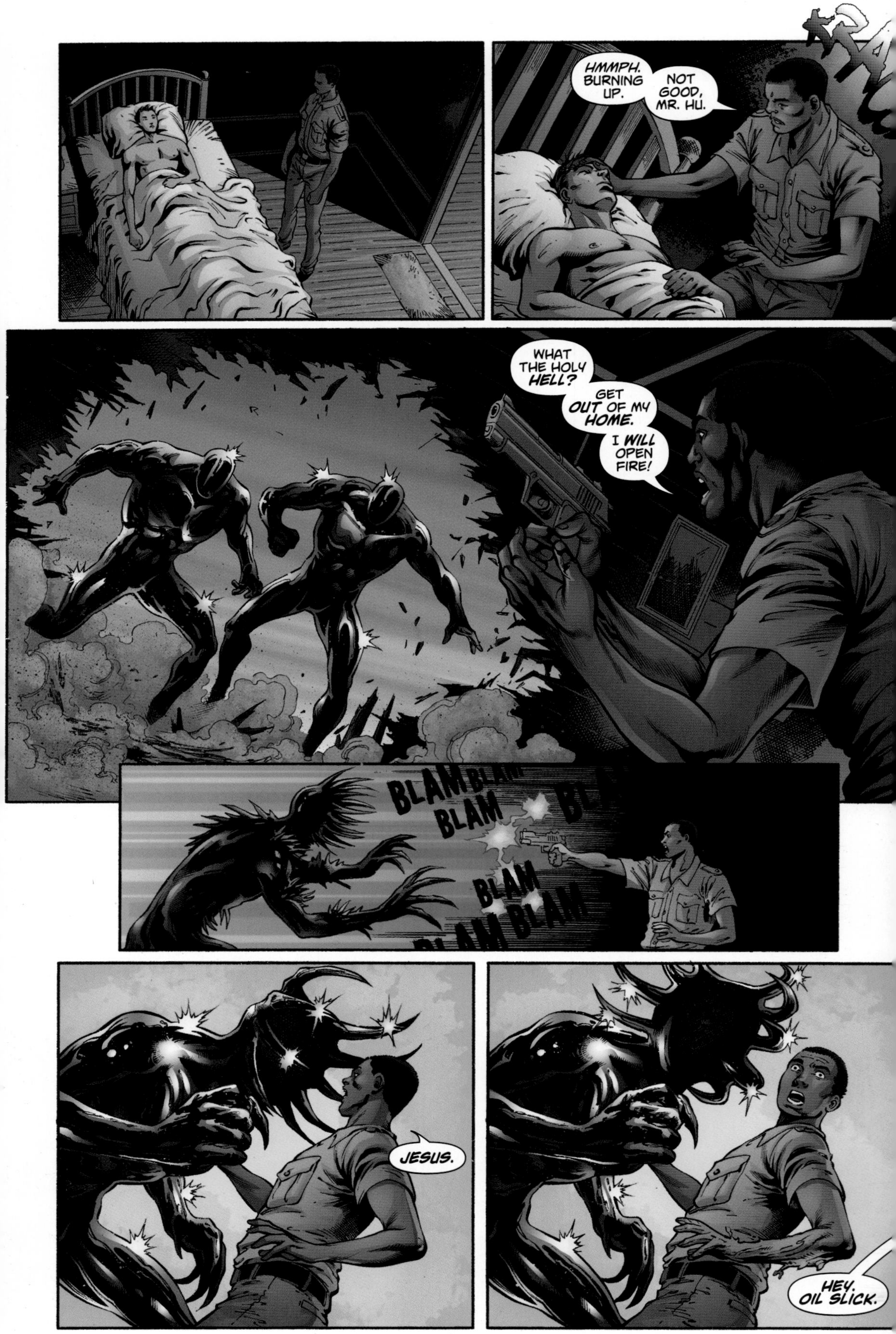

HMMPH. BURNING UP.
NOT GOOD, MR. HU.
WHAT THE HOLY HELL?
GET OUT OF MY HOME.
I WILL OPEN FIRE!
BLAM BLAM
BLAM
BLAM
BLAM BLAM
JESUS.
HEY, OIL SLICK.

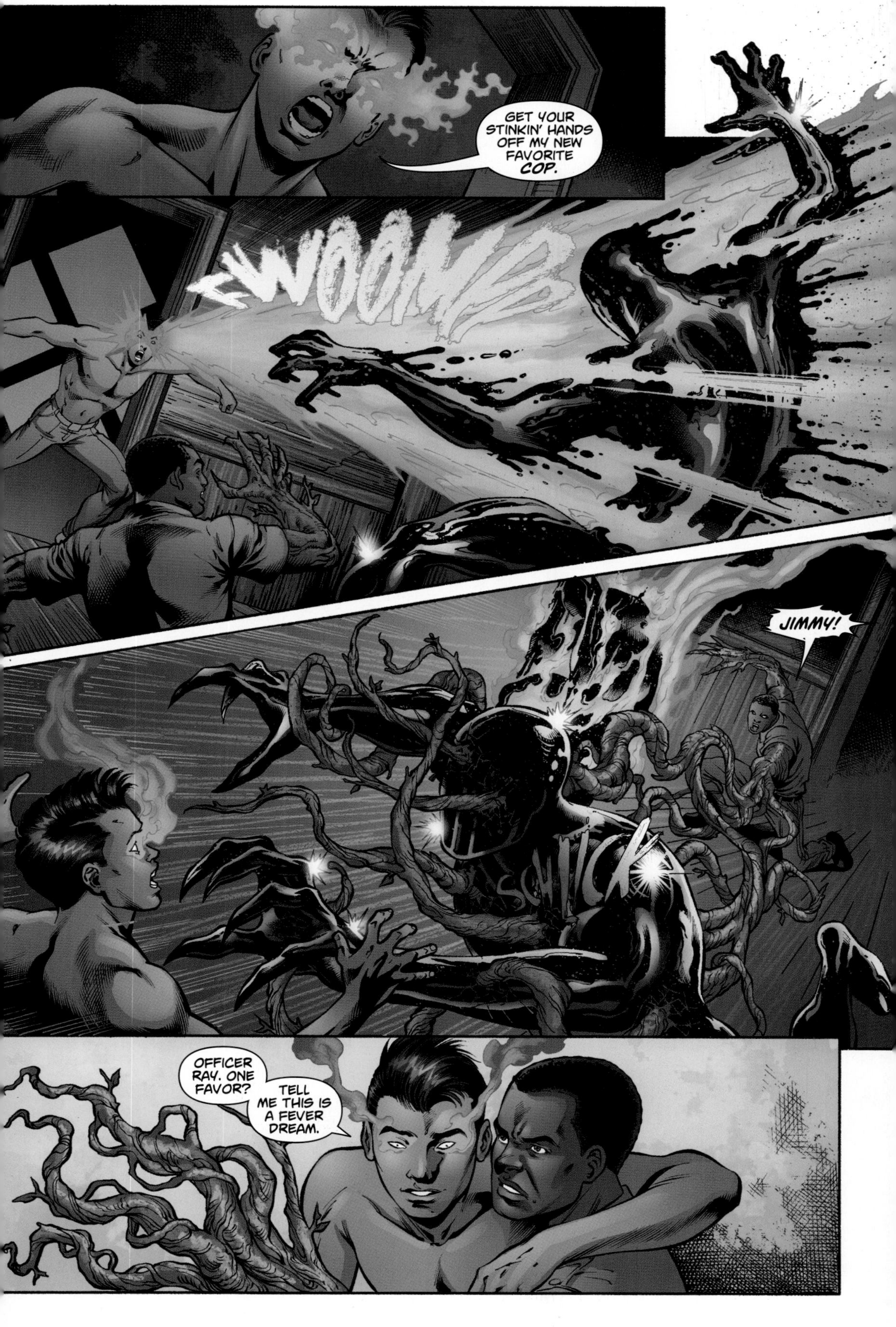
GET YOUR STINKIN' HANDS OFF MY NEW FAVORITE COP.
WOOMB
JIMMY!
SCHLICK
OFFICER RAY. ONE FAVOR?
TELL ME THIS IS A FEVER DREAM.

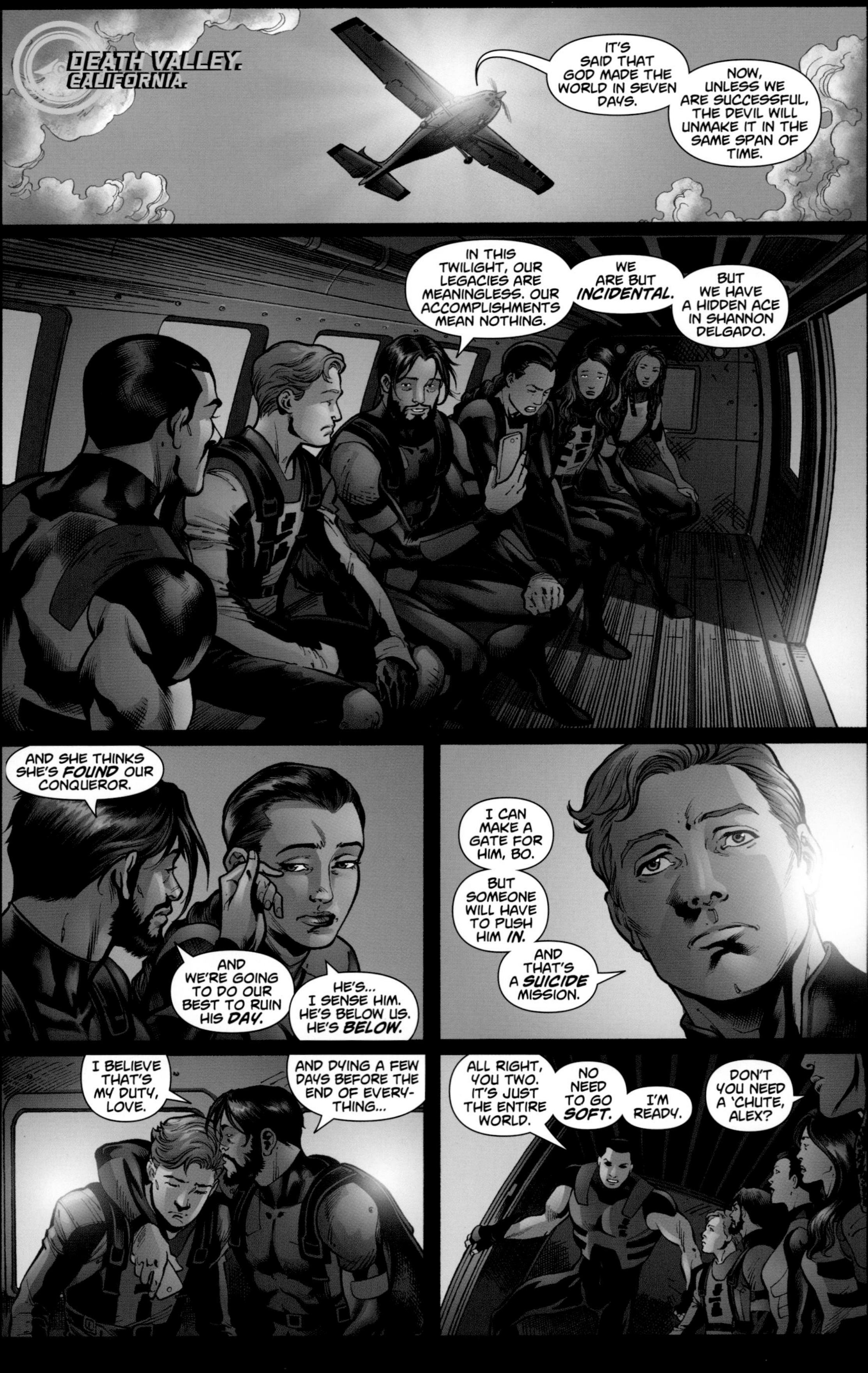
DEATH VALLEY. CALIFORNIA.
IT'S SAID THAT GOD MADE THE WORLD IN SEVEN DAYS.
NOW, UNLESS WE ARE SUCCESSFUL, THE DEVIL WILL UNMAKE IT IN THE SAME SPAN OF TIME.
IN THIS TWILIGHT, OUR LEGACIES ARE MEANINGLESS. OUR ACCOMPLISHMENTS MEAN NOTHING.
WE ARE BUT INCIDENTAL.
BUT WE HAVE A HIDDEN ACE IN SHANNON DELGADO.
AND SHE THINKS SHE'S FOUND OUR CONQUEROR.
AND WE'RE GOING TO DO OUR BEST TO RUIN HIS DAY.
HE'S... I SENSE HIM. HE'S BELOW US. HE'S BELOW.
I CAN MAKE A GATE FOR HIM, BO.
BUT SOMEONE WILL HAVE TO PUSH HIM IN.
AND THAT'S A SUICIDE MISSION.
I BELIEVE THAT'S MY DUTY, LOVE.
AND DYING A FEW DAYS BEFORE THE END OF EVERY-THING...
ALL RIGHT, YOU TWO. IT'S JUST THE ENTIRE WORLD.
NO NEED TO GO SOFT.
I'M READY.
DON'T YOU NEED A 'CHUTE, ALEX?

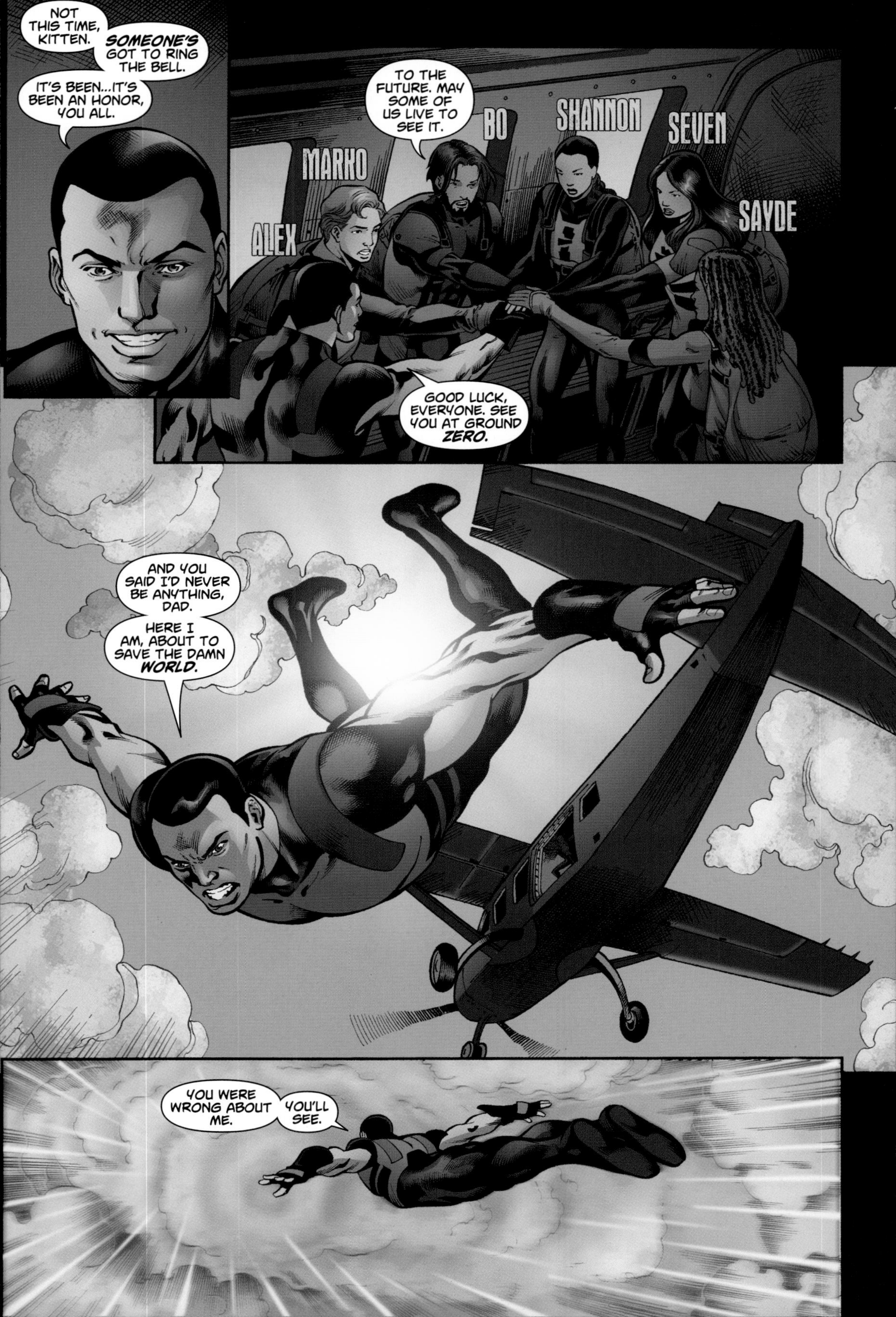
NOT THIS TIME, KITTEN.
SOMEONE'S GOT TO RING THE BELL.
IT'S BEEN...IT'S BEEN AN HONOR, YOU ALL.
TO THE FUTURE. MAY SOME OF US LIVE TO SEE IT.
MARKO
BO
SHANNON
SEVEN
SAYDE
ALEX
GOOD LUCK, EVERYONE. SEE YOU AT GROUND ZERO.
AND YOU SAID I'D NEVER BE ANYTHING, DAD.
HERE I AM, ABOUT TO SAVE THE DAMN WORLD.
YOU WERE WRONG ABOUT ME.
YOU'LL SEE.

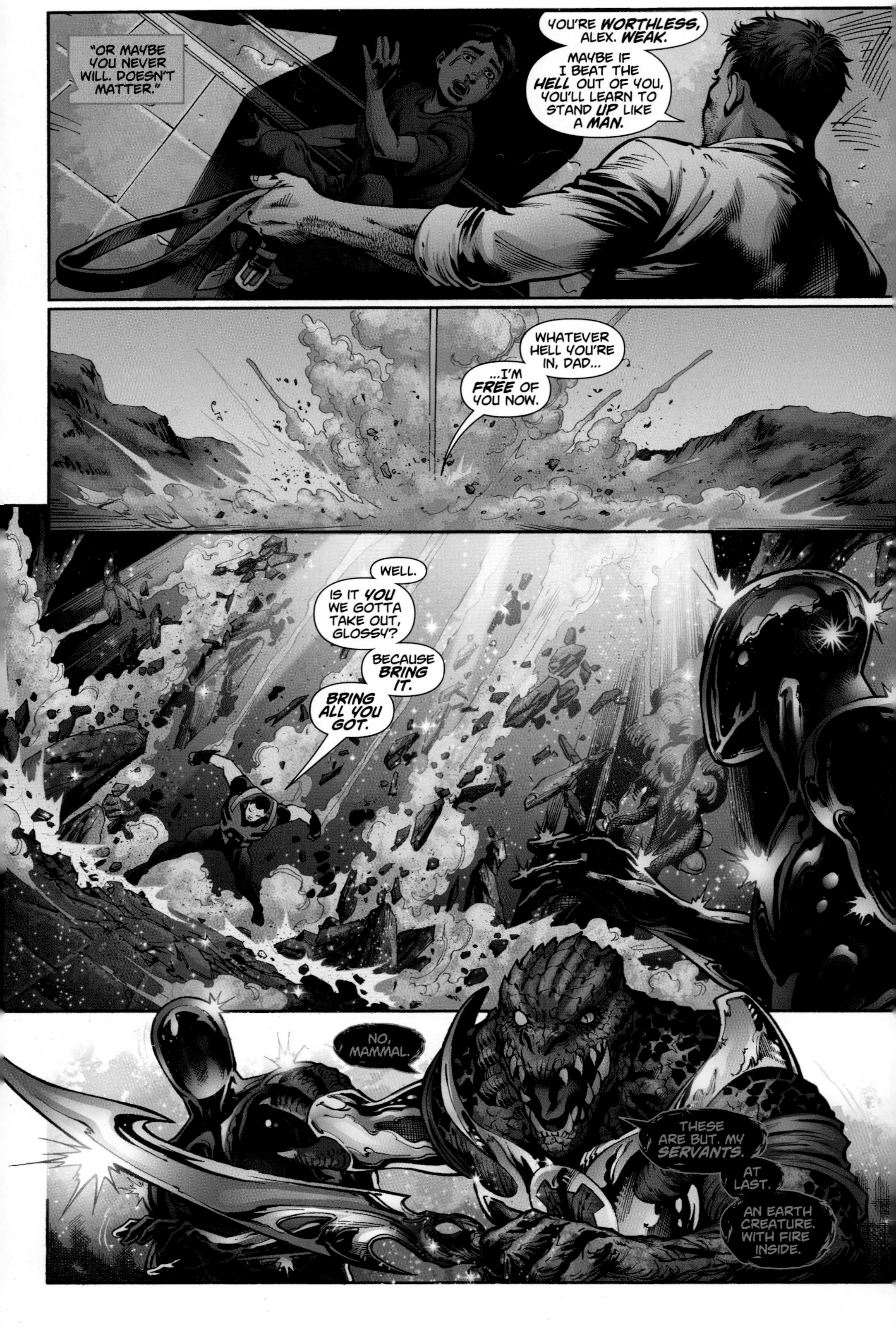
"OR MAYBE YOU NEVER WILL. DOESN'T MATTER."
YOU'RE WORTHLESS, ALEX. WEAK.
MAYBE IF I BEAT THE HELL OUT OF YOU, YOU'LL LEARN TO STAND UP LIKE A MAN.
WHATEVER HELL YOU'RE IN, DAD...
...I'M FREE OF YOU NOW.
WELL.
IS IT YOU WE GOTTA TAKE OUT, GLOSSY?
BECAUSE BRING IT.
BRING ALL YOU GOT.
NO, MAMMAL.
THESE ARE BUT MY SERVANTS.
AT LAST.
AN EARTH CREATURE. WITH FIRE INSIDE.

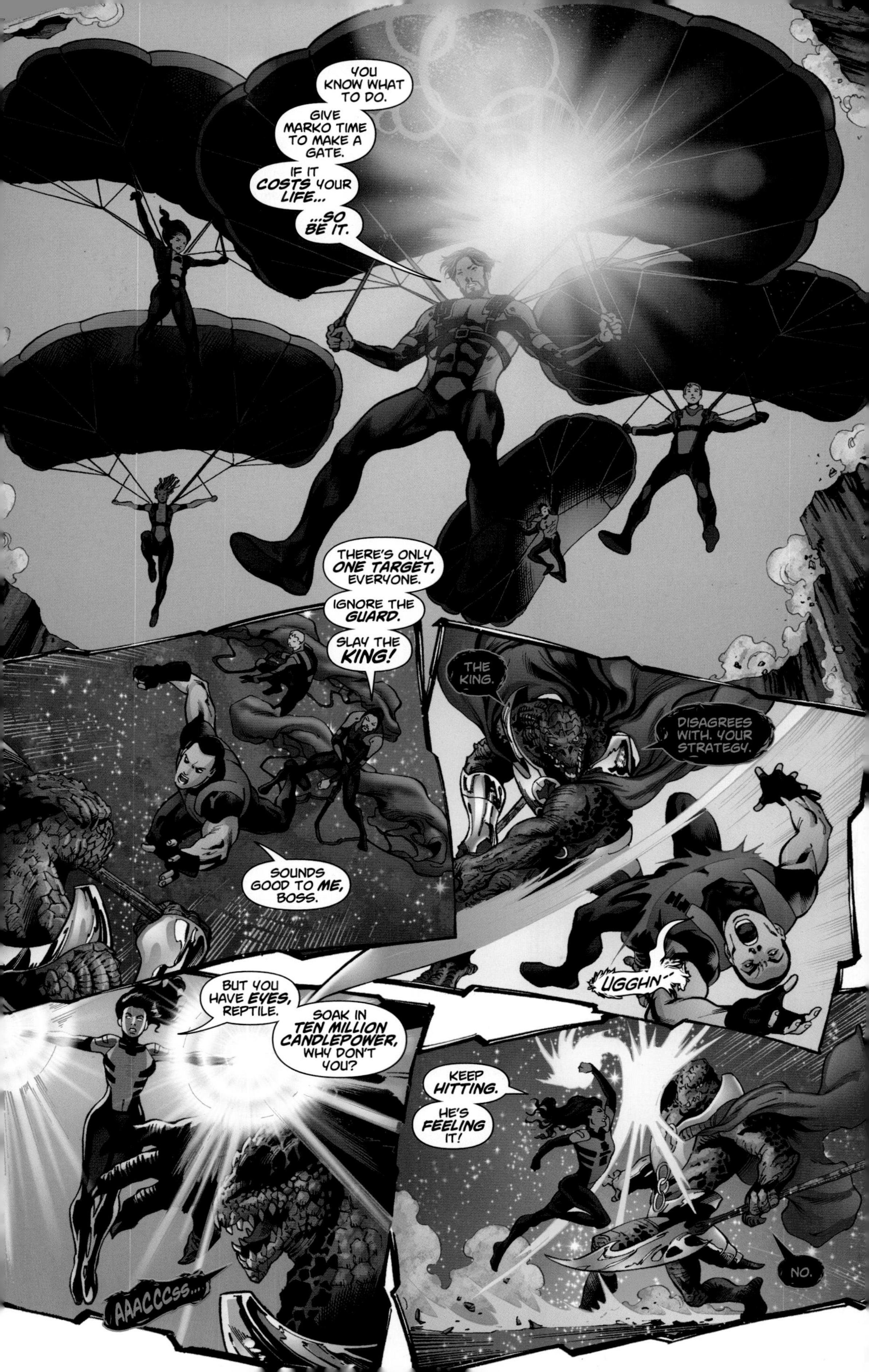
YOU KNOW WHAT TO DO.
GIVE MARKO TIME TO MAKE A GATE.
IF IT **COSTS** YOUR **LIFE...**
...SO BE IT.
THERE'S ONLY **ONE TARGET,** EVERYONE.
IGNORE THE **GUARD.**
SLAY THE **KING!**
SOUNDS GOOD TO **ME,** BOSS.
THE. KING.
DISAGREES WITH. YOUR STRATEGY.
UGGHN
BUT YOU HAVE **EYES,** REPTILE.
SOAK IN **TEN MILLION CANDLEPOWER,** WHY DON'T YOU?
AAACCCSS...
KEEP **HITTING.**
HE'S **FEELING** IT!
NO.

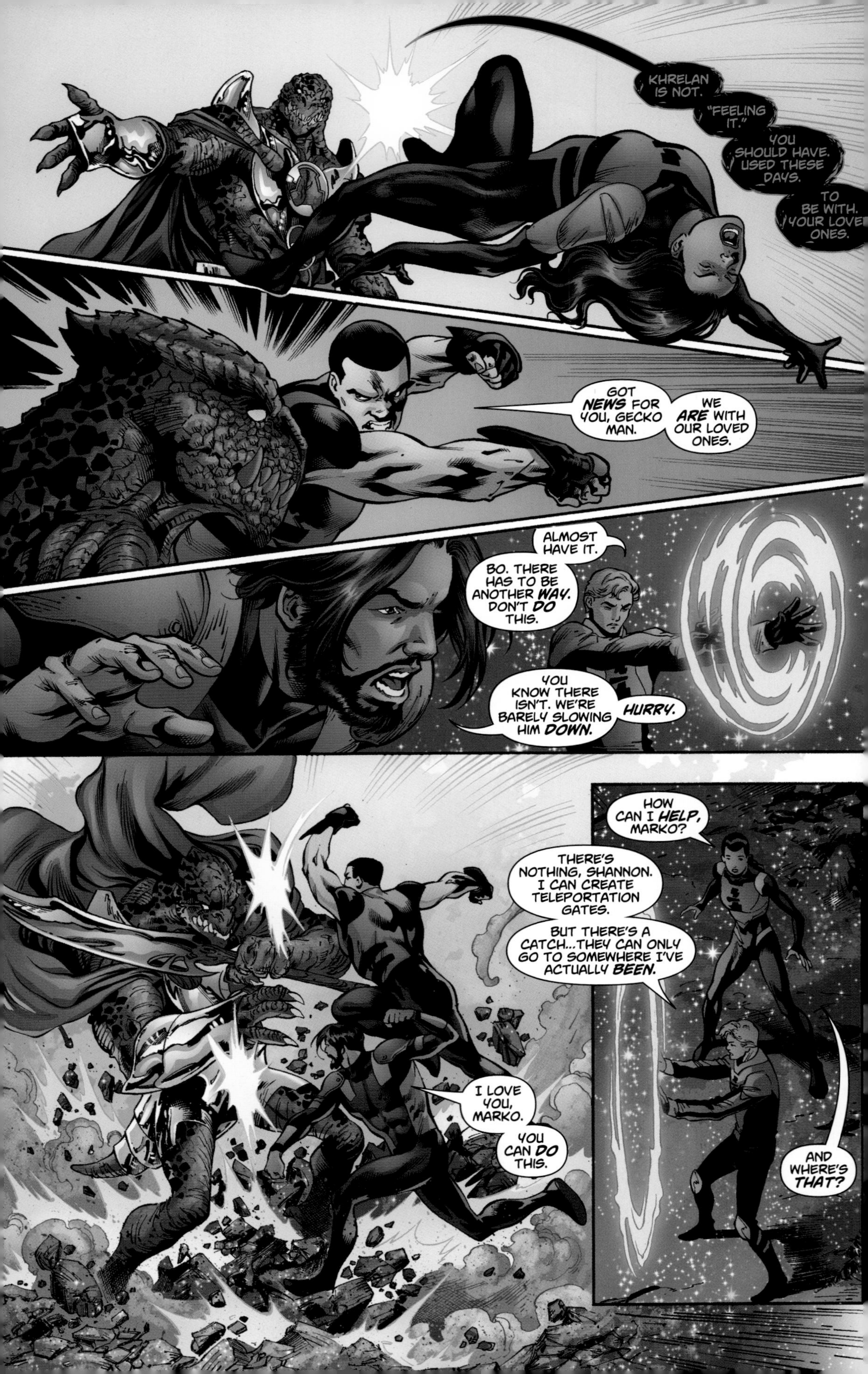
KHRELAN IS NOT.
"FEELING IT."
YOU SHOULD HAVE. USED THESE _DAYS.
TO BE WITH. YOUR LOVE _ONES.
GOT NEWS FOR YOU, GECKO MAN.
WE ARE WITH OUR LOVED ONES.
ALMOST HAVE IT.
BO. THERE HAS TO BE ANOTHER WAY. DON'T DO THIS.
YOU KNOW THERE ISN'T. WE'RE BARELY SLOWING HIM DOWN.
HURRY.
HOW CAN I HELP, MARKO?
THERE'S NOTHING, SHANNON. I CAN CREATE TELEPORTATION GATES.
BUT THERE'S A CATCH...THEY CAN ONLY GO TO SOMEWHERE I'VE ACTUALLY BEEN.
I LOVE YOU, MARKO.
YOU CAN DO THIS.
AND WHERE'S THAT?

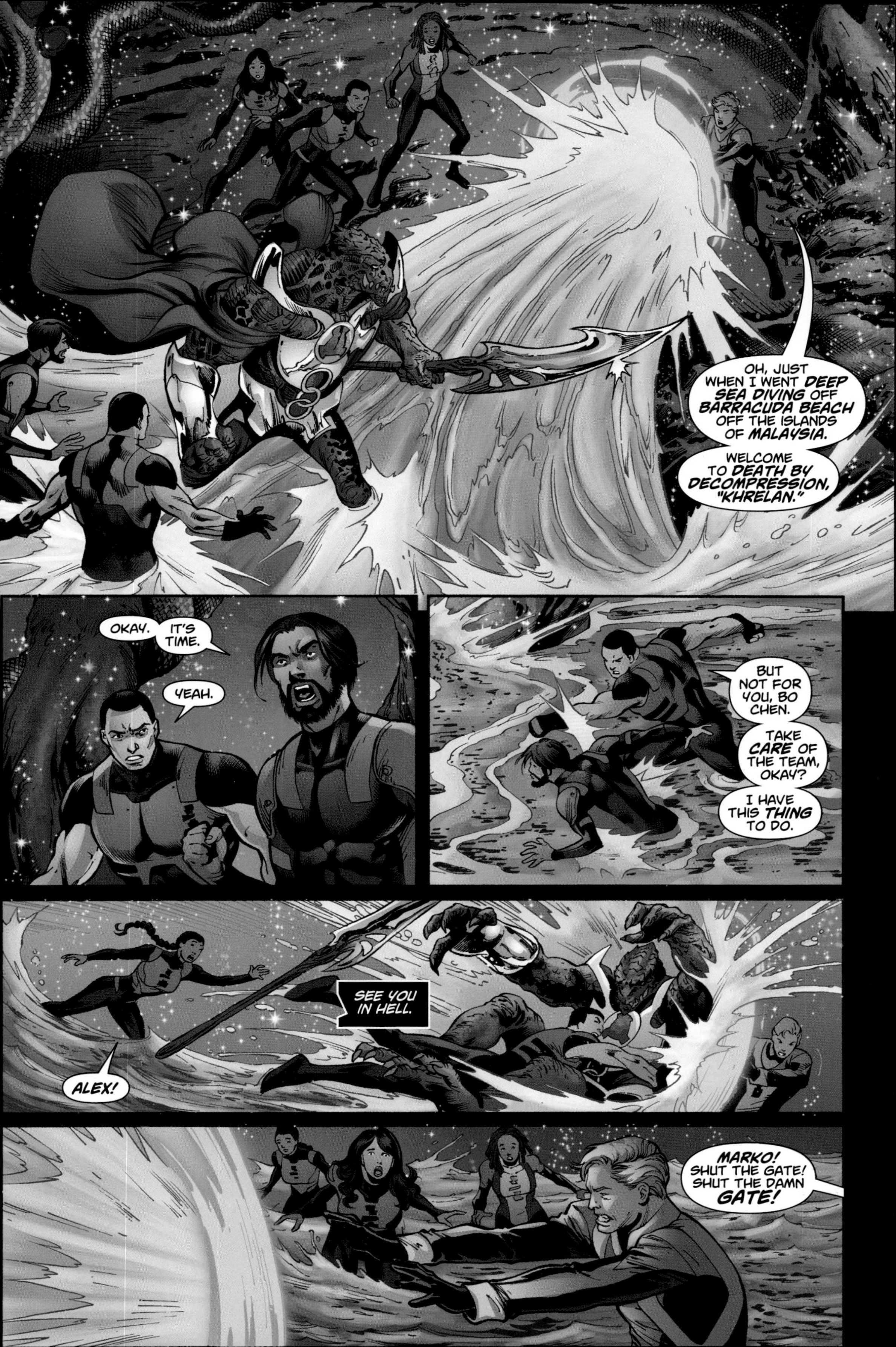
OH, JUST WHEN I WENT DEEP SEA DIVING OFF BARRACUDA BEACH OFF THE ISLANDS OF MALAYSIA.
WELCOME TO DEATH BY DECOMPRESSION, "KHRELAN."
OKAY. IT'S TIME.
YEAH.
BUT NOT FOR YOU, BO CHEN.
TAKE CARE OF THE TEAM, OKAY?
I HAVE THIS THING TO DO.
SEE YOU IN HELL.
ALEX!
MARKO! SHUT THE GATE! SHUT THE DAMN GATE!

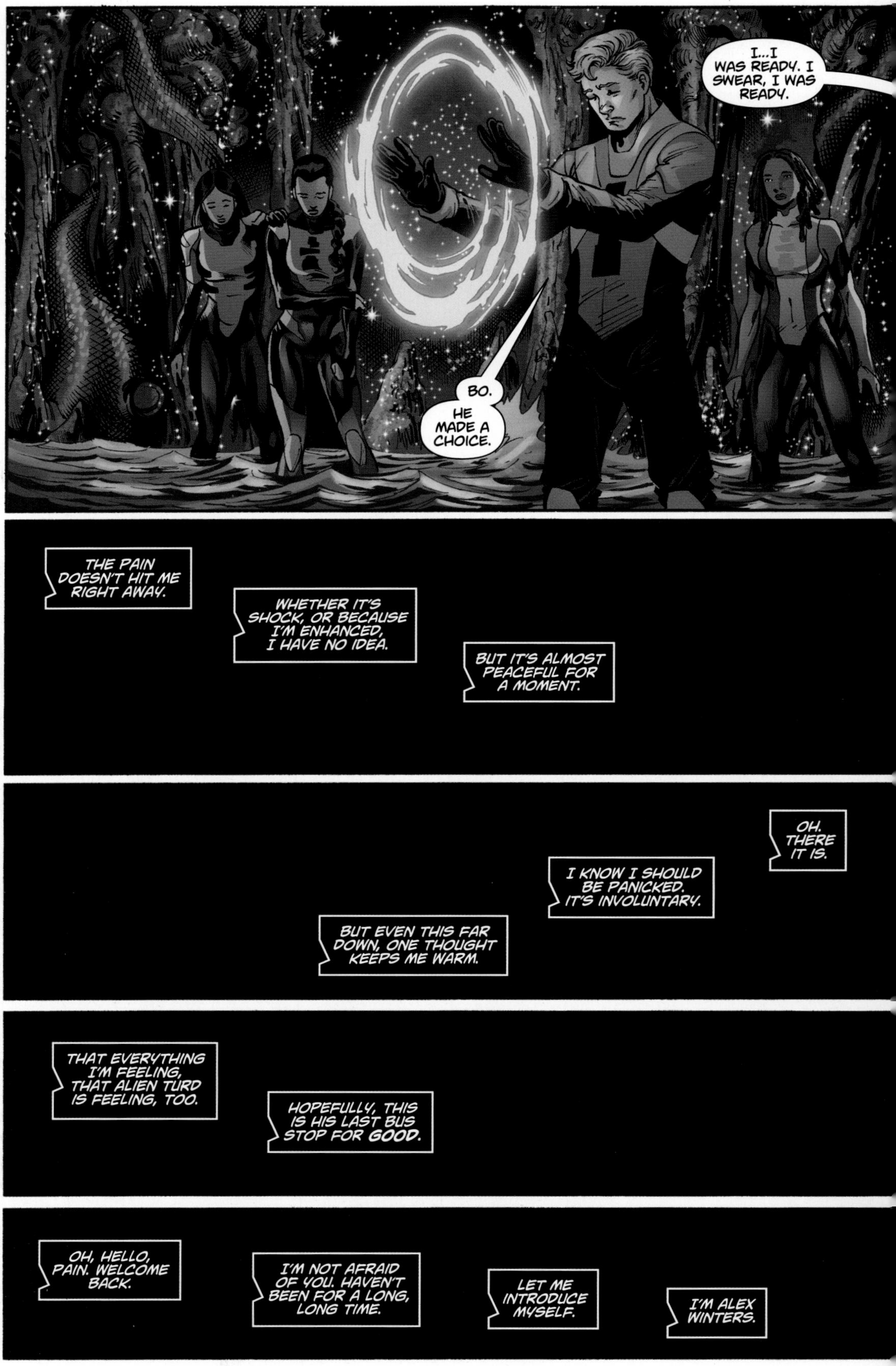
I...I WAS READY. I SWEAR, I WAS READY.
BO.
HE MADE A CHOICE.
THE PAIN DOESN'T HIT ME RIGHT AWAY.
WHETHER IT'S SHOCK, OR BECAUSE I'M ENHANCED, I HAVE NO IDEA.
BUT IT'S ALMOST PEACEFUL FOR A MOMENT.
OH. THERE IT IS.
I KNOW I SHOULD BE PANICKED. IT'S INVOLUNTARY.
BUT EVEN THIS FAR DOWN, ONE THOUGHT KEEPS ME WARM.
THAT EVERYTHING I'M FEELING, THAT ALIEN TURD IS FEELING, TOO.
HOPEFULLY, THIS IS HIS LAST BUS STOP FOR GOOD.
OH, HELLO, PAIN. WELCOME BACK.
I'M NOT AFRAID OF YOU. HAVEN'T BEEN FOR A LONG, LONG TIME.
LET ME INTRODUCE MYSELF.
I'M ALEX WINTERS.

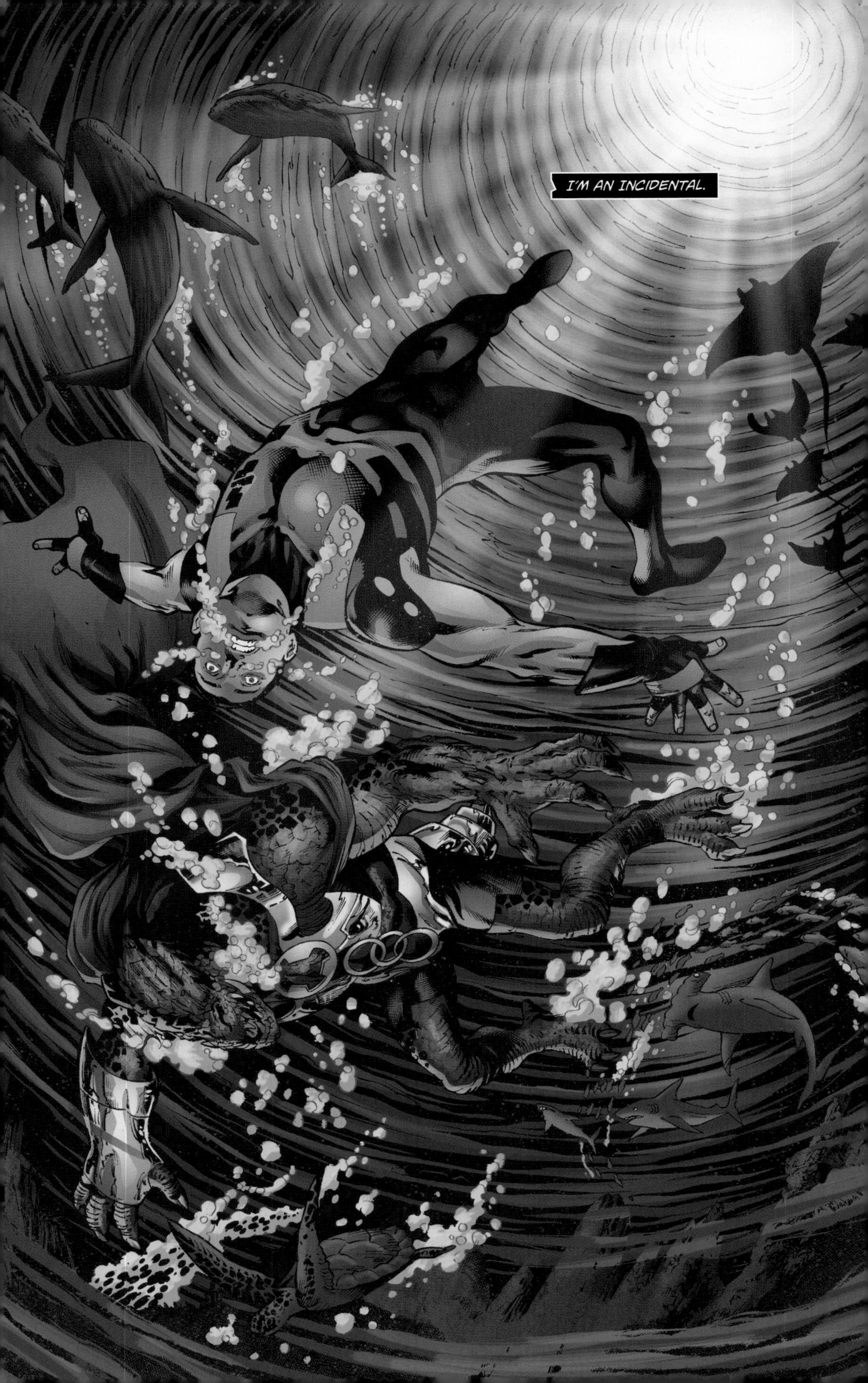
I'M AN INCIDENTAL.

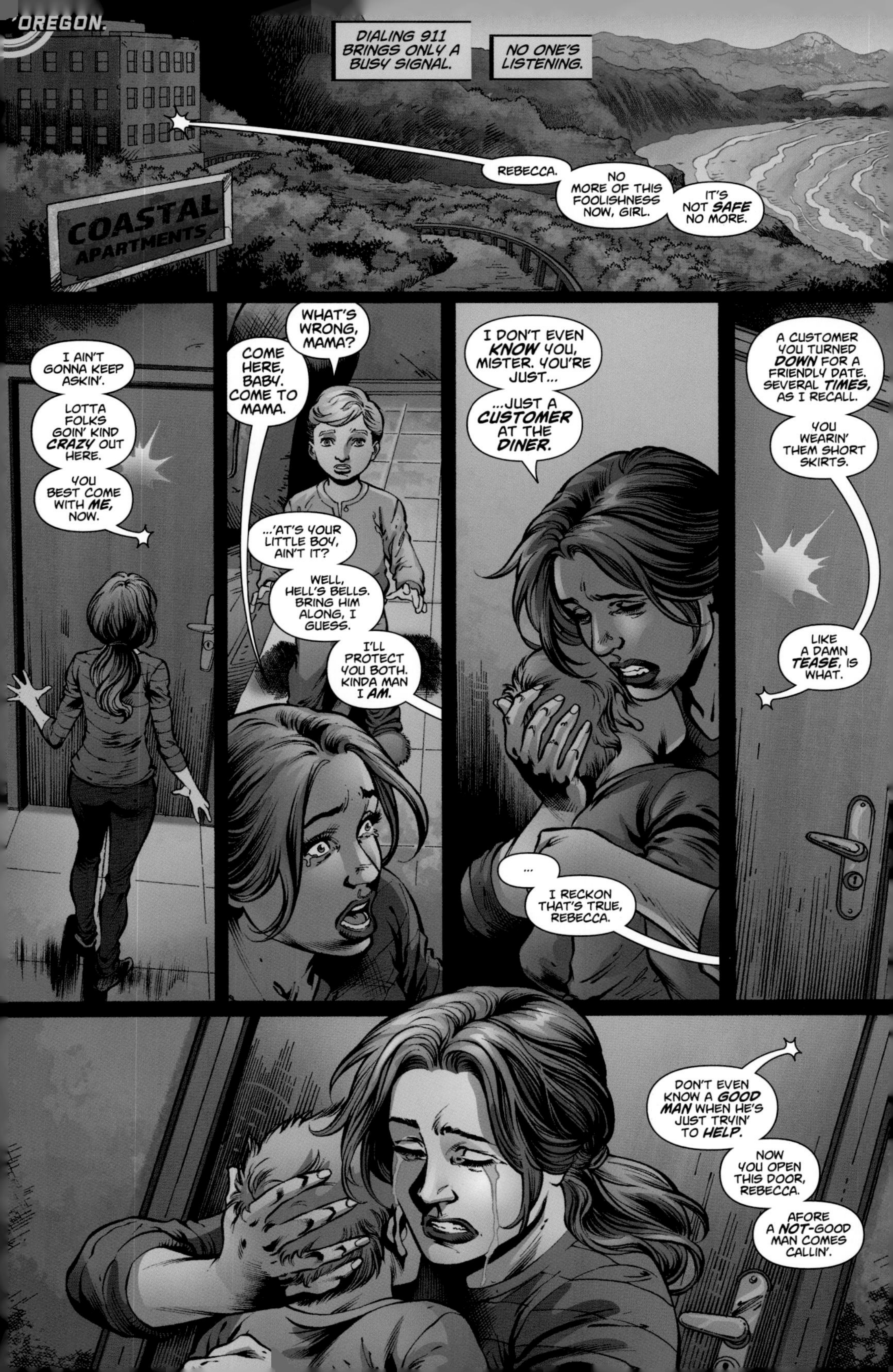
OREGON.
DIALING 911 BRINGS ONLY A BUSY SIGNAL.
NO ONE'S LISTENING.
COASTAL APARTMENTS
REBECCA.
NO MORE OF THIS FOOLISHNESS NOW, GIRL.
IT'S NOT SAFE NO MORE.
I AIN'T GONNA KEEP ASKIN'.
LOTTA FOLKS GOIN' KIND CRAZY OUT HERE.
YOU BEST COME WITH ME, NOW.
WHAT'S WRONG, MAMA?
COME HERE, BABY. COME TO MAMA.
...'AT'S YOUR LITTLE BOY, AIN'T IT?
WELL, HELL'S BELLS. BRING HIM ALONG, I GUESS.
I'LL PROTECT YOU BOTH. KINDA MAN I AM.
I DON'T EVEN KNOW YOU, MISTER. YOU'RE JUST...
...JUST A CUSTOMER AT THE DINER.
...
I RECKON THAT'S TRUE, REBECCA.
A CUSTOMER YOU TURNED DOWN FOR A FRIENDLY DATE. SEVERAL TIMES, AS I RECALL.
YOU WEARIN' THEM SHORT SKIRTS.
LIKE A DAMN TEASE, IS WHAT.
DON'T EVEN KNOW A GOOD MAN WHEN HE'S JUST TRYIN' TO HELP.
NOW YOU OPEN THIS DOOR, REBECCA.
AFORE A NOT-GOOD MAN COMES CALLIN'.

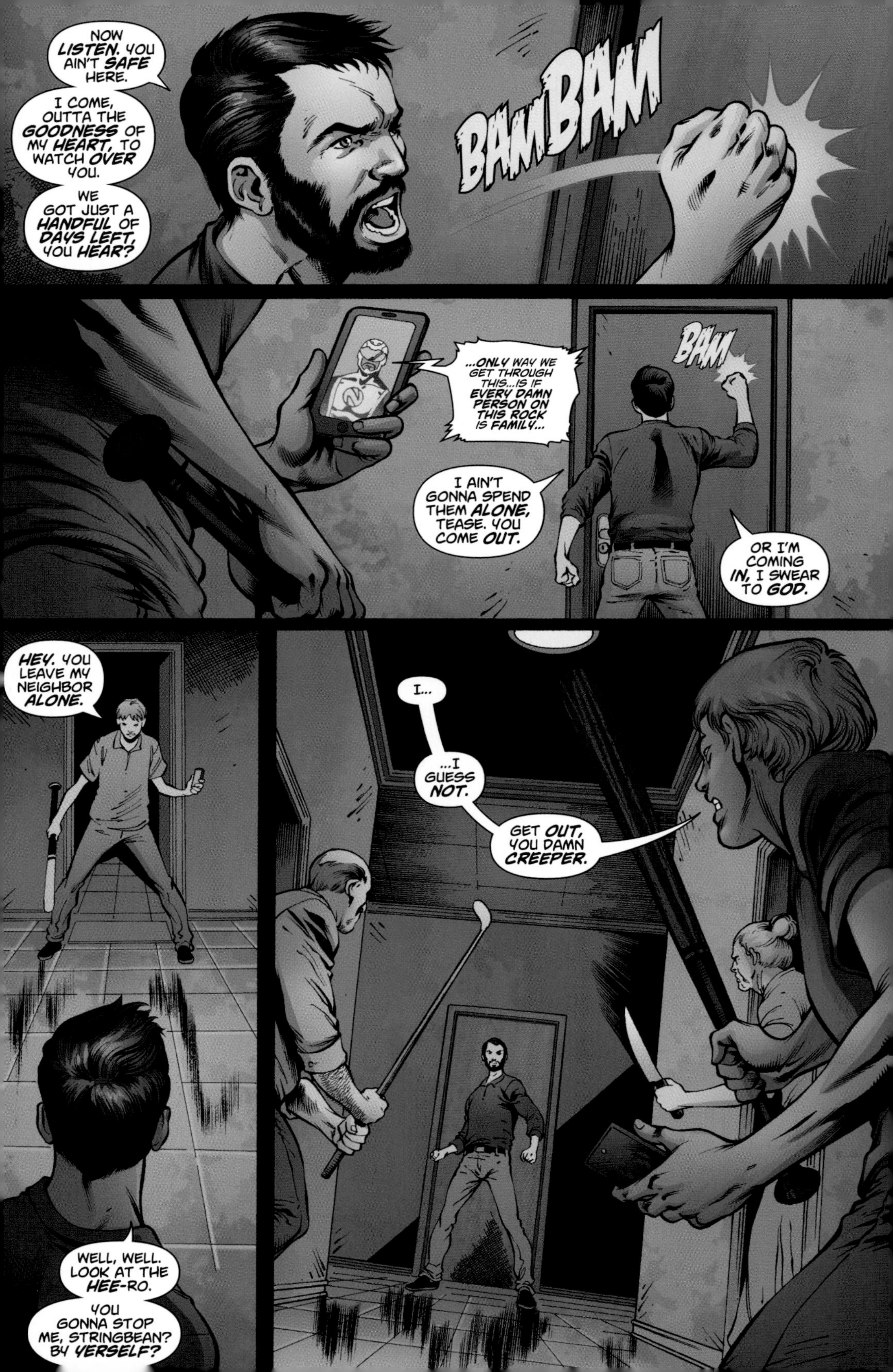
NOW LISTEN. YOU AIN'T SAFE HERE.
I COME, OUTTA THE GOODNESS OF MY HEART, TO WATCH OVER YOU.
WE GOT JUST A HANDFUL OF DAYS LEFT, YOU HEAR?
BAMBAM
...ONLY WAY WE GET THROUGH THIS...IS IF EVERY DAMN PERSON ON THIS ROCK IS FAMILY...
BAM
I AIN'T GONNA SPEND THEM ALONE, TEASE. YOU COME OUT.
OR I'M COMING IN, I SWEAR TO GOD.
HEY. YOU LEAVE MY NEIGHBOR ALONE.
WELL, WELL. LOOK AT THE HEE-RO.
YOU GONNA STOP ME, STRINGBEAN? BY YERSELF?
I...
...I GUESS NOT.
GET OUT, YOU DAMN CREEPER.

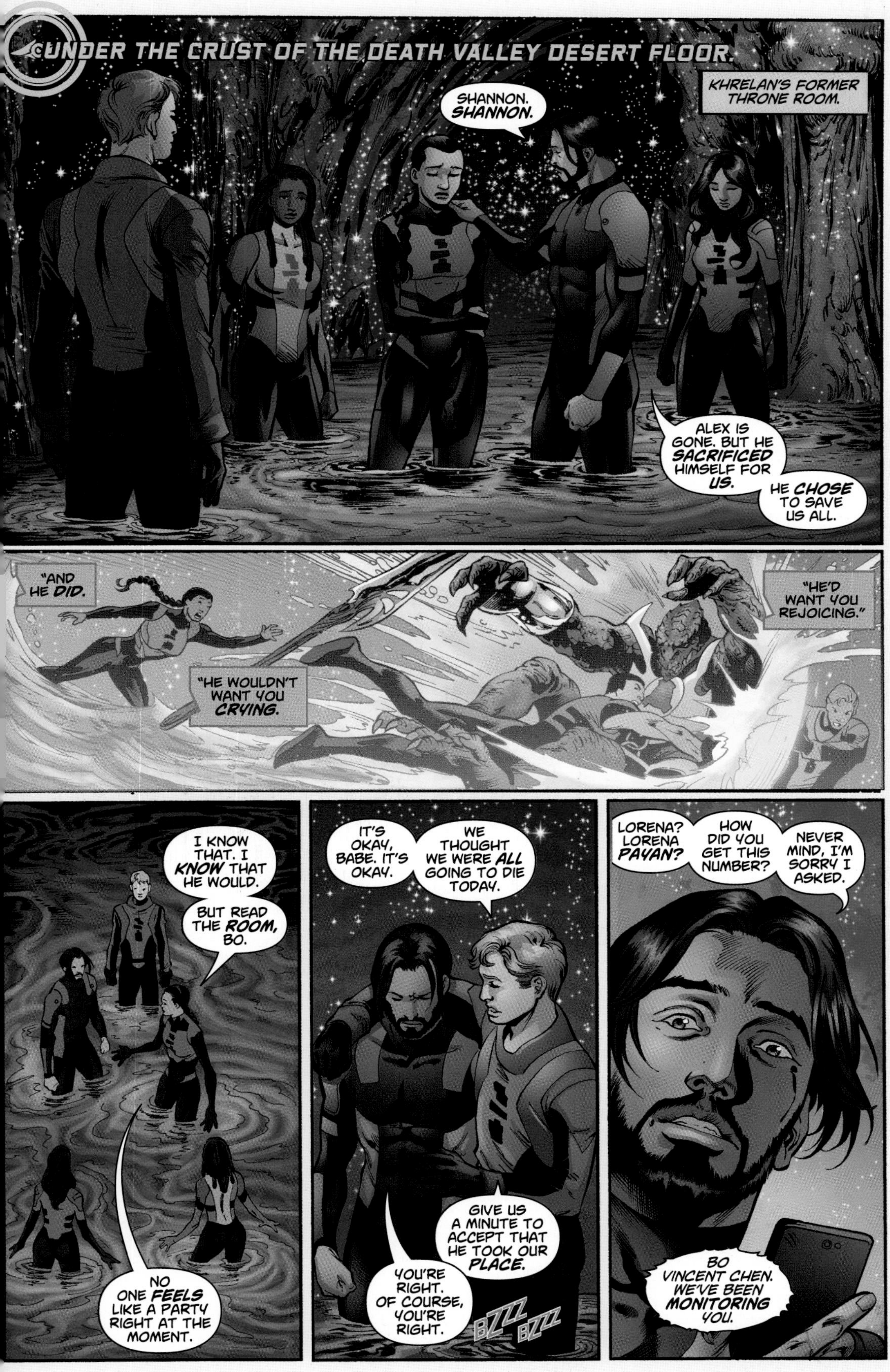
UNDER THE CRUST OF THE DEATH VALLEY DESERT FLOOR.
KHRELAN'S FORMER THRONE ROOM.
SHANNON. SHANNON.
ALEX IS GONE. BUT HE SACRIFICED HIMSELF FOR US.
HE CHOSE TO SAVE US ALL.
"AND HE DID.
"HE WOULDN'T WANT YOU CRYING.
"HE'D WANT YOU REJOICING."
I KNOW THAT. I KNOW THAT HE WOULD.
BUT READ THE ROOM, BO.
NO ONE FEELS LIKE A PARTY RIGHT AT THE MOMENT.
IT'S OKAY, BABE. IT'S OKAY.
WE THOUGHT WE WERE ALL GOING TO DIE TODAY.
GIVE US A MINUTE TO ACCEPT THAT HE TOOK OUR PLACE.
YOU'RE RIGHT. OF COURSE, YOU'RE RIGHT.
BZZZ BZZZ
LORENA? LORENA PAYAN?
HOW DID YOU GET THIS NUMBER?
NEVER MIND, I'M SORRY I ASKED.
BO VINCENT CHEN. WE'VE BEEN MONITORING YOU.

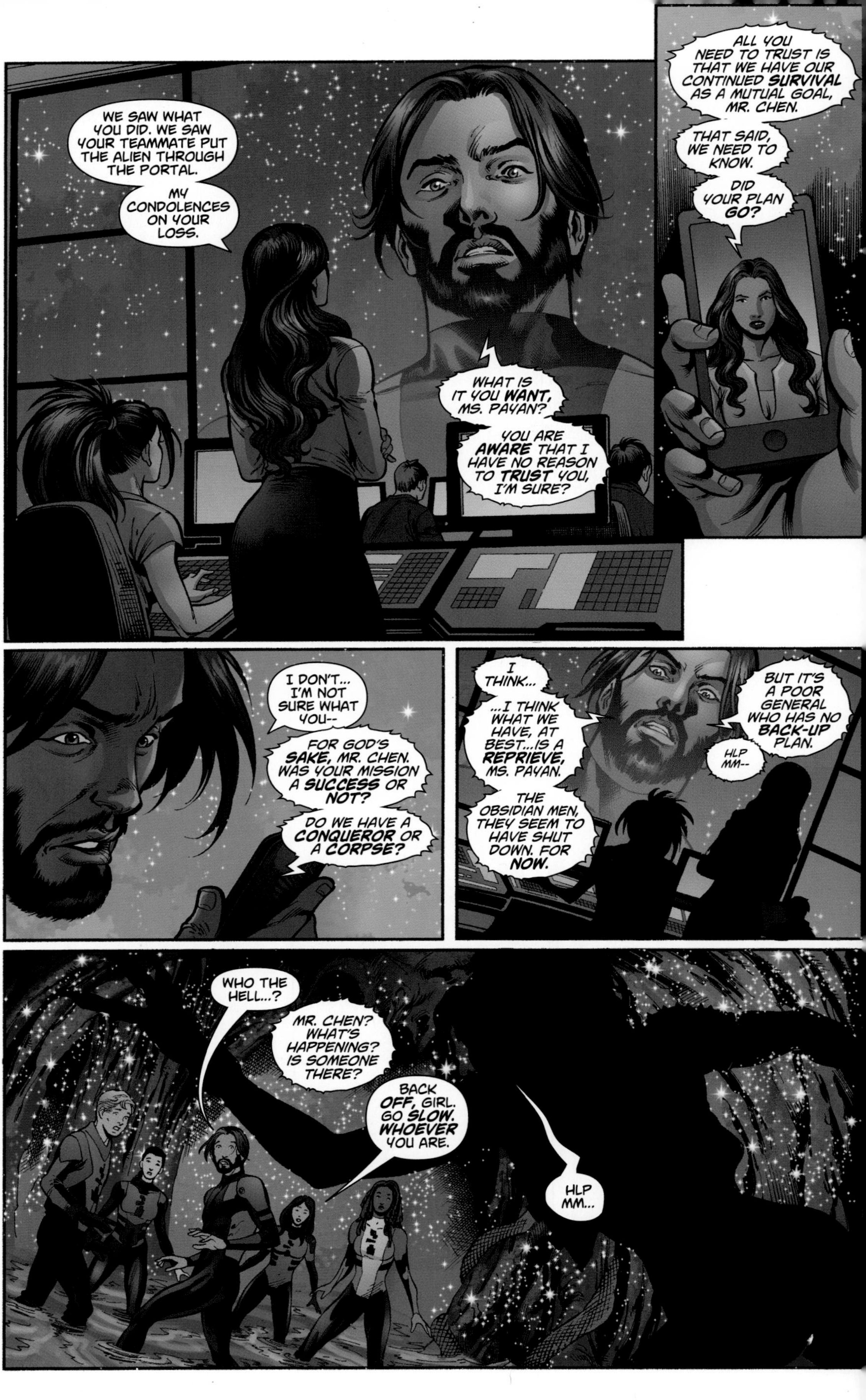
WE SAW WHAT YOU DID. WE SAW YOUR TEAMMATE PUT THE ALIEN THROUGH THE PORTAL.
MY CONDOLENCES ON YOUR LOSS.
WHAT IS IT YOU **WANT**, MS. PAYAN?
YOU ARE **AWARE** THAT I HAVE NO REASON TO **TRUST** YOU, I'M SURE?
ALL YOU NEED TO TRUST IS THAT WE HAVE OUR CONTINUED **SURVIVAL** AS A MUTUAL GOAL, MR. CHEN.
THAT SAID, WE NEED TO KNOW.
DID YOUR PLAN **GO?**
I DON'T... I'M NOT SURE WHAT YOU--
FOR GOD'S **SAKE**, MR. CHEN. WAS YOUR MISSION A **SUCCESS** OR **NOT?**
DO WE HAVE A **CONQUEROR** OR A **CORPSE?**
I THINK...
...I THINK WHAT WE HAVE, AT BEST...IS A **REPRIEVE**, MS. PAYAN.
THE OBSIDIAN MEN, THEY SEEM TO HAVE SHUT DOWN. FOR **NOW**.
BUT IT'S A POOR GENERAL WHO HAS NO **BACK-UP** PLAN.
HLP MM--
WHO THE HELL...?
MR. CHEN? WHAT'S HAPPENING? IS SOMEONE THERE?
BACK **OFF**, GIRL. GO **SLOW**. **WHOEVER** YOU ARE.
HLP MM...

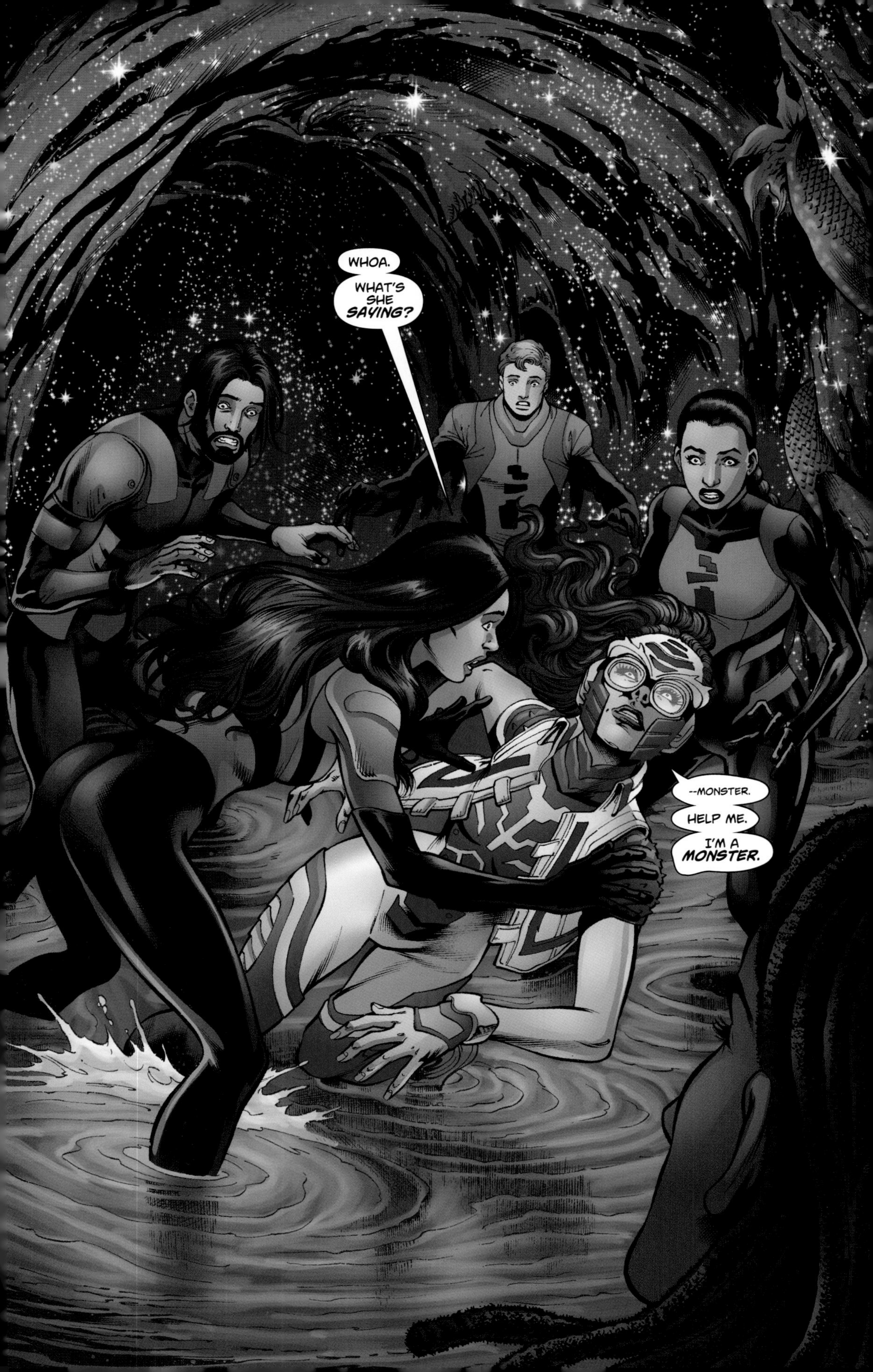
WHOA.
WHAT'S SHE SAYING?
--MONSTER.
HELP ME.
I'M A MONSTER.

DAY FIVE.

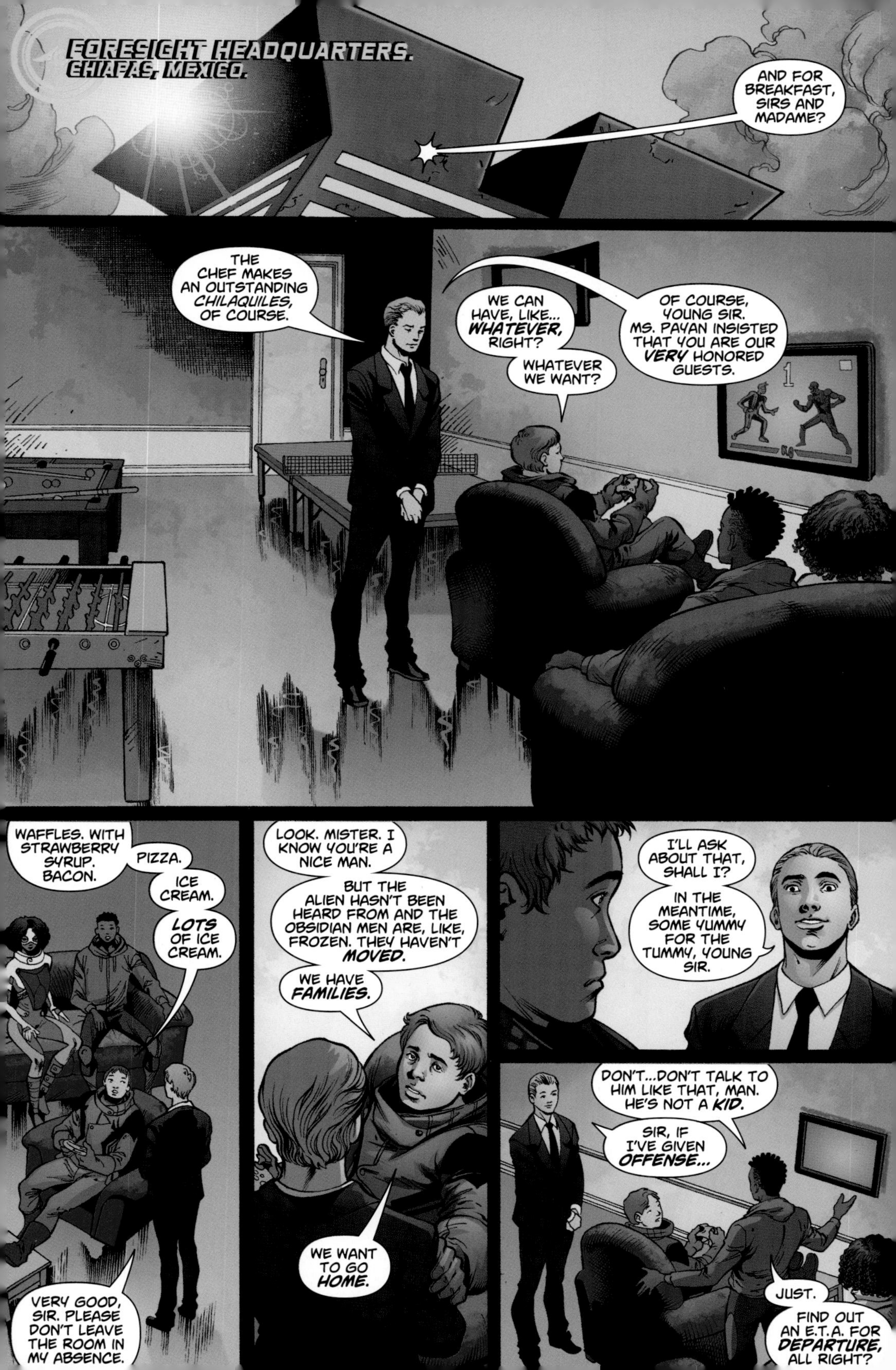
FORESIGHT HEADQUARTERS.
CHIAPAS, MEXICO.
AND FOR BREAKFAST, SIRS AND MADAME?
THE CHEF MAKES AN OUTSTANDING CHILAQUILES, OF COURSE.
WE CAN HAVE, LIKE... WHATEVER, RIGHT?
WHATEVER WE WANT?
OF COURSE, YOUNG SIR. MS. PAYAN INSISTED THAT YOU ARE OUR VERY HONORED GUESTS.
WAFFLES. WITH STRAWBERRY SYRUP. BACON.
PIZZA.
ICE CREAM.
LOTS OF ICE CREAM.
VERY GOOD, SIR. PLEASE DON'T LEAVE THE ROOM IN MY ABSENCE.
LOOK. MISTER. I KNOW YOU'RE A NICE MAN.
BUT THE ALIEN HASN'T BEEN HEARD FROM AND THE OBSIDIAN MEN ARE, LIKE, FROZEN. THEY HAVEN'T MOVED.
WE HAVE FAMILIES.
WE WANT TO GO HOME.
I'LL ASK ABOUT THAT, SHALL I?
IN THE MEANTIME, SOME YUMMY FOR THE TUMMY, YOUNG SIR.
DON'T...DON'T TALK TO HIM LIKE THAT, MAN. HE'S NOT A KID.
SIR, IF I'VE GIVEN OFFENSE...
JUST.
FIND OUT AN E.T.A. FOR DEPARTURE, ALL RIGHT?

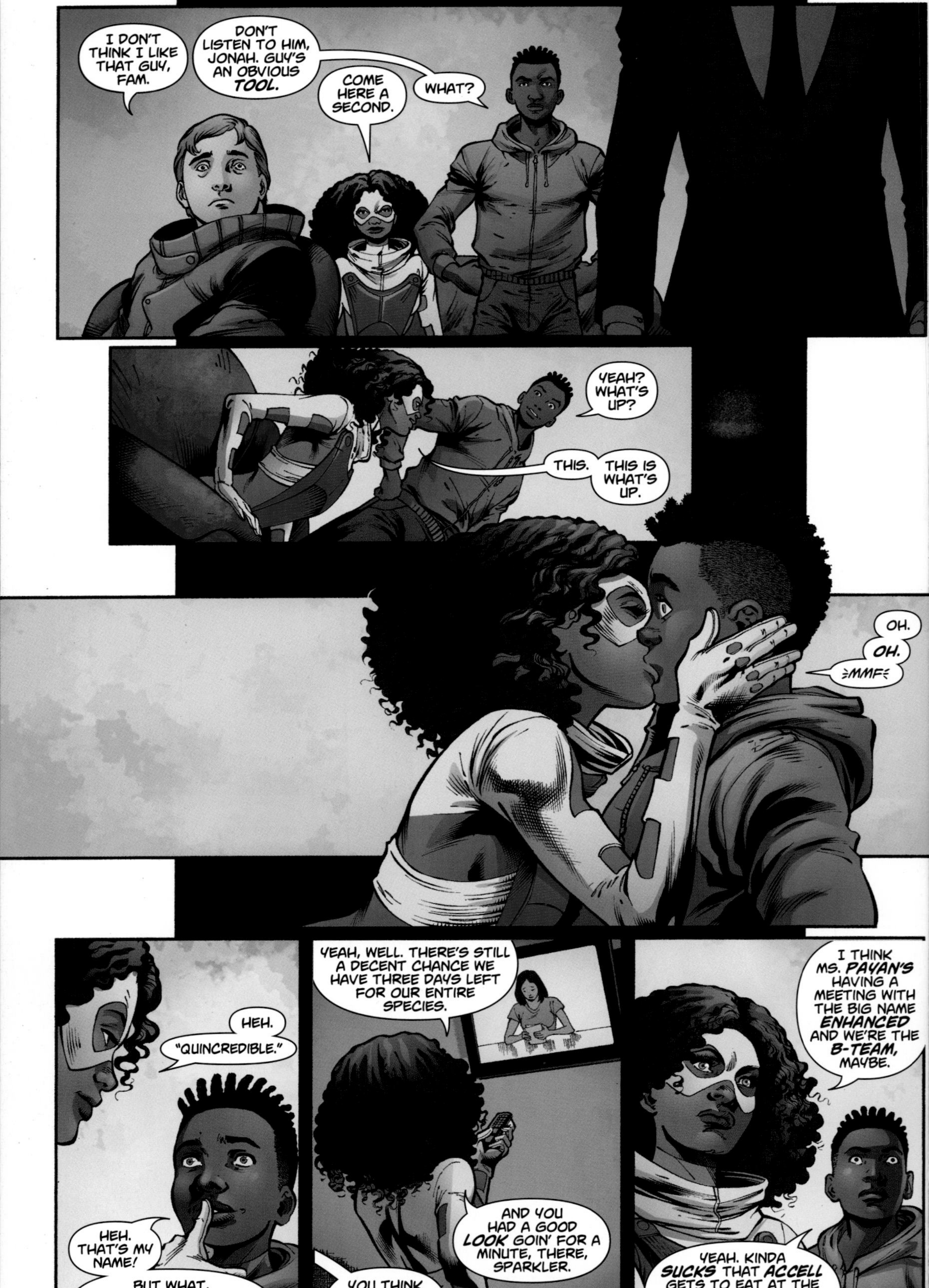
I DON'T THINK I LIKE THAT GUY, FAM.
DON'T LISTEN TO HIM, JONAH. GUY'S AN OBVIOUS TOOL.
WHAT?
COME HERE A SECOND.
YEAH? WHAT'S UP?
THIS. THIS IS WHAT'S UP.
OH.
OH.
MMF
HEH. "QUINCREDIBLE."
HEH. THAT'S MY NAME!
BUT WHAT, AMINA, YOU DIDN'T EVEN WANNA KNOW THE WHOLE TIME WE'VE BEEN HERE!
YEAH, WELL. THERE'S STILL A DECENT CHANCE WE HAVE THREE DAYS LEFT FOR OUR ENTIRE SPECIES.
AND YOU HAD A GOOD LOOK GOIN' FOR A MINUTE, THERE, SPARKLER.
YOU THINK IT'S STILL ON WITH THE LIZARD MAN?
I THINK MS. PAYAN'S HAVING A MEETING WITH THE BIG NAME ENHANCED AND WE'RE THE B-TEAM, MAYBE.
YEAH. KINDA SUCKS THAT ACCELL GETS TO EAT AT THE ADULT TABLE AND WE'RE STUCK IN HERE, TOO, AM I RIGHT?

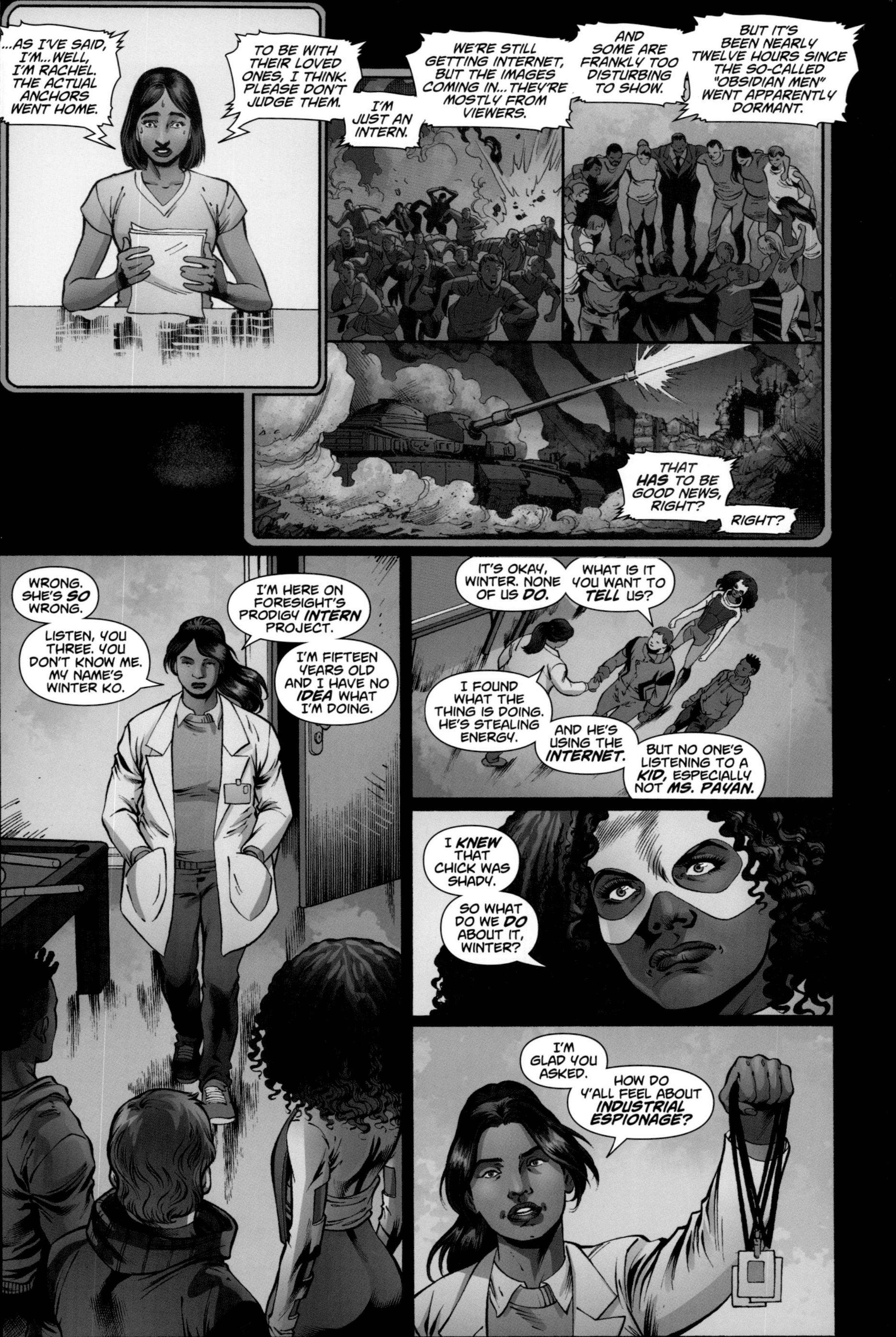
...AS I'VE SAID, I'M... WELL, I'M RACHEL. THE ACTUAL ANCHORS WENT HOME.
TO BE WITH THEIR LOVED ONES, I THINK. PLEASE DON'T JUDGE THEM.
I'M JUST AN INTERN.
WE'RE STILL GETTING INTERNET, BUT THE IMAGES COMING IN... THEY'RE MOSTLY FROM VIEWERS.
AND SOME ARE FRANKLY TOO DISTURBING TO SHOW.
BUT IT'S BEEN NEARLY TWELVE HOURS SINCE THE SO-CALLED "OBSIDIAN MEN" WENT APPARENTLY DORMANT.
THAT HAS TO BE GOOD NEWS, RIGHT?
RIGHT?
WRONG. SHE'S SO WRONG.
LISTEN, YOU THREE. YOU DON'T KNOW ME. MY NAME'S WINTER KO.
I'M HERE ON FORESIGHT'S PRODIGY INTERN PROJECT.
I'M FIFTEEN YEARS OLD AND I HAVE NO IDEA WHAT I'M DOING.
IT'S OKAY, WINTER. NONE OF US DO.
WHAT IS IT YOU WANT TO TELL US?
I FOUND WHAT THE THING IS DOING. HE'S STEALING ENERGY.
AND HE'S USING THE INTERNET.
BUT NO ONE'S LISTENING TO A KID, ESPECIALLY NOT MS. PAYAN.
I KNEW THAT CHICK WAS SHADY.
SO WHAT DO WE DO ABOUT IT, WINTER?
I'M GLAD YOU ASKED.
HOW DO Y'ALL FEEL ABOUT INDUSTRIAL ESPIONAGE?

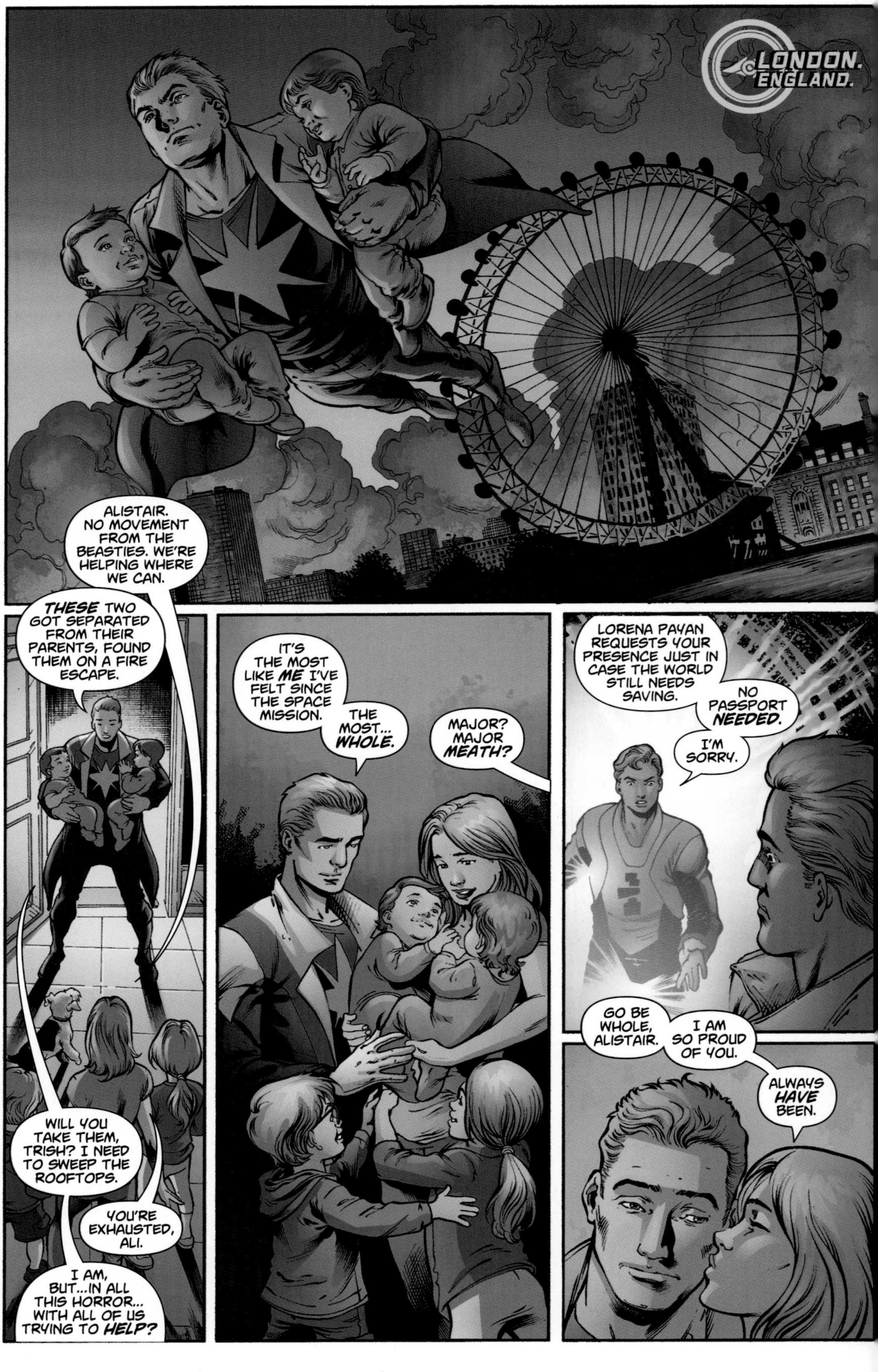
LONDON. ENGLAND.
ALISTAIR. NO MOVEMENT FROM THE BEASTIES. WE'RE HELPING WHERE WE CAN.
THESE TWO GOT SEPARATED FROM THEIR PARENTS, FOUND THEM ON A FIRE ESCAPE.
WILL YOU TAKE THEM, TRISH? I NEED TO SWEEP THE ROOFTOPS.
YOU'RE EXHAUSTED, ALI.
I AM, BUT...IN ALL THIS HORROR... WITH ALL OF US TRYING TO HELP?
IT'S THE MOST LIKE ME I'VE FELT SINCE THE SPACE MISSION.
THE MOST... WHOLE.
MAJOR? MAJOR MEATH?
LORENA PAYAN REQUESTS YOUR PRESENCE JUST IN CASE THE WORLD STILL NEEDS SAVING.
NO PASSPORT NEEDED.
I'M SORRY.
GO BE WHOLE, ALISTAIR.
I AM SO PROUD OF YOU.
ALWAYS HAVE BEEN.

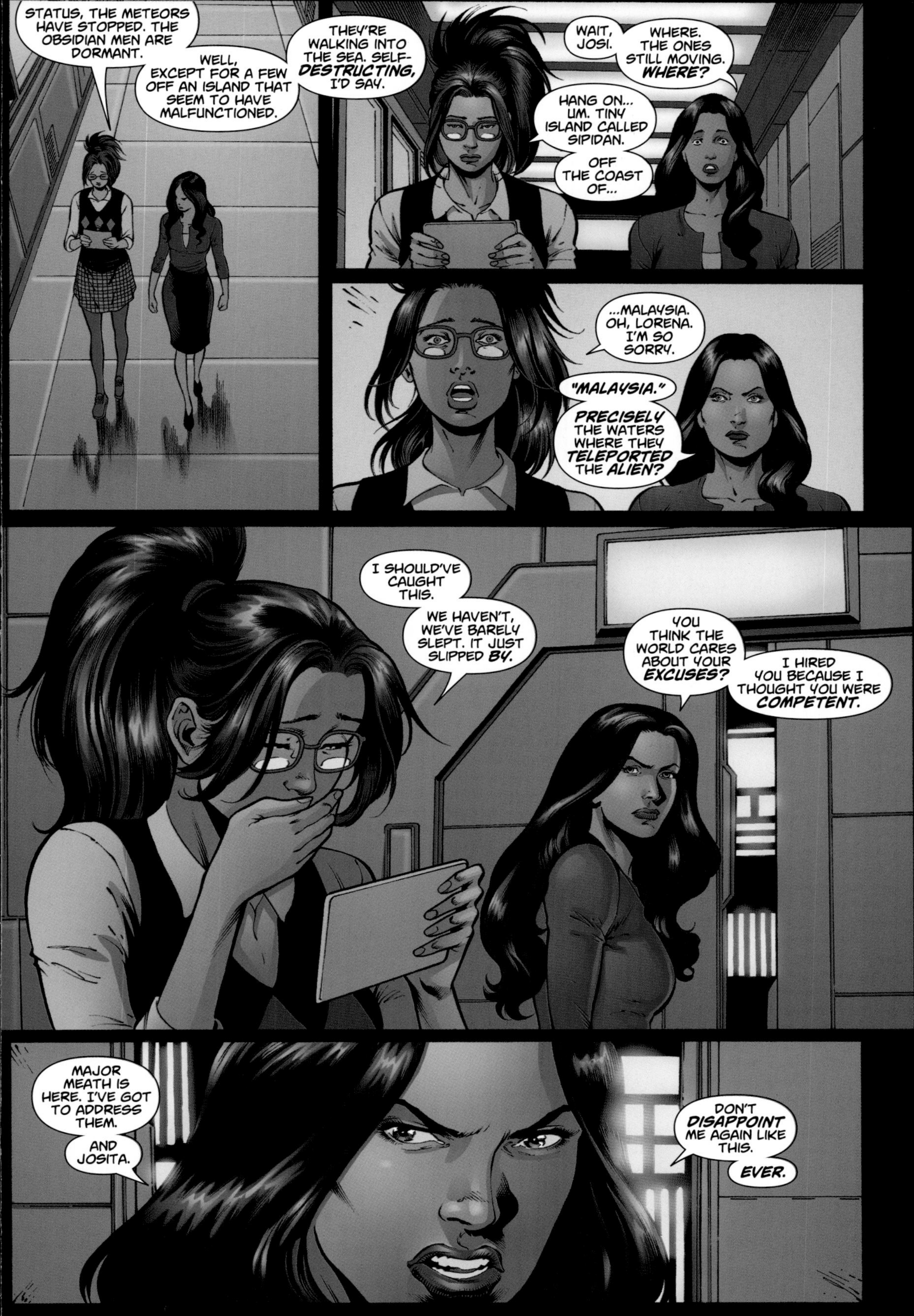
STATUS, THE METEORS HAVE STOPPED. THE OBSIDIAN MEN ARE DORMANT.
WELL, EXCEPT FOR A FEW OFF AN ISLAND THAT SEEM TO HAVE MALFUNCTIONED.
THEY'RE WALKING INTO THE SEA. SELF-DESTRUCTING, I'D SAY.
WAIT, JOSI.
WHERE. THE ONES STILL MOVING. WHERE?
HANG ON... UM. TINY ISLAND CALLED SIPIDAN.
OFF THE COAST OF...
...MALAYSIA. OH, LORENA. I'M SO SORRY.
"MALAYSIA."
PRECISELY THE WATERS WHERE THEY TELEPORTED THE ALIEN?
I SHOULD'VE CAUGHT THIS.
WE HAVEN'T, WE'VE BARELY SLEPT. IT JUST SLIPPED BY.
YOU THINK THE WORLD CARES ABOUT YOUR EXCUSES?
I HIRED YOU BECAUSE I THOUGHT YOU WERE COMPETENT.
MAJOR MEATH IS HERE. I'VE GOT TO ADDRESS THEM.
AND JOSITA.
DON'T DISAPPOINT ME AGAIN LIKE THIS.
EVER.

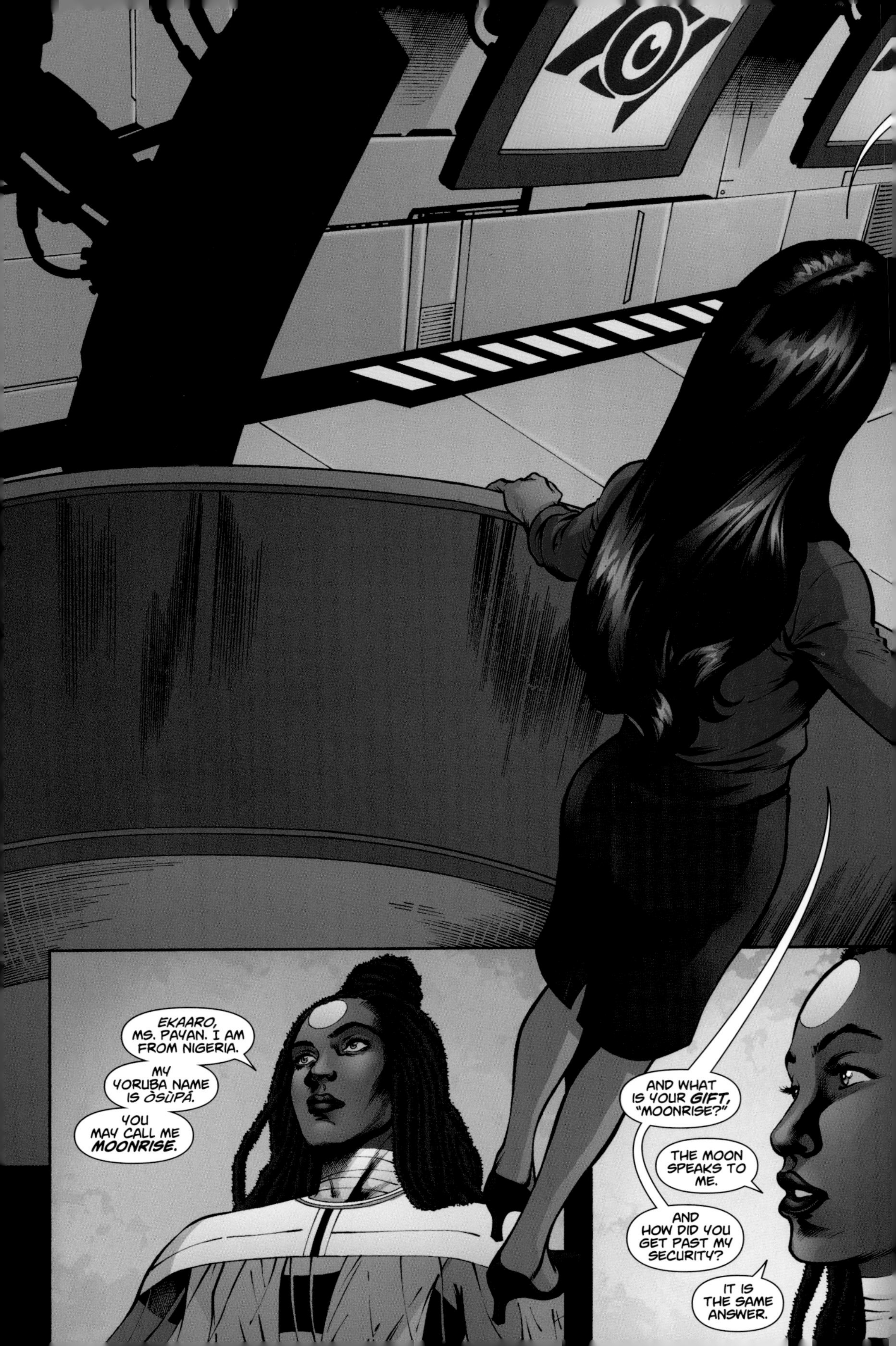
EKAARO, MS. PAYAN. I AM FROM NIGERIA.
MY YORUBA NAME IS ÒSÙPÁ.
YOU MAY CALL ME MOONRISE.
AND WHAT IS YOUR GIFT, "MOONRISE?"
THE MOON SPEAKS TO ME.
AND HOW DID YOU GET PAST MY SECURITY?
IT IS THE SAME ANSWER.

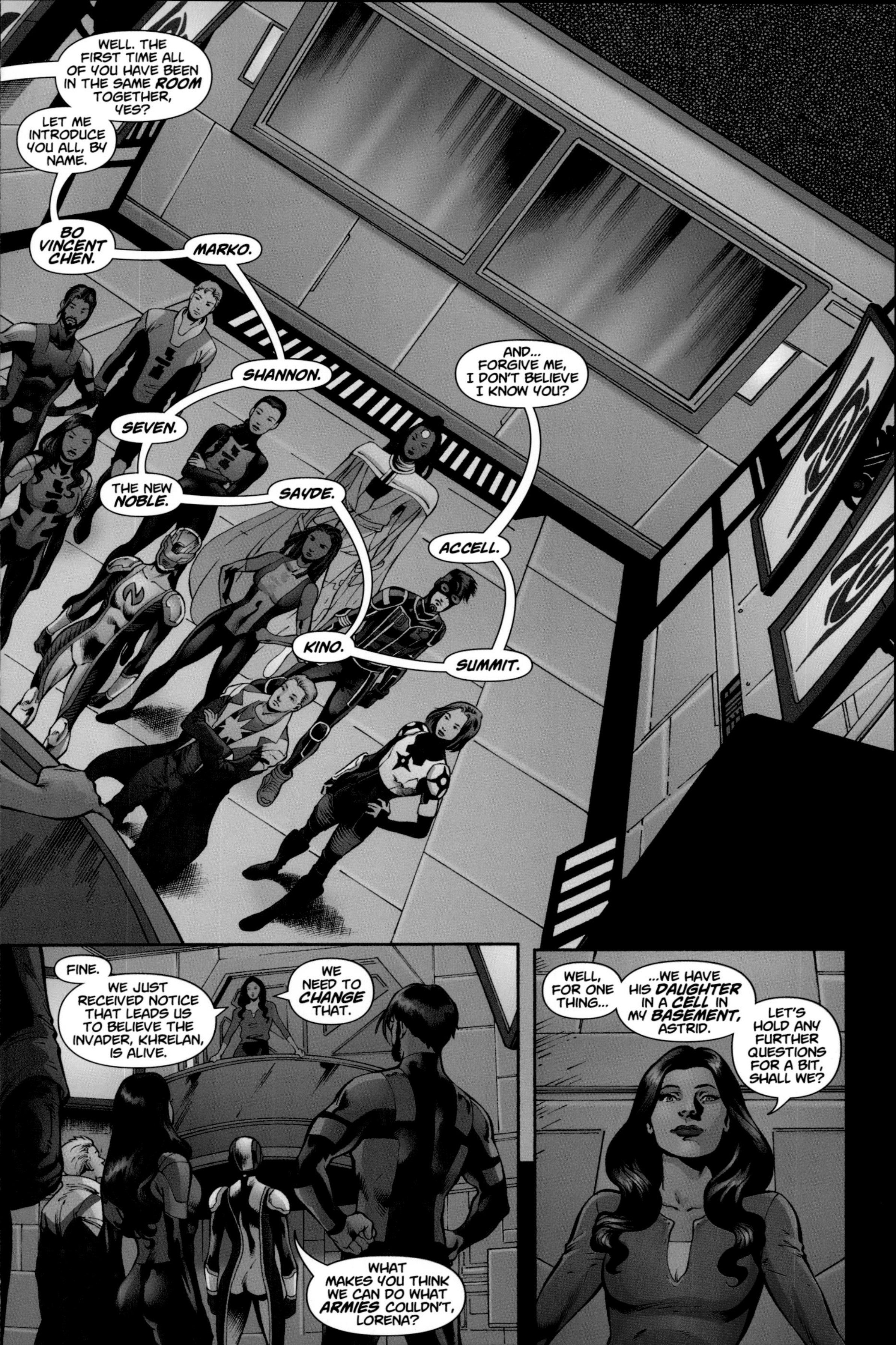
WELL. THE FIRST TIME ALL OF YOU HAVE BEEN IN THE SAME ROOM TOGETHER, YES?
LET ME INTRODUCE YOU ALL, BY NAME.
BO VINCENT CHEN.
MARKO.
SHANNON.
SEVEN.
THE NEW NOBLE.
SAYDE.
KINO.
SUMMIT.
ACCELL.
AND... FORGIVE ME, I DON'T BELIEVE I KNOW YOU?
FINE.
WE JUST RECEIVED NOTICE THAT LEADS US TO BELIEVE THE INVADER, KHRELAN, IS ALIVE.
WE NEED TO CHANGE THAT.
WHAT MAKES YOU THINK WE CAN DO WHAT ARMIES COULDN'T, LORENA?
WELL, FOR ONE THING...
...WE HAVE HIS DAUGHTER IN A CELL IN MY BASEMENT, ASTRID.
LET'S HOLD ANY FURTHER QUESTIONS FOR A BIT, SHALL WE?

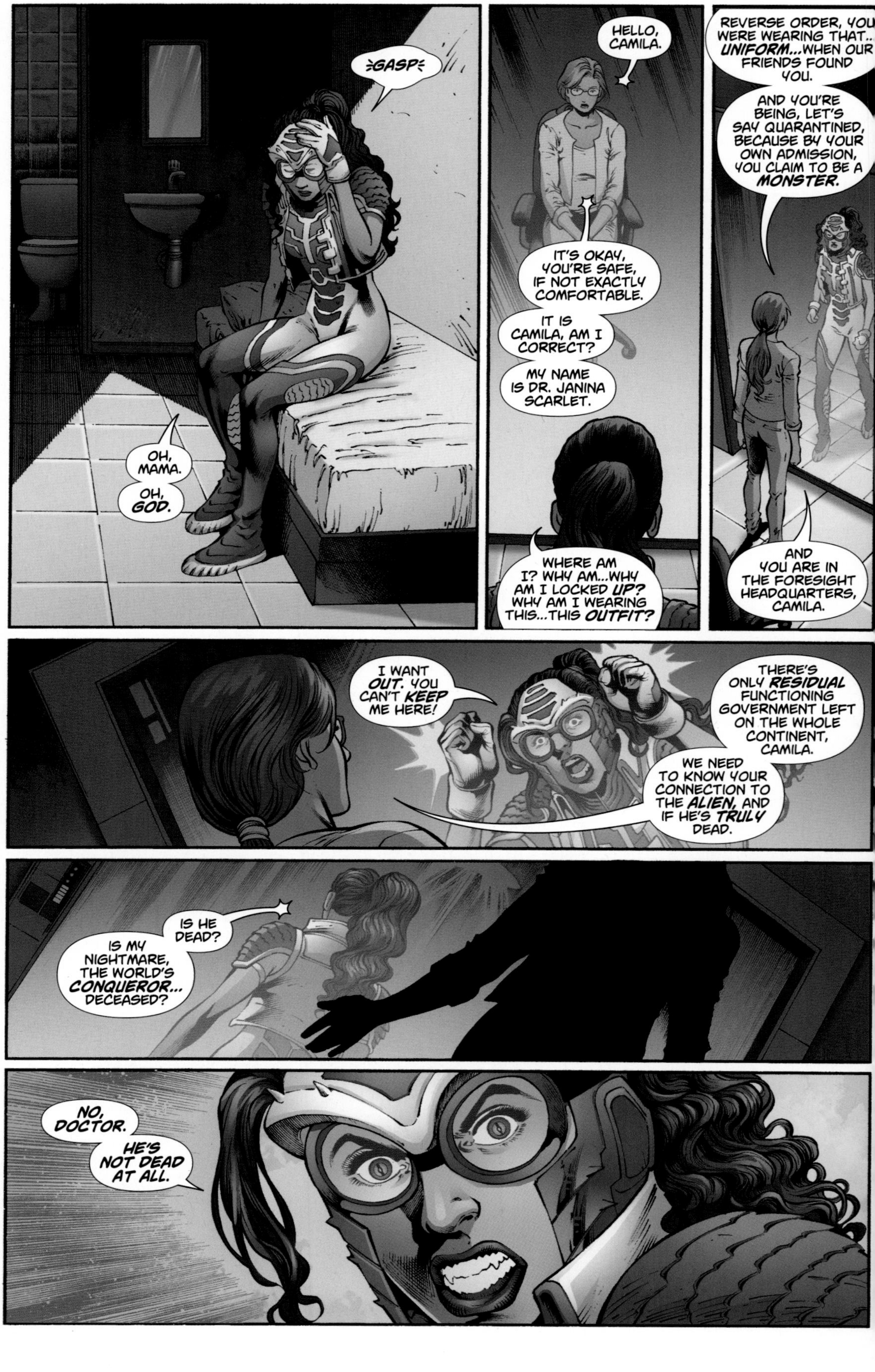

GASP
OH, MAMA.
OH, GOD.
HELLO, CAMILA.
IT'S OKAY, YOU'RE SAFE, IF NOT EXACTLY COMFORTABLE.
IT IS CAMILA, AM I CORRECT?
MY NAME IS DR. JANINA SCARLET.
WHERE AM I? WHY AM...WHY AM I LOCKED UP? WHY AM I WEARING THIS...THIS OUTFIT?
REVERSE ORDER, YOU WERE WEARING THAT... UNIFORM...WHEN OUR FRIENDS FOUND YOU.
AND YOU'RE BEING, LET'S SAY QUARANTINED, BECAUSE BY YOUR OWN ADMISSION, YOU CLAIM TO BE A MONSTER.
AND YOU ARE IN THE FORESIGHT HEADQUARTERS, CAMILA.
I WANT OUT. YOU CAN'T KEEP ME HERE!
THERE'S ONLY RESIDUAL FUNCTIONING GOVERNMENT LEFT ON THE WHOLE CONTINENT, CAMILA.
WE NEED TO KNOW YOUR CONNECTION TO THE ALIEN, AND IF HE'S TRULY DEAD.
IS HE DEAD?
IS MY NIGHTMARE, THE WORLD'S CONQUEROR... DECEASED?
NO, DOCTOR.
HE'S NOT DEAD AT ALL.

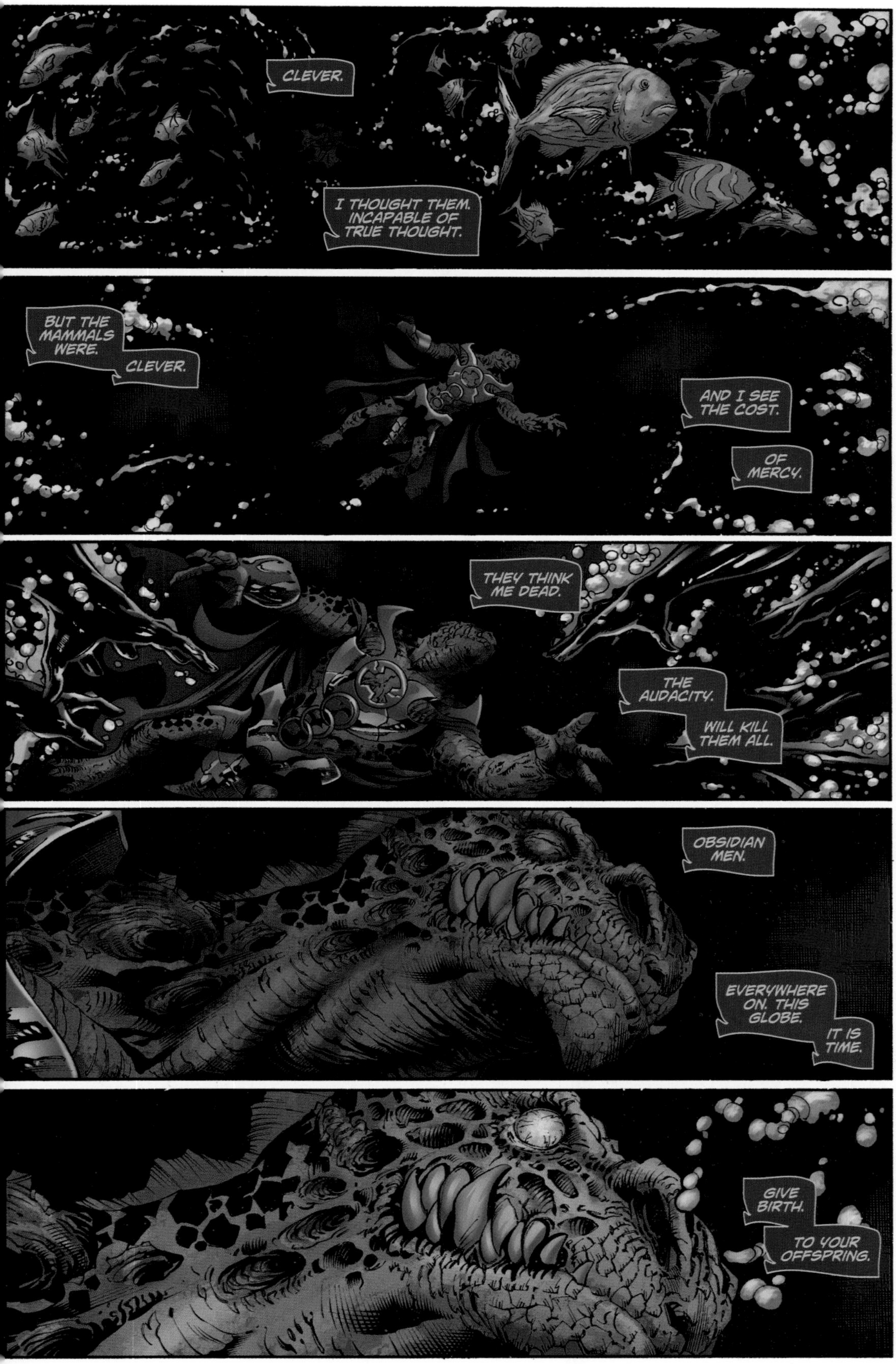
CLEVER.
I THOUGHT THEM. INCAPABLE OF TRUE THOUGHT.
BUT THE MAMMALS WERE.
CLEVER.
AND I SEE THE COST.
OF MERCY.
THEY THINK ME DEAD.
THE AUDACITY.
WILL KILL THEM ALL.
OBSIDIAN MEN.
EVERYWHERE ON. THIS GLOBE.
IT IS TIME.
GIVE BIRTH.
TO YOUR OFFSPRING.

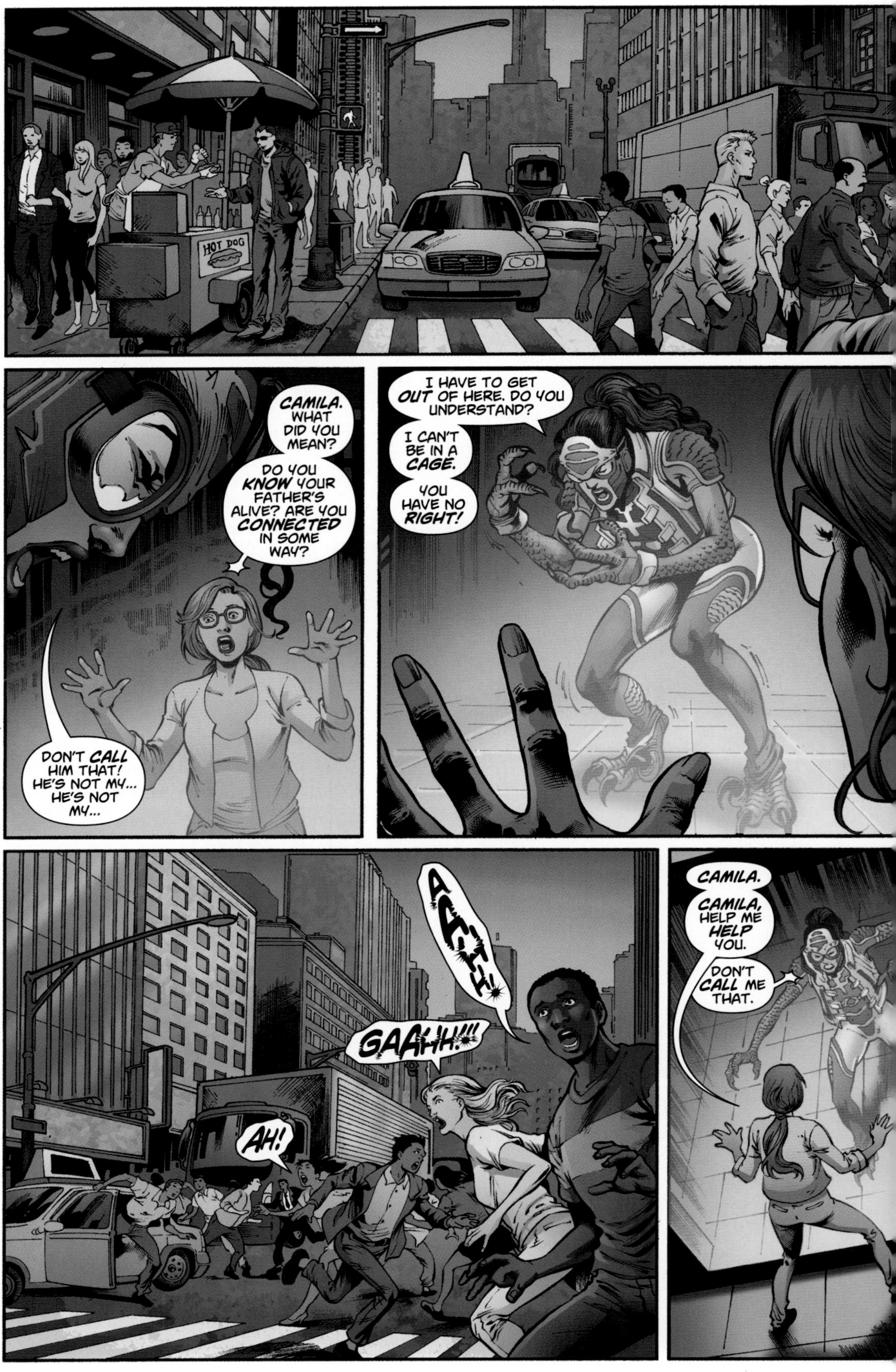
CAMILA. WHAT DID YOU MEAN?
DO YOU KNOW YOUR FATHER'S ALIVE? ARE YOU CONNECTED IN SOME WAY?
DON'T CALL HIM THAT! HE'S NOT MY... HE'S NOT MY...
I HAVE TO GET OUT OF HERE. DO YOU UNDERSTAND?
I CAN'T BE IN A CAGE.
YOU HAVE NO RIGHT!
AAHH!
GAAHH!!
AH!
CAMILA.
CAMILA, HELP ME HELP YOU.
DON'T CALL ME THAT.

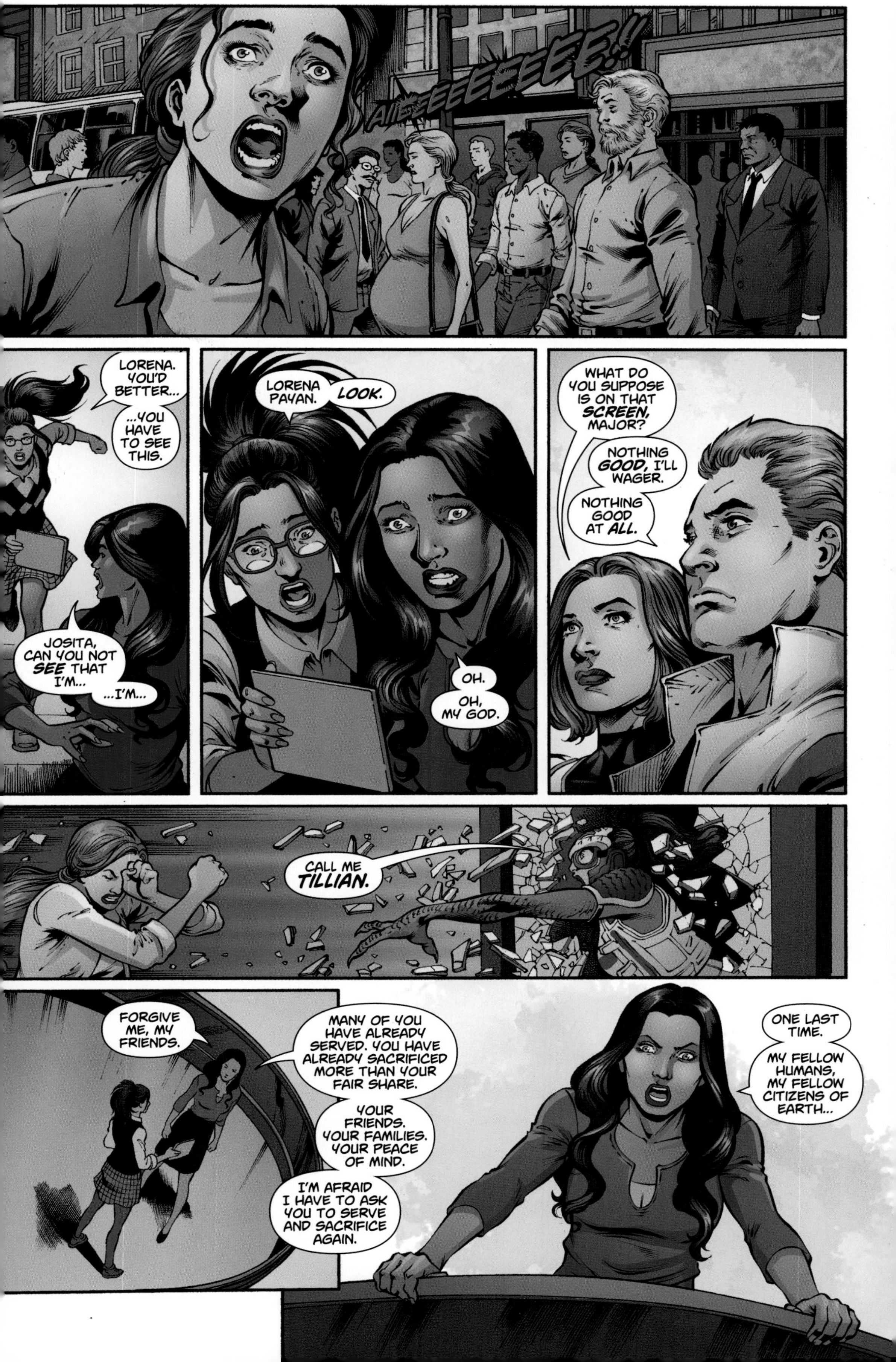
AIIEEEEEEEEEE!!
LORENA. YOU'D BETTER...
...YOU HAVE TO SEE THIS.
JOSITA, CAN YOU NOT SEE THAT I'M...
...I'M...
LORENA PAYAN.
LOOK.
OH.
OH, MY GOD.
WHAT DO YOU SUPPOSE IS ON THAT SCREEN, MAJOR?
NOTHING GOOD, I'LL WAGER.
NOTHING GOOD AT ALL.
CALL ME TILLIAN.
FORGIVE ME, MY FRIENDS.
MANY OF YOU HAVE ALREADY SERVED. YOU HAVE ALREADY SACRIFICED MORE THAN YOUR FAIR SHARE.
YOUR FRIENDS. YOUR FAMILIES. YOUR PEACE OF MIND.
I'M AFRAID I HAVE TO ASK YOU TO SERVE AND SACRIFICE AGAIN.
ONE LAST TIME.
MY FELLOW HUMANS, MY FELLOW CITIZENS OF EARTH...

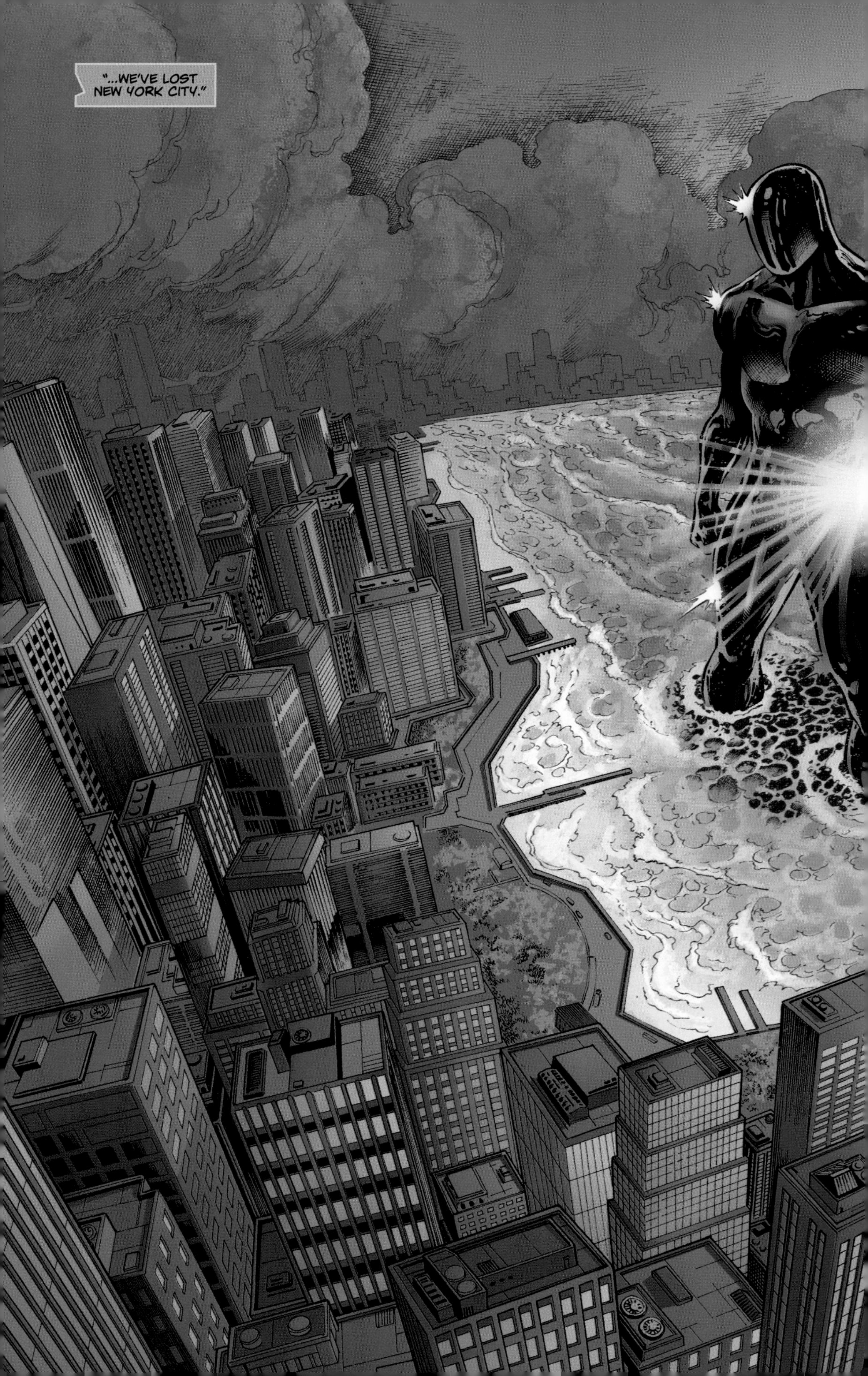
"...WE'VE LOST NEW YORK CITY."

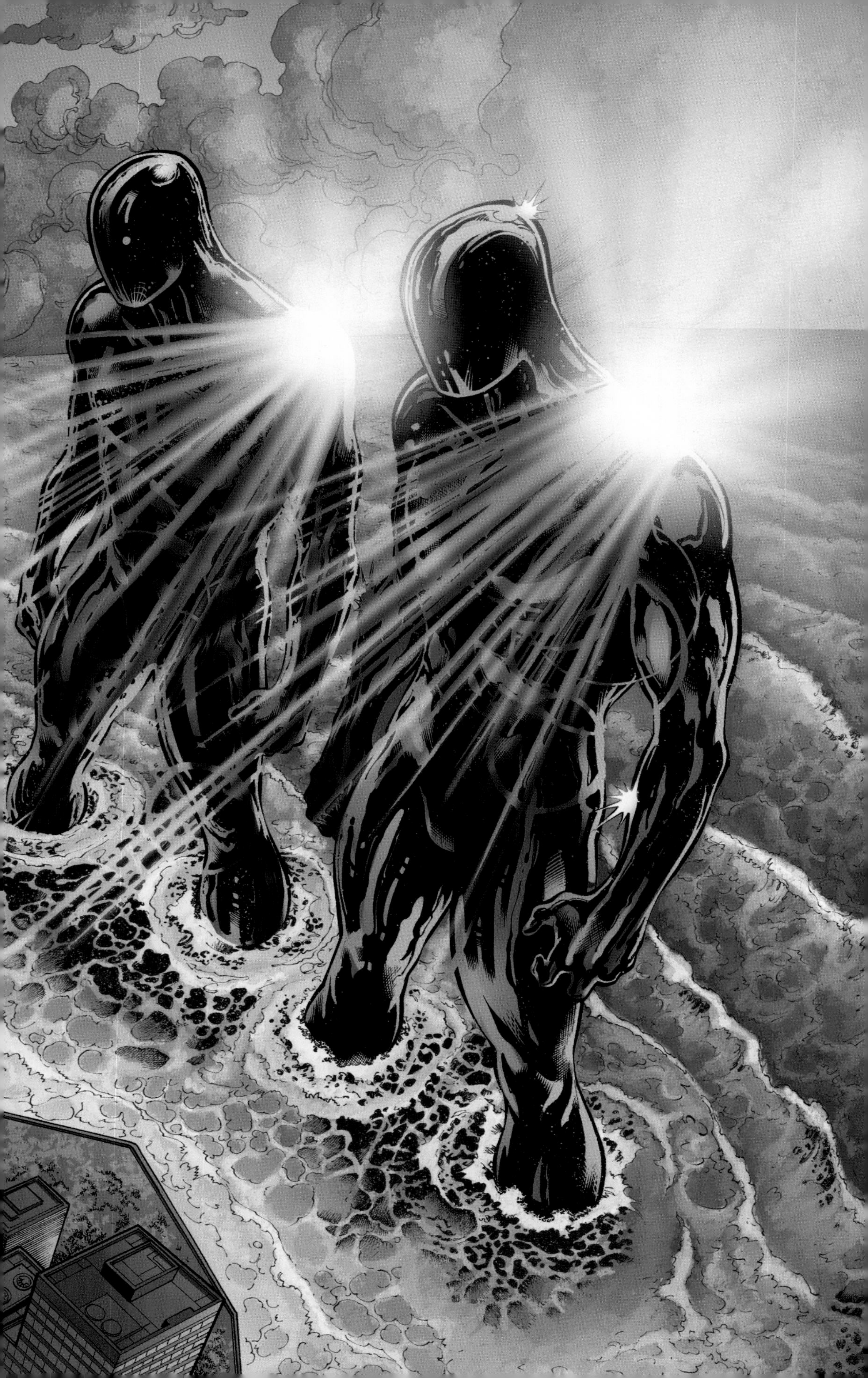

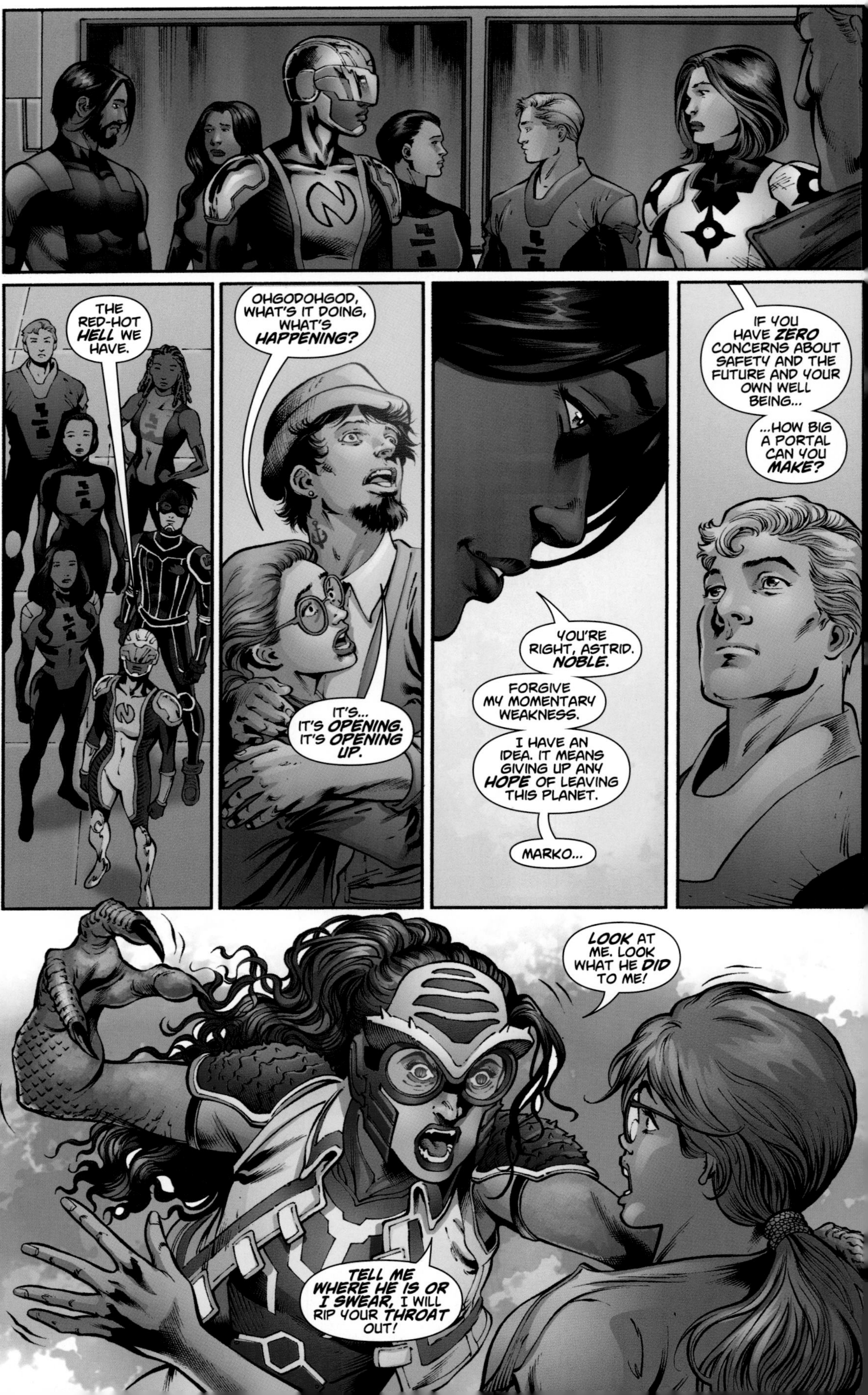
THE RED-HOT HELL WE HAVE.
OHGODOHGOD, WHAT'S IT DOING, WHAT'S HAPPENING?
IT'S... IT'S OPENING. IT'S OPENING UP.
YOU'RE RIGHT, ASTRID. NOBLE.
FORGIVE MY MOMENTARY WEAKNESS.
I HAVE AN IDEA. IT MEANS GIVING UP ANY HOPE OF LEAVING THIS PLANET.
MARKO...
IF YOU HAVE ZERO CONCERNS ABOUT SAFETY AND THE FUTURE AND YOUR OWN WELL BEING...
...HOW BIG A PORTAL CAN YOU MAKE?
LOOK AT ME. LOOK WHAT HE DID TO ME!
TELL ME WHERE HE IS OR I SWEAR, I WILL RIP YOUR THROAT OUT!

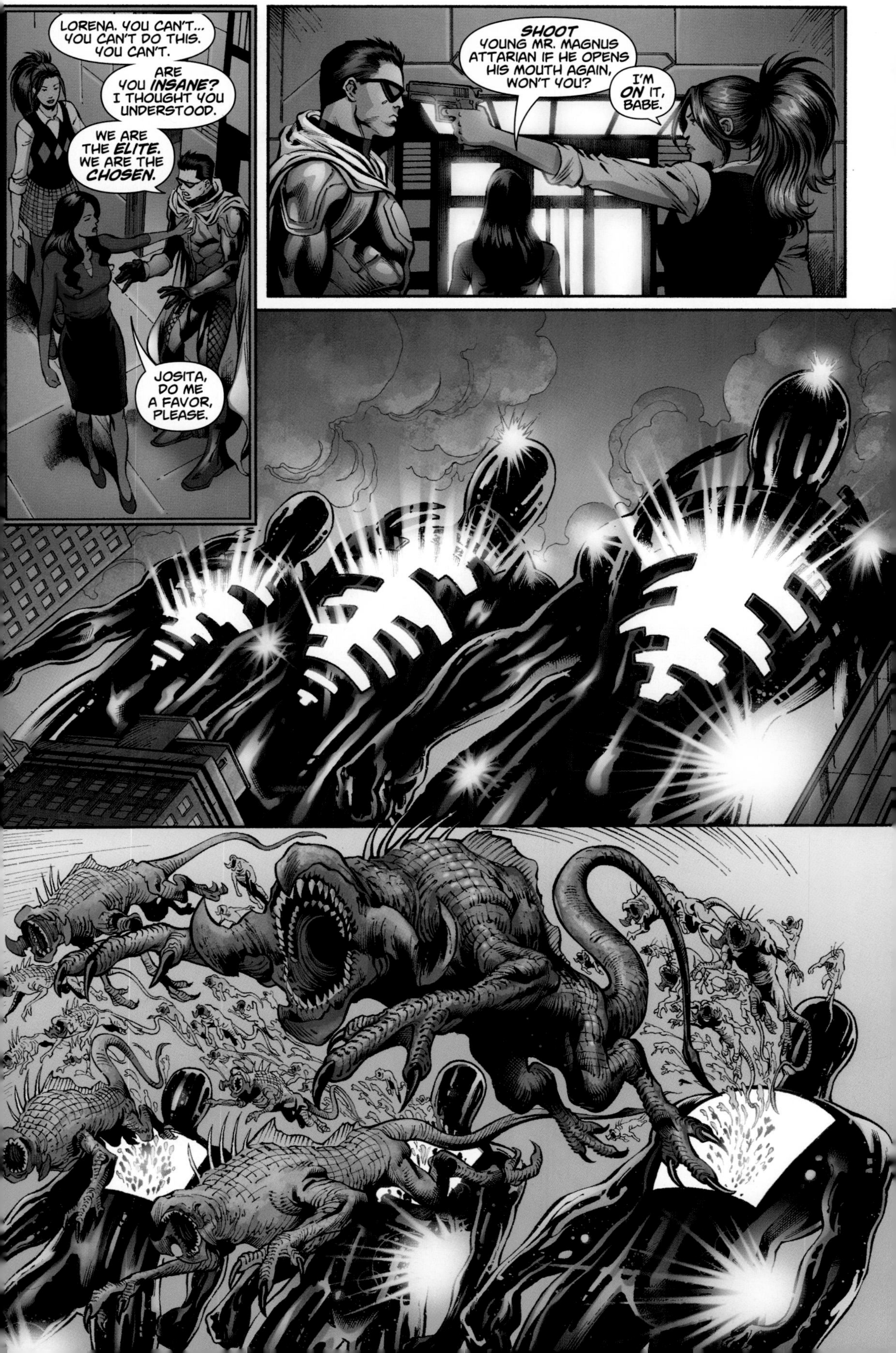
LORENA. YOU CAN'T... YOU CAN'T DO THIS. YOU CAN'T.
ARE YOU INSANE? I THOUGHT YOU UNDERSTOOD.
WE ARE THE ELITE. WE ARE THE CHOSEN.
JOSITA, DO ME A FAVOR, PLEASE.
SHOOT YOUNG MR. MAGNUS ATTARIAN IF HE OPENS HIS MOUTH AGAIN, WON'T YOU?
I'M ON IT, BABE.

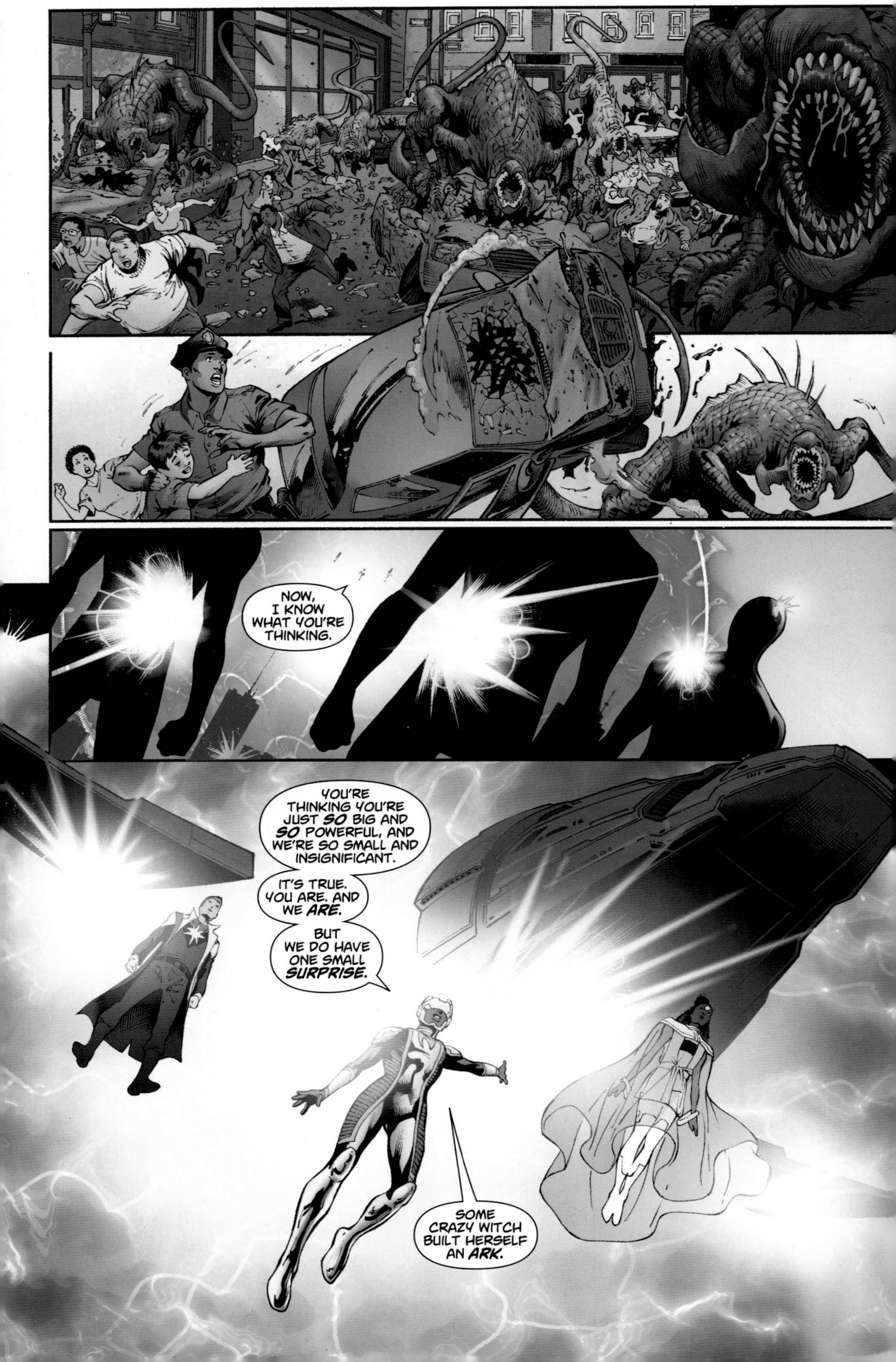
NOW, I KNOW WHAT YOU'RE THINKING.
YOU'RE THINKING YOU'RE JUST SO BIG AND SO POWERFUL, AND WE'RE SO SMALL AND INSIGNIFICANT.
IT'S TRUE. YOU ARE. AND WE ARE.
BUT WE DO HAVE ONE SMALL SURPRISE.
SOME CRAZY WITCH BUILT HERSELF AN ARK.

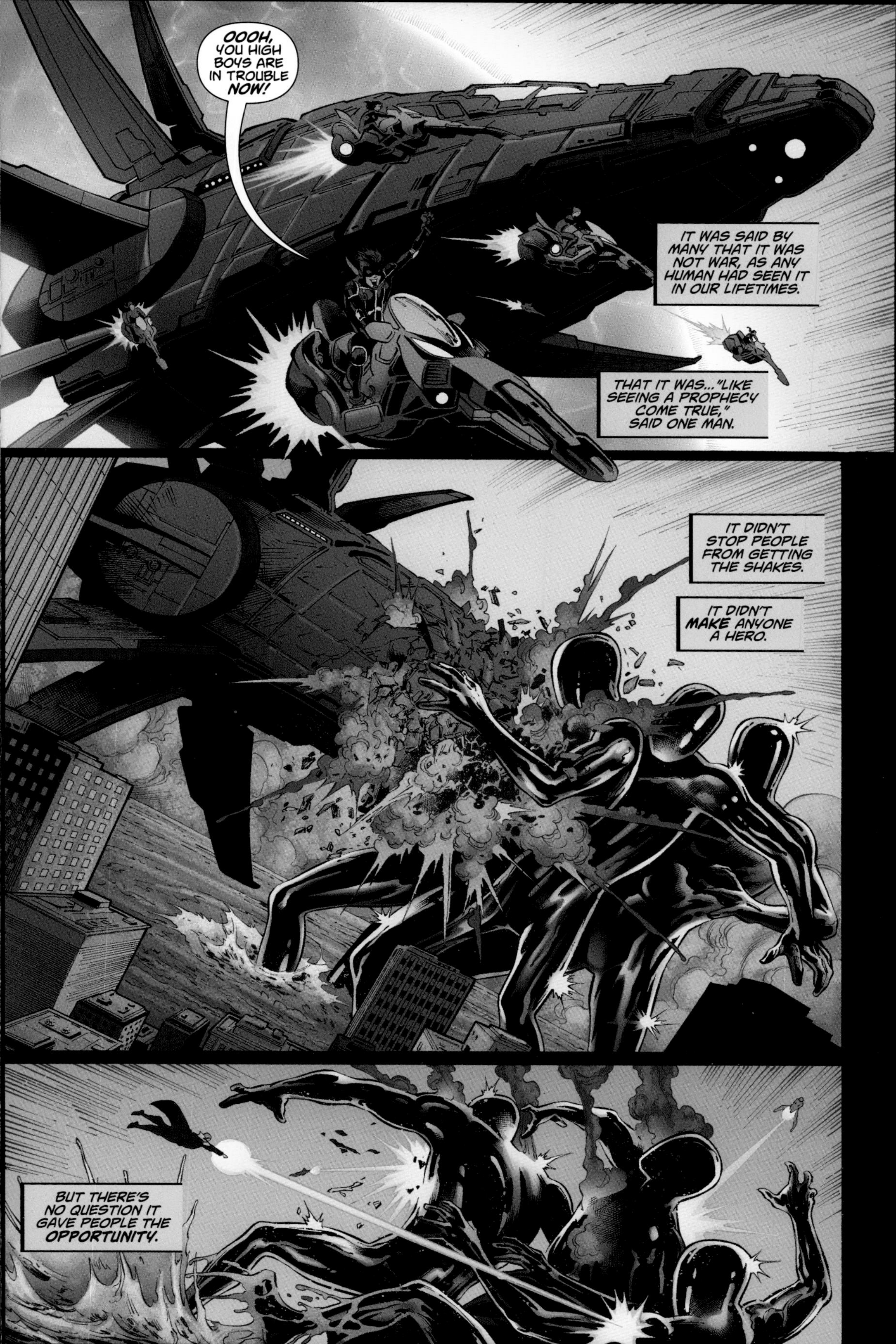
OOOH, YOU HIGH BOYS ARE IN TROUBLE NOW!
IT WAS SAID BY MANY THAT IT WAS NOT WAR, AS ANY HUMAN HAD SEEN IT IN OUR LIFETIMES.
THAT IT WAS..."LIKE SEEING A PROPHECY COME TRUE," SAID ONE MAN.
IT DIDN'T STOP PEOPLE FROM GETTING THE SHAKES.
IT DIDN'T MAKE ANYONE A HERO.
BUT THERE'S NO QUESTION IT GAVE PEOPLE THE OPPORTUNITY.

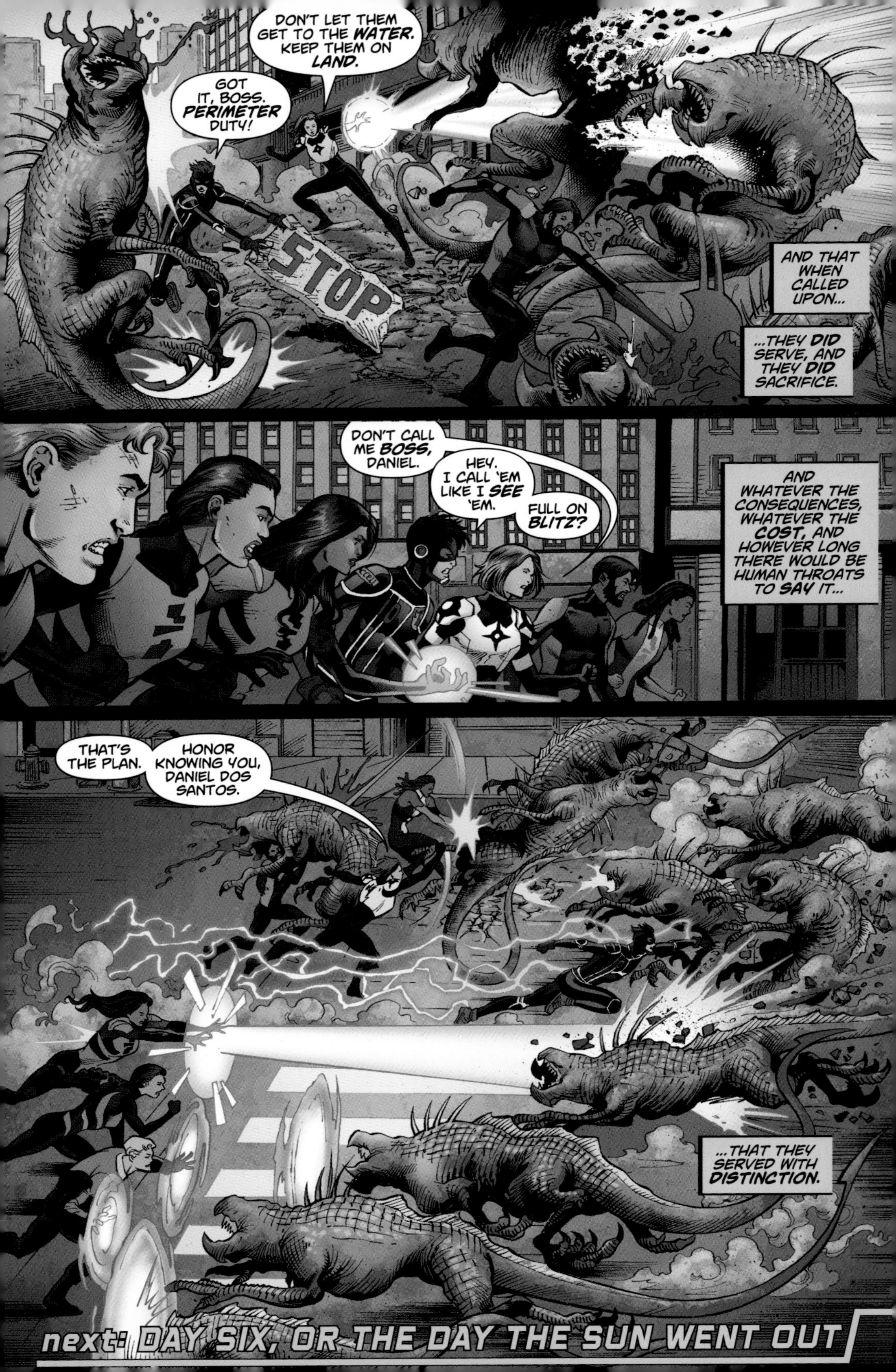
DON'T LET THEM GET TO THE WATER. KEEP THEM ON LAND.
GOT IT, BOSS. PERIMETER DUTY!
STOP
AND THAT WHEN CALLED UPON...
...THEY DID SERVE, AND THEY DID SACRIFICE.
DON'T CALL ME BOSS, DANIEL.
HEY. I CALL 'EM LIKE I SEE 'EM.
FULL ON BLITZ?
AND WHATEVER THE CONSEQUENCES, WHATEVER THE COST, AND HOWEVER LONG THERE WOULD BE HUMAN THROATS TO SAY IT...
THAT'S THE PLAN.
HONOR KNOWING YOU, DANIEL DOS SANTOS.
...THAT THEY SERVED WITH DISTINCTION.
next: DAY SIX, OR THE DAY THE SUN WENT OUT

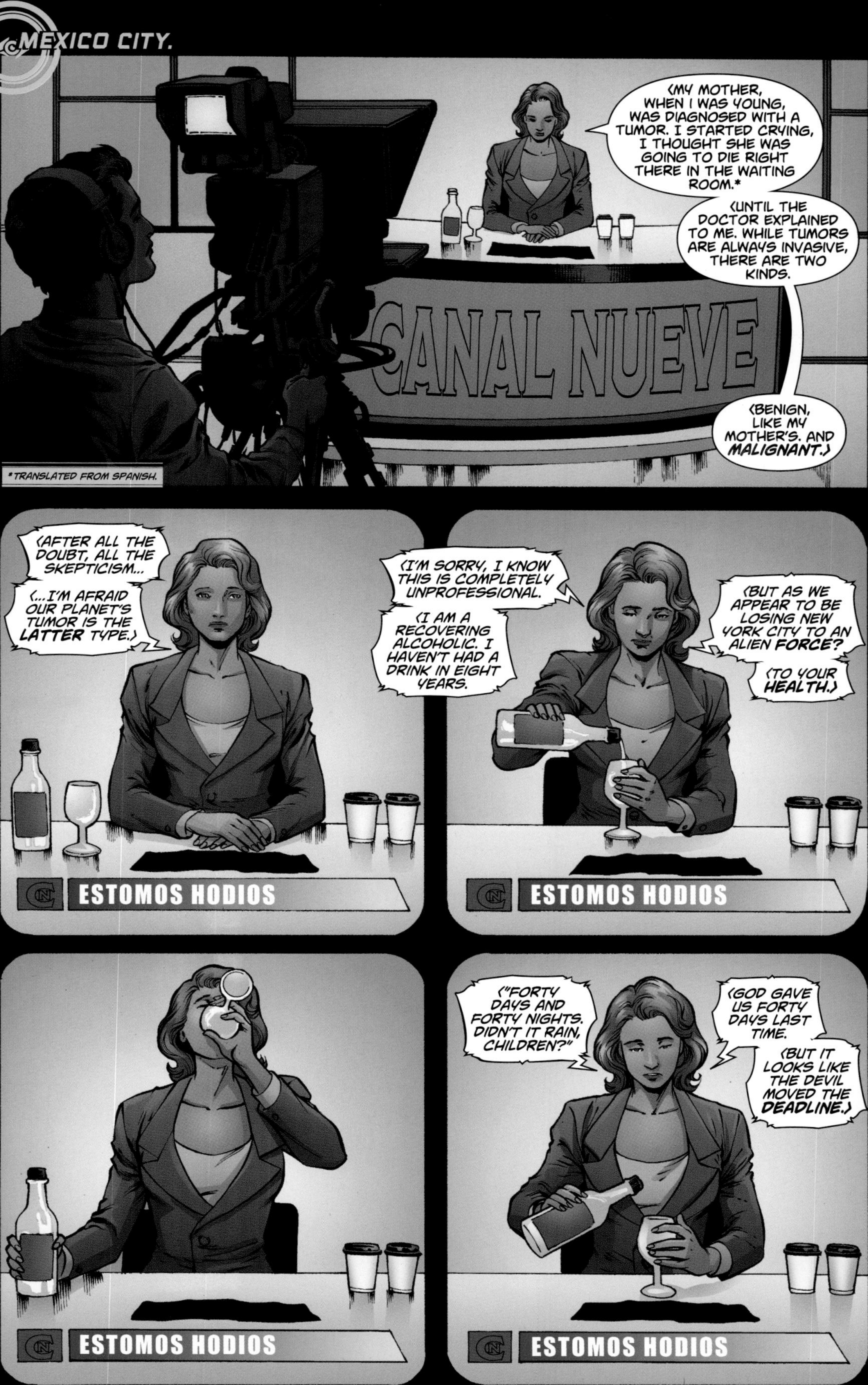
MEXICO CITY.
‹MY MOTHER, WHEN I WAS YOUNG, WAS DIAGNOSED WITH A TUMOR. I STARTED CRYING, I THOUGHT SHE WAS GOING TO DIE RIGHT THERE IN THE WAITING ROOM.*
‹UNTIL THE DOCTOR EXPLAINED TO ME. WHILE TUMORS ARE ALWAYS INVASIVE, THERE ARE TWO KINDS.
CANAL NUEVE
‹BENIGN, LIKE MY MOTHER'S. AND MALIGNANT.›
*TRANSLATED FROM SPANISH.
‹AFTER ALL THE DOUBT, ALL THE SKEPTICISM...
‹...I'M AFRAID OUR PLANET'S TUMOR IS THE LATTER TYPE.›
ESTOMOS HODIOS
‹I'M SORRY, I KNOW THIS IS COMPLETELY UNPROFESSIONAL.
‹I AM A RECOVERING ALCOHOLIC. I HAVEN'T HAD A DRINK IN EIGHT YEARS.
‹BUT AS WE APPEAR TO BE LOSING NEW YORK CITY TO AN ALIEN FORCE?
‹TO YOUR HEALTH.›
ESTOMOS HODIOS
ESTOMOS HODIOS
‹"FORTY DAYS AND FORTY NIGHTS. DIDN'T IT RAIN, CHILDREN?"
‹GOD GAVE US FORTY DAYS LAST TIME.
‹BUT IT LOOKS LIKE THE DEVIL MOVED THE DEADLINE.›
ESTOMOS HODIOS

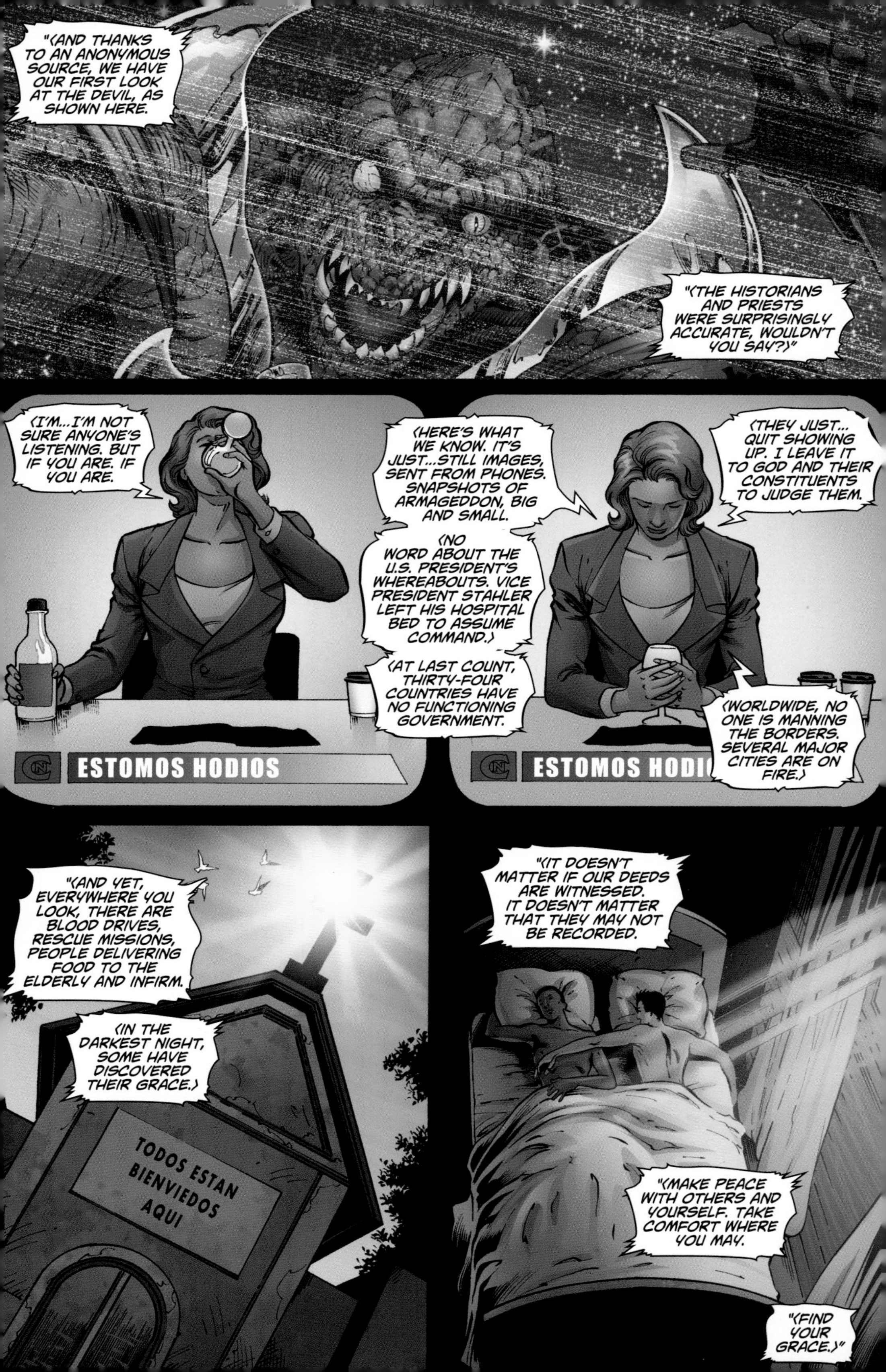
"‹AND THANKS TO AN ANONYMOUS SOURCE, WE HAVE OUR FIRST LOOK AT THE DEVIL, AS SHOWN HERE.
"‹THE HISTORIANS AND PRIESTS WERE SURPRISINGLY ACCURATE, WOULDN'T YOU SAY?›"
‹I'M...I'M NOT SURE ANYONE'S LISTENING. BUT IF YOU ARE. IF YOU ARE.
ESTOMOS HODIOS
‹HERE'S WHAT WE KNOW. IT'S JUST...STILL IMAGES, SENT FROM PHONES. SNAPSHOTS OF ARMAGEDDON, BIG AND SMALL.
‹NO WORD ABOUT THE U.S. PRESIDENT'S WHEREABOUTS. VICE PRESIDENT STAHLER LEFT HIS HOSPITAL BED TO ASSUME COMMAND.›
‹AT LAST COUNT, THIRTY-FOUR COUNTRIES HAVE NO FUNCTIONING GOVERNMENT.
‹THEY JUST... QUIT SHOWING UP. I LEAVE IT TO GOD AND THEIR CONSTITUENTS TO JUDGE THEM.
‹WORLDWIDE, NO ONE IS MANNING THE BORDERS. SEVERAL MAJOR CITIES ARE ON FIRE.›
ESTOMOS HODIO
"‹AND YET, EVERYWHERE YOU LOOK, THERE ARE BLOOD DRIVES, RESCUE MISSIONS, PEOPLE DELIVERING FOOD TO THE ELDERLY AND INFIRM.
‹IN THE DARKEST NIGHT, SOME HAVE DISCOVERED THEIR GRACE.›
TODOS ESTAN BIENVIEDOS AQUI
"‹IT DOESN'T MATTER IF OUR DEEDS ARE WITNESSED. IT DOESN'T MATTER THAT THEY MAY NOT BE RECORDED.
"‹MAKE PEACE WITH OTHERS AND YOURSELF. TAKE COMFORT WHERE YOU MAY.
"‹FIND YOUR GRACE.›"

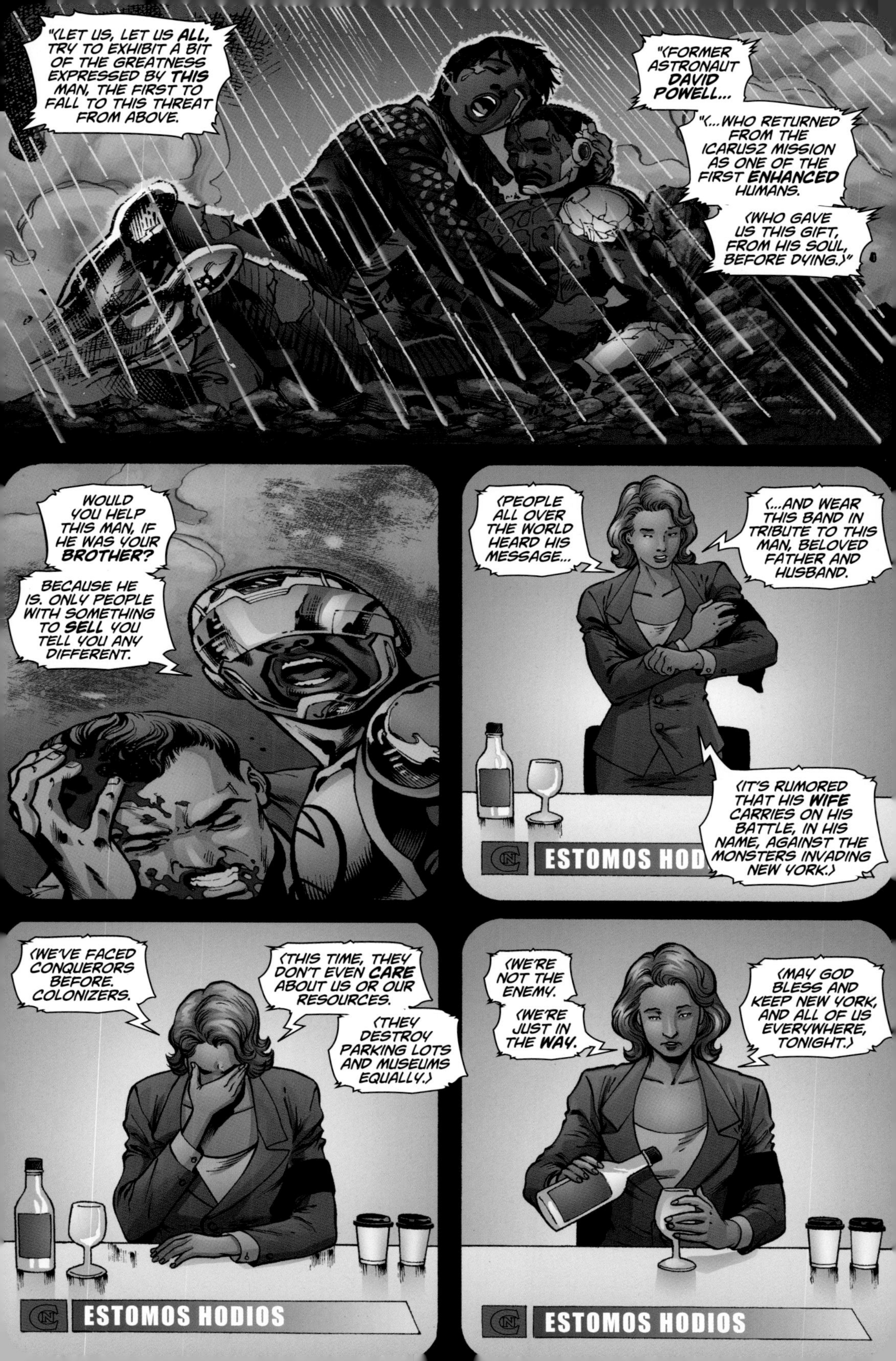
"‹LET US, LET US ALL, TRY TO EXHIBIT A BIT OF THE GREATNESS EXPRESSED BY THIS MAN, THE FIRST TO FALL TO THIS THREAT FROM ABOVE.
"‹FORMER ASTRONAUT DAVID POWELL...
"‹...WHO RETURNED FROM THE ICARUS2 MISSION AS ONE OF THE FIRST ENHANCED HUMANS.
‹WHO GAVE US THIS GIFT, FROM HIS SOUL, BEFORE DYING.›"
WOULD YOU HELP THIS MAN, IF HE WAS YOUR BROTHER?
BECAUSE HE IS. ONLY PEOPLE WITH SOMETHING TO SELL YOU TELL YOU ANY DIFFERENT.
‹PEOPLE ALL OVER THE WORLD HEARD HIS MESSAGE...
‹...AND WEAR THIS BAND IN TRIBUTE TO THIS MAN, BELOVED FATHER AND HUSBAND.
‹IT'S RUMORED THAT HIS WIFE CARRIES ON HIS BATTLE, IN HIS NAME, AGAINST THE MONSTERS INVADING NEW YORK.›
ESTOMOS HOD
‹WE'VE FACED CONQUERORS BEFORE. COLONIZERS.
‹THIS TIME, THEY DON'T EVEN CARE ABOUT US OR OUR RESOURCES.
‹THEY DESTROY PARKING LOTS AND MUSEUMS EQUALLY.›
ESTOMOS HODIOS
‹WE'RE NOT THE ENEMY.
‹WE'RE JUST IN THE WAY.
‹MAY GOD BLESS AND KEEP NEW YORK, AND ALL OF US EVERYWHERE, TONIGHT.›
ESTOMOS HODIOS

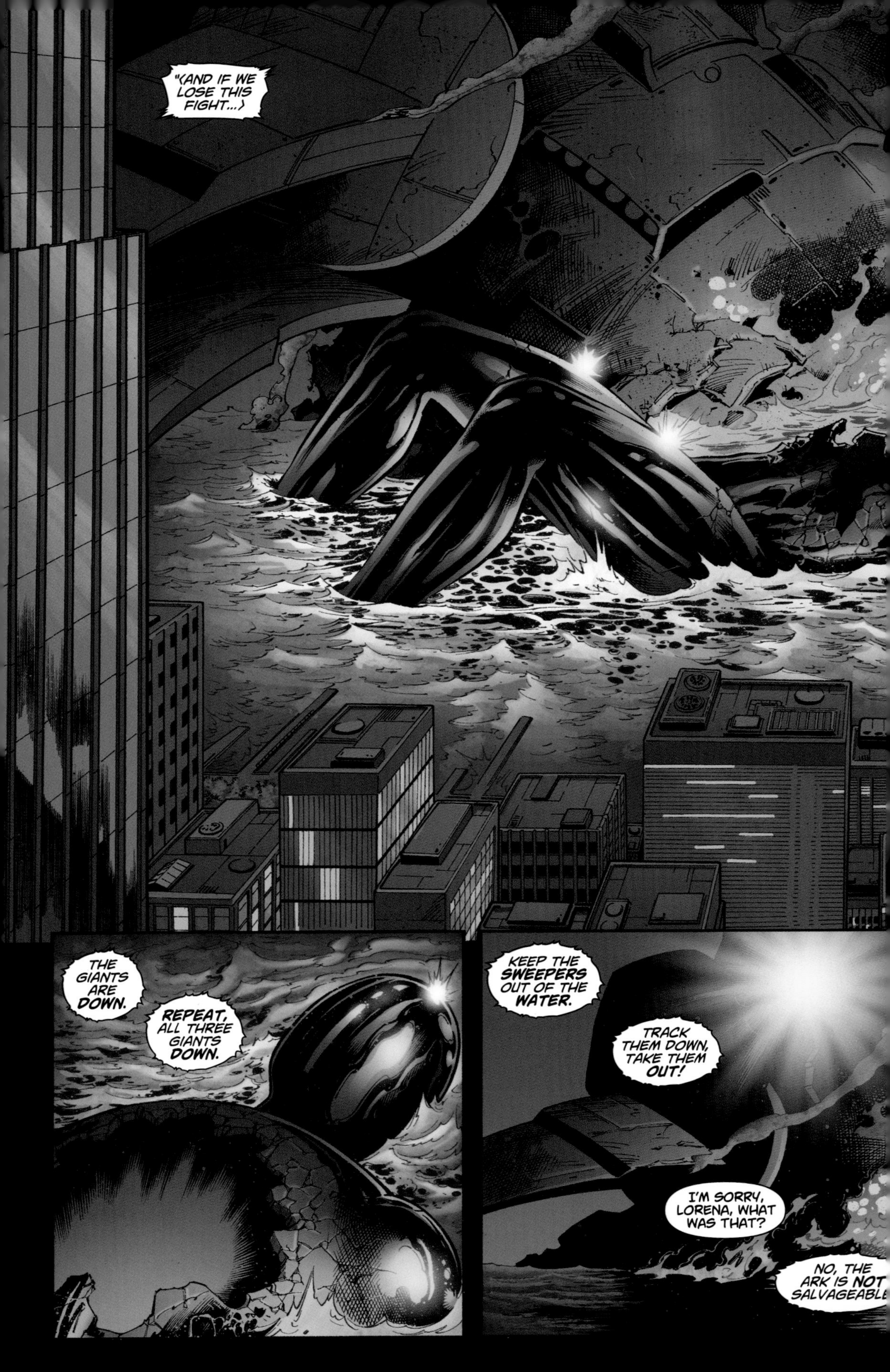
"(AND IF WE LOSE THIS FIGHT...)
THE GIANTS ARE DOWN.
REPEAT, ALL THREE GIANTS DOWN.
KEEP THE SWEEPERS OUT OF THE WATER.
TRACK THEM DOWN, TAKE THEM OUT!
I'M SORRY, LORENA, WHAT WAS THAT?
NO, THE ARK IS NOT SALVAGEABLE

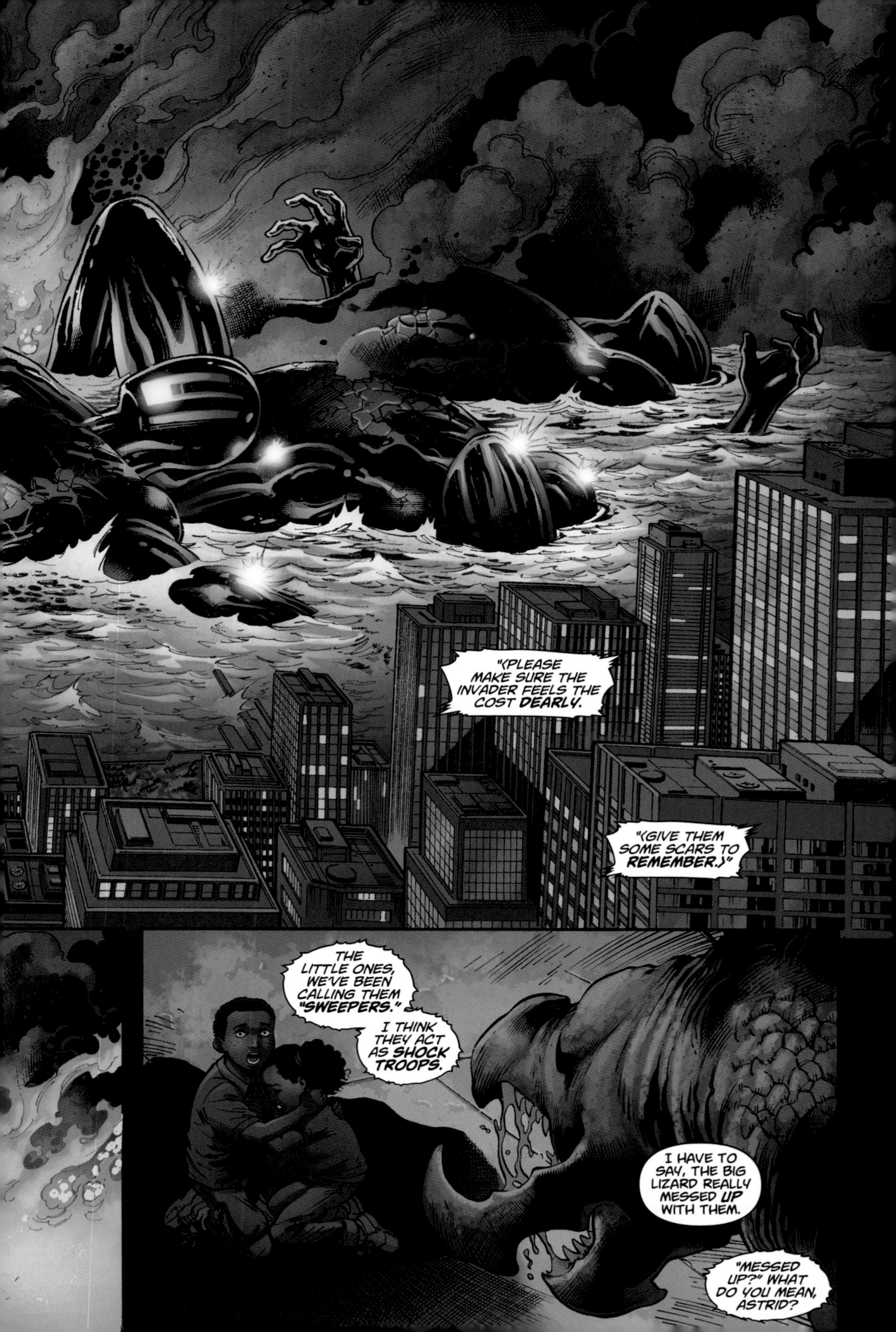
"‹PLEASE MAKE SURE THE INVADER FEELS THE COST DEARLY.
"‹GIVE THEM SOME SCARS TO REMEMBER.›"
THE LITTLE ONES, WE'VE BEEN CALLING THEM "SWEEPERS."
I THINK THEY ACT AS SHOCK TROOPS.
I HAVE TO SAY, THE BIG LIZARD REALLY MESSED UP WITH THEM.
"MESSED UP?" WHAT DO YOU MEAN, ASTRID?

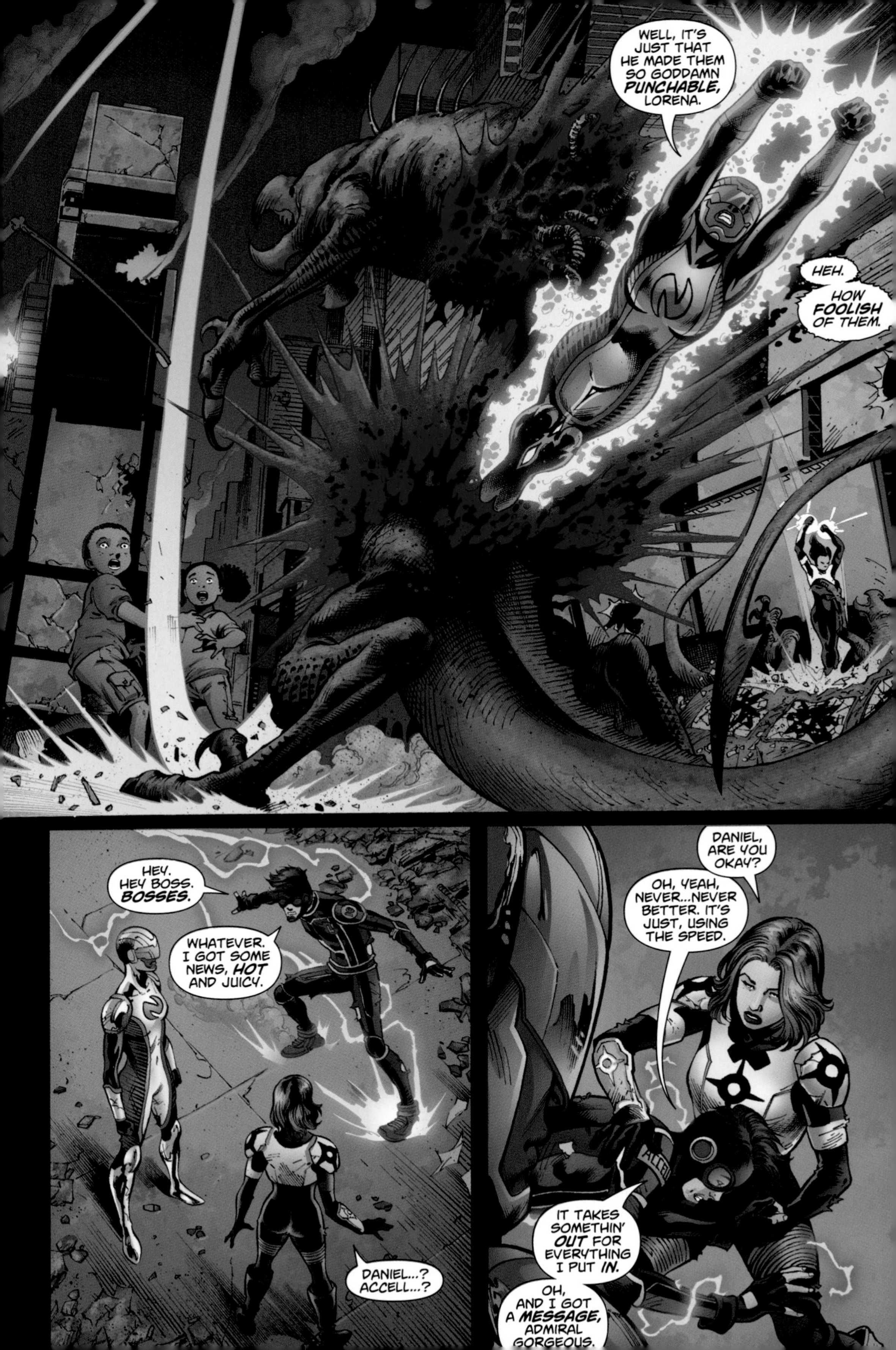
WELL, IT'S JUST THAT HE MADE THEM SO GODDAMN **PUNCHABLE,** LORENA.
HEH.
HOW **FOOLISH** OF THEM.
HEY. HEY BOSS. **BOSSES.**
WHATEVER. I GOT SOME NEWS, **HOT** AND JUICY.
DANIEL...? ACCELL...?
DANIEL, ARE YOU OKAY?
OH, YEAH, NEVER...NEVER BETTER. IT'S JUST, USING THE SPEED.
IT TAKES SOMETHIN' **OUT** FOR EVERYTHING I PUT **IN.**
OH, AND I GOT A **MESSAGE,** ADMIRAL GORGEOUS.

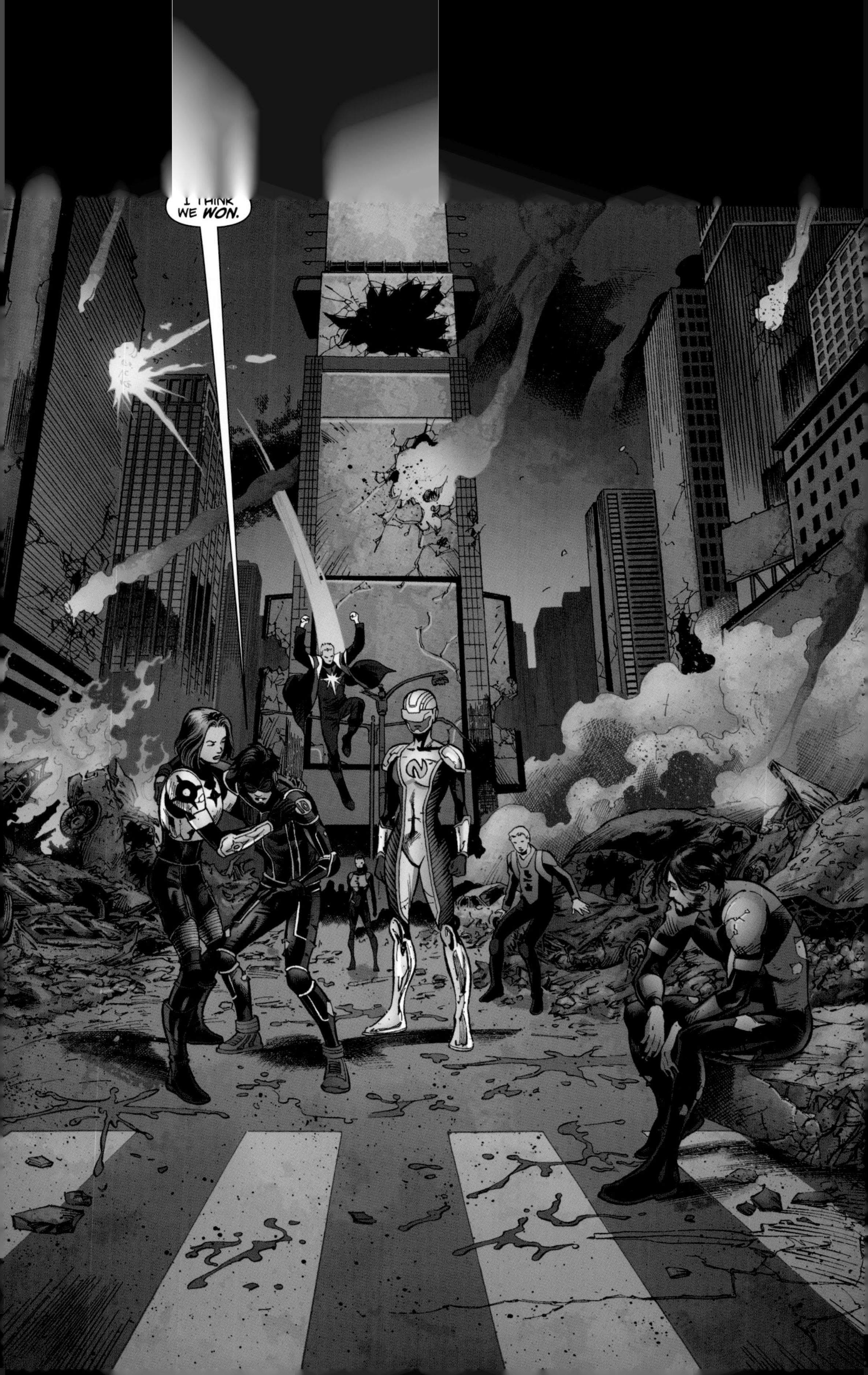
I THINK WE WON.

DAY SIX.

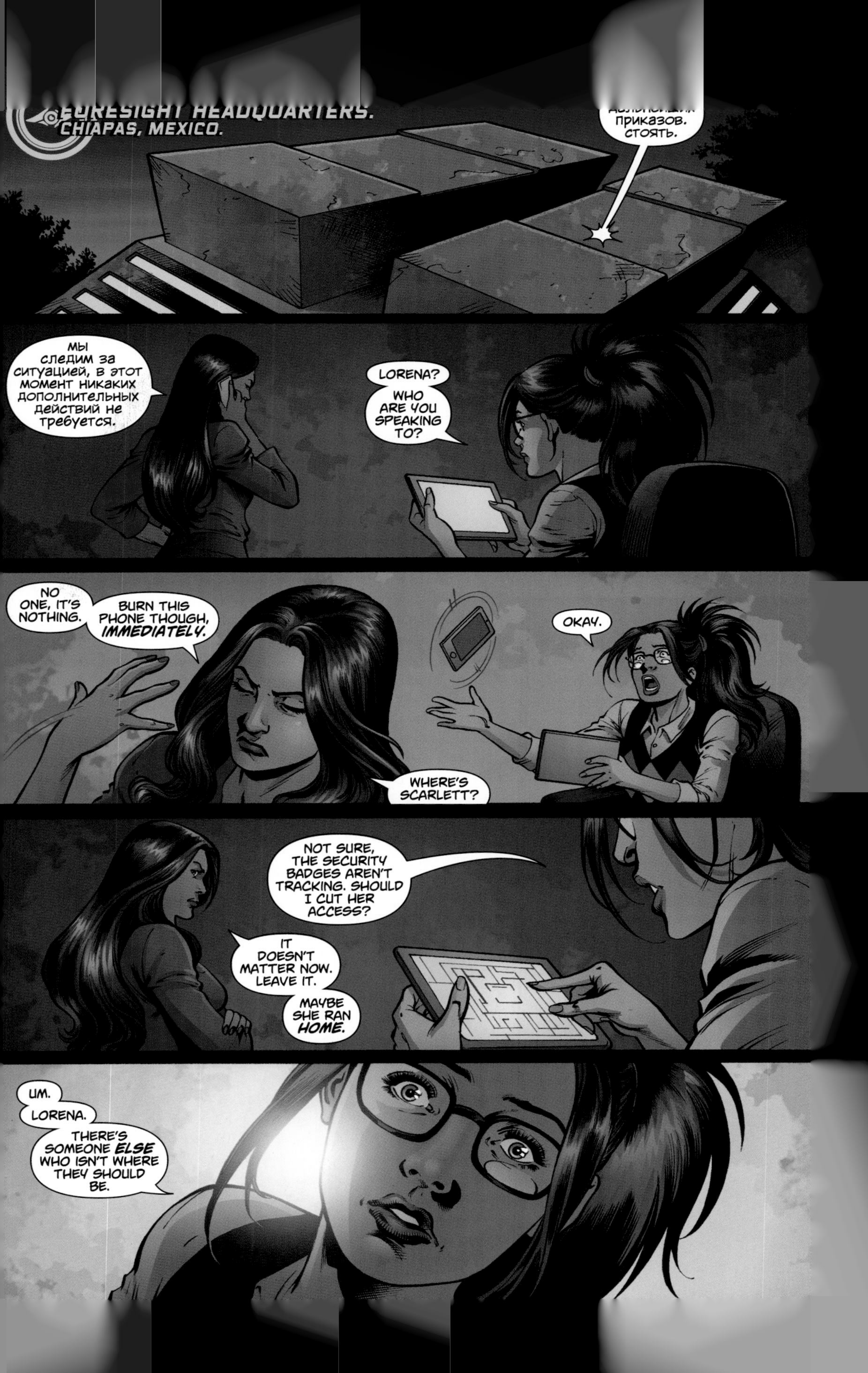

FORESIGHT HEADQUARTERS. CHIAPAS, MEXICO.
приказов. стоять.
Мы следим за ситуацией, в этот момент никаких дополнительных действий не требуется.
LORENA?
WHO ARE YOU SPEAKING TO?
NO ONE, IT'S NOTHING.
BURN THIS PHONE THOUGH, IMMEDIATELY.
OKAY.
WHERE'S SCARLETT?
NOT SURE, THE SECURITY BADGES AREN'T TRACKING. SHOULD I CUT HER ACCESS?
IT DOESN'T MATTER NOW. LEAVE IT.
MAYBE SHE RAN HOME.
UM.
LORENA.
THERE'S SOMEONE ELSE WHO ISN'T WHERE THEY SHOULD BE.

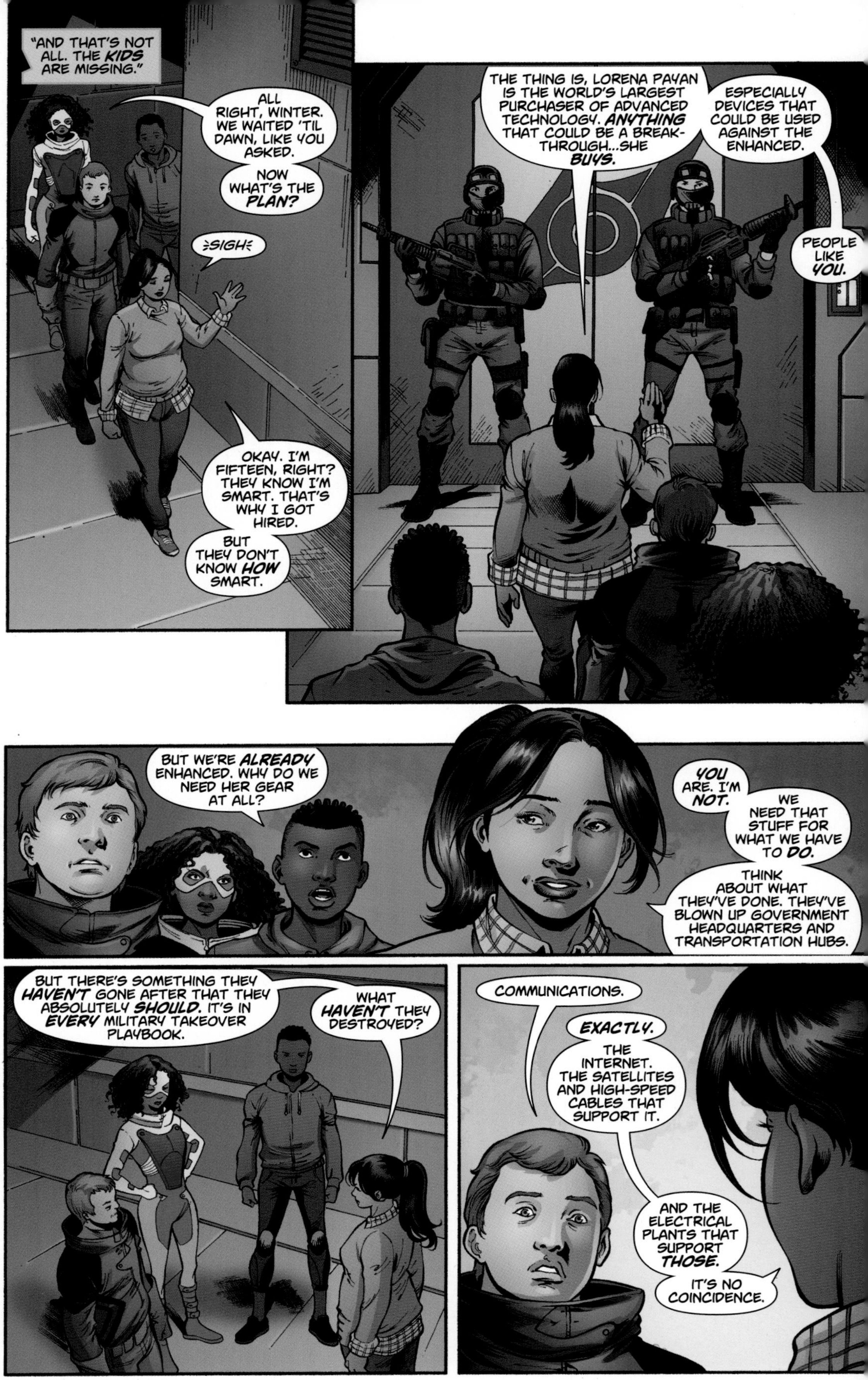
"AND THAT'S NOT ALL. THE KIDS ARE MISSING."
ALL RIGHT, WINTER. WE WAITED 'TIL DAWN, LIKE YOU ASKED.
NOW WHAT'S THE PLAN?
SIGH
OKAY. I'M FIFTEEN, RIGHT? THEY KNOW I'M SMART. THAT'S WHY I GOT HIRED.
BUT THEY DON'T KNOW HOW SMART.
THE THING IS, LORENA PAYAN IS THE WORLD'S LARGEST PURCHASER OF ADVANCED TECHNOLOGY. ANYTHING THAT COULD BE A BREAK-THROUGH...SHE BUYS.
ESPECIALLY DEVICES THAT COULD BE USED AGAINST THE ENHANCED.
PEOPLE LIKE YOU.
BUT WE'RE ALREADY ENHANCED. WHY DO WE NEED HER GEAR AT ALL?
YOU ARE. I'M NOT.
WE NEED THAT STUFF FOR WHAT WE HAVE TO DO.
THINK ABOUT WHAT THEY'VE DONE. THEY'VE BLOWN UP GOVERNMENT HEADQUARTERS AND TRANSPORTATION HUBS.
BUT THERE'S SOMETHING THEY HAVEN'T GONE AFTER THAT THEY ABSOLUTELY SHOULD. IT'S IN EVERY MILITARY TAKEOVER PLAYBOOK.
WHAT HAVEN'T THEY DESTROYED?
COMMUNICATIONS.
EXACTLY.
THE INTERNET. THE SATELLITES AND HIGH-SPEED CABLES THAT SUPPORT IT.
AND THE ELECTRICAL PLANTS THAT SUPPORT THOSE.
IT'S NO COINCIDENCE.

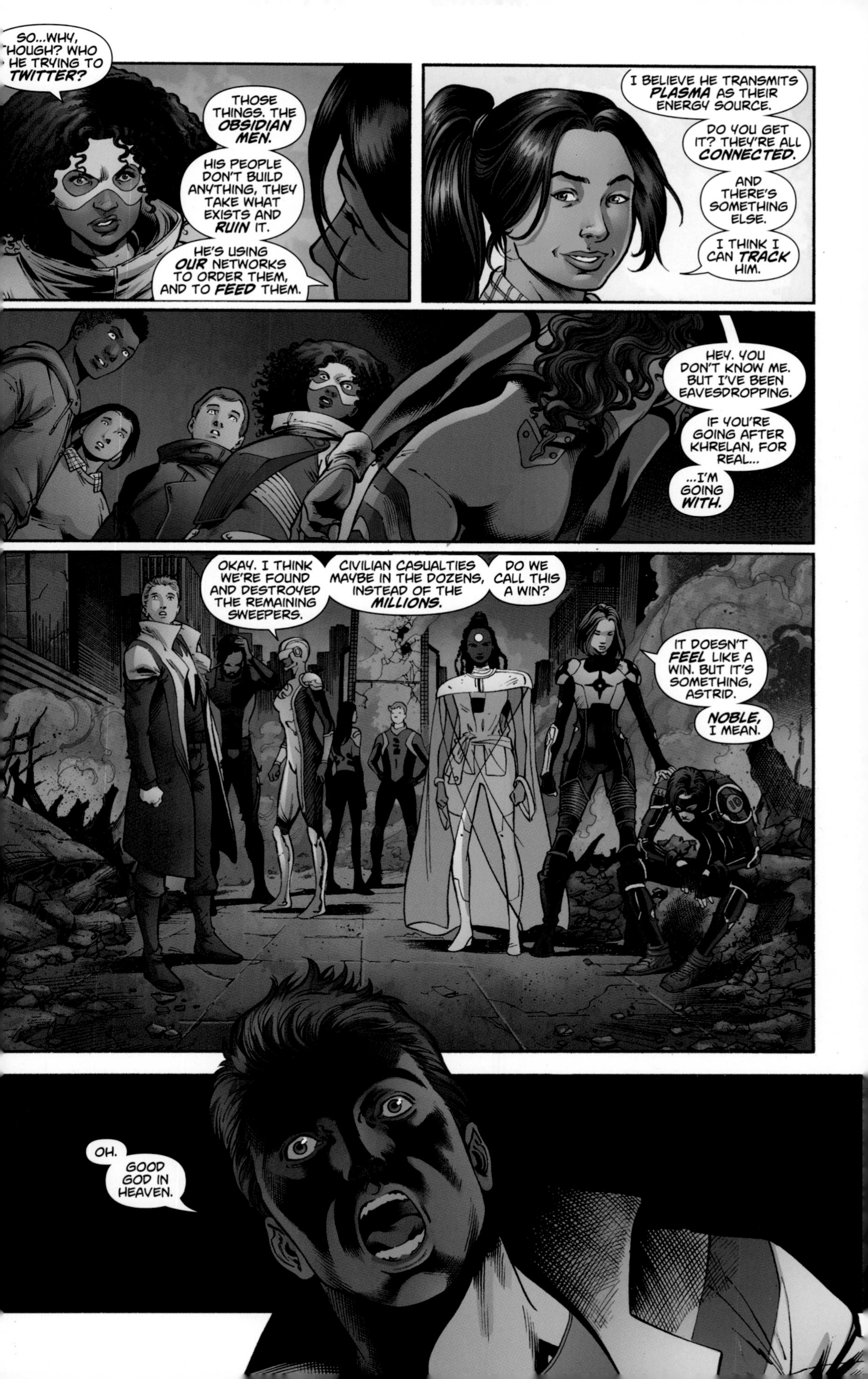
SO...WHY, HOUGH? WHO HE TRYING TO TWITTER?
THOSE THINGS. THE OBSIDIAN MEN.
HIS PEOPLE DON'T BUILD ANYTHING, THEY TAKE WHAT EXISTS AND RUIN IT.
HE'S USING OUR NETWORKS TO ORDER THEM, AND TO FEED THEM.
I BELIEVE HE TRANSMITS PLASMA AS THEIR ENERGY SOURCE.
DO YOU GET IT? THEY'RE ALL CONNECTED.
AND THERE'S SOMETHING ELSE.
I THINK I CAN TRACK HIM.
HEY. YOU DON'T KNOW ME. BUT I'VE BEEN EAVESDROPPING.
IF YOU'RE GOING AFTER KHRELAN, FOR REAL...
...I'M GOING WITH.
OKAY. I THINK WE'RE FOUND AND DESTROYED THE REMAINING SWEEPERS.
CIVILIAN CASUALTIES MAYBE IN THE DOZENS, INSTEAD OF THE MILLIONS.
DO WE CALL THIS A WIN?
IT DOESN'T FEEL LIKE A WIN. BUT IT'S SOMETHING, ASTRID.
NOBLE, I MEAN.
OH.
GOOD GOD IN HEAVEN.

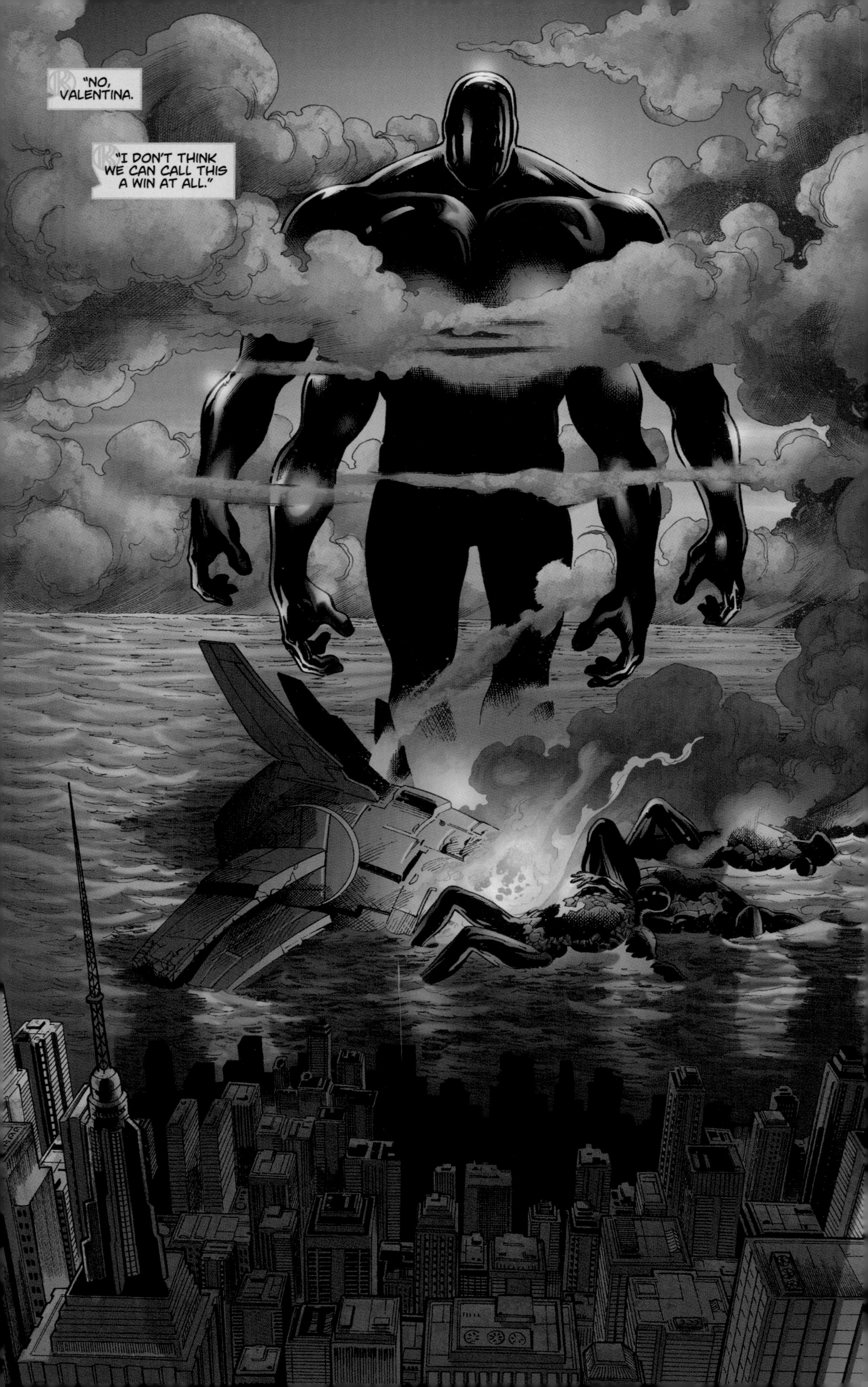
"NO, VALENTINA.
"I DON'T THINK WE CAN CALL THIS A WIN AT ALL."

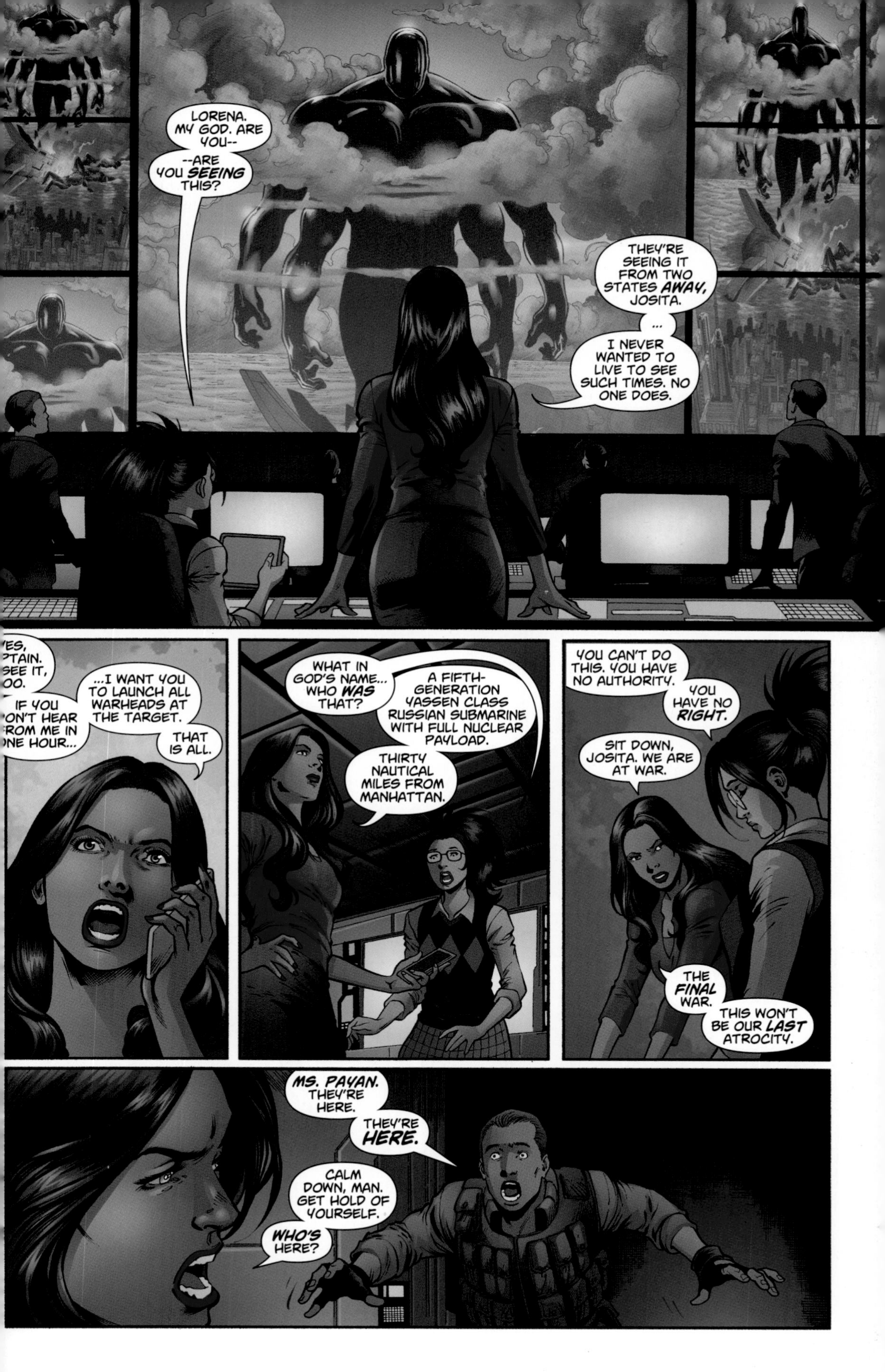
LORENA. MY GOD. ARE YOU--
--ARE YOU SEEING THIS?
THEY'RE SEEING IT FROM TWO STATES AWAY, JOSITA.
...
I NEVER WANTED TO LIVE TO SEE SUCH TIMES. NO ONE DOES.
YES, CAPTAIN. I SEE IT, TOO.
...I WANT YOU TO LAUNCH ALL WARHEADS AT THE TARGET.
IF YOU DON'T HEAR FROM ME IN ONE HOUR...
THAT IS ALL.
WHAT IN GOD'S NAME... WHO WAS THAT?
A FIFTH-GENERATION YASSEN CLASS RUSSIAN SUBMARINE WITH FULL NUCLEAR PAYLOAD.
THIRTY NAUTICAL MILES FROM MANHATTAN.
YOU CAN'T DO THIS. YOU HAVE NO AUTHORITY.
YOU HAVE NO RIGHT.
SIT DOWN, JOSITA. WE ARE AT WAR.
THE FINAL WAR.
THIS WON'T BE OUR LAST ATROCITY.
MS. PAYAN. THEY'RE HERE.
THEY'RE HERE.
CALM DOWN, MAN. GET HOLD OF YOURSELF.
WHO'S HERE?

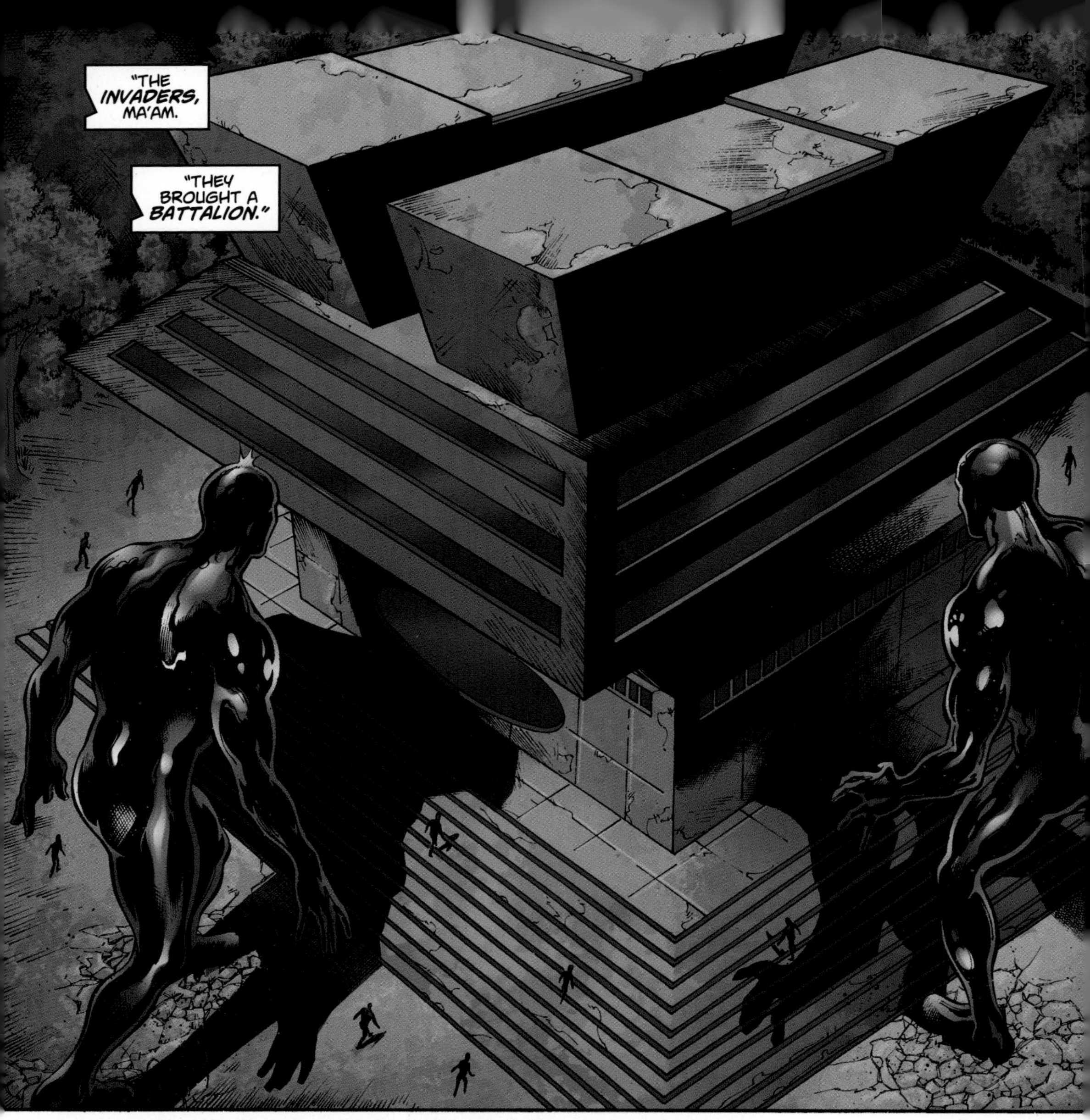
"THE INVADERS, MA'AM.
"THEY BROUGHT A BATTALION."

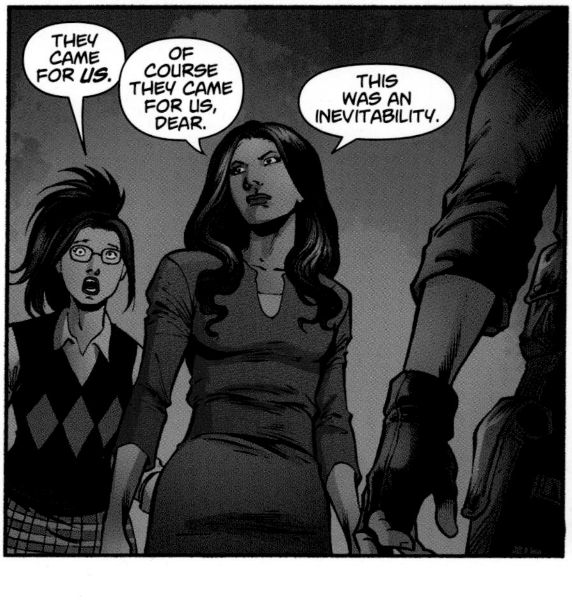
THEY CAME FOR US.
OF COURSE THEY CAME FOR US, DEAR.
THIS WAS AN INEVITABILITY.

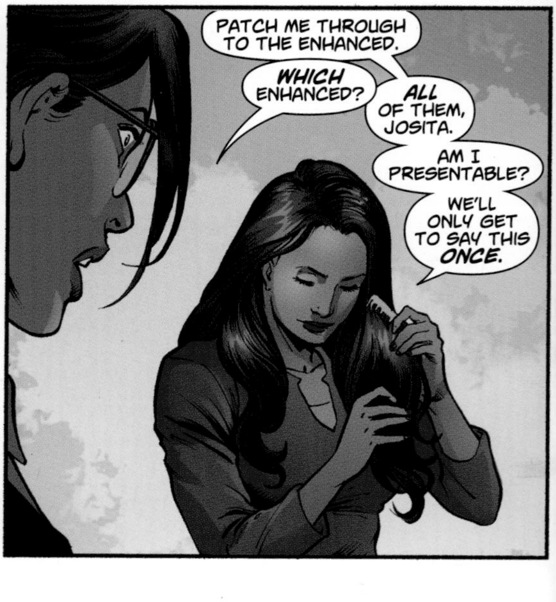
PATCH ME THROUGH TO THE ENHANCED.
WHICH ENHANCED?
ALL OF THEM, JOSITA.
AM I PRESENTABLE?
WE'LL ONLY GET TO SAY THIS ONCE.

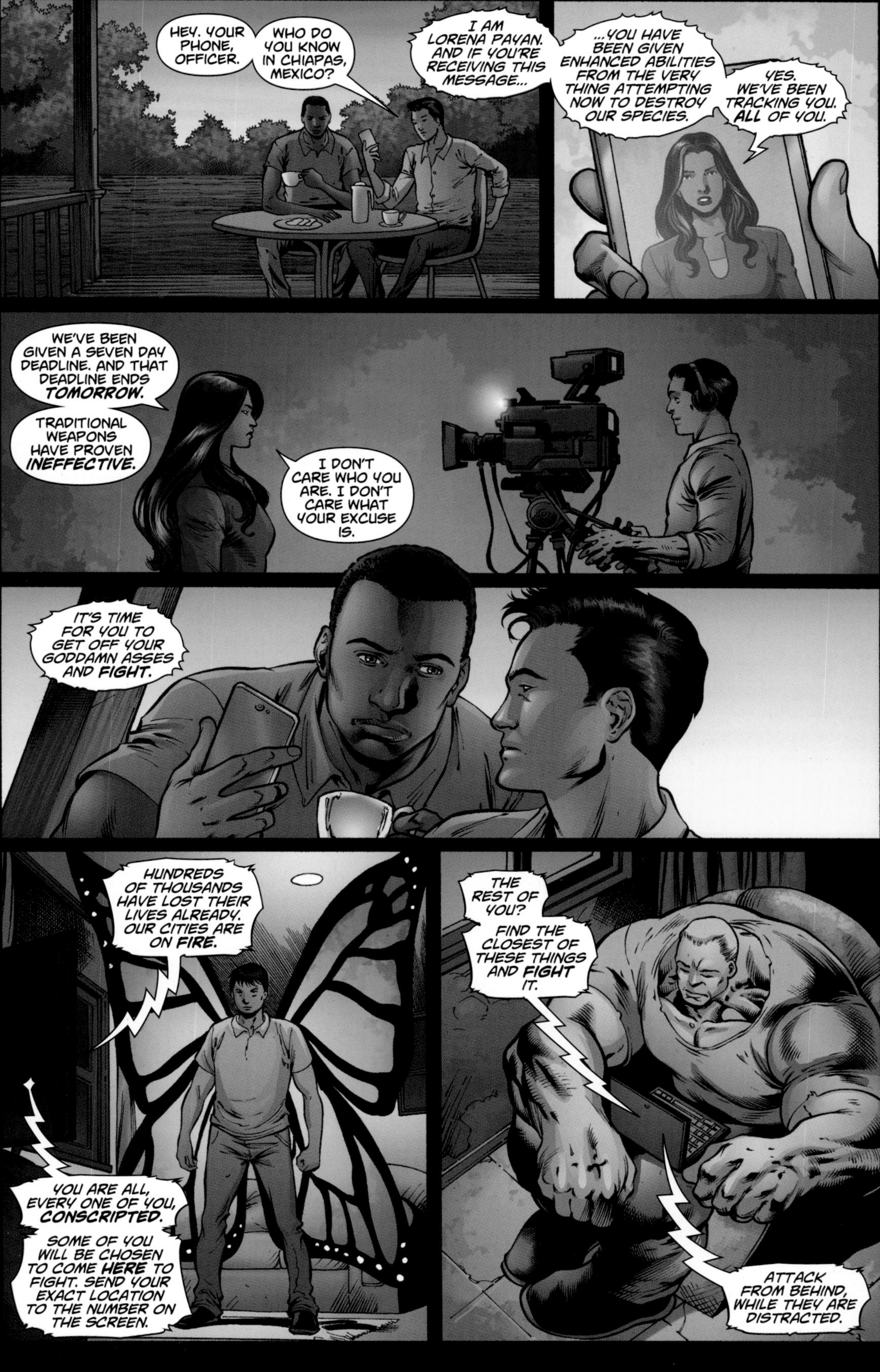
HEY. YOUR PHONE, OFFICER.
WHO DO YOU KNOW IN CHIAPAS, MEXICO?
I AM LORENA PAYAN. AND IF YOU'RE RECEIVING THIS MESSAGE...
...YOU HAVE BEEN GIVEN ENHANCED ABILITIES FROM THE VERY THING ATTEMPTING NOW TO DESTROY OUR SPECIES.
YES. WE'VE BEEN TRACKING YOU. ALL OF YOU.
WE'VE BEEN GIVEN A SEVEN DAY DEADLINE. AND THAT DEADLINE ENDS TOMORROW.
TRADITIONAL WEAPONS HAVE PROVEN INEFFECTIVE.
I DON'T CARE WHO YOU ARE. I DON'T CARE WHAT YOUR EXCUSE IS.
IT'S TIME FOR YOU TO GET OFF YOUR GODDAMN ASSES AND FIGHT.
HUNDREDS OF THOUSANDS HAVE LOST THEIR LIVES ALREADY. OUR CITIES ARE ON FIRE.
YOU ARE ALL, EVERY ONE OF YOU, CONSCRIPTED.
SOME OF YOU WILL BE CHOSEN TO COME HERE TO FIGHT. SEND YOUR EXACT LOCATION TO THE NUMBER ON THE SCREEN.
THE REST OF YOU?
FIND THE CLOSEST OF THESE THINGS AND FIGHT IT.
ATTACK FROM BEHIND, WHILE THEY ARE DISTRACTED.

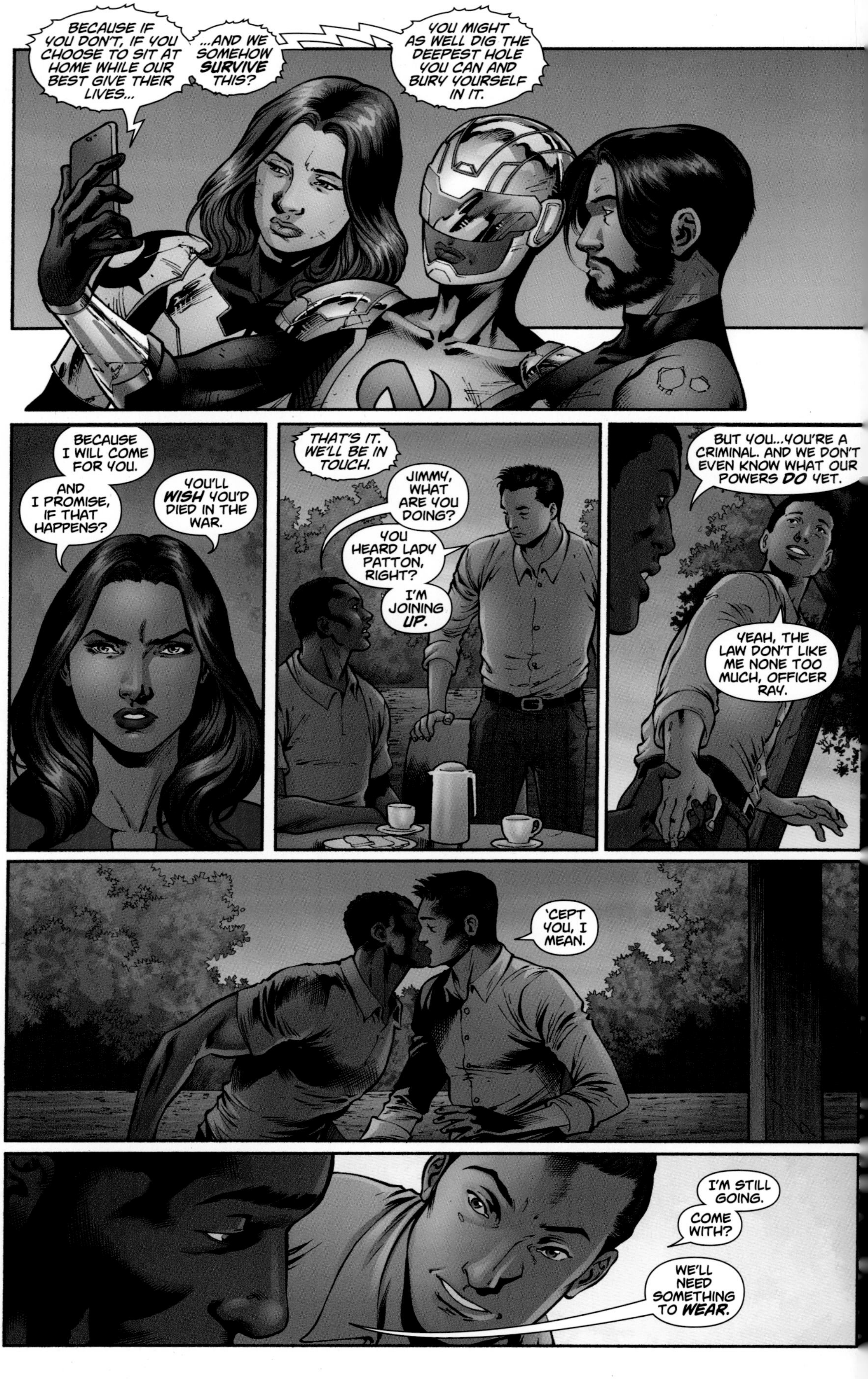
BECAUSE IF YOU DON'T, IF YOU CHOOSE TO SIT AT HOME WHILE OUR BEST GIVE THEIR LIVES...
...AND WE SOMEHOW **SURVIVE** THIS?
YOU MIGHT AS WELL DIG THE DEEPEST HOLE YOU CAN AND BURY YOURSELF IN IT.
BECAUSE I WILL COME FOR YOU.
AND I PROMISE, IF THAT HAPPENS?
YOU'LL **WISH** YOU'D DIED IN THE WAR.
THAT'S IT. WE'LL BE IN TOUCH.
JIMMY, WHAT ARE YOU DOING?
YOU HEARD LADY PATTON, RIGHT?
I'M JOINING **UP.**
BUT YOU...YOU'RE A CRIMINAL. AND WE DON'T EVEN KNOW WHAT OUR POWERS **DO** YET.
YEAH, THE LAW DON'T LIKE ME NONE TOO MUCH, OFFICER RAY.
'CEPT YOU, I MEAN.
I'M STILL GOING.
COME WITH?
WE'LL NEED SOMETHING TO **WEAR.**

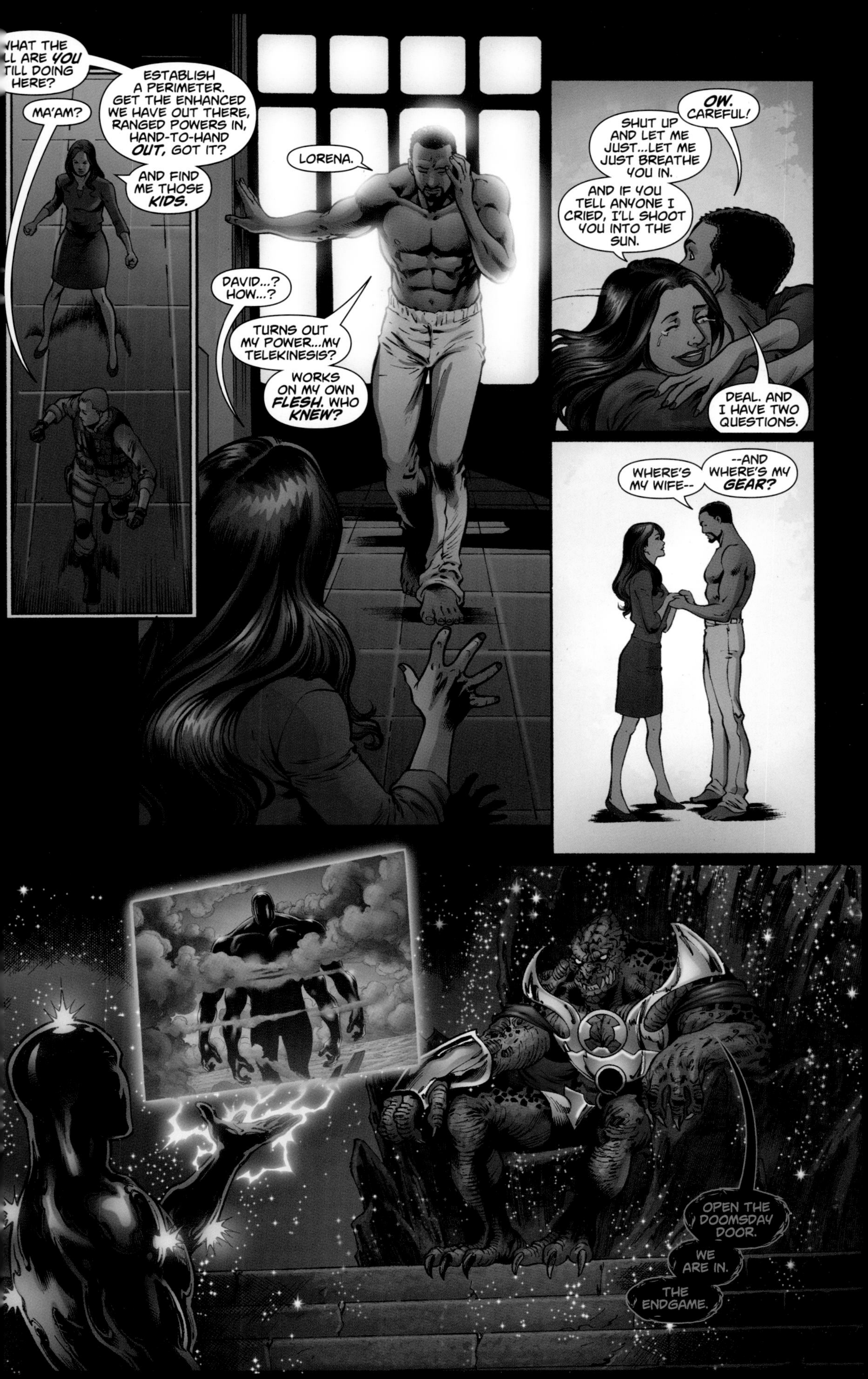
WHAT THE
LL ARE YOU
TILL DOING
HERE?
MA'AM?
ESTABLISH A PERIMETER. GET THE ENHANCED WE HAVE OUT THERE, RANGED POWERS IN, HAND-TO-HAND OUT, GOT IT?
AND FIND ME THOSE KIDS.
LORENA.
DAVID...? HOW...?
TURNS OUT MY POWER...MY TELEKINESIS?
WORKS ON MY OWN FLESH. WHO KNEW?
OW. CAREFUL!
SHUT UP AND LET ME JUST...LET ME JUST BREATHE YOU IN.
AND IF YOU TELL ANYONE I CRIED, I'LL SHOOT YOU INTO THE SUN.
DEAL. AND I HAVE TWO QUESTIONS.
WHERE'S MY WIFE--
--AND WHERE'S MY GEAR?
OPEN THE DOOMSDAY DOOR.
WE ARE IN.
THE ENDGAME.

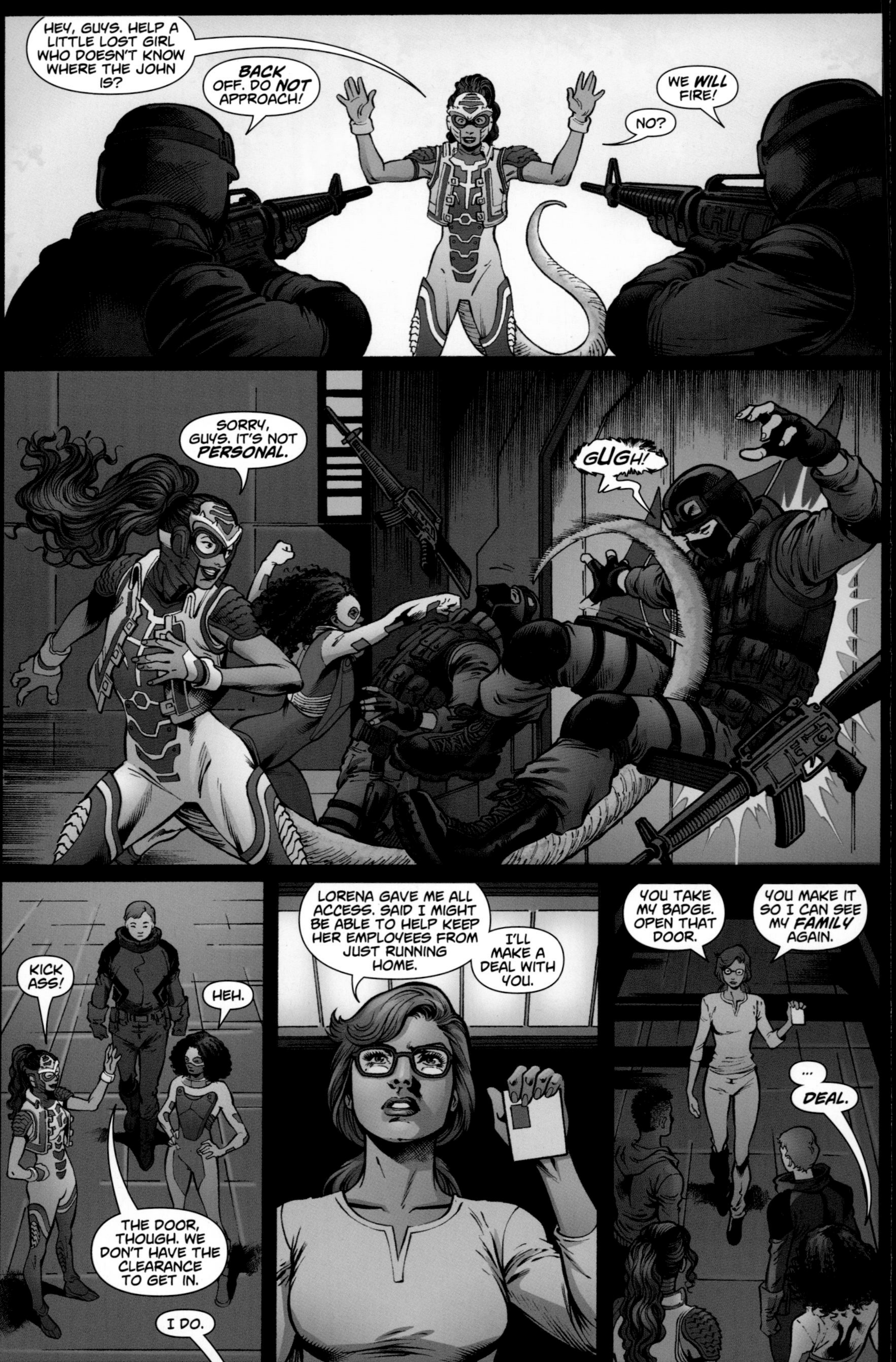
HEY, GUYS. HELP A LITTLE LOST GIRL WHO DOESN'T KNOW WHERE THE JOHN IS?
BACK OFF. DO NOT APPROACH!
NO?
WE WILL FIRE!
SORRY, GUYS. IT'S NOT PERSONAL.
GUGH!
KICK ASS!
HEH.
THE DOOR, THOUGH. WE DON'T HAVE THE CLEARANCE TO GET IN.
I DO.
LORENA GAVE ME ALL ACCESS. SAID I MIGHT BE ABLE TO HELP KEEP HER EMPLOYEES FROM JUST RUNNING HOME.
I'LL MAKE A DEAL WITH YOU.
YOU TAKE MY BADGE. OPEN THAT DOOR.
YOU MAKE IT SO I CAN SEE MY FAMILY AGAIN.
... DEAL.

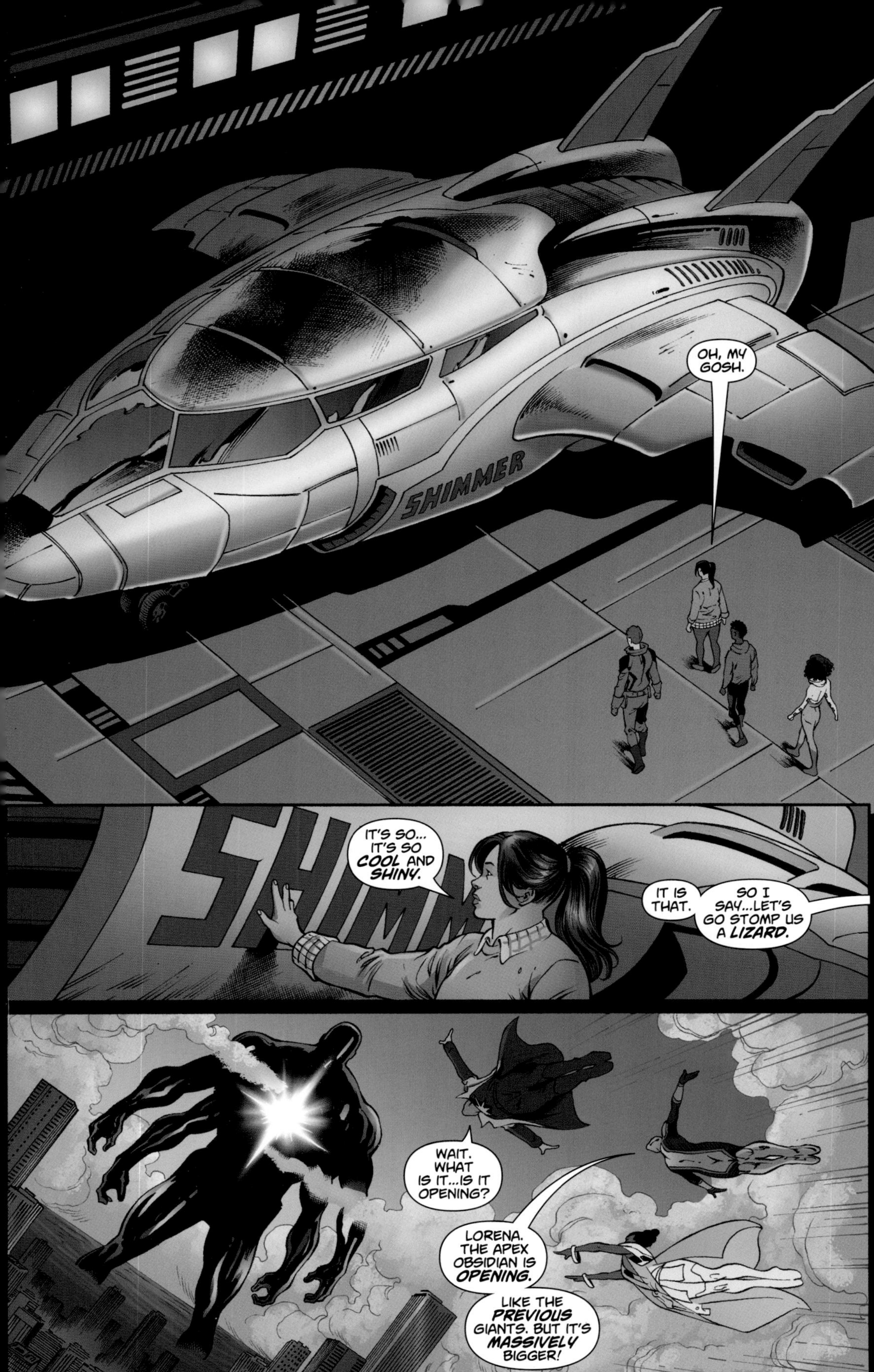
SHIMMER
OH, MY GOSH.
IT'S SO... IT'S SO COOL AND SHINY.
IT IS THAT.
SO I SAY...LET'S GO STOMP US A LIZARD.
WAIT. WHAT IS IT...IS IT OPENING?
LORENA. THE APEX OBSIDIAN IS OPENING.
LIKE THE PREVIOUS GIANTS. BUT IT'S MASSIVELY BIGGER!

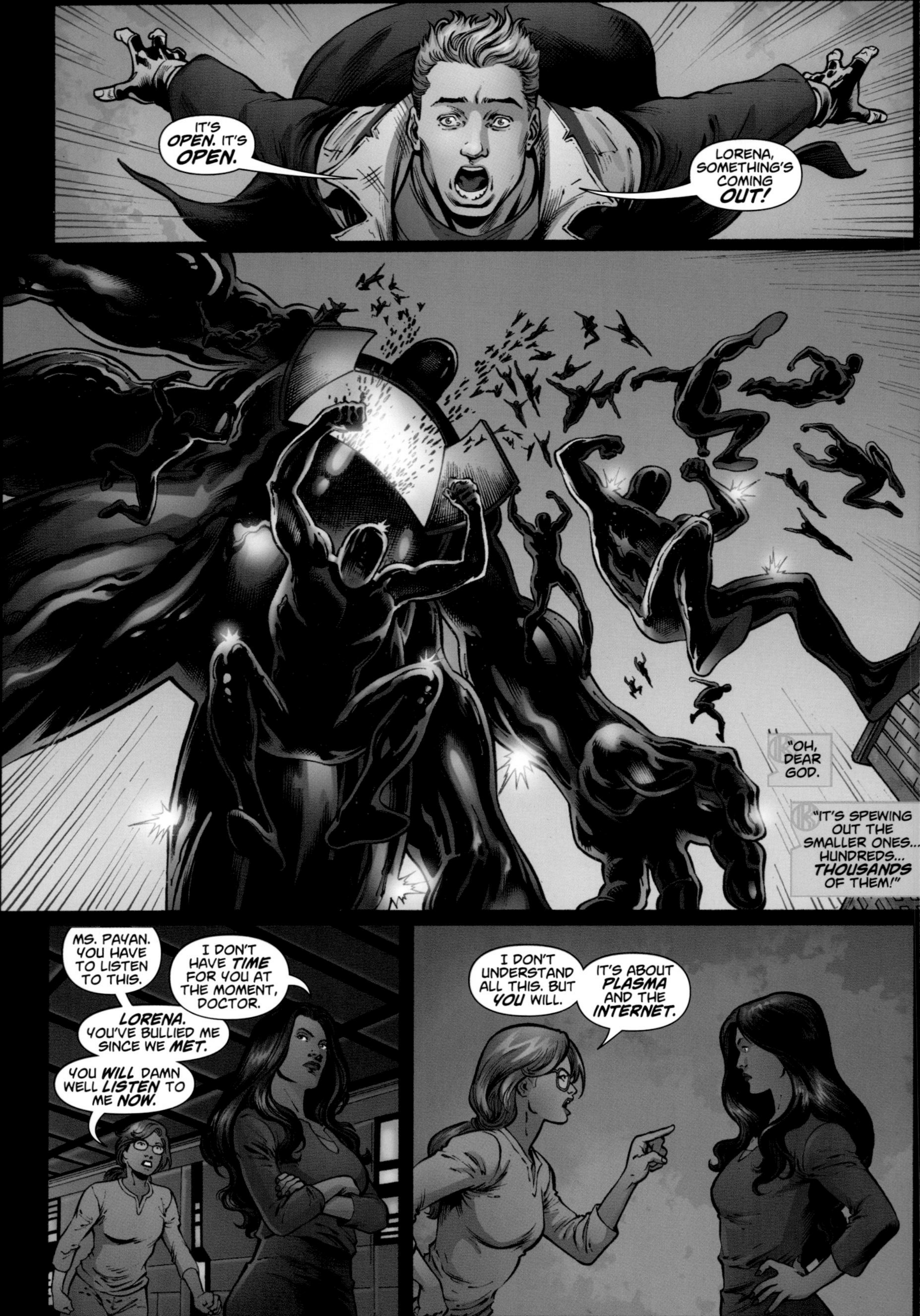

IT'S OPEN. IT'S OPEN.
LORENA, SOMETHING'S COMING OUT!
"OH, DEAR GOD.
"IT'S SPEWING OUT THE SMALLER ONES... HUNDREDS... THOUSANDS OF THEM!"
MS. PAYAN. YOU HAVE TO LISTEN TO THIS.
I DON'T HAVE TIME FOR YOU AT THE MOMENT, DOCTOR.
LORENA. YOU'VE BULLIED ME SINCE WE MET.
YOU WILL DAMN WELL LISTEN TO ME NOW.
I DON'T UNDERSTAND ALL THIS. BUT YOU WILL.
IT'S ABOUT PLASMA AND THE INTERNET.

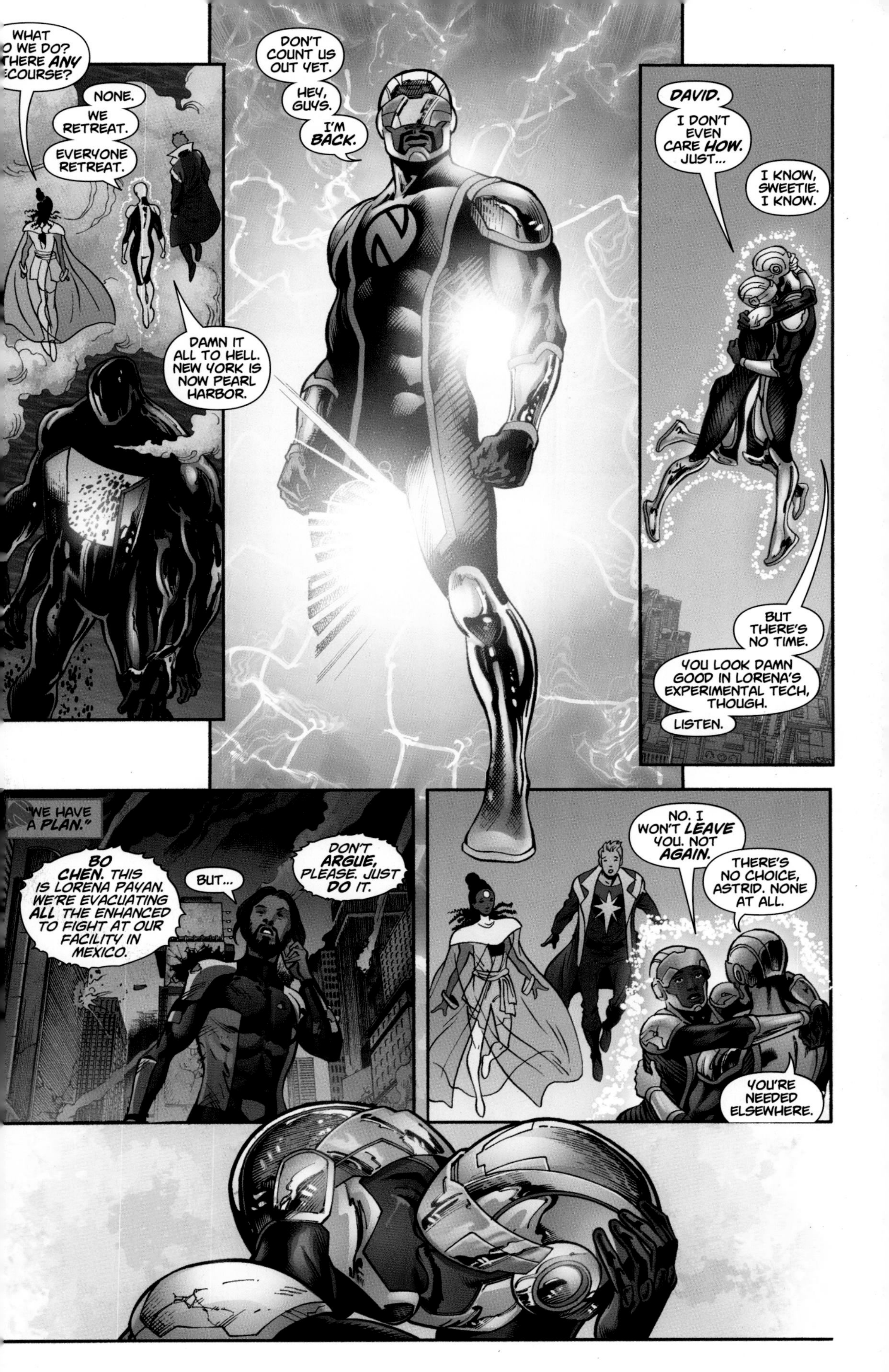
WHAT
O WE DO?
THERE ANY
ECOURSE?
NONE.
WE RETREAT.
EVERYONE RETREAT.
DAMN IT ALL TO HELL. NEW YORK IS NOW PEARL HARBOR.
DON'T COUNT US OUT YET.
HEY, GUYS.
I'M BACK.
DAVID.
I DON'T EVEN CARE HOW. JUST...
I KNOW, SWEETIE. I KNOW.
BUT THERE'S NO TIME.
YOU LOOK DAMN GOOD IN LORENA'S EXPERIMENTAL TECH, THOUGH.
LISTEN.
"WE HAVE A PLAN."
BO CHEN. THIS IS LORENA PAYAN. WE'RE EVACUATING ALL THE ENHANCED TO FIGHT AT OUR FACILITY IN MEXICO.
BUT...
DON'T ARGUE, PLEASE. JUST DO IT.
NO. I WON'T LEAVE YOU. NOT AGAIN.
THERE'S NO CHOICE, ASTRID. NONE AT ALL.
YOU'RE NEEDED ELSEWHERE.

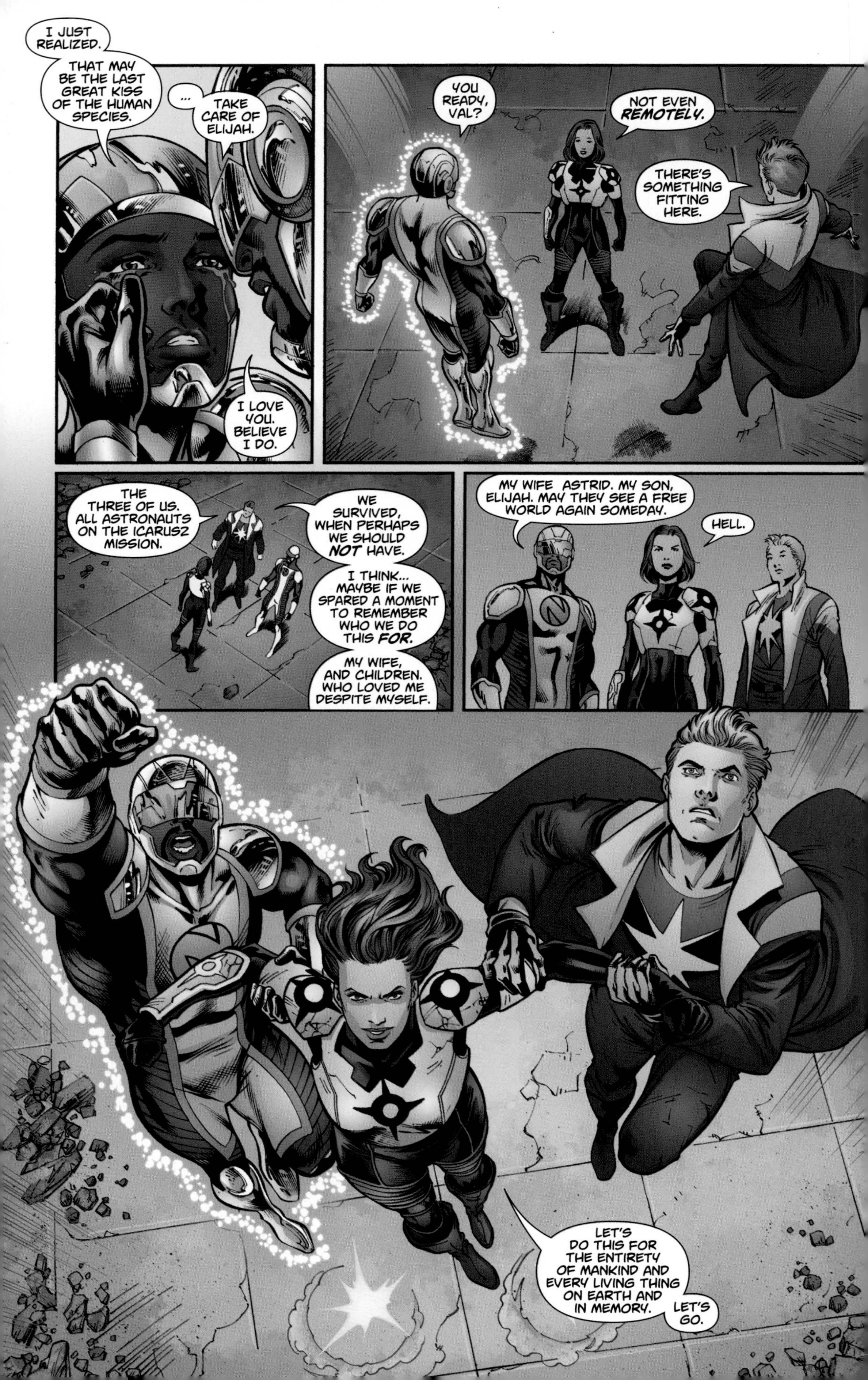
I JUST REALIZED.
THAT MAY BE THE LAST GREAT KISS OF THE HUMAN SPECIES.
...
TAKE CARE OF ELIJAH.
I LOVE YOU. BELIEVE I DO.
YOU READY, VAL?
NOT EVEN REMOTELY.
THERE'S SOMETHING FITTING HERE.
THE THREE OF US. ALL ASTRONAUTS ON THE ICARUS2 MISSION.
WE SURVIVED, WHEN PERHAPS WE SHOULD NOT HAVE.
I THINK... MAYBE IF WE SPARED A MOMENT TO REMEMBER WHO WE DO THIS FOR.
MY WIFE, AND CHILDREN. WHO LOVED ME DESPITE MYSELF.
MY WIFE ASTRID. MY SON, ELIJAH. MAY THEY SEE A FREE WORLD AGAIN SOMEDAY.
HELL.
LET'S DO THIS FOR THE ENTIRETY OF MANKIND AND EVERY LIVING THING ON EARTH AND IN MEMORY.
LET'S GO.

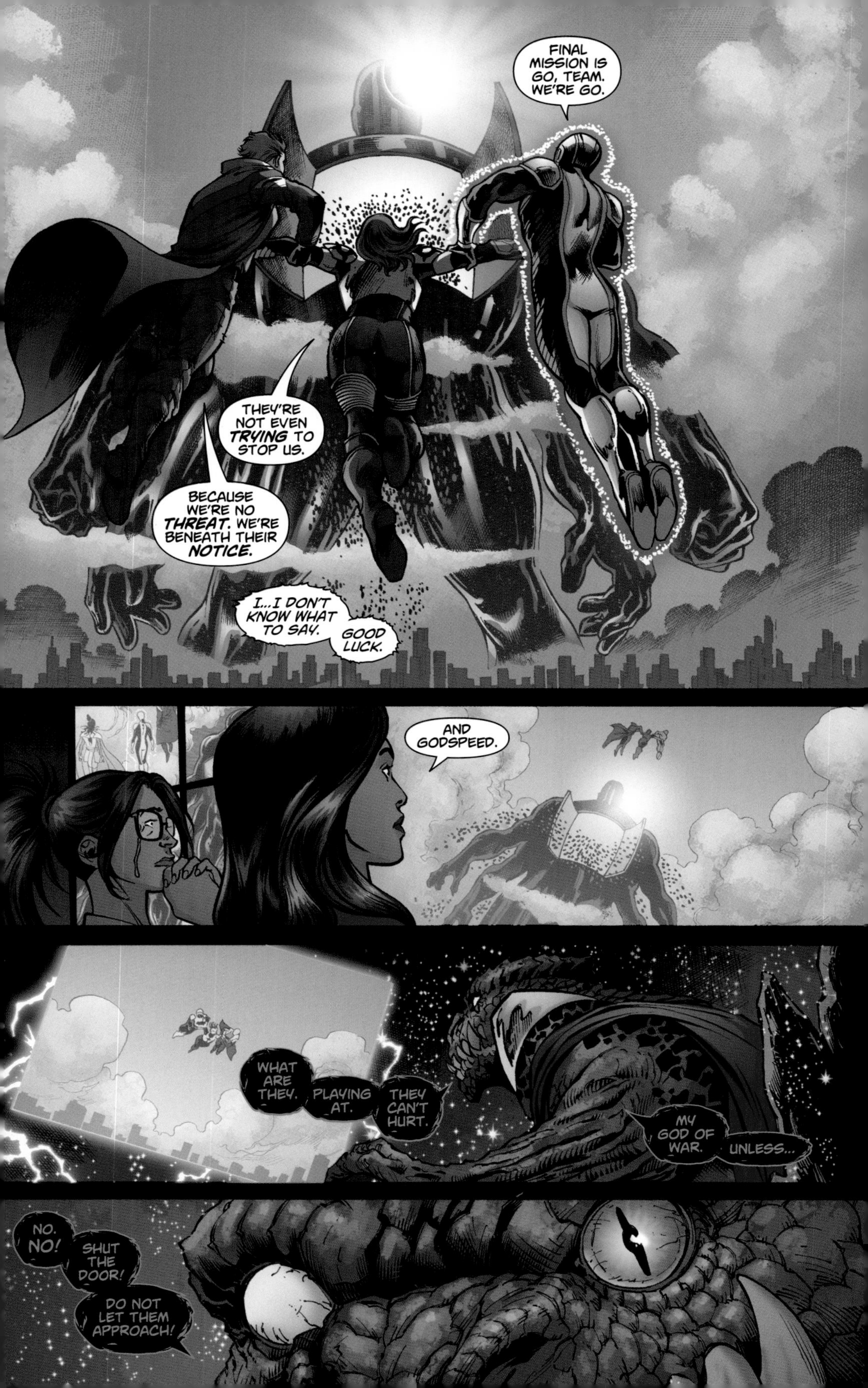
FINAL MISSION IS GO, TEAM. WE'RE GO.
THEY'RE NOT EVEN TRYING TO STOP US.
BECAUSE WE'RE NO THREAT. WE'RE BENEATH THEIR NOTICE.
I...I DON'T KNOW WHAT TO SAY.
GOOD LUCK.
AND GODSPEED.
WHAT ARE THEY.
PLAYING AT.
THEY CAN'T HURT.
MY GOD OF WAR.
UNLESS...
NO. NO!
SHUT THE DOOR!
DO NOT LET THEM APPROACH!

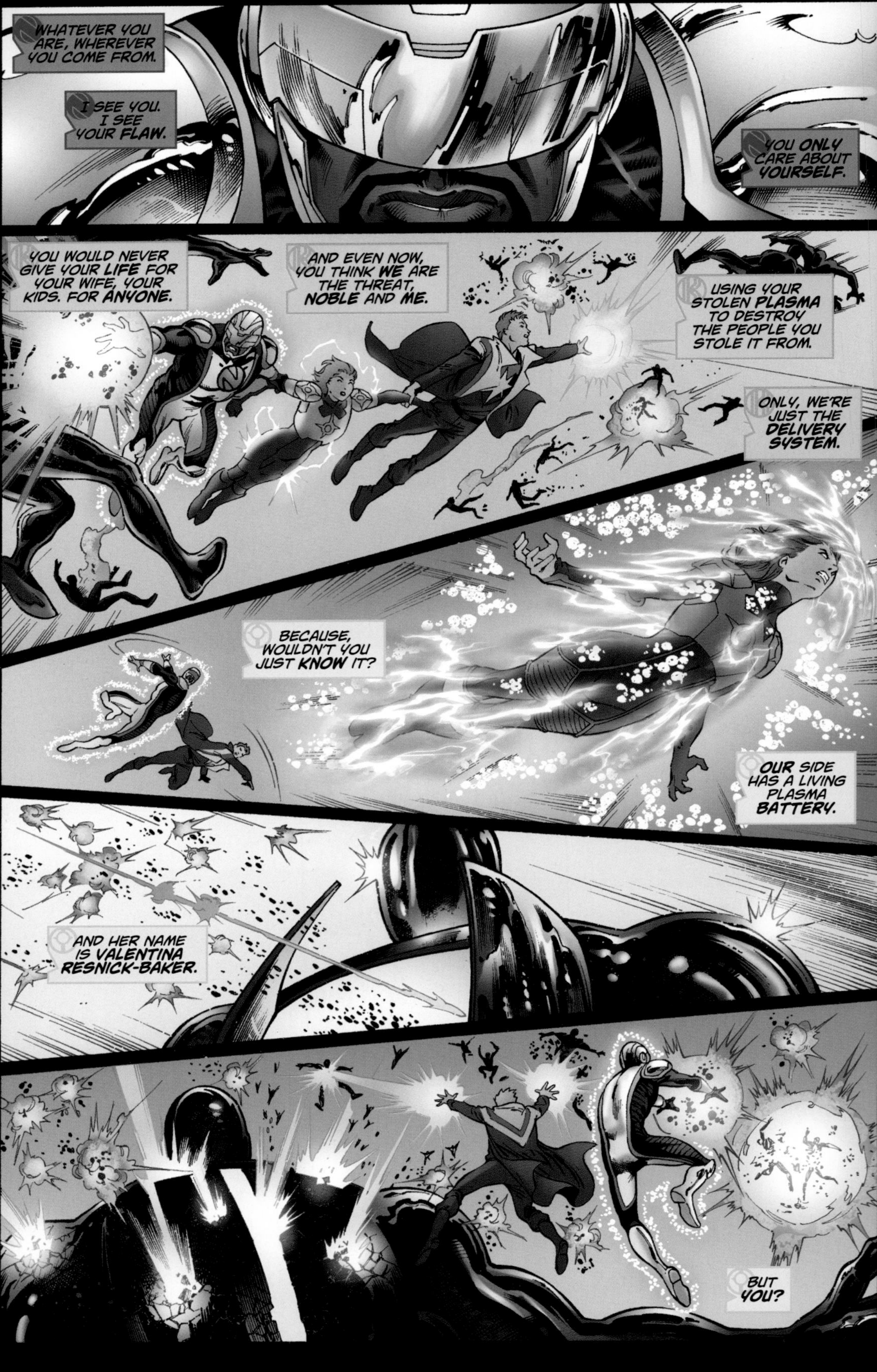
WHATEVER YOU ARE, WHEREVER YOU COME FROM.
I SEE YOU. I SEE YOUR FLAW.
YOU ONLY CARE ABOUT YOURSELF.
YOU WOULD NEVER GIVE YOUR LIFE FOR YOUR WIFE, YOUR KIDS. FOR ANYONE.
AND EVEN NOW, YOU THINK WE ARE THE THREAT, NOBLE AND ME.
USING YOUR STOLEN PLASMA TO DESTROY THE PEOPLE YOU STOLE IT FROM.
ONLY, WE'RE JUST THE DELIVERY SYSTEM.
BECAUSE, WOULDN'T YOU JUST KNOW IT?
OUR SIDE HAS A LIVING PLASMA BATTERY.
AND HER NAME IS VALENTINA RESNICK-BAKER.
BUT YOU?

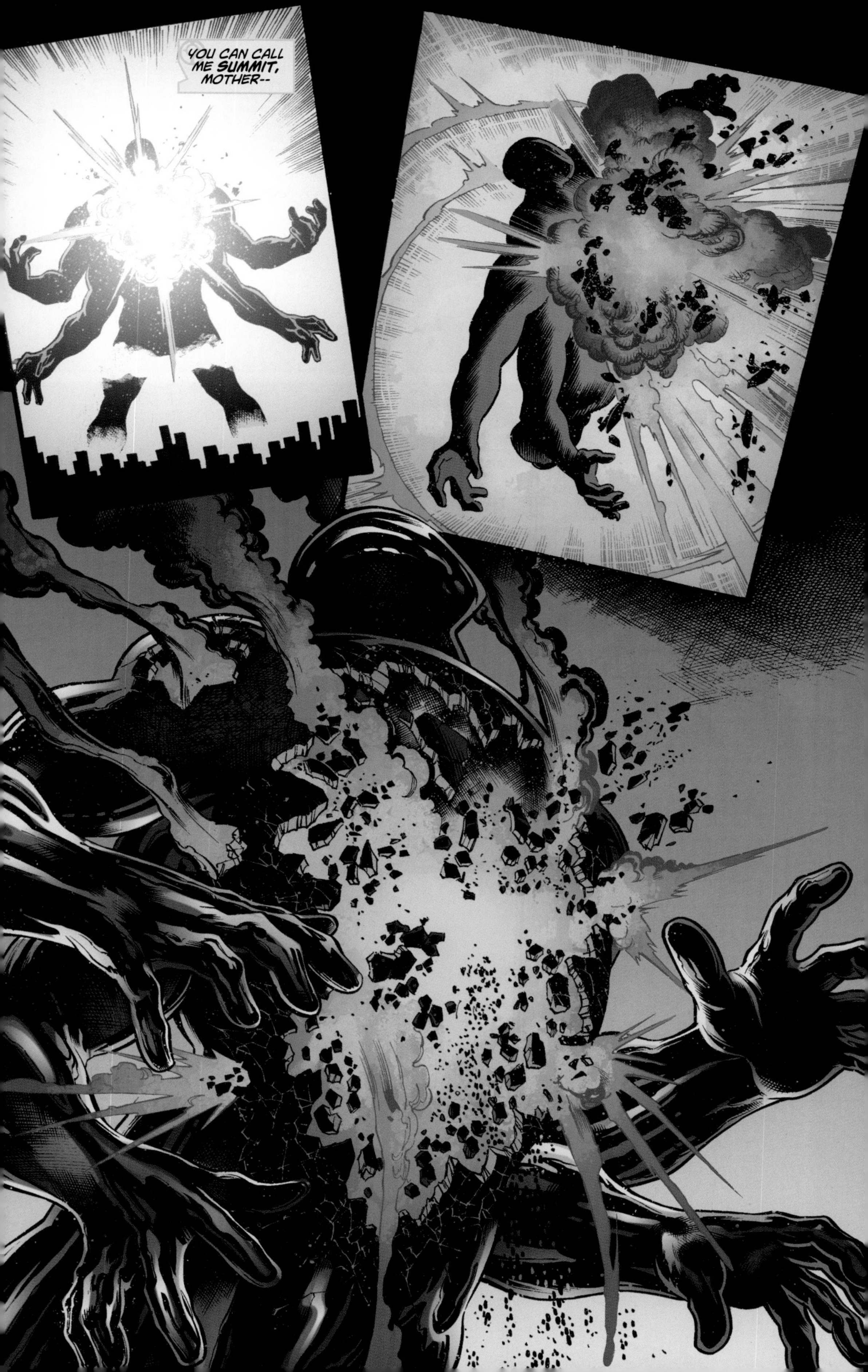
YOU CAN CALL ME SUMMIT, MOTHER--

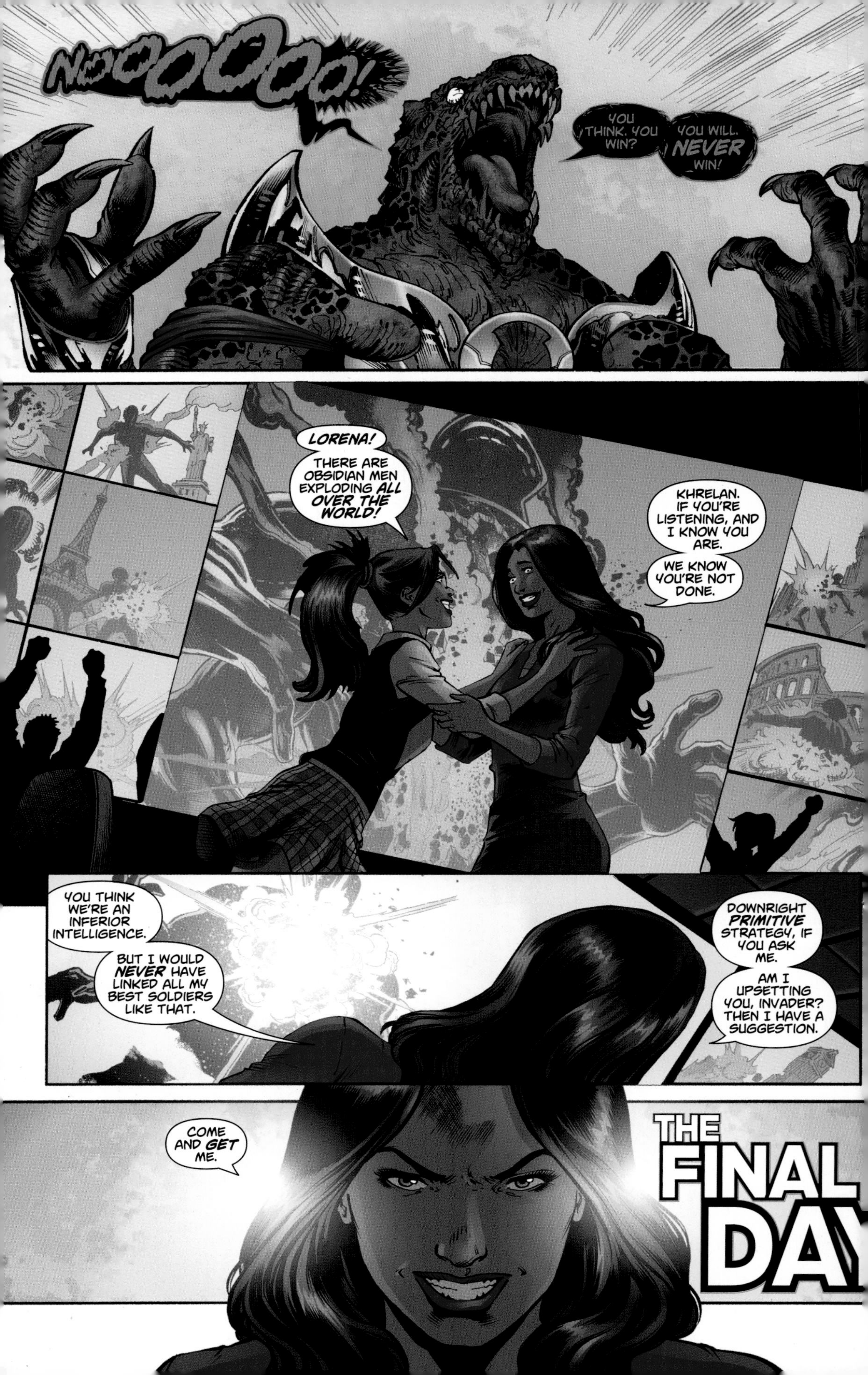
NOOOOOOO!
YOU THINK. YOU WIN?
YOU WILL. NEVER WIN!
LORENA! THERE ARE OBSIDIAN MEN EXPLODING ALL OVER THE WORLD!
KHRELAN. IF YOU'RE LISTENING, AND I KNOW YOU ARE.
WE KNOW YOU'RE NOT DONE.
YOU THINK WE'RE AN INFERIOR INTELLIGENCE.
BUT I WOULD NEVER HAVE LINKED ALL MY BEST SOLDIERS LIKE THAT.
DOWNRIGHT PRIMITIVE STRATEGY, IF YOU ASK ME.
AM I UPSETTING YOU, INVADER? THEN I HAVE A SUGGESTION.
COME AND GET ME.
THE FINAL DAY

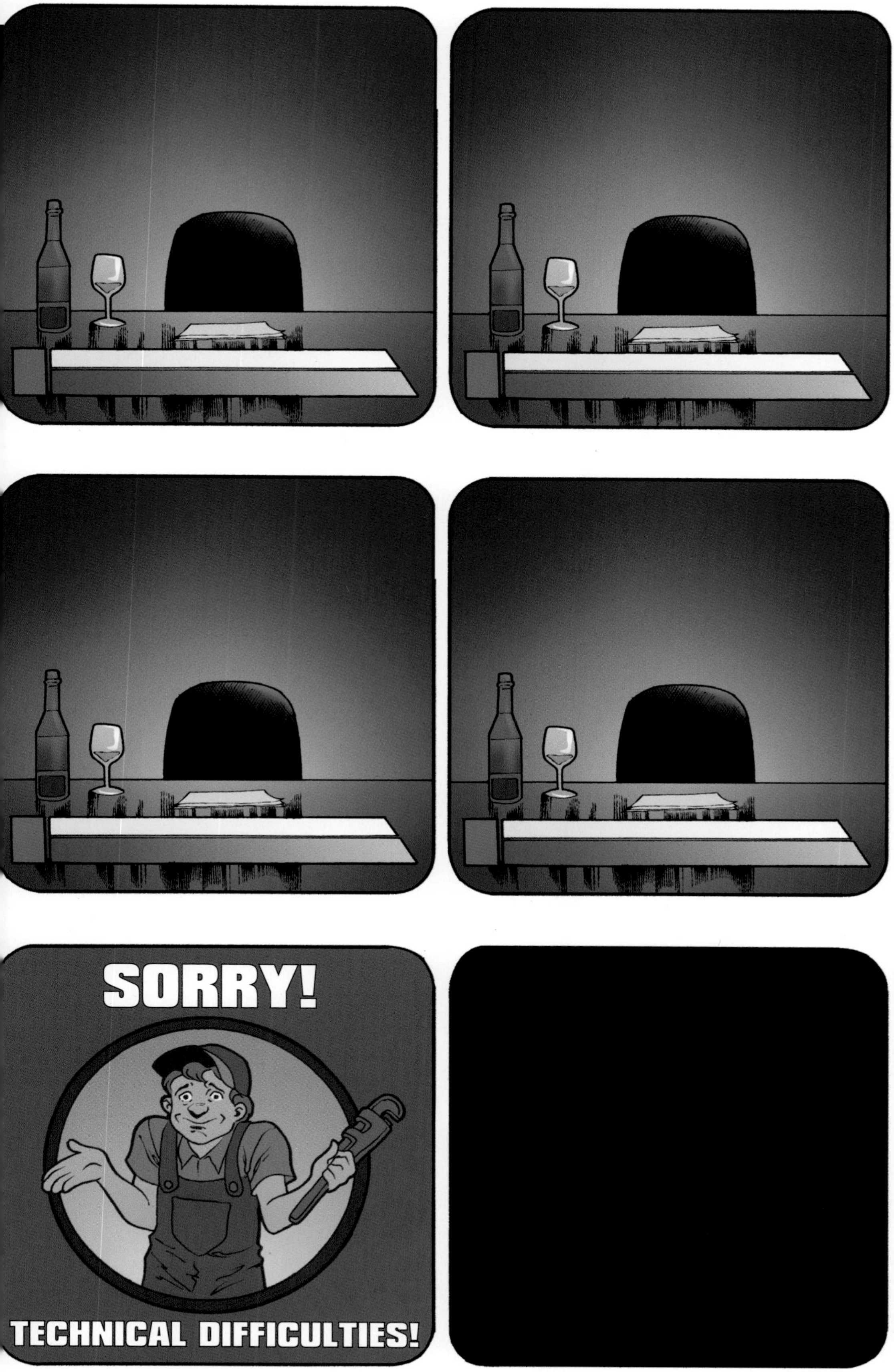
SORRY!
TECHNICAL DIFFICULTIES!

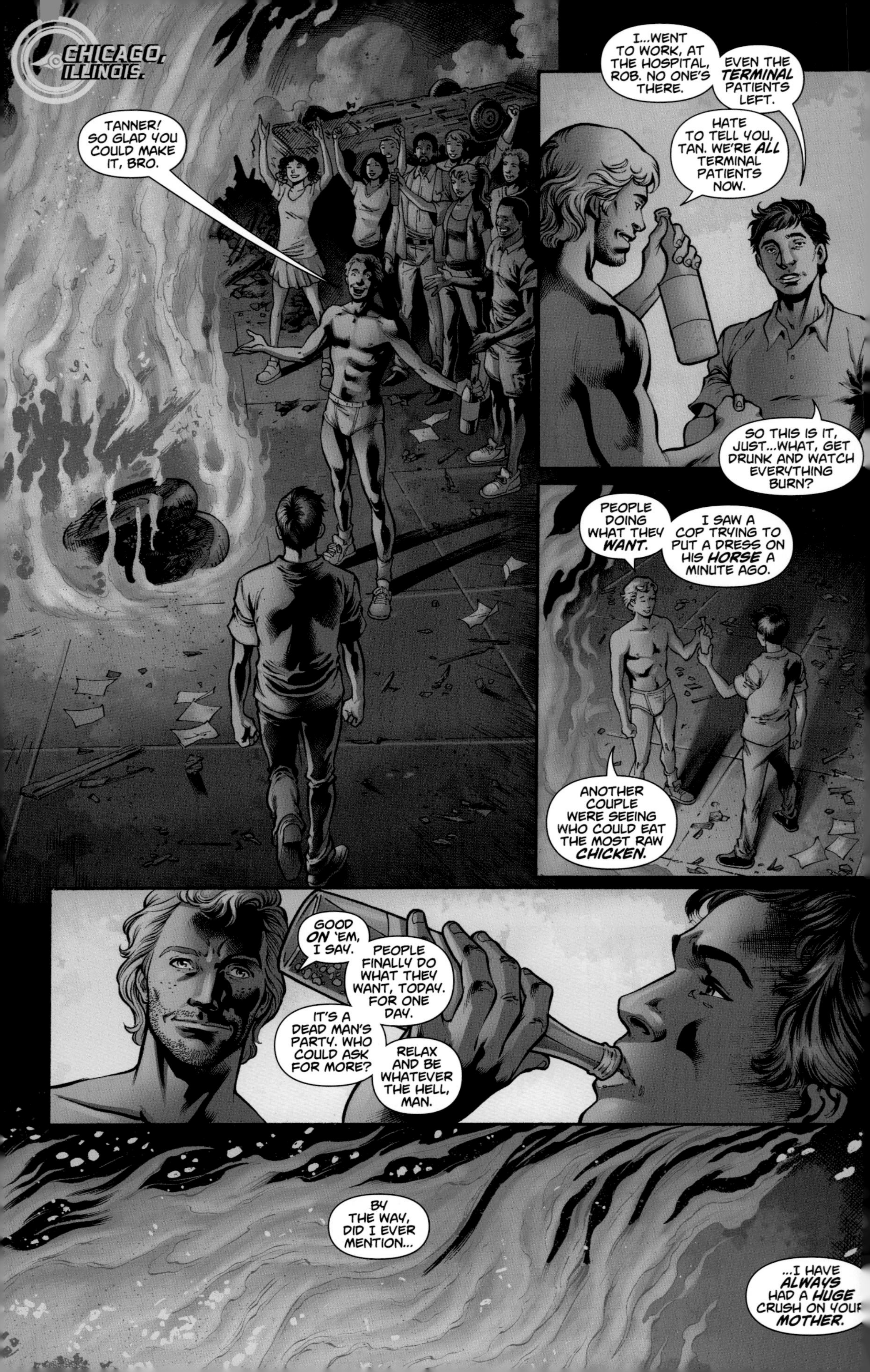
CHICAGO, ILLINOIS.
TANNER! SO GLAD YOU COULD MAKE IT, BRO.
I...WENT TO WORK, AT THE HOSPITAL, ROB. NO ONE'S THERE.
EVEN THE TERMINAL PATIENTS LEFT.
HATE TO TELL YOU, TAN. WE'RE ALL TERMINAL PATIENTS NOW.
SO THIS IS IT, JUST...WHAT, GET DRUNK AND WATCH EVERYTHING BURN?
PEOPLE DOING WHAT THEY WANT.
I SAW A COP TRYING TO PUT A DRESS ON HIS HORSE A MINUTE AGO.
ANOTHER COUPLE WERE SEEING WHO COULD EAT THE MOST RAW CHICKEN.
GOOD ON 'EM, I SAY.
PEOPLE FINALLY DO WHAT THEY WANT, TODAY. FOR ONE DAY.
IT'S A DEAD MAN'S PARTY. WHO COULD ASK FOR MORE?
RELAX AND BE WHATEVER THE HELL, MAN.
BY THE WAY, DID I EVER MENTION...
...I HAVE ALWAYS HAD A HUGE CRUSH ON YOUR MOTHER.

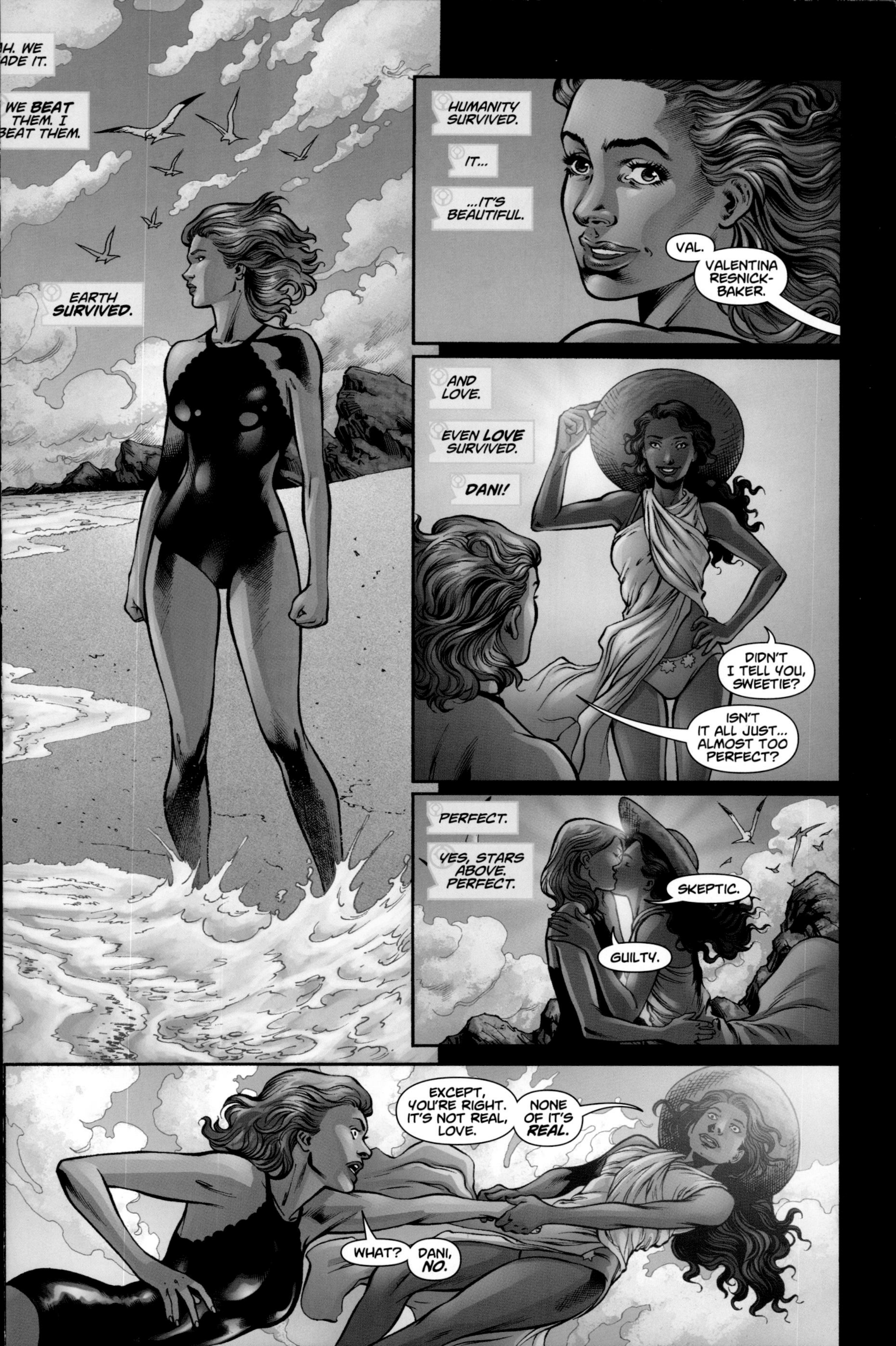

...H. WE ...ADE IT.
WE BEAT THEM. I BEAT THEM.
EARTH SURVIVED.
HUMANITY SURVIVED.
IT...
...IT'S BEAUTIFUL.
VAL.
VALENTINA RESNICK-BAKER.
AND LOVE.
EVEN LOVE SURVIVED.
DANI!
DIDN'T I TELL YOU, SWEETIE?
ISN'T IT ALL JUST... ALMOST TOO PERFECT?
PERFECT.
YES, STARS ABOVE. PERFECT.
SKEPTIC.
GUILTY.
EXCEPT, YOU'RE RIGHT. IT'S NOT REAL, LOVE.
NONE OF IT'S REAL.
WHAT?
DANI, NO.

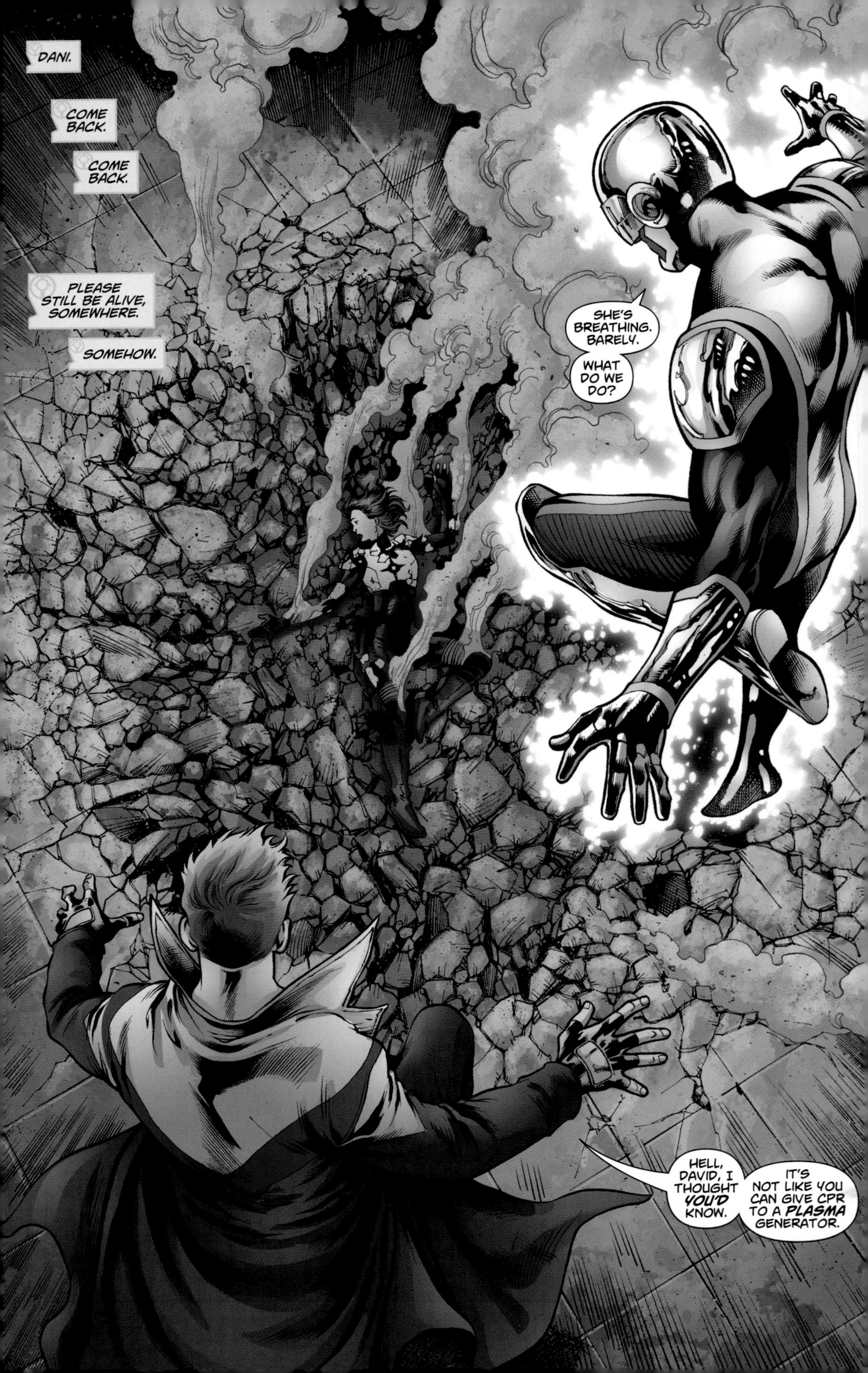
DANI.
COME BACK.
COME BACK.
PLEASE STILL BE ALIVE, SOMEWHERE.
SOMEHOW.
SHE'S BREATHING. BARELY.
WHAT DO WE DO?
HELL, DAVID, I THOUGHT YOU'D KNOW.
IT'S NOT LIKE YOU CAN GIVE CPR TO A PLASMA GENERATOR.

≥MMF≤

WELCOME BACK TO HELL, RESNICK-BAKER. IF I COULD HAND OUT MEDALS, YOU'D CARRY HOME A BUSHEL.

KIDDO, YOU OKAY?

OH. DELUSIONS.

WE SORT OF THREW YOU INTO THE HEART OF A STAR, VAL.

"I'M NOT SURPRISED IT LEFT YOU A BIT SHOOK."

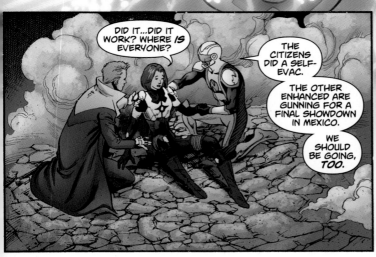

DID IT...DID IT WORK? WHERE IS EVERYONE?

THE CITIZENS DID A SELF-EVAC. THE OTHER ENHANCED ARE GUNNING FOR A FINAL SHOWDOWN IN MEXICO.

WE SHOULD BE GOING, TOO.

NOBLE. DAVID. MY POWER. MY PLASMA.

I CAN'T FEEL IT.

IT'S GONE!

DAY SEVEN.

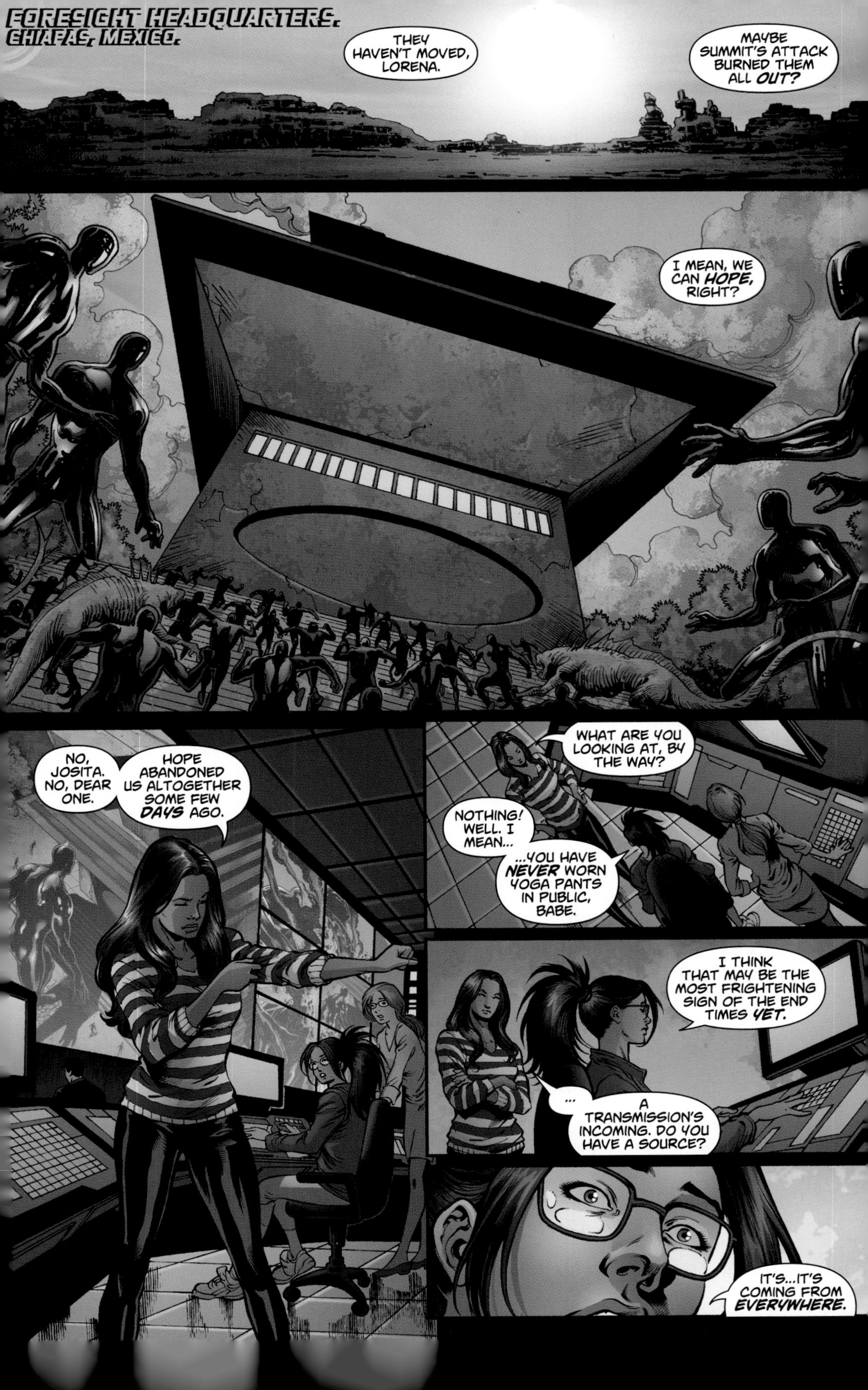
FORESIGHT HEADQUARTERS. CHIAPAS, MEXICO.
THEY HAVEN'T MOVED, LORENA.
MAYBE SUMMIT'S ATTACK BURNED THEM ALL OUT?
I MEAN, WE CAN HOPE, RIGHT?
NO, JOSITA. NO, DEAR ONE.
HOPE ABANDONED US ALTOGETHER SOME FEW DAYS AGO.
WHAT ARE YOU LOOKING AT, BY THE WAY?
NOTHING! WELL. I MEAN...
...YOU HAVE NEVER WORN YOGA PANTS IN PUBLIC, BABE.
I THINK THAT MAY BE THE MOST FRIGHTENING SIGN OF THE END TIMES YET.
...
A TRANSMISSION'S INCOMING. DO YOU HAVE A SOURCE?
IT'S...IT'S COMING FROM EVERYWHERE.

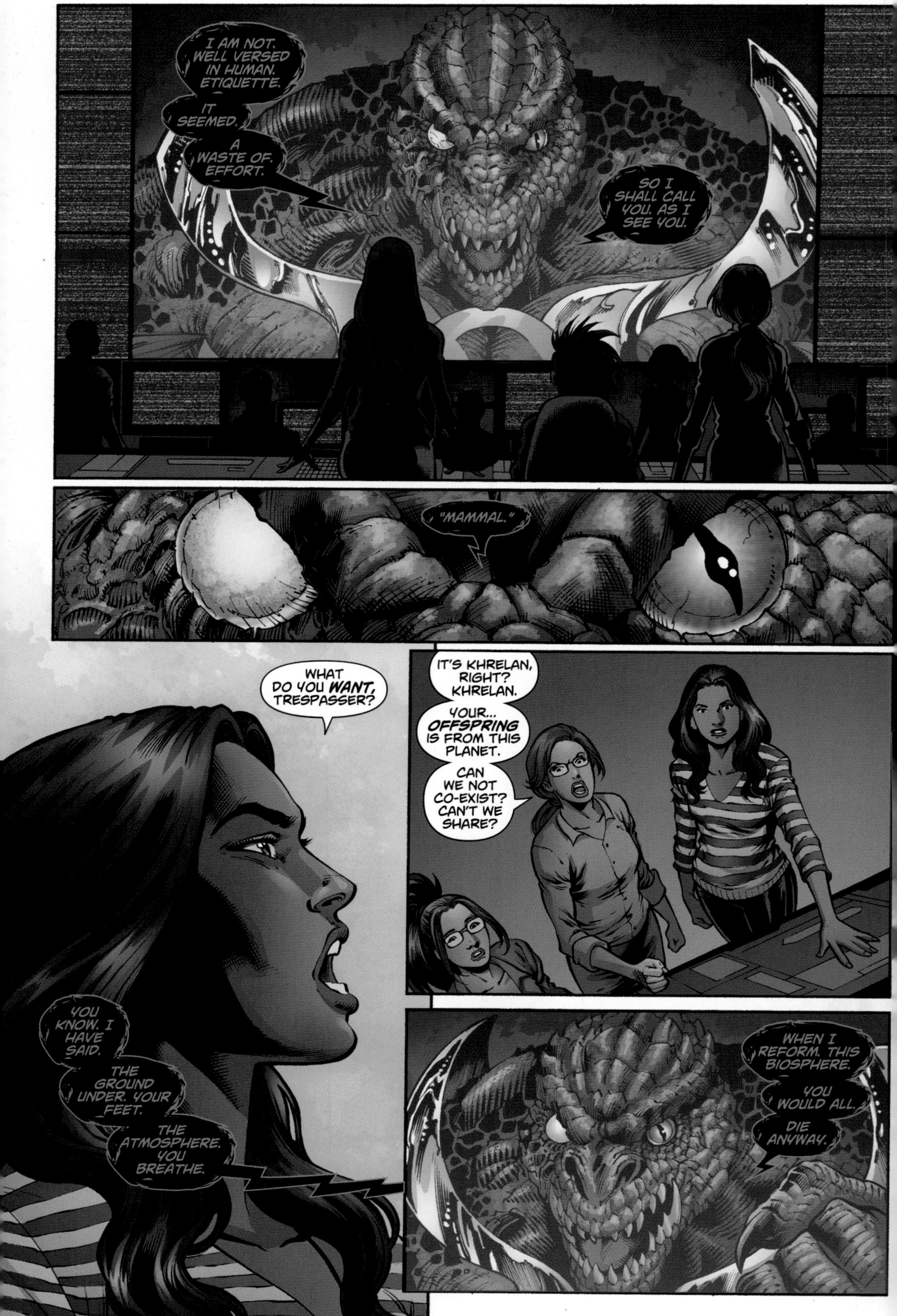
I AM NOT. WELL VERSED IN HUMAN. ETIQUETTE.
IT SEEMED.
A WASTE OF. EFFORT.
SO I SHALL CALL YOU. AS I SEE YOU.
"MAMMAL."
WHAT DO YOU WANT, TRESPASSER?
IT'S KHRELAN, RIGHT? KHRELAN.
YOUR... OFFSPRING IS FROM THIS PLANET.
CAN WE NOT CO-EXIST? CAN'T WE SHARE?
YOU KNOW. I HAVE SAID.
THE GROUND UNDER. YOUR FEET.
THE ATMOSPHERE. YOU BREATHE.
WHEN I REFORM. THIS BIOSPHERE.
YOU WOULD ALL.
DIE ANYWAY.

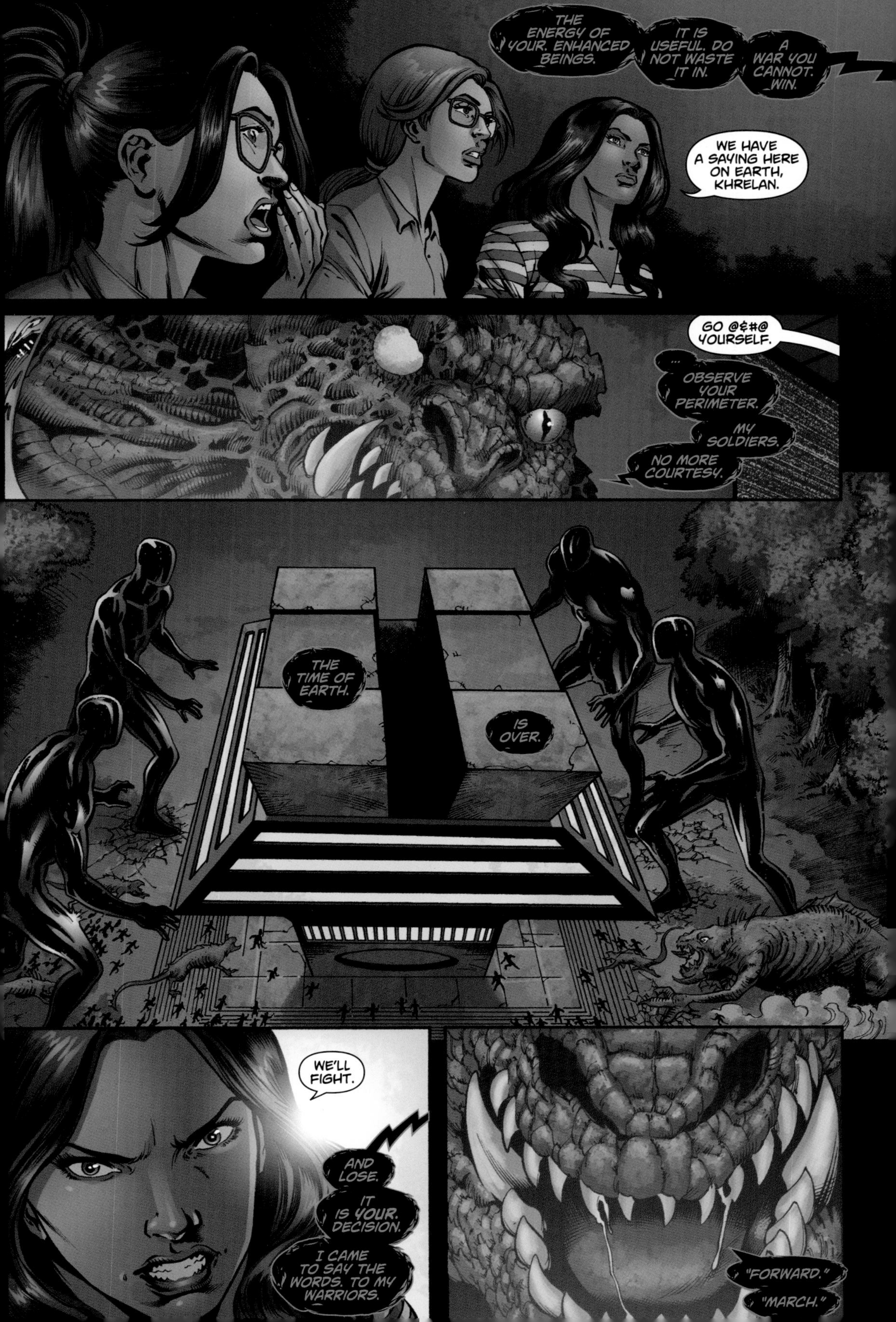
THE ENERGY OF YOUR. ENHANCED BEINGS.
IT IS USEFUL. DO NOT WASTE IT IN.
A WAR YOU CANNOT. WIN.
WE HAVE A SAYING HERE ON EARTH, KHRELAN.
GO @&#@ YOURSELF.
... OBSERVE YOUR PERIMETER.
MY SOLDIERS.
NO MORE COURTESY.
THE TIME OF EARTH.
IS OVER.
WE'LL FIGHT.
AND LOSE.
IT IS YOUR. DECISION.
I CAME TO SAY THE WORDS. TO MY WARRIORS.
"FORWARD."
"MARCH."

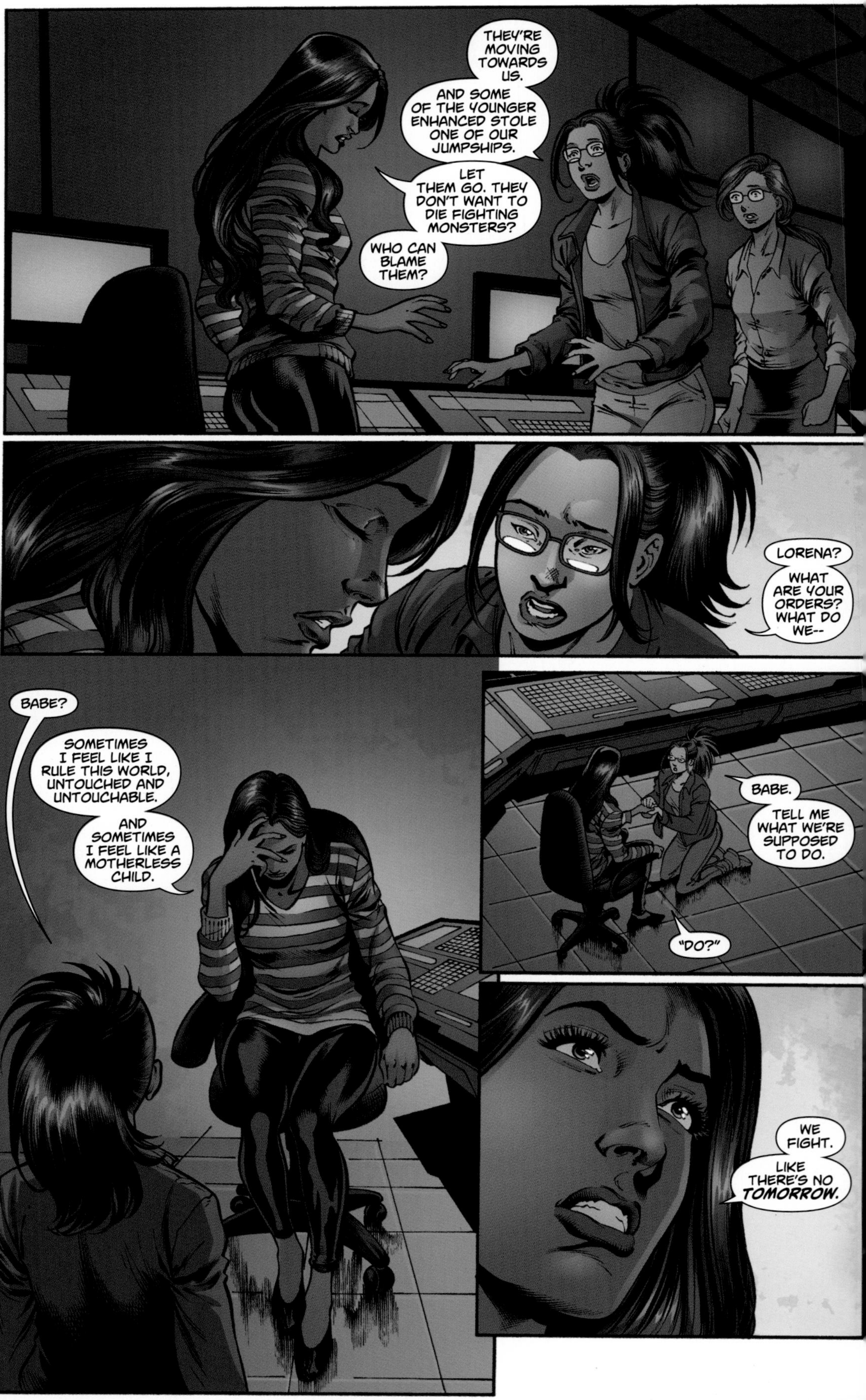
THEY'RE MOVING TOWARDS US.
AND SOME OF THE YOUNGER ENHANCED STOLE ONE OF OUR JUMPSHIPS.
LET THEM GO. THEY DON'T WANT TO DIE FIGHTING MONSTERS?
WHO CAN BLAME THEM?
LORENA? WHAT ARE YOUR ORDERS? WHAT DO WE--
BABE?
SOMETIMES I FEEL LIKE I RULE THIS WORLD, UNTOUCHED AND UNTOUCHABLE.
AND SOMETIMES I FEEL LIKE A MOTHERLESS CHILD.
BABE.
TELL ME WHAT WE'RE SUPPOSED TO DO.
"DO?"
WE FIGHT.
LIKE THERE'S NO TOMORROW.

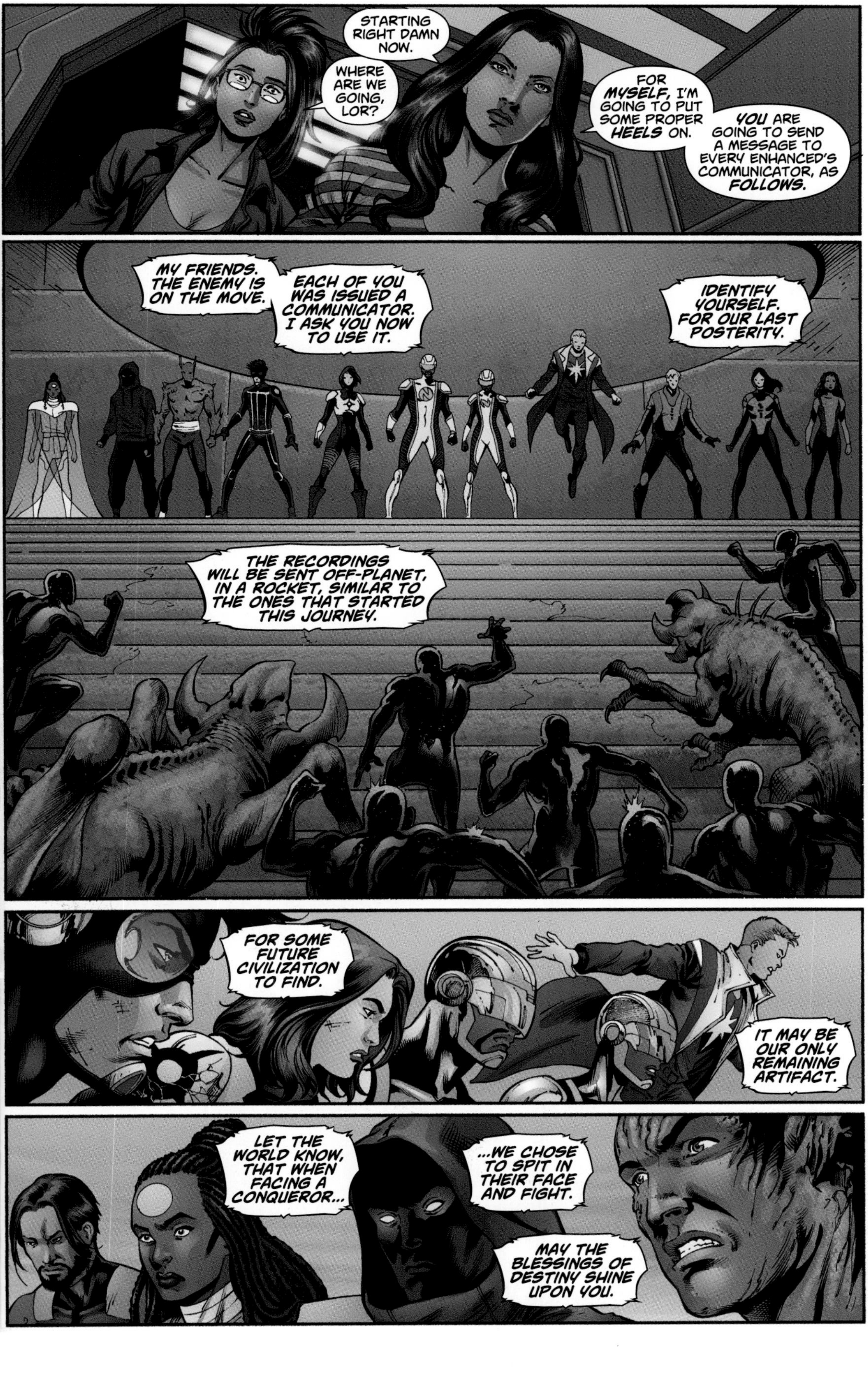
STARTING RIGHT DAMN NOW.
WHERE ARE WE GOING, LOR?
FOR MYSELF, I'M GOING TO PUT SOME PROPER HEELS ON.
YOU ARE GOING TO SEND A MESSAGE TO EVERY ENHANCED'S COMMUNICATOR, AS FOLLOWS.
MY FRIENDS. THE ENEMY IS ON THE MOVE.
EACH OF YOU WAS ISSUED A COMMUNICATOR. I ASK YOU NOW TO USE IT.
IDENTIFY YOURSELF. FOR OUR LAST POSTERITY.
THE RECORDINGS WILL BE SENT OFF-PLANET, IN A ROCKET, SIMILAR TO THE ONES THAT STARTED THIS JOURNEY.
FOR SOME FUTURE CIVILIZATION TO FIND.
IT MAY BE OUR ONLY REMAINING ARTIFACT.
LET THE WORLD KNOW, THAT WHEN FACING A CONQUEROR...
...WE CHOSE TO SPIT IN THEIR FACE AND FIGHT.
MAY THE BLESSINGS OF DESTINY SHINE UPON YOU.

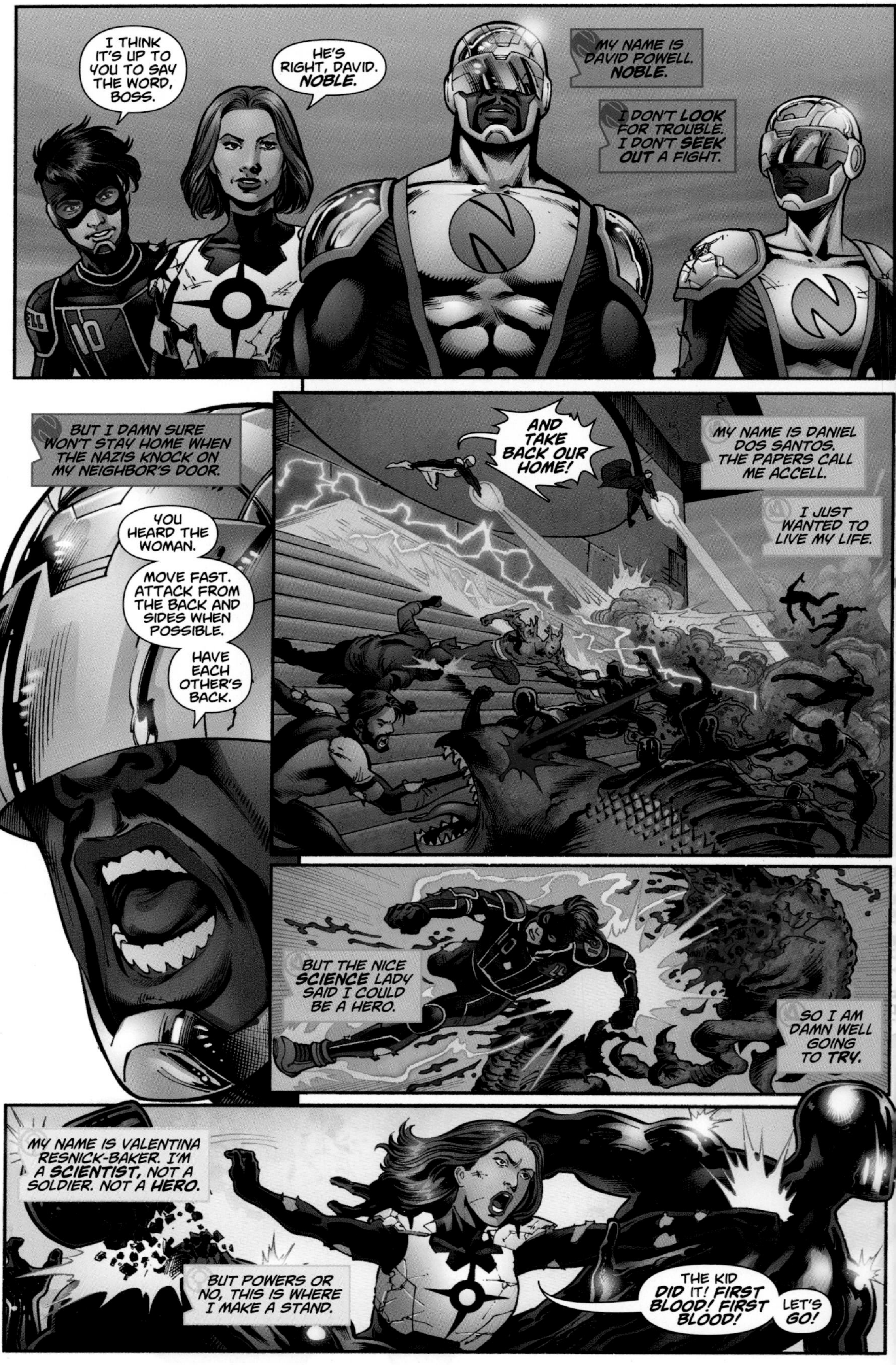
I THINK IT'S UP TO YOU TO SAY THE WORD, BOSS.
HE'S RIGHT, DAVID. NOBLE.
MY NAME IS DAVID POWELL. NOBLE.
I DON'T LOOK FOR TROUBLE. I DON'T SEEK OUT A FIGHT.
BUT I DAMN SURE WON'T STAY HOME WHEN THE NAZIS KNOCK ON MY NEIGHBOR'S DOOR.
YOU HEARD THE WOMAN.
MOVE FAST. ATTACK FROM THE BACK AND SIDES WHEN POSSIBLE.
HAVE EACH OTHER'S BACK.
AND TAKE BACK OUR HOME!
MY NAME IS DANIEL DOS SANTOS. THE PAPERS CALL ME ACCELL.
I JUST WANTED TO LIVE MY LIFE.
BUT THE NICE SCIENCE LADY SAID I COULD BE A HERO.
SO I AM DAMN WELL GOING TO TRY.
MY NAME IS VALENTINA RESNICK-BAKER. I'M A SCIENTIST, NOT A SOLDIER. NOT A HERO.
BUT POWERS OR NO, THIS IS WHERE I MAKE A STAND.
THE KID DID IT! FIRST BLOOD! FIRST BLOOD!
LET'S GO!

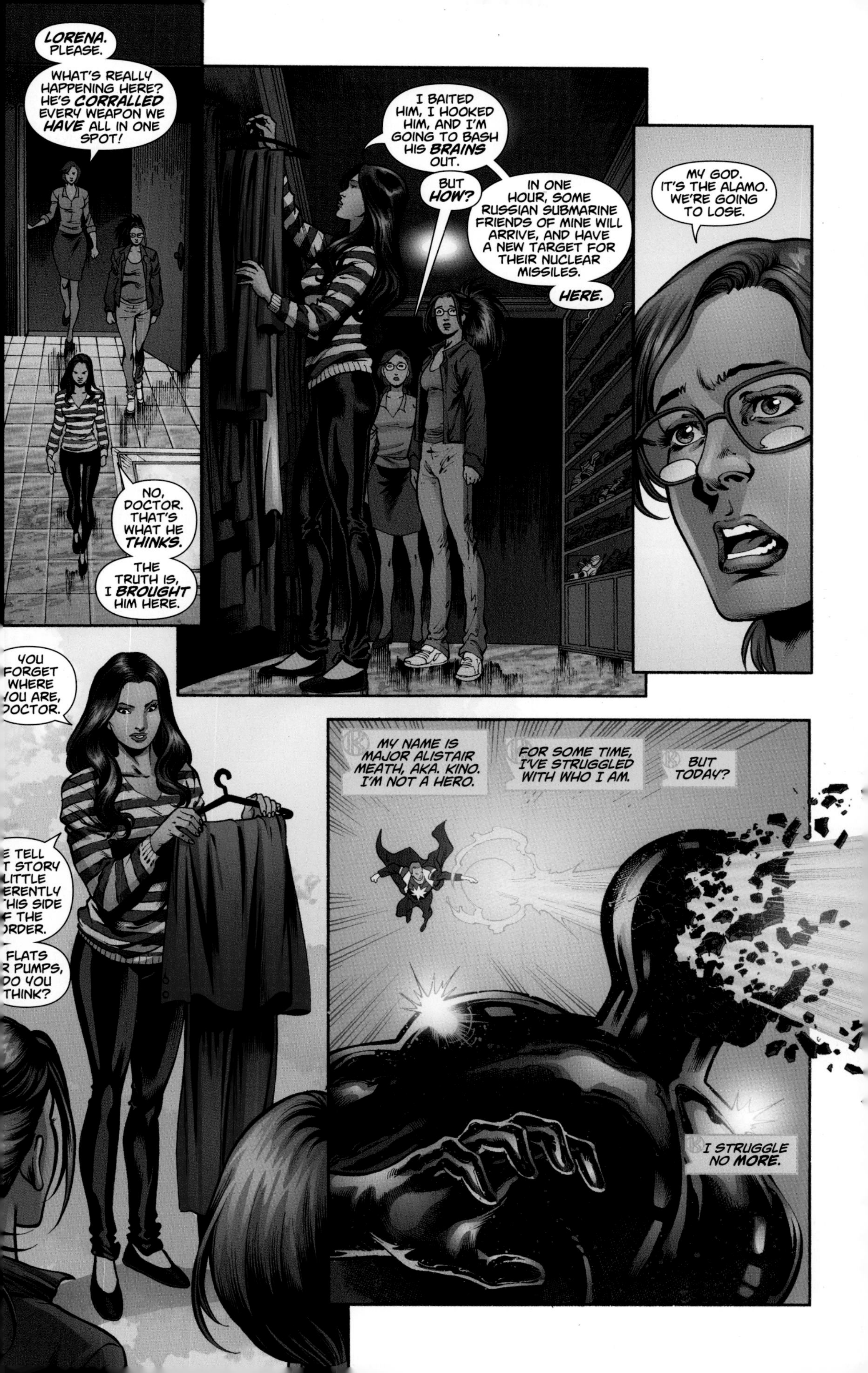
LORENA. PLEASE.
WHAT'S REALLY HAPPENING HERE? HE'S CORRALLED EVERY WEAPON WE HAVE ALL IN ONE SPOT!
NO, DOCTOR. THAT'S WHAT HE THINKS.
THE TRUTH IS, I BROUGHT HIM HERE.
I BAITED HIM, I HOOKED HIM, AND I'M GOING TO BASH HIS BRAINS OUT.
BUT HOW?
IN ONE HOUR, SOME RUSSIAN SUBMARINE FRIENDS OF MINE WILL ARRIVE, AND HAVE A NEW TARGET FOR THEIR NUCLEAR MISSILES.
HERE.
MY GOD. IT'S THE ALAMO. WE'RE GOING TO LOSE.
YOU FORGET WHERE YOU ARE, DOCTOR.
FLATS
MY NAME IS MAJOR ALISTAIR MEATH, AKA. KINO. I'M NOT A HERO.
FOR SOME TIME, I'VE STRUGGLED WITH WHO I AM.
BUT TODAY?
I STRUGGLE NO MORE.

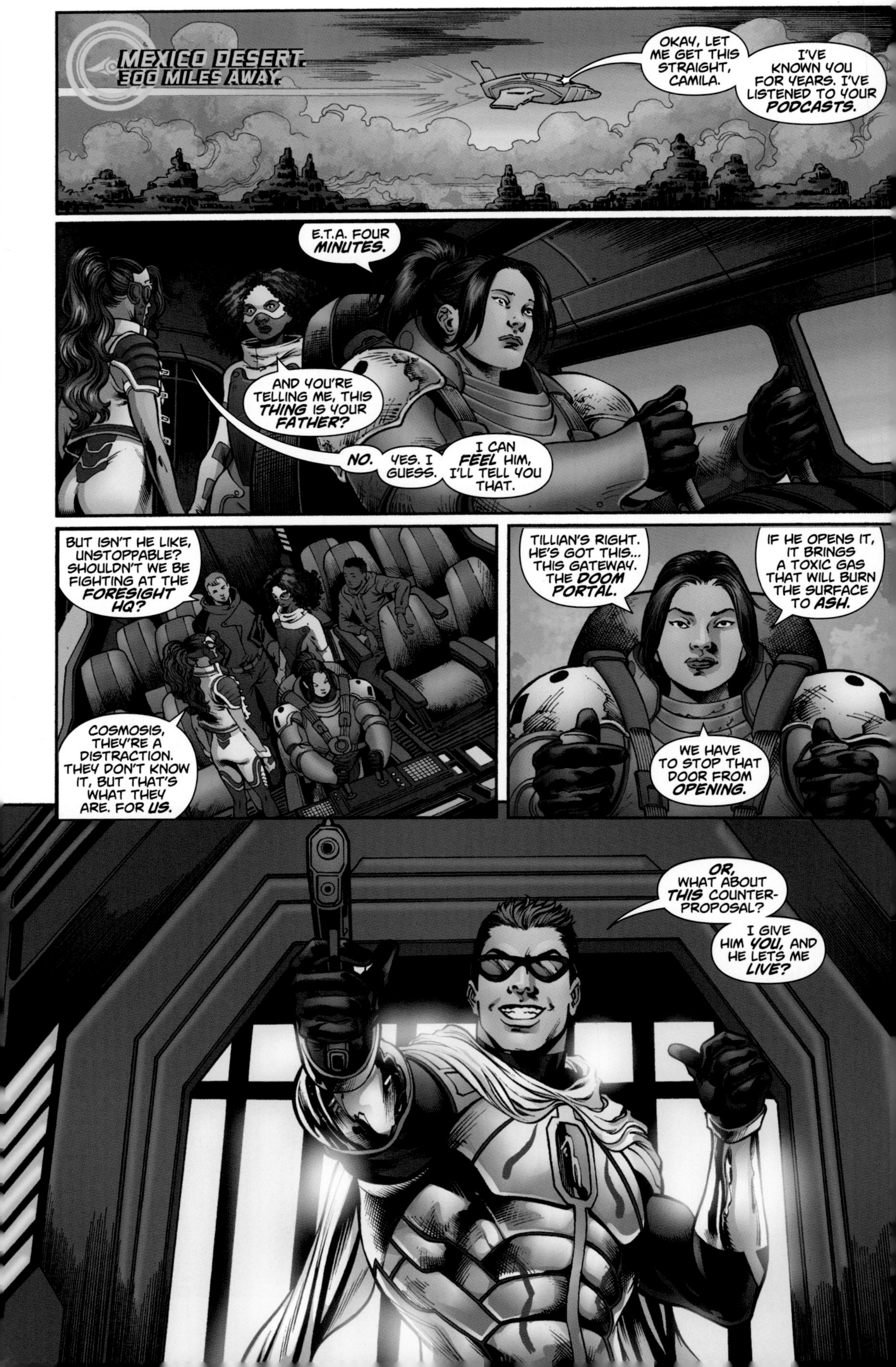
MEXICO DESERT. 300 MILES AWAY.
OKAY, LET ME GET THIS STRAIGHT, CAMILA.
I'VE KNOWN YOU FOR YEARS. I'VE LISTENED TO YOUR PODCASTS.
E.T.A. FOUR MINUTES.
AND YOU'RE TELLING ME, THIS THING IS YOUR FATHER?
NO.
YES. I GUESS.
I CAN FEEL HIM, I'LL TELL YOU THAT.
BUT ISN'T HE LIKE, UNSTOPPABLE? SHOULDN'T WE BE FIGHTING AT THE FORESIGHT HQ?
COSMOSIS, THEY'RE A DISTRACTION. THEY DON'T KNOW IT, BUT THAT'S WHAT THEY ARE. FOR US.
TILLIAN'S RIGHT. HE'S GOT THIS... THIS GATEWAY. THE DOOM PORTAL.
IF HE OPENS IT, IT BRINGS A TOXIC GAS THAT WILL BURN THE SURFACE TO ASH.
WE HAVE TO STOP THAT DOOR FROM OPENING.
OR, WHAT ABOUT THIS COUNTER-PROPOSAL?
I GIVE HIM YOU, AND HE LETS ME LIVE?

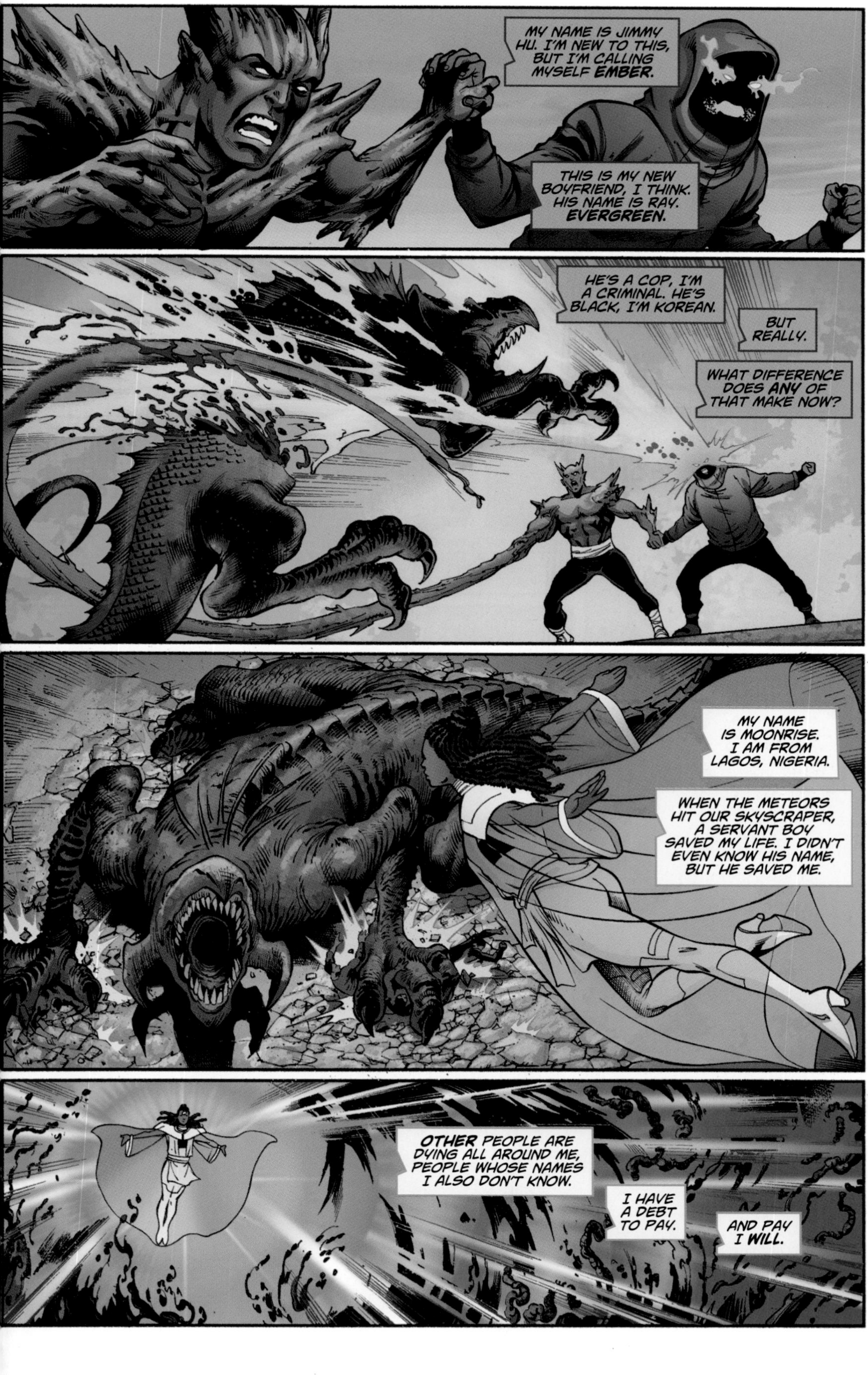
MY NAME IS JIMMY HU. I'M NEW TO THIS, BUT I'M CALLING MYSELF EMBER.
THIS IS MY NEW BOYFRIEND, I THINK. HIS NAME IS RAY. EVERGREEN.
HE'S A COP, I'M A CRIMINAL. HE'S BLACK, I'M KOREAN.
BUT REALLY.
WHAT DIFFERENCE DOES ANY OF THAT MAKE NOW?
MY NAME IS MOONRISE. I AM FROM LAGOS, NIGERIA.
WHEN THE METEORS HIT OUR SKYSCRAPER, A SERVANT BOY SAVED MY LIFE. I DIDN'T EVEN KNOW HIS NAME, BUT HE SAVED ME.
OTHER PEOPLE ARE DYING ALL AROUND ME, PEOPLE WHOSE NAMES I ALSO DON'T KNOW.
I HAVE A DEBT TO PAY.
AND PAY I WILL.

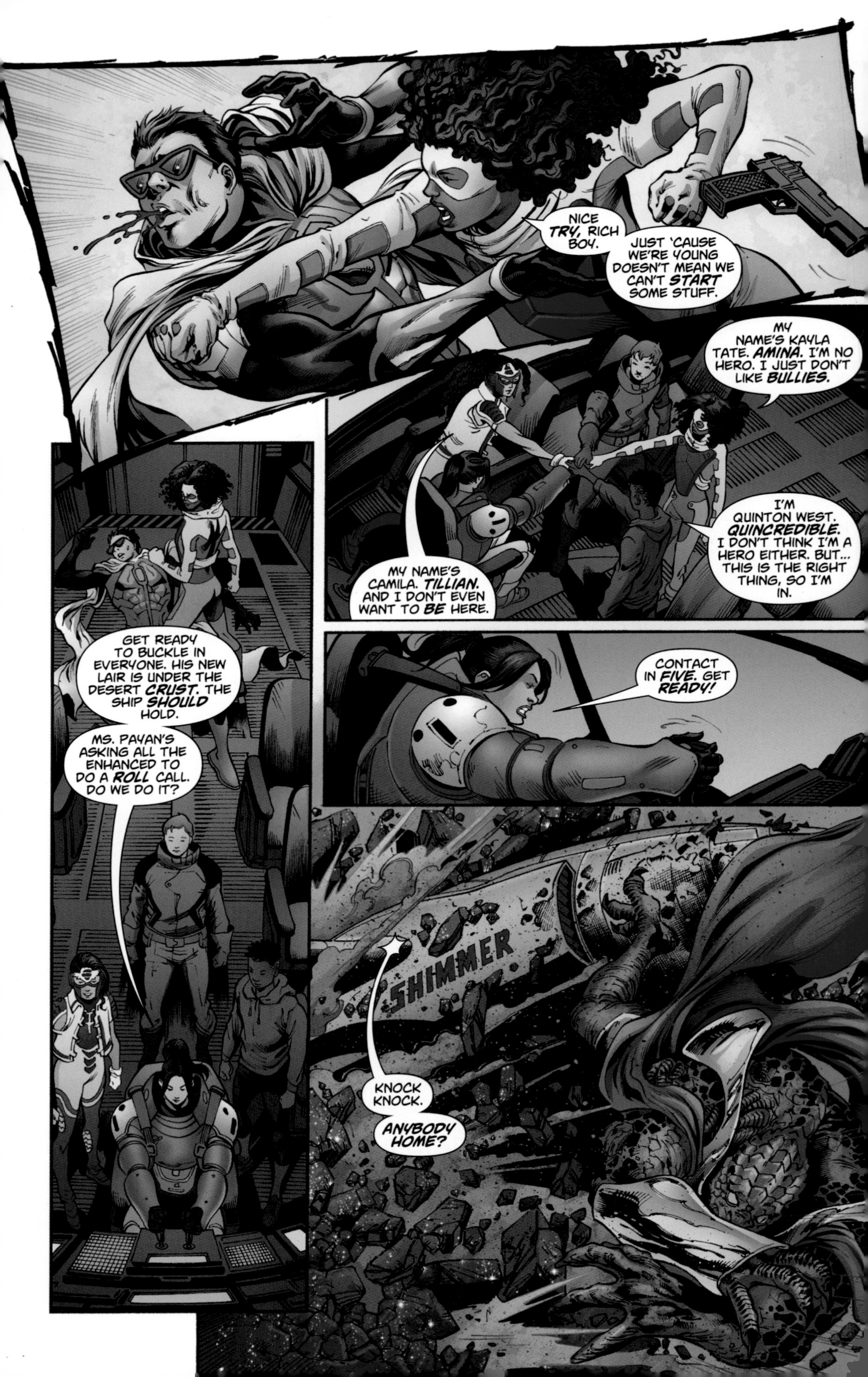
NICE TRY, RICH BOY.
JUST 'CAUSE WE'RE YOUNG DOESN'T MEAN WE CAN'T START SOME STUFF.
MY NAME'S KAYLA TATE. AMINA. I'M NO HERO. I JUST DON'T LIKE BULLIES.
MY NAME'S CAMILA. TILLIAN. AND I DON'T EVEN WANT TO BE HERE.
I'M QUINTON WEST. QUINCREDIBLE. I DON'T THINK I'M A HERO EITHER. BUT... THIS IS THE RIGHT THING, SO I'M IN.
GET READY TO BUCKLE IN EVERYONE. HIS NEW LAIR IS UNDER THE DESERT CRUST. THE SHIP SHOULD HOLD.
MS. PAYAN'S ASKING ALL THE ENHANCED TO DO A ROLL CALL. DO WE DO IT?
CONTACT IN FIVE. GET READY!
SHIMMER
KNOCK KNOCK.
ANYBODY HOME?

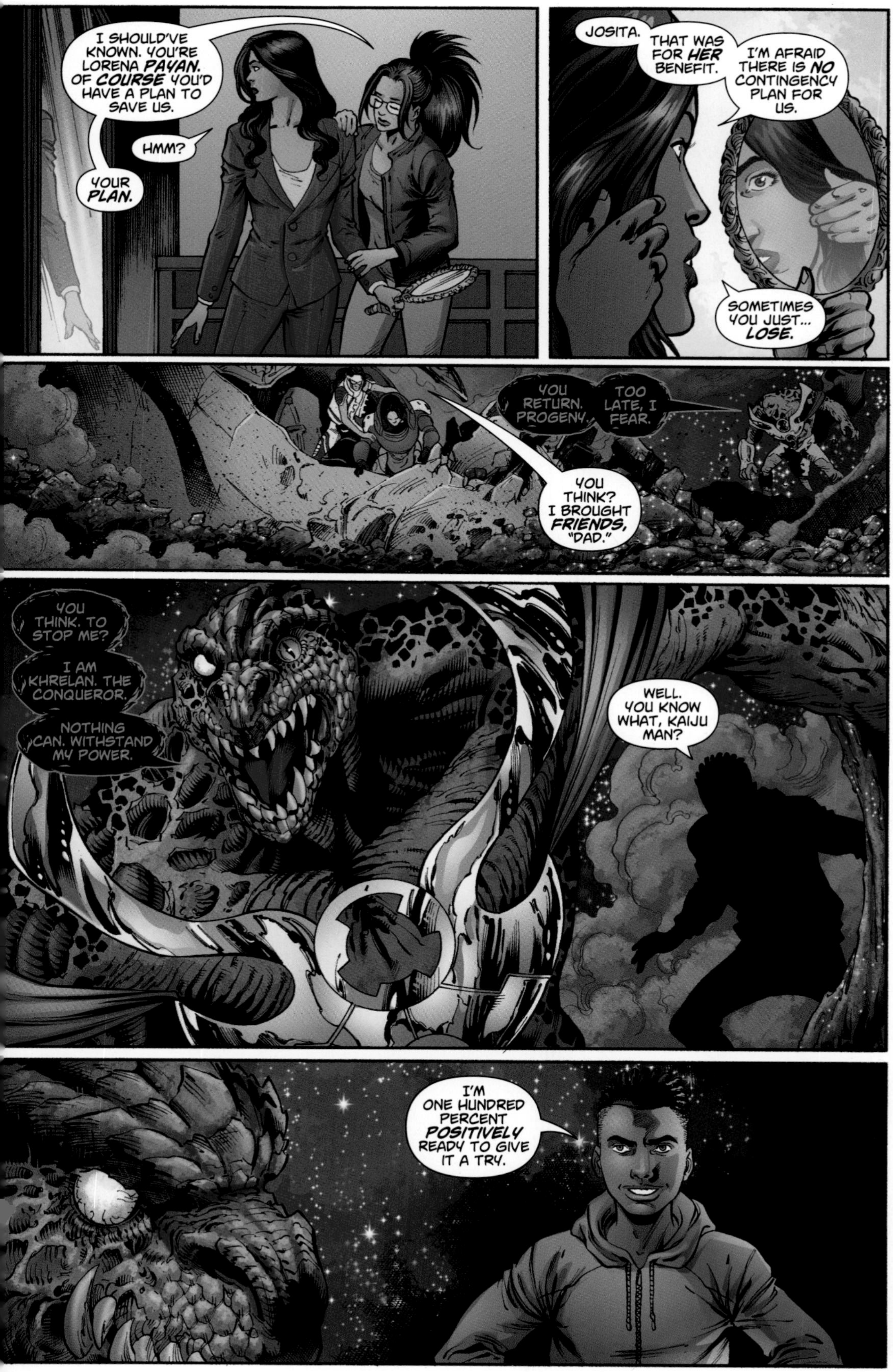
I SHOULD'VE KNOWN. YOU'RE LORENA PAYAN. OF COURSE YOU'D HAVE A PLAN TO SAVE US.
HMM?
YOUR PLAN.
JOSITA.
THAT WAS FOR HER BENEFIT.
I'M AFRAID THERE IS NO CONTINGENCY PLAN FOR US.
SOMETIMES YOU JUST... LOSE.
YOU RETURN. PROGENY.
TOO LATE, I FEAR.
YOU THINK? I BROUGHT FRIENDS, "DAD."
YOU THINK. TO STOP ME?
I AM KHRELAN. THE CONQUEROR.
NOTHING CAN. WITHSTAND MY POWER.
WELL. YOU KNOW WHAT, KAIJU MAN?
I'M ONE HUNDRED PERCENT POSITIVELY READY TO GIVE IT A TRY.

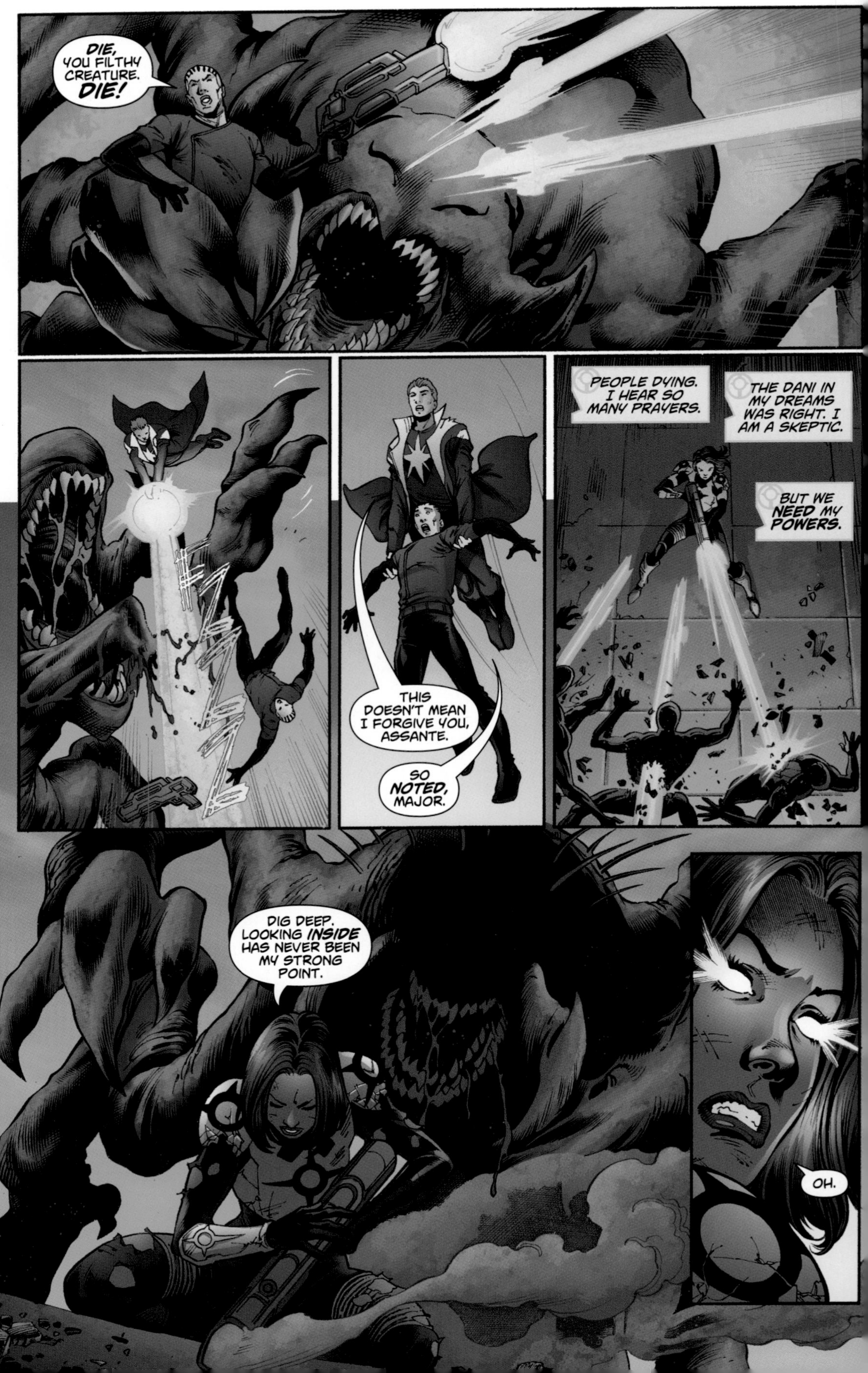

DIE, YOU FILTHY CREATURE. DIE!
PEOPLE DYING. I HEAR SO MANY PRAYERS.
THE DANI IN MY DREAMS WAS RIGHT. I AM A SKEPTIC.
BUT WE NEED MY POWERS.
FZZZZZZ
THIS DOESN'T MEAN I FORGIVE YOU, ASSANTE.
SO NOTED, MAJOR.
DIG DEEP. LOOKING INSIDE HAS NEVER BEEN MY STRONG POINT.
OH.

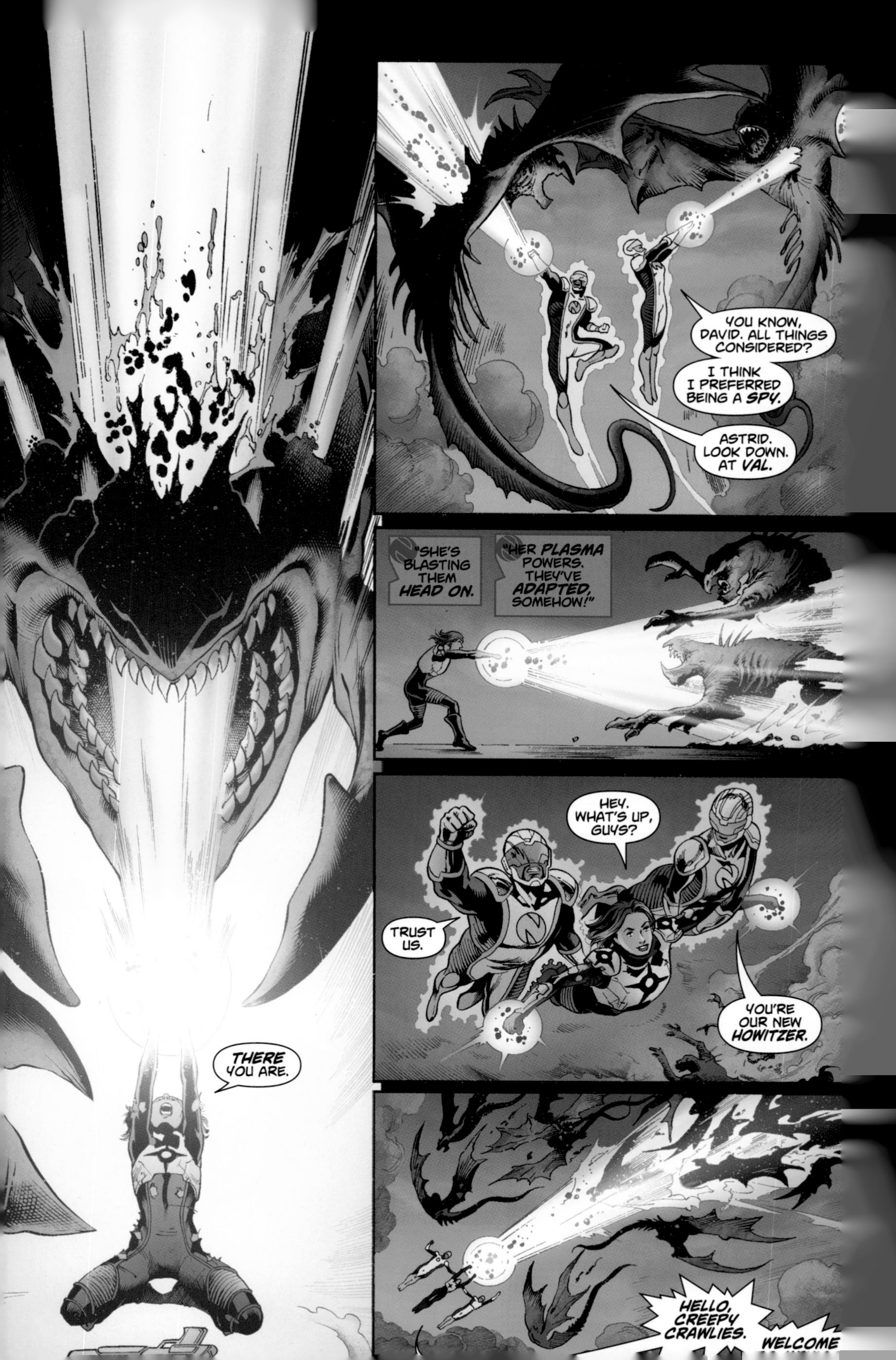
YOU KNOW, DAVID. ALL THINGS CONSIDERED?
I THINK I PREFERRED BEING A SPY.
ASTRID. LOOK DOWN. AT VAL.
"SHE'S BLASTING THEM HEAD ON.
"HER PLASMA POWERS. THEY'VE ADAPTED, SOMEHOW!"
HEY. WHAT'S UP, GUYS?
TRUST US.
YOU'RE OUR NEW HOWITZER.
HELLO, CREEPY CRAWLIES.
WELCOME
THERE YOU ARE.

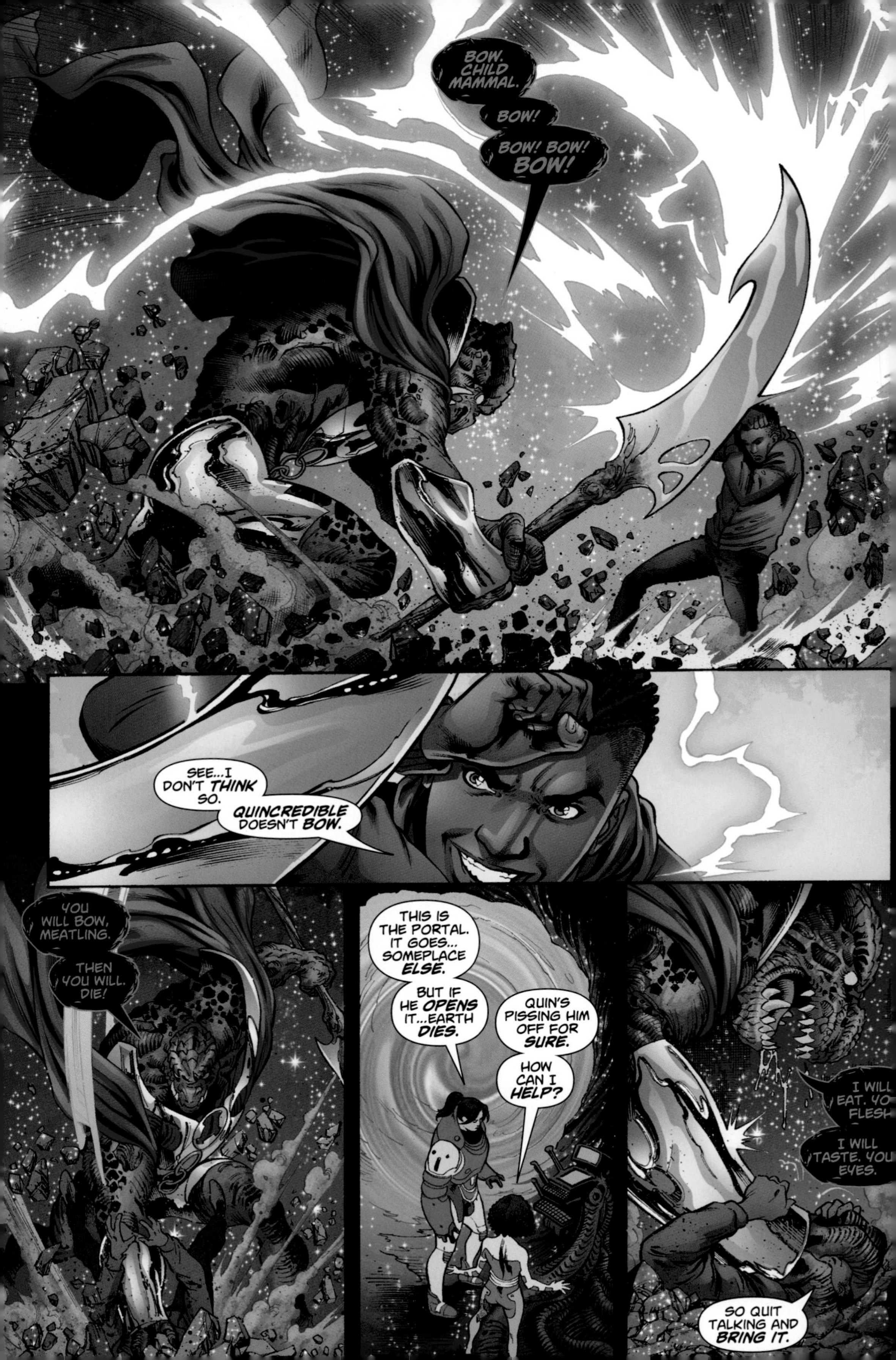
BOW. CHILD MAMMAL.
BOW!
BOW! BOW! BOW!
SEE...I DON'T THINK SO.
QUINCREDIBLE DOESN'T BOW.
YOU WILL BOW, MEATLING.
THEN YOU WILL. DIE!
THIS IS THE PORTAL. IT GOES... SOMEPLACE ELSE.
BUT IF HE OPENS IT...EARTH DIES.
QUIN'S PISSING HIM OFF FOR SURE.
HOW CAN I HELP?
I WILL EAT. YO FLESH
I WILL TASTE. YOU EYES.
SO QUIT TALKING AND BRING IT.

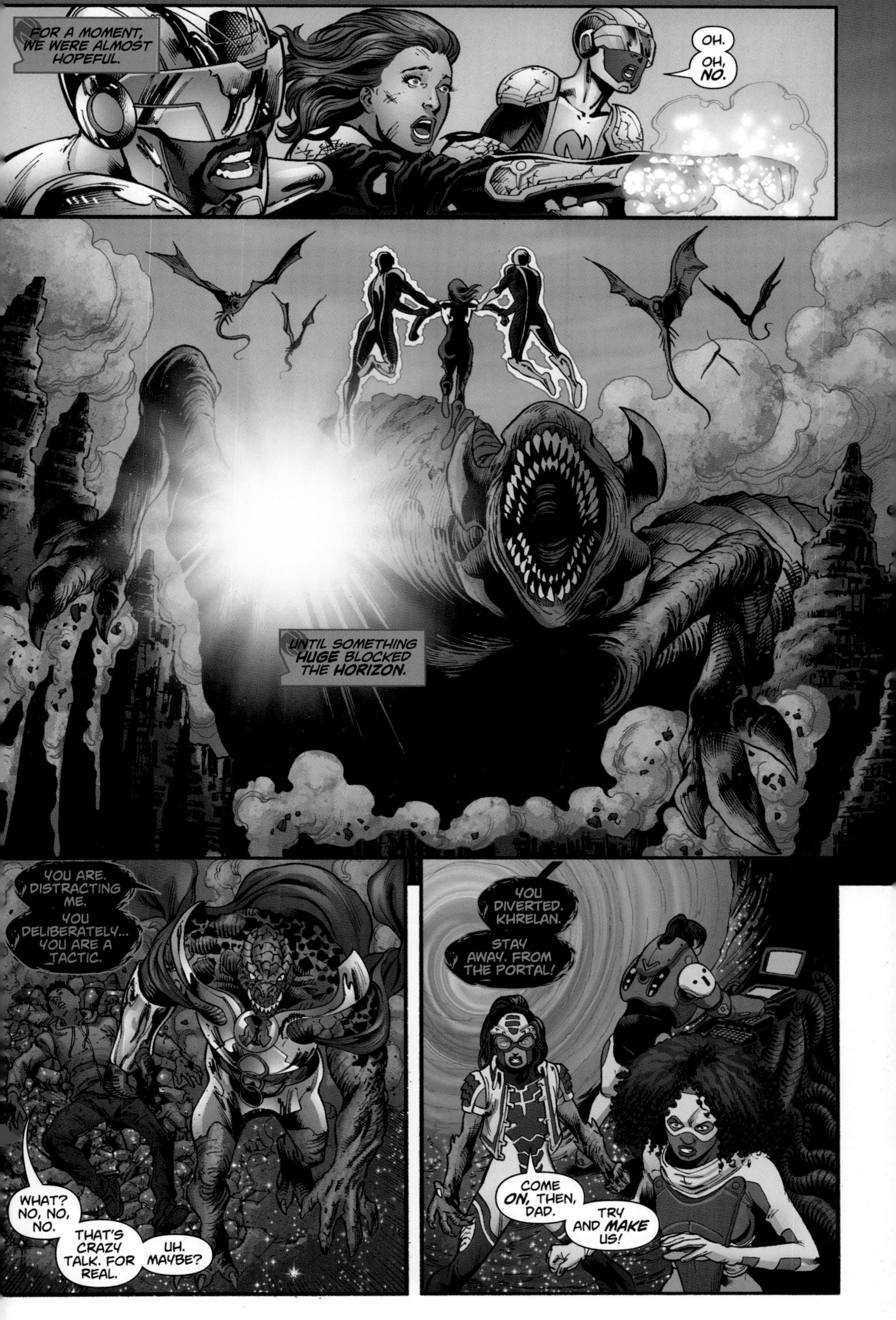
FOR A MOMENT, WE WERE ALMOST HOPEFUL.
OH. OH, NO.
UNTIL SOMETHING HUGE BLOCKED THE HORIZON.
YOU ARE. DISTRACTING ME.
YOU DELIBERATELY... YOU ARE A TACTIC.
WHAT? NO, NO, NO.
THAT'S CRAZY TALK. FOR REAL.
UH. MAYBE?
YOU DIVERTED. KHRELAN.
STAY AWAY. FROM THE PORTAL!
COME ON, THEN, DAD.
TRY AND MAKE US!

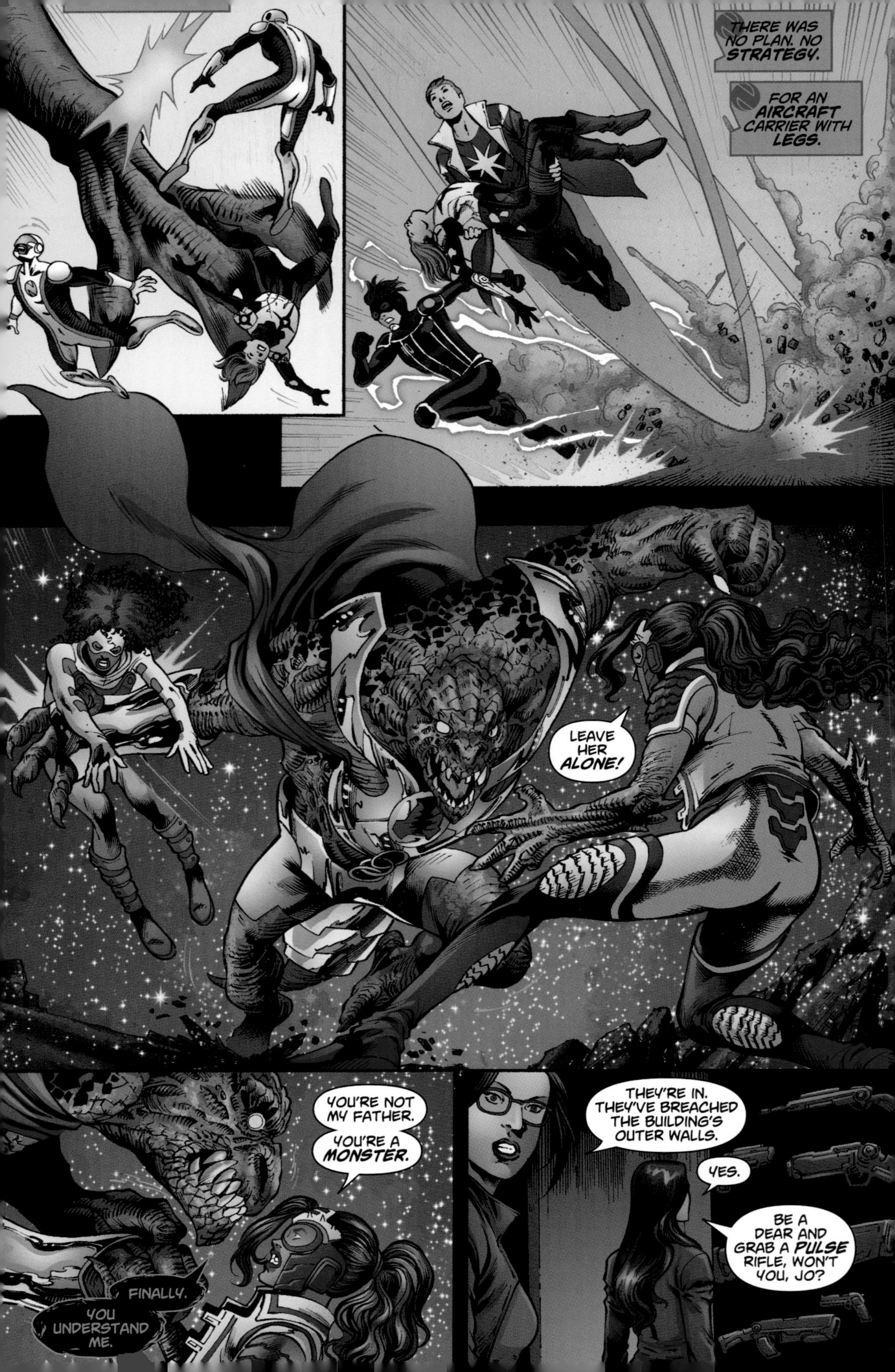
THERE WAS NO PLAN. NO STRATEGY.
FOR AN AIRCRAFT CARRIER WITH LEGS.
LEAVE HER ALONE!
YOU'RE NOT MY FATHER.
YOU'RE A MONSTER.
FINALLY.
YOU UNDERSTAND ME.
THEY'RE IN. THEY'VE BREACHED THE BUILDING'S OUTER WALLS.
YES.
BE A DEAR AND GRAB A PULSE RIFLE, WON'T YOU, JO?

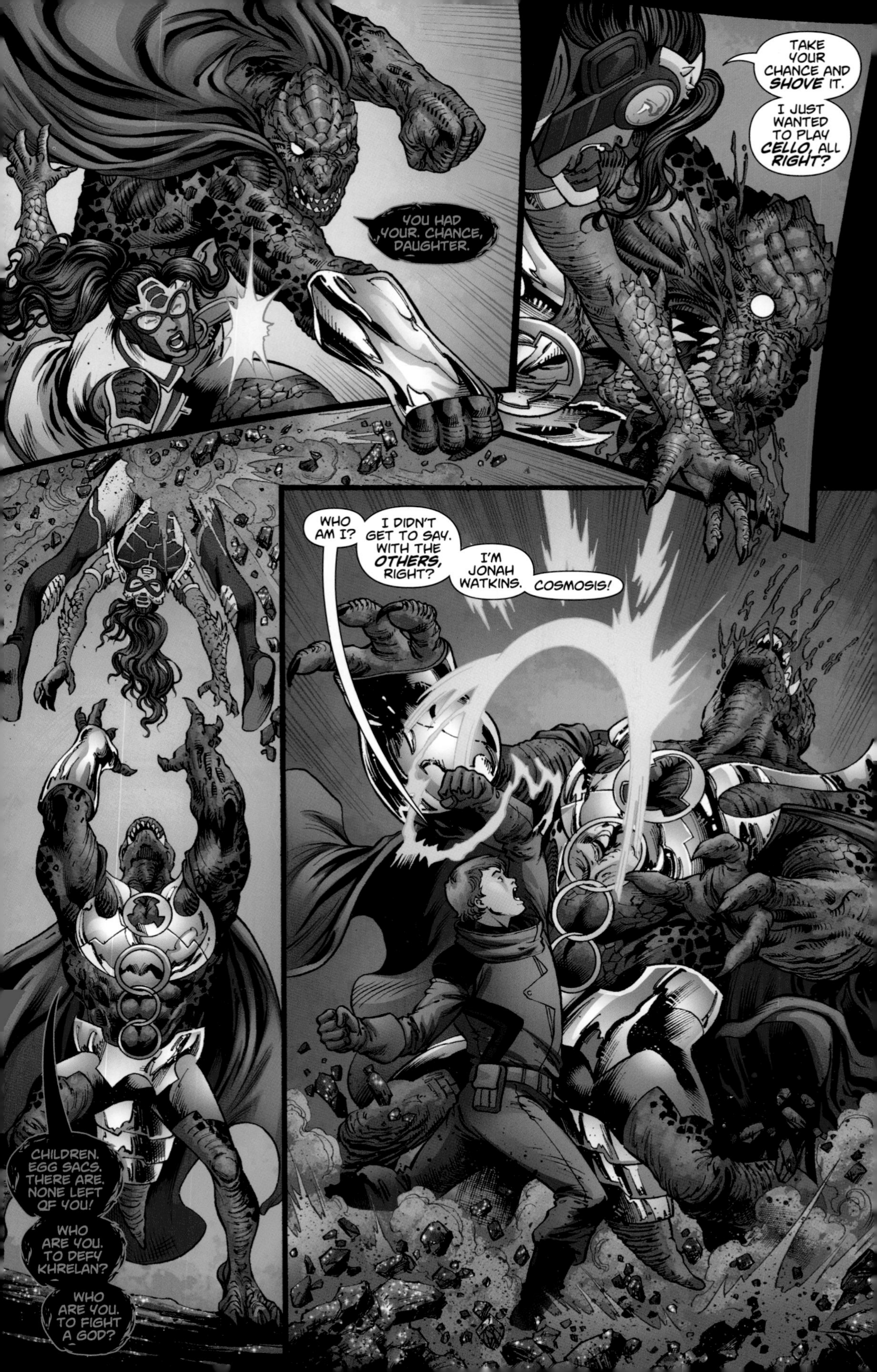
YOU HAD YOUR. CHANCE, DAUGHTER.
TAKE YOUR CHANCE AND SHOVE IT.
I JUST WANTED TO PLAY CELLO, ALL RIGHT?
CHILDREN. EGG SACS. THERE ARE. NONE LEFT OF YOU!
WHO ARE YOU. TO DEFY KHRELAN?
WHO ARE YOU. TO FIGHT A GOD?
WHO AM I?
I DIDN'T GET TO SAY. WITH THE OTHERS, RIGHT?
I'M JONAH WATKINS.
COSMOSIS!

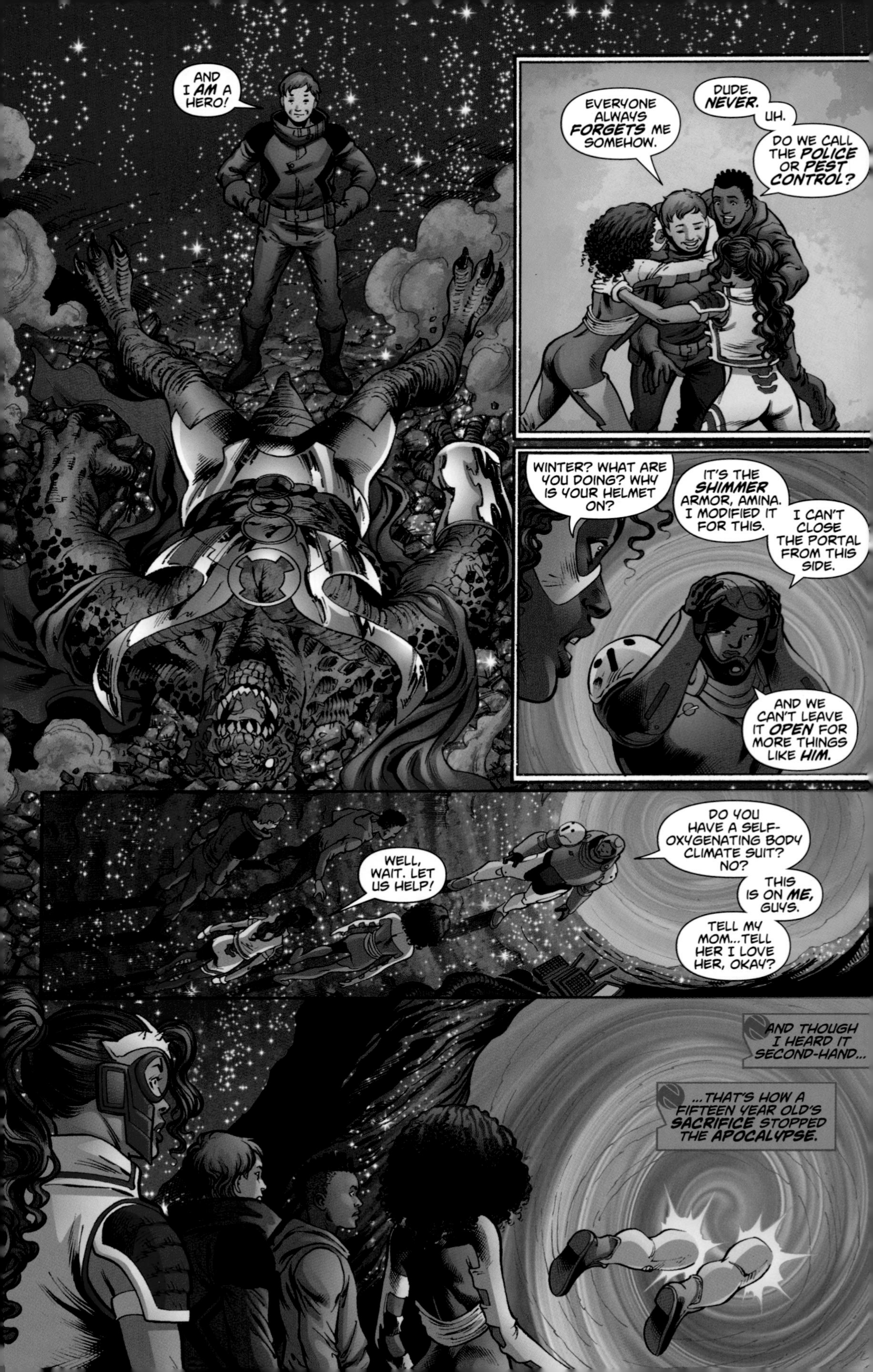
AND I AM A HERO!
EVERYONE ALWAYS FORGETS ME SOMEHOW.
DUDE. NEVER.
UH.
DO WE CALL THE POLICE OR PEST CONTROL?
WINTER? WHAT ARE YOU DOING? WHY IS YOUR HELMET ON?
IT'S THE SHIMMER ARMOR, AMINA. I MODIFIED IT FOR THIS.
I CAN'T CLOSE THE PORTAL FROM THIS SIDE.
AND WE CAN'T LEAVE IT OPEN FOR MORE THINGS LIKE HIM.
WELL, WAIT. LET US HELP!
DO YOU HAVE A SELF-OXYGENATING BODY CLIMATE SUIT? NO?
THIS IS ON ME, GUYS.
TELL MY MOM...TELL HER I LOVE HER, OKAY?
AND THOUGH I HEARD IT SECOND-HAND...
...THAT'S HOW A FIFTEEN YEAR OLD'S SACRIFICE STOPPED THE APOCALYPSE.

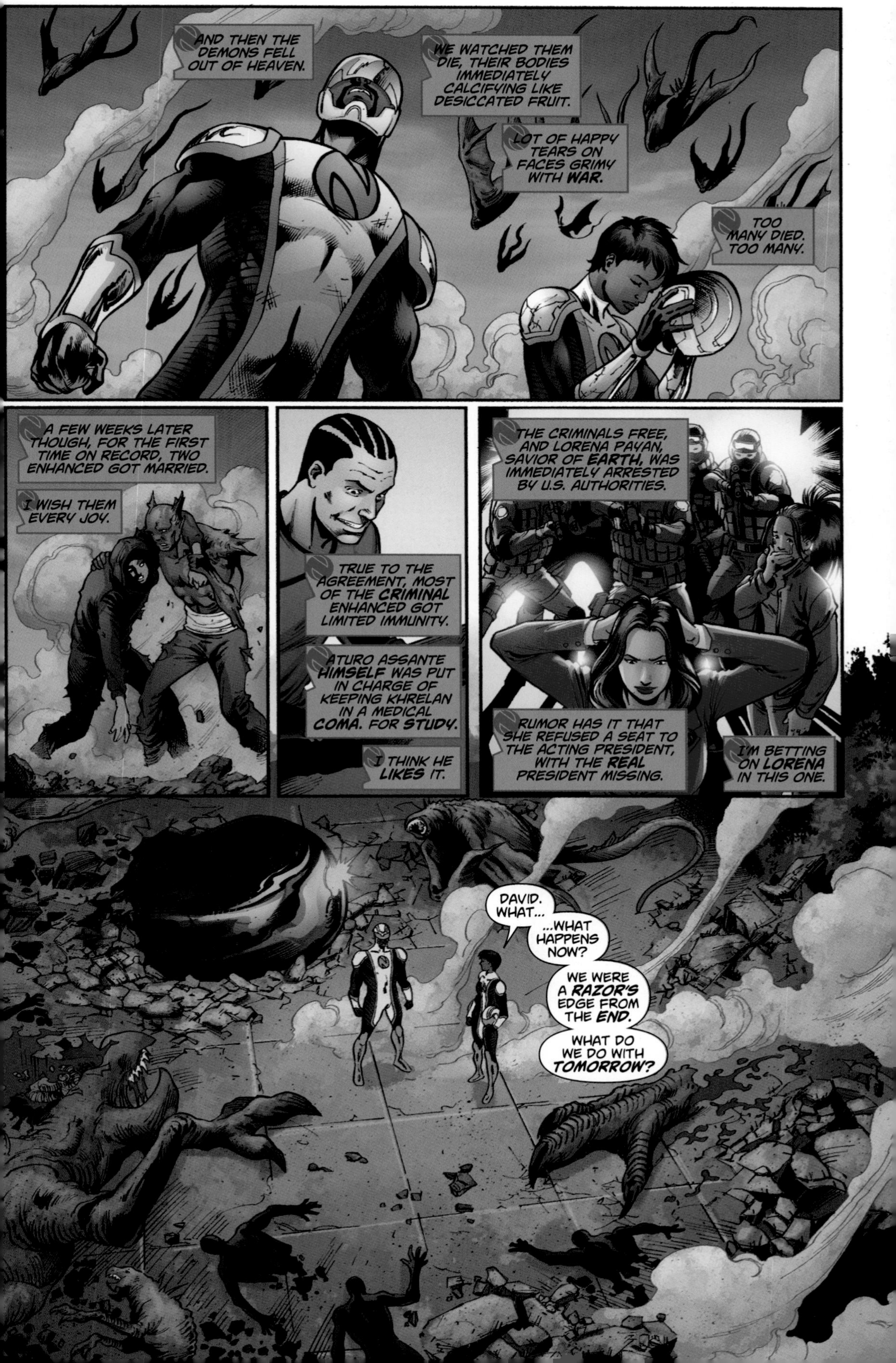

AND THEN THE DEMONS FELL OUT OF HEAVEN.
WE WATCHED THEM DIE, THEIR BODIES IMMEDIATELY CALCIFYING LIKE DESICCATED FRUIT.
LOT OF HAPPY TEARS ON FACES GRIMY WITH WAR.
TOO MANY DIED. TOO MANY.
A FEW WEEKS LATER THOUGH, FOR THE FIRST TIME ON RECORD, TWO ENHANCED GOT MARRIED.
I WISH THEM EVERY JOY.
TRUE TO THE AGREEMENT, MOST OF THE CRIMINAL ENHANCED GOT LIMITED IMMUNITY.
ATURO ASSANTE HIMSELF WAS PUT IN CHARGE OF KEEPING KHRELAN IN A MEDICAL COMA. FOR STUDY.
I THINK HE LIKES IT.
THE CRIMINALS FREE, AND LORENA PAYAN, SAVIOR OF EARTH, WAS IMMEDIATELY ARRESTED BY U.S. AUTHORITIES.
RUMOR HAS IT THAT SHE REFUSED A SEAT TO THE ACTING PRESIDENT, WITH THE REAL PRESIDENT MISSING.
I'M BETTING ON LORENA IN THIS ONE.
DAVID. WHAT...
...WHAT HAPPENS NOW?
WE WERE A RAZOR'S EDGE FROM THE END.
WHAT DO WE DO WITH TOMORROW?

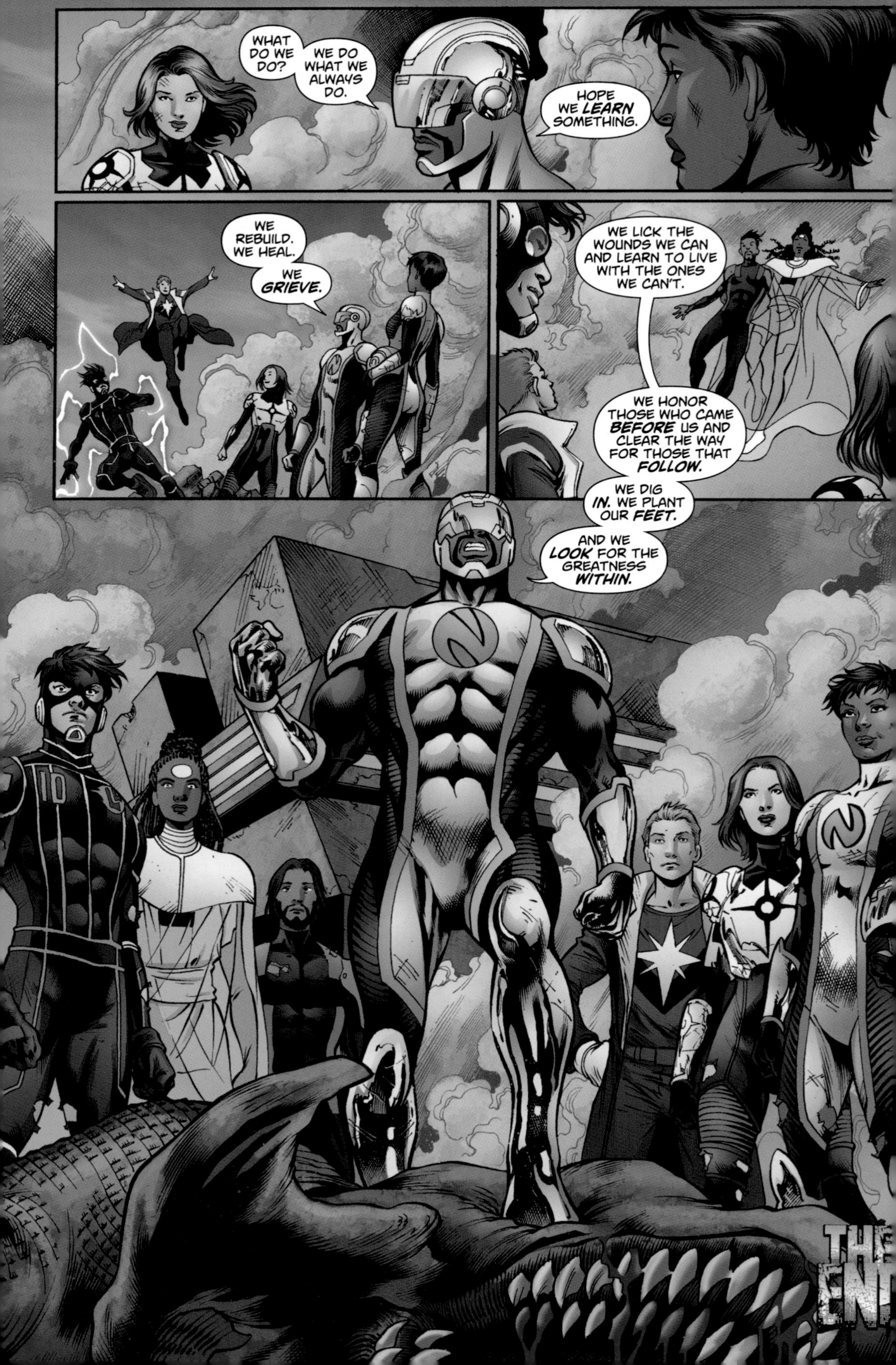
WHAT DO WE DO?
WE DO WHAT WE ALWAYS DO.
HOPE WE LEARN SOMETHING.
WE REBUILD. WE HEAL.
WE GRIEVE.
WE LICK THE WOUNDS WE CAN AND LEARN TO LIVE WITH THE ONES WE CAN'T.
WE HONOR THOSE WHO CAME BEFORE US AND CLEAR THE WAY FOR THOSE THAT FOLLOW.
WE DIG IN. WE PLANT OUR FEET.
AND WE LOOK FOR THE GREATNESS WITHIN.
THE END

DAY
~~SEVEN.~~

ZERO.

COVERS GALLERY